PUTTING IT ALL TOGETHER (pp. 121–169)

WRITING THE VARIOUS FORMS OF DISCOURSE (pp. 170–237)

SPECIAL KINDS OF WRITING ASSIGNMENTS (pp. 238–303)

ALPHABETICAL LIST OF CORRECTION SYMBOLS

(The numbers following the translation of the symbols
refer to the pertinent sections of the handbook.)

agr/pn	faulty pronoun-noun agreement **23** (p. 570)
agr/sv	faulty subject-verb agreement **22** (p. 564)
apos	use apostrophe for possessive case of noun **20** (p. 561)
awk	awkward expression **45** (p. 621)
coh	coherence of the paragraph is weak **55** (p. 637)
CS	comma splice **30** (p. 591)
Da	use appropriate diction **42** (p. 614)
dangl	dangling modifier **25** (p. 576)
Dev	inadequate development of the paragraph **52** (p. 642)
div	improper division of word at end of sentence **88** (p. 699)
Dx	use exact, precise diction **41** (p. 612)
fig	faulty figure of speech **48** (p. 628)
frag	sentence fragment **29** (p. 586)
FS	fused sentence **31** (p. 594)
hyph	use hyphen for the compound word **87** (p. 695)
id	unidiomatic expression **43** (p. 617)
ital	use italics **83, 85, 86,** (pp. 688, 692, 694)
MS	improper manuscript form **10–16** (pp. 554–556)
num	improper use of arabic numeral **89** (p. 700)
p/C	use comma here **60, 61, 63, 64** (pp. 651, 654, 659, 662)
p/Col	use colon here **68** (p. 675)
p/d	use dash here **69, 70, 71** (pp. 677, 679, 681)
p/sc	use semicolon here **66, 67** (pp. 670, 673)
paral	breakdown of parallel structure **27** (p. 579)
pass	questionable use of passive verb **49** (p. 629)
pred	faulty predication **40** (p. 609)
quot	quotation mark placed improperly in relation to punctuation mark **80, 81, 82** (pp. 684, 686, 687)
ref	faulty reference of pronoun **24** (p. 573)
rep	careless repetition **47** (p. 626)
trite	trite expression **44** (p. 619)
U	unity of the paragraph is weak **50** (p. 633)
wordy	unnecessarily wordy sentence **46** (p. 624)
WW	wrong word **40** (p. 609)

THE LITTLE RHETORIC
&
HANDBOOK
WITH
READINGS

Edward P. J. Corbett
The Ohio State University

Scott, Foresman and Company
Glenview, Illinois

Dallas, Tex.   Oakland, N.J.
Palo Alto, Calif.   Tucker, Ga.   London, England

A Double Dedication

> —*to Aristotle, who taught me most of what I know about rhetoric.*
>
> —*to all my students over the years, whose written prose sometimes mystified me, often enlightened me, and invariably beguiled me. Bless them all.*

An Instructor's Manual is available. It may be obtained through your local Scott, Foresman representative or by writing to English Editor, College Division, Scott, Foresman and Company, 1900 E. Lake Avenue, Glenview, IL 60025.

Library of Congress Cataloging in Publication Data

Corbett, Edward P. J.
  The little rhetoric and handbook with readings.

  "A combination of the second edition of The little rhetoric, the third edition of The little English handbook, and a gathering of about thirty prose readings"—Pref.
  Includes index.
  1. English language—Rhetoric. 2. College readers.
I. Title.
PE1408.C587 1983   808'.042   82-23089
ISBN 0-673-15830-6

Printed in the United States of America.
2345678910-HPI-9089888786858483

ISBN 0-673-15830-6

Preface

The Little Rhetoric and Handbook with Readings is a combination of the second edition of *The Little Rhetoric and Handbook* and a gathering of some thirty prose readings. By adding readings to *The Little Rhetoric and Handbook*, I hope to enhance its usefulness for those who appreciate having a rhetoric and a reader and a handbook all under a single cover. At the same time, I hope that I have preserved those features that teachers and students valued most in earlier editions.

The readings I have chosen illustrate the four modes of discourse treated in Chapter Seven: Narration, Description, Exposition, and Argumentation. There is a balance among the selections between classic and contemporary essays, well-known and new authors, topics of weight and topics of levity, and long and short pieces. You will also notice that the Exposition and Argumentation essays cover a wide variety of rhetorical patterns—from Analogy and Example to Comparison and Contrast and Testimony.

The selection of readings includes familiar classics by writers such as Swift, Virginia Woolf, and Langston Hughes, but also some not-so-familiar pieces by popular writers such as E. B. White, Lewis Thomas, and Ashley Montagu. There are also essays by infrequently anthologized contemporary writers, ranging from topics lyrical (N. Scott Momaday's "Yellowstone and the Kiowas") or humorous (Jean Shepherd's "Easter Ham and the Bumpus Hounds") to issues of

Preface

serious concern (Ellen Goodman's "Drafting Daughters," Richard Rodriguez's "Achievement of Desire," and Jonathan Schell's "Destructive Power of a Nuclear Bomb").

In order to keep the structure flexible, I have placed the readings in a separate, middle part, where they are accessible but not cemented to a particular section. For the same reason, I have chosen not to subdivide the readings beyond the four modes of discourse—Narration, Description, Exposition, and Argumentation: since many of the essays feature more than one rhetorical device (e.g., the selection by Judith Viorst uses Classification, Definition, and Example), I feel further categorization limits their usefulness. Instead, I have indicated in the table of contents the rhetorical patterns used in each Exposition and Argumentation essay, thus enabling the user to select essays suitable for his or her own purpose.

The rhetoric portion of the text deals, in a brief and sometimes schematic way, with the whole process of effective writing. Basically, my approach is a traditional, familiar one: a step-by-step linear sequence, beginning with the initial assignment and moving progressively through the stages of Fixing on a Subject, Finding Something to Say, Selecting and Arranging the Material, and Expressing What Has Been Discovered, Selected, and Arranged. In Chapter Six, entitled Putting It All Together, a specific topic is carried through all of those stages, from initiating assignment to final product. Chapter Seven deals with the basic strategies of discovery, arrangement, and style in relation to four kinds of discourse, Narration, Description, Exposition, and Argumentation. Chapter Eight goes on to deal with four special kinds of writing assignments: writing about literature, writing essay examinations, writing formal reports, and writing abstracts. Chapter Nine deals with some special forms of writ-

Preface

ing: the research paper, the business letter, the résumé, and the memorandum.

I have incorporated into this commonplace approach to the writing process several of the traditional and recent techniques of invention or discovery and a variety of imitative and sentence-combining exercises in style. In addition to the MLA style of documenting a research paper, I have introduced the system of documentation recommended by the American Psychological Association (APA), the second most widely used system in the United States. In accordance with the directions given in the latest edition of the *MLA Handbook,* the notes for the sample research paper in this edition have been presented not as footnotes at the bottom of the page, but as endnotes on separate pages at the end of the paper.

From the variety of methods of "composition" offered in this text, I trust that writers will find a method—or combination of methods—that works for them.

In the handbook section, I concentrate on those matters of grammar, style, paragraphing, punctuation, and mechanics that I know from my years of experience in reading student papers and responding to telephone queries from people in the business world to be the most common and persistent problems in the expressive part of the writing process. Following the handbook is a brief Glossary of Usage.

An essential feature of this book has always been its small size, and of course, even with minor deletions, the addition of readings has enlarged the book somewhat. However, I think you will still find *The Little Rhetoric and Handbook with Readings* a compact—and now more useful and complete—text for teaching composition.

Edward P. J. Corbett

Acknowledgments

The rhetoric part of this book has benefited immeasurably from the criticisms and suggestions of a number of experienced teachers: Elizabeth Wooten Cowan and the late Greg Cowan of Texas A & M University, Richard Lloyd-Jones of the University of Iowa, Joseph F. Trimmer of Ball State University, Betty Renshaw of Prince George's Community College, James Raymond of the University of Alabama, W. G. Schermbrucker of Capilano College in British Columbia, Caroline Eckhardt of Pennsylvania State University, Margaret Blickle of Ohio State University, Elizabeth K. Burton of Montclair High School, C. Jeriel Howard of Northeastern Illinois University, John D. Groppe of St. Joseph's College, Robert J. Reddick of the University of Texas at Arlington, Ronald S. Woodland of Edinboro State College, Joyce S. Beck of the University of Texas at Arlington, Patricia Robinson of St. Joseph's College, Marie Secor of Pennsylvania State University, Thomas P. Adler of Purdue University, Timothy Donovan of Northeastern University, and Gary Tate of Texas Christian University.

At all stages, the handbook has profited immensely from the advice of knowledgeable teachers, but if I were to name all the teachers who offered me helpful advice as far back as the prospectus stage, the list would be prohibitively long. So while I continue to be grateful to all those reviewers who guided me in preparing the first edition of the handbook, I want to acknowledge here those people who gave me detailed suggestions for improving the handbook in its second and third editions: Peter DeBlois of Syracuse University, Evelyn Claxton of Rend Lake College, George Miller of the

Acknowledgments

University of Delaware, Annette Rottenberg of the University of Massachusetts, W. G. Schermbrucker of Capilano College in British Columbia, Maureen Waters Oser of Queens College, Sarah M. Wallace and her colleagues at Volunteer Community College in Tennessee, Peter T. Zoller of Wichita State University, Robert Fox of St. Francis College, James Nardin of Louisiana State University, and Paul Sorrentino of Pennsylvania State University.

I was judiciously guided in choosing readings for this edition by the following people: Jay Balderson, Western Illinois University; Thomas Carnicelli, University of New Hampshire; Toni A. Lopez, University of Florida; Donovan J. Ochs, University of Iowa; Robert S. Rudolph, University of Toledo; John J. Ruszkiewicz, University of Texas; Jack Selzer, Pennsylvania State University; David Skwire, Cuyahoga Community College; James M. Williams, Johnson County Community College; James C. Work, Colorado State University.

I want to thank Stephen G. Perine and Stephen Lunsford for preparing the Teacher's Manual for this edition of *The Little Rhetoric and Handbook with Readings* and Kathryn N. Benzel and Janne Goldbeck for preparing *The Little English Workbook* for the third edition of the handbook. Both of these aids have considerably enhanced the classroom usefulness of the texts.

I am immeasurably indebted to countless members of the staff at Scott, Foresman, but I want to single out for special mention Harriett Prentiss and Amanda Clark, who strongly supported me at all stages of preparing this edition, and Lydia Webster, who edited the manuscript with meticulous care and infallible common sense.

Edward P. J. Corbett

Contents

Contents

Contents

Contents

Contents

Contents

The Readings

Contents

Chapter 12
Exposition   433

Contents

Contents

The Handbook

Legend   **549**

Contents

Contents

THE LITTLE
RHETORIC
&
HANDBOOK
WITH
READINGS

The Rhetoric

Chapter 1
What is Rhetoric?

What is rhetoric? One definition is that **rhetoric is the art of effective communication**. That brief, rather general definition demands explanation. First of all, to say that rhetoric is an *art* means that it is a skill—one that enables us to make wise choice of the means to achieve a desired end.

Choice is a key term in rhetoric. When there is no choice available, we are probably in a realm where we have to do something in a single, invariable way. For instance, if we want to produce water chemically, we must fuse two parts of hydrogen with one part of oxygen; we have no choice in the matter. But in the realm of art, we do have the choice of two or more means to achieve the desired end, and throughout this book, you will be made aware of these choices and will be shown how to make the best choice of the means available to you.

The word **communication** in our definition derives from two Latin words that together mean "making one with." When we say that we communicate with someone, we are suggesting that through words or some other set of symbols or actions, we are, in a sense, making that person at-one with us. We are using symbols or actions to make someone understand or appreciate our thoughts and feelings. When that state of at-

1

What Is Rhetoric?

oneness is not completely achieved, we are still "at odds" with one another. In other words, our communication has not been wholly *effective*. In some way, we have failed to make the right choice of the means of transmitting our message to someone.

There are of course many symbol systems that we can use to convey our message. We can, for instance, use gestures or facial expressions or pictures or sounds or black squiggles on a piece of paper. The most efficient system of symbols that man has devised for conveying most messages is the system of words—either spoken words or written words. This text will deal almost exclusively with effective communication through the medium of *written* words.

Most of the communicating you will do during your lifetime will be through the medium of spoken words. But occasionally you will have to resort to written words. If you find it difficult to communicate with written words, remember that most people find it difficult. One reason for this difficulty is that they have had much more practice in speaking than in writing. They probably speak more words in a single month than they will ever write in a lifetime. No wonder they feel so much more at ease in speaking than in writing: frequent practice in any skill is bound to improve the skill.

Another reason why speaking words is easier than writing words is that in speaking, we usually have to produce only short bursts of words—perhaps only a word or phrase at a time, at most only two or three consecutive sentences. And we usually don't have to search for something to say, nor do we have to arrange the order of sentences. Our grasp of the vocabulary and the grammar of our native language has been so internalized after years of oral practice that we have only to open our mouths and the words trip off our tongues.

But the written medium is another matter. Except for short notes we sometimes dash off or tack up on a bulletin board, most writing demands an extensive, uninterrupted sequence of sentences—two or three or ten pages of words with a beginning, a middle, and an end, which must have a certain measure of unity and coherence. It is that kind of sustained writing that is difficult for most of us and that this text mainly deals with.

This text tries to help you *compose*—that is, *put together*—an extended piece of writing—the kind of writing that requires many words, many sentences, many paragraphs, many divisions.

●

The rhetorical interrelationships

What might help you at the outset to grasp the art of effective writing is some understanding of the interrelationships that are involved in any act of communication with words. The rhetorical act—the kind of act we are concerned with here—involves *someone* saying *something* to *someone else*. As you can see, there are three distinct elements—a **writer**, a **message**, and a **reader**. These three can be put in pronoun terms—an *I*, an *it*, and a *you*. (Although a singular noun or pronoun is used here for the third element—*reader, you*—most of the time in a sustained piece of writing, the writer is addressing a *group* of readers. A word that carries this idea of plurality is **audience**, and it is this word that we will most often use for the third element.)

But there is another, fourth, term that should now be introduced into this rhetorical set of relationships. We will use the word **universe** for this fourth element. The *universe* is the "world out there" in which the writer and the audience exist and about which the message is perhaps talking; but sometimes the message may not be talking about the "world out

What Is Rhetoric?

there." Occasionally, it may be talking only about the thoughts and feelings within the private self of the writer. A writer who says, "The sun is shining today," is obviously saying something about the condition of the "world out there." But the writer who says, "I am happy today," is saying something about the condition of the "world within." Diaries and journals are examples of this latter kind of writing, especially when they are mere recordings of the thoughts, reactions, and feelings of the writer. Eventually, of course, some journals and diaries are read by an audience, and so they take on a communicative aspect that they did not have when they were first composed; but still, what they record is primarily the inner world of the writer rather than the outer world that can be perceived by both the writer and the audience. Sometimes this kind of writing is called "expressive discourse"—discourse that "pushes out" what is inside the mind of the writer.

There is a value to, and a place for, expressive writing. We are all richer because of the "personal" writing that has come down to us from the past, whether in elegant prose or in lyric verse. But the writing that most of us have to do deals with the "world out there." We have to give information about, or urge a course of action in relation to, an object, a situation, or an idea that exists in that world. The response of readers to this kind of writing will partly depend on how accurately our description or interpretation corresponds with the reality that they know or perceive. Our view of the world will be rejected if readers say to themselves, "That just isn't so." For that reason alone, the communication will be judged as something less than *effective*.

The four elements of **writer**, **message**, **audience**, and **universe** not only shed light on the communication process and the rhetoric that governs effective communication but also provide reference points to help us make a wise choice of options. A diagram may help us see how the four elements serve as reference points:

4

● The Rhetorical Interrelationships

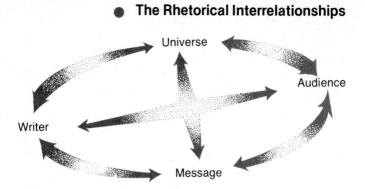

The two-way arrows in this diagram indicate the reciprocal—the back-and-forth—relationships among the four elements.

As a result of the relationships in the communication process, we have a number of standards to help us make wise choices from among the means at our disposal. We may decide, for instance, to adopt one kind of approach rather than another kind

Choices

1 because we feel that this approach is closer to **reality** as we see it in the universe than the other is, or

2 because we sense that this particular **audience** is more likely to accept this approach than the other, or

3 because this approach fits better (than the other) with the **other approaches** already in the message, or   ?

4 because this approach better suits our own **value system**.

In writing, we may not always, or even often, consciously make our choices in reference to the other elements, but if we are to be effective, we must at least *unconsciously* or *subconsciously* do so. Our writing will hang together and do its job to the extent that we deliberately or intuitively make our choices in relation to the audience, the message, the universe, and ourselves. In order to assess these relationships accurately, we must, of course, *know* something about

What Is Rhetoric?

1 **the nature of the universe**,
2 **the disposition of our audience**,
3 **the possible structures of our message**,
4 **our own disposition**.

These reference points also work when choices have to be made among units as small as the word or the sentence. Why do writers choose a certain word rather than another, synonymous, word? Perhaps this word is more consistent with their own personality than the other word is ("I don't like big, pretentious words"). Or they might choose one over the other because they sense that it will be better understood by the particular audience they are addressing at the moment. Or they might choose it because it fits better with the level of vocabulary that they have been using or because it more precisely conveys the comment they want to make about the "world out there." Their choices of sentence structure for their message may also be guided by their conscious or unconscious consideration of one or other of the above four elements. But along with those features of style that represent more or less conscious choices, there will be others that represent *habit*. A writer's style is therefore a combination of habitual and chosen features.

The art of rhetoric had its beginnings with Greek and Roman practitioners of the art (called *rhetoricians*), such as Aristotle, Isocrates, Cicero, and Quintilian. Rhetoric, with them, dealt primarily with persuasive public speaking. It presented theoretical principles and practical suggestions for composing and delivering speeches that would confirm or change an audience's mind or that would move an audience to act or not to act. As rhetoric developed throughout the Middle Ages and the Renaissance, its principles and practices were extended to written, and other than just persuasive, kinds of discourse. By the third quarter of the eighteenth century, George Campbell, the Scottish rhetorician, could define rhetoric as "that art or talent by which the discourse is adapted to its end," the ends of discourse being reducible to four: "to enlighten the understanding, to please the imagination, to move the passions, or to influence the will." Thus rhetoric had been expanded to embrace a wide range of functions: **instructing**, **informing**, **entertaining**, **persuading**, and **moving to action**, and during the third quarter of the nineteenth century, these functions became the basis of the four types of discourse that have been a staple of twentieth-century rhetoric texts: **exposition**, **description**, **narration**, and **argumentation**. This text also regards rhetoric as applicable to a wide range of functions and to the full range of the types of discourse.

So we return to our definition of rhetoric as the *art of effective communication*; but now we have a better understanding of all that is included in that broad, general definition. We see that **effective communication involves a concern for the interrelations among the writer, the audience, the message, and the universe, that it depends on wise choices being made from among the available means, and that it embraces a wide range of functional types of written prose**. We must now move on to the particulars of this *art of effective communication*.

Classical
 to please (middle)
 to convince (plain)
 to move (grand)

epideictic
deliberative
judicial

Chapter 2
Fixing on a Subject

Sometimes when you have to write something, the choice of a subject will be entirely your own. You may feel the urge to write a letter to the editor of the local newspaper about the miserable condition of the city streets. You may have agreed to write to the manager of a department store to recommend a friend who is applying for a summer position at the store. You may have to write a letter to a friend to explain why you didn't stop by for a visit on your trip West. In each case, the choice of *whether* to write was your own, and the choice of *what* to write about was your own. Under such circumstances, you usually experience little or no difficulty in composing the letter. The words just seem to flow onto the paper.

But it seems safe to say that on at least ninety percent of the occasions when you have to write something, either in school or on the job, both the decision to write and the choice of a subject are *not* yours to make. Someone asks or requires you to write something and determines, at least in a general way, the subject you are to write about. A teacher requires you to write a paper on the history of progressive income tax; an employer asks you to prepare a written report on annual sales patterns for the forthcoming board meeting; an editor commissions you to write an article on predatory sharks at resort beaches. You can of course refuse to write, but for your refusal, you may have to pay the penalty of failing the course, losing your job, or forgoing a royalty check.

Even when you don't have a choice of subject to make, many choices about the *treatment* of the subject will be left up to you. One of the most crucial decisions you will have to make—even when the choice of subject is up to you—is what *aspect* of the subject you are going to treat. Almost always, you will have to put some limitations on the subject, because usually you will not be able, or even required, to treat it exhaustively.

Let us set forth in outline form some of the considerations that can help you limit your subject:

1 **The amount of wordage you are allotted.**
2 **The purpose of the writing.**
3 **The occasion of the writing.**
4 **The nature of the audience for whom you are writing.**
5 **The extent and depth of your knowledge of the subject.**
6 **The thesis or central point you want to make about the subject.**

Other considerations may help to limit the subject, but these are the common ones.

Let us take a subject and show how these considerations might help you to fix the limits of your treatment. Suppose that you were asked to write about the subject of *capital punishment*.

(1) Usually when you are assigned a subject, some **word limit** is suggested: a 500-word theme, a 3000-word research paper, a 6000-word article, a 10,000-word pamphlet, a 70,000-word book. Obviously, the amount of wordage allotted to you will greatly influence how much you have to restrict your sub-

Fixing on a Subject

ject. If you have only 500 words to work with, you may have to treat only one aspect of the subject, and your treatment of that one aspect will have to be more general than if you had 6000 words to work with.

(2) What (besides doing an assignment) is your **purpose** in writing about capital punishment? Do you wish merely *to inform* your audience about the present status or the past history of capital punishment in your state? Or do you wish *to argue* for a particular position on the issue of whether capital punishment should be continued? Your answers to the question of purpose will have some influence on the aspect or aspects of your subject that you will write about.

(3) The **occasion** of your writing will also suggest some limitations. If, for instance, you were writing a letter to the editor about capital punishment—a subject that was being hotly debated in your state legislature—you would choose a smaller portion of the subject than if you were writing a term paper about capital punishment. For one thing, the letter would not require any extensive review of the situation or any definition of key terms, for these would be familiar to newspaper readers from reports about the debate. And, of course, a letter treating the subject in 150 words would have a better chance of being published than would a letter of 500 or more words.

(4) The **audience** for whom you are writing will have a great influence on the limits you set for your subject. For whom *are* you writing? For your sociology teacher? For a group of concerned university students? For the general public? For the state legislators? For a group of clergymen gathered at a national convention? Once you have determined who your main audience will be, you will have to estimate the extent of that audience's *knowledge* of the subject and its *attitude* toward the subject. Those estimates will help determine what should be included in, and what excluded from, your treatment. For a group

of lawyers, you might want to concentrate on the legal aspects of capital punishment; for a group of clergymen, you might decide to concentrate on the moral issues.

(5) Obviously, the extent and depth of your **knowledge** of the subject will help to determine what aspects you will select to write about. As the old saying goes, "You can't give what you don't have." A professional penologist knows more about capital punishment than the ordinary citizen does. You can extend and deepen your knowledge of the subject by research, of course, but you will still probably have less knowledge of the subject than the professional penologist has. You will tend to select that segment of the subject which you know most about or feel most strongly about.

(6) Determining the **thesis** or central point of your discourse is one of the best ways to establish the limits of a subject. The very nature of a thesis statement—a single declarative sentence in which the predicate asserts or denies something about the subject—sets severe limits on a subject. The subject "capital punishment" covers a vast territory. But as soon as you predicate something of that subject—as in the thesis statement "Capital punishment is not an effective deterrent to crimes of violence"—you fence off a portion of that territory, a manageable part of the subject for purposes of writing. The thesis statement "Capital punishment is morally indefensible" stakes out another manageable portion of the vast territory. **The mere formulation of a thesis statement helps you to define your subject more narrowly.**

●
Applying the six considerations to a specific topic

Having been shown in a general way how the six considerations might help you to define and limit your subject, you can

11

Fixing on a Subject

now take the broad subject of capital punishment and apply these considerations to it in order to determine what aspect of it you will treat. These considerations need not be explored in the same order in which they are laid out above, nor need all six of them be explored. But by way of illustration, we will explore all six considerations and take them in the order in which they occur above.

1 You are asked to write a twenty-minute speech on capital punishment to be delivered to the members of an upper-division Speech course you are taking. At a normal speaking rate, eight double-spaced typewritten pages (2000–2500 words) can be delivered in approximately twenty minutes. So you have a fair idea of **how long** a speech you have to write.

2 You are told that the **purpose** of your speech is to inform your audience about the history of capital punishment in the state.

3 The **occasion** of your speech is a classroom exercise. You recognize that this is a rather artificial situation, so you know that the information you convey will not serve any real function, except perhaps to educate the audience to some extent. (On another occasion, such a historical survey might serve a real function—for instance, as background information for your fellow-legislators who are faced with the decision of whether to reinstate capital punishment for certain crimes.) However, the very artificiality of this occasion might help suggest to you the particular aspect of the subject you should concentrate on in your speech.

4 Your **audience** will be classmates with a wide variety of backgrounds and academic, social, religious, and political viewpoints. Almost anything you tell this audience about capital punishment in your state will be news to them; consequently, the historical details you present will not seem trite to them.

● Applying the Six Considerations to a Topic

5 As for your **knowledge** of the subject, you are not an expert on capital punishment; in fact, the only thing you know about capital punishment in your state is something you recall hearing or reading recently: that no one has been executed in the state penitentiary in the last four years. So almost everything you tell your audience about the history of capital punishment in your state will have to be found out from the research you do between now and the time of your speech. You decide that in the time available you can research only the history of the laws about capital punishment passed in your state.

6 You may not be able to formulate a **thesis** until you have done your research, but let us suppose that you tentatively set the following as the thesis of your speech: ''The punishments for capital offenses in our state have become more lenient.'' Your research will then turn up evidence either to support your thesis or to change it.

After running through these six considerations, you have a clearer idea of the kinds of limitation you must put on your treatment of the assigned subject. You know that you have to limit your speech to eight pages **(1)** Accordingly, you know that you can give more details than you could if you had to write an 800-word essay on the subject but fewer details than if you had to write a 6000-word term paper. You will have to touch on only the landmarks in the 150-year history of capital punishment in your state **(2)** Since the most natural arrangement for your speech will be to take events as they occurred over the years, perhaps you can present your history in a sequence of 25-year segments—about a page for each segment, leaving some space for an introduction and a conclusion. Since the speech is a classroom exercise for a grade **(3)** even though your audience will be your classmates **(4)** you will have to impress the instructor, who is likely to be impressed in proportion to how

Fixing on a Subject

well you hold the interest of your audience. You are not likely to hold their interest if you merely recite facts and statistics; so in your research, you will have to look out for human-interest details **(5)**. Your tentative thesis too will help you to set limits on those aspects of your general subject that you will explore in your speech **(6)**

You begin now to see the dimensions of your treatment of the subject. You have reduced the once sprawling subject to a manageable area; the fences are staked out around it. You know now what aspects of the subject you are going to talk about and what aspects you are *not* going to talk about. In 2000 to 2500 words, you are going to inform your classmates about the progressively lenient laws passed by the state legislature over the last 150 years.

You are now ready for the next stage in the writing process: finding something to say about your delimited subject. But before we go on to that, let us review the considerations that may help you to fix limits to the subject you are going to write on:

1 **The specified length of your paper** (how many words are you allotted?).

2 **The purpose of your paper** (what are you seeking to accomplish with this piece of writing—informing? instructing? persuading? entertaining?).

3 **The occasion of your paper** (are there any special circumstances in this occasion that have a bearing on your treatment of the subject?).

4 **The nature of the audience for whom you are writing** (what will your audience be? will it be fairly uniform? what is likely to be its temperament? what is likely to be the extent of its knowledge about your subject?).

● Applying the Six Considerations to a Topic

5 **The extent and depth of your knowledge of the subject** (how much do you know about this subject? how much more will you have to learn? how much research can you do in the time available?).

6 **The thesis or central point you want to make about the subject** (can you now formulate a thesis statement that will help you fix limits to your subject?).

Chapter 3
Finding Something To Say

Once you have fixed the limits of your subject, you face the most difficult part of the composition process: *finding something to say about the subject*. This is the stage that the classical rhetoricians called **invention**, which meant "discovery through a process of search or inquiry." Their texts dealt at great length with this crucial stage of the composing process and suggested a system for generating something to say about a subject. This text will present a simplified form of the classical system and will suggest some other systems for generating ideas. But first let us consider further the problem of finding something pertinent and significant to say about a subject once it has been delimited.

The really hard part of the writing process is, paradoxically enough, the *prewriting* stage—all those things you have to do *before* you put a single word down on paper. But if you do a thorough job in the prewriting stage, you will find that writing the paper becomes, if not easy, certainly easier. You have probably had the experience, at one time or another, of writing that simply flowed onto the paper. What happened in that case is that you had gained a firm grasp on what you wanted to say even before you sat down to write. You had assembled all the bricks, and all you had to do was lay them out in a neat pattern and put mortar between them. If all writing were that easy, many people would try to make their living by writing for publication. But writing never becomes easy; it may, however, become easier. As with any other skill, writing becomes easier if you practice it and if you develop a "discovery" procedure that works for you most of the time.

As we saw in the previous chapter, you will rarely have the opportunity of picking the subject you are going to write about, although you may have the opportunity of delimiting it. If you had the choice of subject, you would naturally write about what you knew best or what you felt compelled to write about. But often when you are handed a subject, you cannot simply write about it off the top of your head. You have to think about it for a while, meditate on it, ponder it, perhaps read something about it. Experienced writers, who necessarily write frequently, develop some system for generating ideas. What works for one writer may not work for another, so you will have to find or devise a system that works for you. What this text will do is acquaint you with some of the systems of search and discovery that have worked for others and invite you to try them out to see if they work for you.

●

Some common informal methods of search and discovery

(A) BRAINSTORMING

One of the systems that have worked for many writers is a system that might be called *brainstorming*. This is the system of taking a subject and **listing, in random, rapid-fire fashion,**

Finding Something To Say

anything you can think of that has even the remotest relation to the subject. The listing can be done in the form of words or phrases or sentences. Relying on the process of free association, you write down as many ideas as come to your mind. You will often be surprised at how many usable ideas about the subject can be turned up by this brainstorming technique.

Suppose that you were assigned to write a paper on "The Influence of Music on My Life." If you put your mind in gear, you might come up with a random list like this:

First hooked on music by the
    "singing commercials" on
    TV
Memories of sing-alongs
    around the family piano
A prisoner of piano-practice
    on Saturday mornings
My tone-deaf music teacher
My first piano recital
The "big deal" on my first
    record-player
My Elton John phase
Nostalgia for the Beatles
Into "hard-rock"
Music and my first date
Family crisis about the
    loudness of my record-
    player
Attending my first outdoor
    concert
Hooked on Earl Scruggs and
    Doc Watson
My bluegrass phase
Strumming a friend's guitar

● Informal Methods of Search and Discovery

Buying my first guitar
Pilgrimage to Grand Ole Opry
   in Nashville
Jam-sessions at parties
My growing record library
Three-finger picking
Music for my lonely hours

The list could go on and on, but almost any young man or woman could produce a list that long in ten or fifteen minutes of scribbling "off the top of one's head."

The brainstorming technique works best, of course, with subjects you know something about just from your own experiences. (You probably couldn't come up with a very long list on the subject of nuclear fission.) You might not be able to use all, or even most, of the items you compiled on the subject of music, especially if you had been told to confine your essay to 500–800 words. You would have to do some selecting and grouping. But at least you would have discovered more than enough material for the writing assignment.

(B) MEDITATION

Closely allied to brainstorming is the technique of meditation. You may be aware that the practice of meditation has had a long tradition in monasteries and seminaries in the West, beginning in the Middle Ages and continuing to the present day; and the practice is still prevalent in many Asian religions. Ignatius of Loyola, the founder of the Jesuit order in the sixteenth century, wrote a training manual called *The Spiritual Exercises*, in which he gave detailed instructions about the technique of meditation. In general, the technique consists in taking a short passage from the Scriptures or from the text of the day's Mass and, in an atmosphere of silence and freedom from distraction, thinking about it in a serious, persistent way, trying to see the relevance of that passage to one's own life and spiritual growth. If engaged in conscientiously, meditation can be a wonderfully effective way of discovering one's self and one's relations with other people and with God.

Systems of meditation are designed to put people in an atmosphere and a disposition that lead to a heightening of consciousness. For that reason, meditation can be an effective way of turning up ideas for writing about a subject. It differs from brainstorming in that it is a more systematic way of pondering the subject. It will work, however, only if you remove yourself from an atmosphere of noise and distraction. An ideal setting is a small quiet room, with a moderately comfortable chair facing a blank wall, so that you can't gaze out the window. In that kind of setting, put your mind in gear and let it run.

At first, you can just **allow the free-association process to turn out random thoughts concerning the subject you are writing about**, much like the free-wheeling system of brainstorming. But if a particularly fruitful thought turns up, you should **make a deliberate effort to pursue that thought for several minutes**. The concentration on that one line of thought may suggest not only the main *approach* to the development of the topic but also the main *parts* of that development. Some people find that jotting down notes on a pad of paper interrupts their meditation and distracts them from the line of thought they were pursuing, and so they prefer to wait until they have finished the meditation before recording the ideas and images that were turned up.

Meditation requires disciplined concentration, and you probably won't find it very productive the first two or three times. But if you persist, you may find that meditation is an unusually productive method of search and discovery. Like the other systems reviewed in this chapter, it is a way of cultivating the mind and thereby generating ideas.

● Informal Methods of Search and Discovery

(C) RESEARCH

One of the commonest methods of search and discovery is research. But since research includes a variety of procedures, we will break it down into various categories and discuss each separately.

(1) Observation

The usual way we learn things about the world outside ourselves is by observation and contemplation of what comes to us through our senses of sight, hearing, taste, touch, and smell. Observation is an especially useful method when we have to narrate or report physical events or when we have to describe some physical object or scene.

Sometimes you may be assigned to attend a certain event and write a report of what happened. In that case, you will have to **observe carefully and perhaps take notes on what you observe**. What you see and hear will depend partly on your keenness of observation and partly on your physical and psychological point of view. It is well known that three people can witness the same event and report three different versions of it. One reason for the differences is that one of the observers may have developed keener powers of observation. Another reason is that one observer may have a better vantage point than the others, a better physical position for observing what happened. Another reason is that the various observers may have a certain mental attitude toward the event that influences what they see and hear. They tend to select those details of an event that confirm the attitudes they brought with them and to ignore or forget those details that do not agree with their attitudes.

If observation is the most suitable method of search and discovery for your writing assignment, you will have to force yourself to **observe more closely than you normally do**. Productive observation doesn't just happen; it is a skill that needs to be practiced and refined.

(2) Interviews

Another form of research is the face-to-face interview with a person or group. You can turn to this device when you are assigned to gather and report information or opinions from one or more people, whether they are experts on the subject or simply laypersons. **The usual technique of interviewing is to ask a series of prepared questions and to record the answers on tape, in a notebook, or in the memory.**

There is a real art to conducting the kind of interview that will yield significant information or opinion. Some of the moderators of talk-shows, like Johnny Carson, Barbara Walters, Merv Griffin, and Mike Wallace, have brought this art to a highly refined level. Such authors of "profiles" of prominent people as Truman Capote, Tom Wolfe, Gay Talese, and Rex Reed have also perfected the art of the interview.

Even when conducted on an amateur level, however, the interview can turn up useful material for a writing assignment. But **it is extremely important to select and to phrase questions so that they get at the kind of information or opinion you are seeking and to record as accurately and as fully as possible the answers you receive**. The person you interview may be able to recommend a local restaurant or two, but this information won't be useful if your assignment is to gather opinions about a tax proposal coming up for a vote. And nothing can make the person you interview angrier than to be quoted inaccurately or "out of context." Listen carefully, record accurately, and report fairly.

● Informal Methods of Search and Discovery

(3) Questionnaires

Another device for gathering information and opinions is the written questionnaire. The questionnaire is like the interview in that it presents a series of carefully prepared questions to several people who have been selected either randomly or deliberately. It differs from the interview in that whereas the interview is conducted face to face, **the questionnaire is usually distributed in a written form and often by mail**.

The questionnaire is a less reliable way than the interview for gathering material because while personal interviewers are almost guaranteed some kind of response to their questions, the distributor of a written questionnaire must depend on the goodwill and diligence of the interviewees in filling out and returning the questionnaire. The distributor will be glad if he or she gets even a fifty-percent return. Normally, the shorter the questionnaire and the easier it is to respond to (check-off answers, for instance, rather than written responses), the higher the percentage of returns. Another significant difference is that the personal interviewer usually has to deal with only a few respondents, but the distributor of the questionnaire may have to deal with hundreds. Consequently, **the distributor has to tabulate a great number of responses and then must try to make valid generalizations from the accumulated responses**.

(4) Experiments

The controlled experiment is a common technique used in the hard sciences, and it is becoming increasingly common in the social sciences too. Scientists, doctors, sociologists, and

Finding Something To Say

political scientists regularly conduct **experiments to discover facts or to confirm theories and assumptions. The data provided by an experiment then become the basis for a written report**.

Whereas experimenters in the hard sciences most often deal with inanimate elements or with animals, experimenters in the social sciences most often deal with people. A political scientist, for instance, may want to test a theory about how people respond to a persuasive message in various media. So she will assemble a group of people, often by random choice, will expose each member to the same persuasive message delivered successively in writing, in a cassette recording, in a videotape presentation, and in a live speech, and then will try to measure the impact of the message as presented in the various media.

Even simple experiments could yield material for a fascinating essay. Suppose that you want to test your theory that the workers who come into the city from a newly built northern suburb are more likely to drive subcompact cars, whereas the workers who come into the city from a long-established western suburb are likely to drive large automobiles. You enlist the aid of a friend who can identify cars as well as you can, and between the hours of 7:00 and 8:00 in the morning, from Monday through Friday, both of you stand at the intersection of the main street leading from the northern suburb and the main street leading from the western suburb, and you count the number of large and subcompact cars coming from the north, and your friend counts the number of large and subcompact cars coming from the west. A comparison of your tabulations at the end of the week will confirm or negate your hypothesis and might yield some material for an interesting essay about the sociological significance of your findings.

● Formal Methods of Search and Discovery

(5) Reading

Reading is a great source for discovering facts, opinions, insights, and interpretations, because for centuries, writing or printing was the principal way of recording and transmitting information or judgments. For some writing assignments, books, articles, and other printed matter provide the only, or the main, source of the material you need. The main repository of printed matter is the library. A later chapter of this book carries a section that tells you how to make use of various reference sources in the library in order to find pertinent books and articles for a writing assignment. Once you find the pertinent books and articles, you have to extract from them what may be usable. **You may want to take notes as you read or after you read. From your handwritten notes, you may later want to summarize, paraphrase, or quote some of the material in your own piece of writing.**

●

Some formal, systematic methods of search and discovery

The Journalistic Formula

1 **Who?**   4 **Where?**
2 **What?**   5 **Why?**
3 **When?**   6 **How?**

This formula was once widely used as a guideline for reporters about the key questions that the "lead" part of a news story—the first sentence or the first paragraph—should answer. The formula is less closely followed now than it once was, but it is

Finding Something To Say

still useful for suggesting the main points that should be covered in certain types of writing, especially the reporting of an event.

The six questions do not all have to be answered in a single part of the essay, as they are in this "lead" sentence from a news story:

> John Proxmire [**who**] was critically injured [**what**] in an auto accident [**how**] because of a malfunctioning stoplight [**why**] at the intersection of Maple and Sycamore [**where**] during the evening rush-hour on Friday [**when**].

Nor do all six questions always have to be answered. The formula does suggest, however, those aspects of a happening that you might want to concentrate on and develop in different parts of your narrative. In one part of the narrative, you might want to concentrate on the person (**who**) involved in the happening, supplying details about the person's biography, personality, and achievements; in another part, you might want to concentrate on the causes (**why**) of the event; in other parts, you might want to concentrate on the time (**when**), the setting (**where**), the manner (**how**), or the nature (**what**) of the event.

The journalistic formula is similar to a formula that Kenneth Burke, the literary critic, called the "dramatistic pentad":

1 **Action** (**What** happened?)
2 **Agent** (**Who** did it?)
3 **Means** (**How** did he do it?)
4 **Purpose** (**Why** did he do it?)
5 **Scene** (**Where** and **when** did it happen?)

The journalistic questions and the pentad bear some relation to the four traditional modes of discourse: exposition, argumentation, description, and narration. Although the journalistic questions are especially useful generating devices for reporting events (the narrative mode), they also have a bearing on the other modes. Concentration on the *where* or *when* (to give readers a sense of the "climate of the times") engages you primarily in the descriptive mode. *What* or *how* might lead you into the expository mode. *Why* might lead you into the argumentative mode. But just as there are mixtures of the modes in a single piece of writing (rarely is a piece purely expository or purely argumentative), so there could be interchanges between the six questions and the four modes.

The Classical Topics   *source? (Ad Herennium)*

You are probably familiar with the word *topic* as a synonym for *subject*. But we shall use the term here in a much different sense. *Topic* derives from the Greek word *topos*, meaning "place." Used metaphorically in rhetoric, it came to mean "a place where one went to hunt for arguments." In another sense, *topics* were "suggesters or generators of lines of argument." The topics of **definition, comparison, relationship,** and **testimony** represent the typical ways in which the human mind thinks about something. When you probe a subject, especially an unfamiliar one, you typically ask questions like these:

1 "What is it?" (**definition**).
2 "What is it like or unlike?" (**comparison**).
3 "What caused it?" (**relationship**).
4 "What is said about it?" (**testimony**).

These typical mental operations, arranged as headings or categories, suggest how you might go about developing a subject.

Let us first outline the topics, and then see how they might be used to find something to say about a subject.

Finding Something To Say

DEFINITION—"What is it?"

Types of definition:
> **Synonym**—shortest form of definition.
> **Formal definition**—putting the thing in a general class (*genus*) and then distinguishing it from other members of the class (*differentiation*).
> **Extended definition**—an amplified form of the one-sentence definition.
> **Stipulative definition**—"What I mean by . . ."
> **Classification**—division into distinct groups.
> **Examples**—giving concrete instances of an abstraction.

COMPARISON—"What is it like or unlike?"

Results of comparing things:
> **Similarity in kind**
> —metaphor and simile
> —analogy
> **Difference in kind**
> —antithesis
> —contrast
> **Similarity or difference in degree**
> —more, less, or the same

RELATIONSHIP—"What caused it?"

Types of relationship:
> **Cause and effect**
> —*this* produced *that* (cause to effect)
> —*that* was produced by *this* (effect to cause)
> **Antecedent and consequence**
> —*this* followed from *that*

● Formal Methods of Search and Discovery

TESTIMONY— "What is said about it?"

When you need:
—facts
—precedents
—statistics
—testimonials
—opinions
—documents

What you turn to:
—books
—magazines
—newspapers
—manuscripts
—records
—reports
—interviews
—questionnaires
—observation

Where you go:
—libraries
—private agencies
—government agencies
—museums
—computer centers
—experts
—"man-in-the-street"
—the scene itself

DEFINITION

One line of development that is always open to you is to explain the *nature* of something to someone. Natural human

Finding Something To Say

curiosity prompts us to try to define something and to pass the resulting clarification on to others. Definition is the basic line of development behind **exposition**, which presents information about, or an explanation of, something. An entire essay might be devoted to defining a concept (what is justice?) or a process (how to file for bankruptcy or how to program a computer) or an operation (how a digital watch works). But definition is also a line of development for *parts* of an essay. You might want to offer definitions of some key terms that will figure prominently in the essay.

Here are some common types of definition:

(1) Synonym

The simplest and briefest way to clarify the meaning of a word is to supply a word of similar meaning: *amnesty—pardon, reiterate—repeat, parsimonious—stingy*. There are three things to keep in mind when you are defining by synonym:

1 **Most synonyms are *approximate*, rather than exact, equivalents of the other word.**
2 **The synonym you supply must be the *same part of speech* as the other word—a noun for a noun, a verb for a verb, etc.**
3 **The synonym you supply must be *more familiar* to the audience than the word for which it stands.**

Dictionaries often supply synonyms for some words, and there is a book (called a *thesaurus*) that supplies nothing but synonyms.

(2) Formal Definition

A formal definition is the kind supplied by a dictionary—although instead of quoting verbatim from a dictionary, you could supply a formal definition in your own words. A formal definition is usually presented in a single sentence. A common way of defining concrete and abstract nouns is to put the thing to be defined into a general class (called the **genus**) and then to distinguish it from other members of the class (called the **differentiation**)—e.g. "An automobile is a *vehicle* [genus] with *four wheels*, propelled by an internal-combustion *engine* [differentiating details]"; "Democracy is that *type of government* [genus] in which the ultimate source of rule resides with the *people* [differentiating details]."

(3) Extended Definition

An extended definition is simply an amplified form of the one-sentence definition. It could take up an entire essay; more commonly it occupies several sentences. You often resort to extended definitions when you are dealing with unusually strange, complicated concepts or processes.

(4) Stipulative Definition

A stipulative definition is a definition formulated by the speaker or writer. Knowing that a particular term may have a variety of meanings, the speaker or writer tells the audience what *he* or *she* means in using the term. The audience may not accept the stipulated definition, but at least they know what meaning the author attaches to the term.

(5) Classification

Classification is another way of clarifying the meaning of something. It consists in dividing something into distinct groups according to a common basis. There are a number of ways, for instance, of classifying college students: (1) on the basis of

sex—male and female; (2) on the basis of geographical origin—in-state and out-of-state; (3) on the basis of their year-
standing—freshman, sophomore, junior, senior; (4) on the
basis of the college in which they are enrolled—Arts and Sciences, Business Administration, Law, Medicine, etc.; (5) on the
basis of their religious affiliation—Baptist, Methodist, Catholic,
Jewish, etc. There are many other categories, of course, into
which students could be classified, but the point here is that
classification is a means of clarifying the nature of something.

(6) Examples

One of the best ways to define an abstraction is to supply
one or more concrete examples. The ungrammatical formula
"Justice is when . . . " is an instance of this kind of definition.
Charles Shultz's "Happiness is a warm puppy" is another instance. The example could be something from real life or it
could be an invented fable or story.

COMPARISON

Another process for unfolding a subject is comparison. Especially when probing a new subject, you tend to compare it with
something that you and your audience are more or less familiar
with. And when you compare things, you discover one of the
following: *similarity* or *difference* in kind or *similarity* or *difference* in degree.

(1) Similarity

Similarity is the basic principle behind such figures of speech
as *metaphor* and *simile* and behind all development of a subject by *analogy*. Bringing two things together, you note their
likenesses. If two things were the same in all respects, you

would have *identity* rather than *similarity*. But they are similar in just enough respects to cast some light upon each other.

You can resort to *analogy* for purposes of **description** ("The apartment complex is laid out in the shape of the letter H") or of **exposition** ("A knee operates like the hinge on a door") or of **argumentation** ("If division of labor works efficiently in a bee-hive, we can expect the same kind of efficiency in a society where various groups of people are assigned to perform specific tasks").

One caution to observe in the use of analogy for purposes of description or exposition is that **the thing with which something else is being compared must be familiar to the audience**. (Comparing the layout of an apartment complex to the shape of a Lorraine cross would probably not convey a clear picture to most people.) A caution to observe in using analogy for purposes of argumentation is that **the similarities found between two things must not be overweighed by some crucial differences**. (There might be just enough significant differences between bees and human beings to make the analogy of the beehive invalid and therefore unpersuasive.)

Two questions that are likely to generate a line of development for a subject are **what is this like?** and **in what way are the two things similar?**

(2) Difference

Another possible result of comparison is the detection of differences. Differences disclose the *antitheses* and *contrasts* between things. Pointing out differences can often be as illuminating as pointing out similarities, whether for purposes of description, exposition, or argumentation. To say, "Whereas a football game is completed when a specified number of minutes of play have expired, a baseball game is completed when a specified number of innings have been played, no matter how long that takes,'' certainly gives us an idea of a crucial difference in the structure of these two sports.

Another question that is likely to generate a line of development is **in what significant ways does this thing differ from something else?**

(3) Degree

Sometimes when you compare things, you don't find similarities or differences *in kind*—that is, in the *basic nature or structure* of things—but rather you find similarities and differences *in degree*. Democracy and monarchy are two forms of government that differ *in kind*; but the democracies of two countries might differ only *in degree*—for instance, just in the degree of real power that the poeple have in determining how and by whom they are governed. Often you have to make a choice not between a *good* and an *evil* (a difference in kind) but between one good and another good (a difference of degree).

In general, when you make a judgment about *more* or *less, better* or *worse,* you do so on the basis either that one thing is *inherently more worthy or valuable* than another or that one thing is *more advantageous* (it brings more benefits) than another. In that case, you usually have to establish for yourself and reveal to your audience more specific criteria for making the judgment than those two general ones.

The topic of *degree* suggests another line of development that might be used when you are faced with the task of writing about some subject.

RELATIONSHIP

Like the topic of *comparison*, the topic of *relationship* invites you to bring things together and to note the light that is cast by one thing on another. But whereas comparison results in the

● Formal Methods of Search and Discovery

detection of similarity or difference in kind and degree, relationship may expose a *causal* or *conditional* link between two things.

(1) Cause and Effect

One of the kinds of relationship that may be revealed by juxtaposing things is the *cause-and-effect* relationship. One thing may be seen to be the *cause* of something else or to be the *effect* of something else. In essence, the *cause-and-effect* relationship seeks to establish one or the other of these two kinds of link between two things:

1 ***This* produced *that*.**
2 ***That* was produced by *this*.**

If you see a rock lying under a recently broken window, you naturally suppose that the rock is the "cause" of that broken window (the effect). And if you were looking for someone to pay for that broken window, you would have to search for a further cause—the culprit who heaved the rock through the window. If you detect the presence of a *potential cause* in a particular situation, you may be able to predict the *probable effect* if that potential cause is not removed. Thus, a candle burning dangerously close to some curtains is recognized as a potential cause of an undesirable effect—curtains on fire.

There are certain logical principles that govern cause-and-effect relationships—or at least the arguments that are based on cause-and-effect relationships. For instance, when you are trying to argue that one thing is the probable cause of another (the effect), you may have to establish:

1 That the cause is *capable* of producing the effect.
2 That other causes similarly capable were absent.

Finding Something To Say

A murder mystery is fundamentally an account of the working out of a cause-and-effect relationship—who murdered the man found dead in the library? The detective does not suspect the four-year-old boy of having strangled Lord Carruthers, because the child is physically incapable of such an act. He does not rule out the mild-mannered butler, because although this gentle man is an unlikely suspect, he is physically capable of strangling the lord of the manor. The 250-pound gardener, who quarreled with Lord Carruthers the day before, is the most suspect character in the household. And yet unless he is absolutely the last link in the chain of *capable* and *present* causes, the detective cannot point an accusing finger at the gardener. He may not *assume*, but must *prove*, that the gardener strangled Lord Carruthers.

(2) Antecedent-consequence

Another kind of relationship is the *antecedent-consequence* relationship, which is not so much causal as it is conditional. A consequence, for instance, of reaching a certain age in certain societies is that one becomes eligible to vote. The presence of conjunctions like *because, since, for* in a sentence may signal that the writer is claiming either a cause-and-effect relationship *or* an antecedent-consequence relationship, and you must be able to discriminate between the two. If someone says, "The water in the birdbath froze because the temperature dropped to twenty degrees above zero," he is claiming that the dropping of the temperature *caused* the freezing of the water. If, however, someone says, "Jim voted this year because he turned eighteen," he is not claiming that turning eighteen *caused* Jim to vote. Rather, turning eighteen was the necessary *antecedent* for any voting Jim might do; and with the antecedent condition satisfied, Jim consequently *did* vote.

● Formal Methods of Search and Discovery

It may not always be easy to determine whether a relationship is causal or conditional. Fortunately, in a writing situation, the determination will not always be crucial and will hardly affect how you proceed. It will be sufficient, in other words, to demonstrate that there is some kind of *connection* between things. (On the other hand, the fate of a person on trial for murder might very well depend on whether the alleged connection was merely *conditional*—or *causal*.)

TESTIMONY

Whereas the topics of *definition*, *comparison*, and *relationship* suggest ways of developing a subject from the *inside*, the topic of *testimony* suggests ways of developing a subject from the *outside*. Testimony includes all the material you have to find in sources outside your subject—all such supporting material as facts, precedents, statistics, testimonials, opinions, documents. To find such material, you have to go to sources such as books, magazines, and newspapers and to such places as libraries, agencies, museums, computer centers, and storerooms. Data gathered from interviews, questionnaires, experiments, and observation can also be said to come from *outside* the subject and can also be used in developing the subject.

You simply have to develop a sense of

1 **what kind of outside material can be used in developing your subject,**
2 **when such material will be pertinent to the development of your subject, and**
3 **where to find such material.**

Although formal education cannot provide you with the answers to all of your questions, it should at least acquaint you with the *possible sources* of those answers. Because of the

Finding Something To Say

great reverence that our society has for "facts," you have more and more occasion to discover and to make use of "facts" in writing about the "world out there." Chapter 9 of this book discusses some of the reference books in the library that can supply you with these "facts."

Topical Questions

The classical topics were derived from observation of the typical ways in which the human mind thinks about something. But because they are posed in the form of static labels, they don't work as well for some people in turning up usable material for a writing assignment as some of the other methods of search and discovery do. When the topics are posed in the form of *questions*, however, they seem to work better as generating devices for some writers. You saw such a list of questions in the *journalistic formula* (p. 25). If you found the six questions of the journalistic formula too limited, you may find this fuller list, grouped according to different categories of subjects, more helpful.*

ABOUT PHYSICAL OBJECTS

1 What are the physical characteristics of the object (shape, dimensions, materials, etc.)?
2 What sort of structure does it have?
3 What other object is it similar to?

---

* This list of topical questions has been adapted from a list of 116 questions proposed by Richard L. Larson in his article "Discovery through Questioning: A Plan for Teaching Rhetorical Invention," *College English*, 30 (November 1968), 126–134.

● Formal Methods of Search and Discovery

4 How does it differ from things that resemble it?
5 Who or what produced it?
6 Who uses it? for what?

ABOUT EVENTS

1 Exactly what happened? (who? what? when? where? why? how?)
2 What were its causes?
3 What were its consequences?
4 How was the event like or unlike similar events?
5 To what other events was it connected?
6 How might the event have been changed or avoided?

ABOUT ABSTRACT CONCEPTS *(e.g. democracy, justice)*

1 How has the term been defined by others?
2 How do *you* define the term?
3 What other concepts have been associated with it?
4 In what ways has this concept affected the lives of people?
5 How might the concept be changed to work better?

ABOUT PROPOSITIONS *(statements to be proved or disproved):*

1 What must be established before the reader will believe it?
2 What are the meanings of key words in the proposition?
3 By what kinds of evidence or argument can the proposition be proved or disproved?
4 What counterarguments must be confronted and refuted?
5 What are the practical consequences of the proposition?

Finding Something To Say

These are not the only questions, of course, that can be asked in each of the four main categories, but there are enough here to help you overcome any inertia and to get you moving in the development of your subject. From practice with a system of topical questions like these, you may devise other questions that work well for you.

Problem-solving

In recent years, a number of rhetoricians have explored problem-solving as another fruitful method of search and discovery. It is a rare person who has not had to engage in problem-solving at one time or another, and in some professions and occupations, problem-solving is the principal concern. A TV repairman, for instance, constantly has to troubleshoot defective sets; he may have to run through a whole sequence of checks to discover what is wrong with the set so that he can repair it. A lawyer agrees to accept a case whose nature confronts her with the problem of how best to present it so that she can get a favorable ruling for her client. A student has difficulty in reading, and he comes to his teacher for help in discovering the source of his difficulty and for suggestions of how he can overcome the difficulty.

The process of problem-solving, by its very nature, is a process of discovering—of finding out—something. The "something" that is discovered can, in turn, become usable material for a writing assignment. Many articles in professional journals, for instance, are simply reports of someone's engagement in problem-solving.

In every problem, there are some things that you know or can easily find out, but there is something too that you don't know. It is the *unknown* that creates the problem. **When confronted with a problem, you have to take note of all the**

● Formal Methods of Search and Discovery

things you do know. Then, by a series of inferences from the known, you try to form a hypothesis about what the unknown is. Finally, you test your hypothesis to determine whether your tentative theory leads you to discover the unknown that is causing the problem.

How is the process of solving a problem similar to the process you have to go through in trying to find something to say about a subject? Imagine the following situation. When you first check into your motel room in the evening, you notice that when you flip the light-switch near the door, at one and the same moment the light in the ceiling, the lamp near the bed, and the light on the desk all go on. After dinner that evening, you come back to your room, intending to write a letter. You flip the light-switch, and the ceiling-light goes on, the bed-lamp goes on, but the desk-lamp doesn't go on. Nuts! That's the light you need if you are going to write that letter. You could call the manager, but you are an inquisitive and a resourceful type, and you decide to investigate the problem and see if you can get the desk-lamp working again.

So you have a problem. Let us set up a sequence of procedures that can be used in solving *any* problem—including that of finding something to say about a subject you have to write about—and, by way of illustration, apply the procedures to the problem of the desk-lamp that won't light up.

(A) SPECIFY WHAT THE PROBLEM IS

The desk-lamp doesn't go on when I flip the wall-switch, and I need that light if I am to write a letter.

(B) ANALYZE THE PROBLEM

(1) What Do I Know for Sure?

The wall-switch controls three lights, yet only two went on. I know, then, that the wall-switch works, the fuse is sound, and two of the lights are in working order. Either the electricity is not getting to the lamp, or something is wrong with the lamp itself.

(2) What Is the Unknown?

I suspect that the trouble is with the desk-lamp. It worked earlier. Why doesn't it light now, when I flip on the wall-switch? That's the unknown that needs to be known before the problem can be solved.

(C) FORMULATE ONE OR MORE HYPOTHESES ABOUT THE UNKNOWN

I'm not an electrician, but common sense yields some hypotheses: (1) the lamp-switch is not in the "on" position; (2) the bulb could be burned out; (3) there's a loose connection somewhere that is preventing the electricity from getting to the bulb.

(D) TEST THE HYPOTHESES

Turning the on-off switch several times doesn't make the lamp go on; so my first hypothesis is wrong. Putting in a good bulb doesn't make the lamp go on; so my second hypothesis is wrong. It seems then that the electricity is not getting to the bulb. Shaking the lamp several times to see if it has a loose connection, I find that it still doesn't work. But then I notice the trailing lamp cord. Pulling it from behind the desk, I see that it was not plugged into the wall socket. So my third hypothesis proves to be correct, for there *was* a "loose" connection that prevented the electricity from getting to the bulb. The *unknown* is discovered, and the problem is solved.

What you have traced out here is the solving of a mechanical problem, by a process of observation, inference, guess-

• Formal Methods of Search and Discovery

work, and testing of guesses. If you were asked to write an account of the problem-solving, you would have no difficulty about having something to say. Your written document would simply be a narration of the steps you took.

But writing in general can also be approached in terms of problem-solving. Faced with the assignment, for instance, of writing a speech to persuade the members of your sorority to stop smoking, you might go through the steps outlined above:

1 **Specify what the problem is.**
2 **Analyze the problem.**
3 **Formulate one or more hypotheses about the unknown.**
4 **Test the hypotheses.**

—specifying the problem, analyzing the known and unknown elements in the problem, proposing some tentative solutions, and testing the tentative solutions to discover which one might work best for this particular situation.

You might determine that the main problem is to find arguments that will be convincing to the really confirmed smokers in this group. You might want to tote up first the things you know about the situation. Having lived for several months now in the same house with this group, you know that some of them have never smoked, some have recently stopped smoking, some of them would like to stop smoking and have made efforts to stop, and some are so addicted that they seem to have no will to break the habit.

Almost any arguments you could present would serve to confirm the nonsmokers in their resolution not to smoke. The *unknown* in this situation is the kind of argument that will work on the wavering smokers and the confirmed smokers.

In your efforts to discover the unknown—the kinds of argument that might appeal to the various segments of your audience—your formulation and testing of hypotheses might take the form of rehearsing various arguments and then selecting those that seem likeliest to appeal to that audience. The crucial segments of this selected audience are the group who genuinely want to stop and the group who seem to be incurably addicted. What kind of arguments are likely to be persuasive for these two groups? After reviewing some of the standard arguments against smoking, you finally decide that what is needed is some actual testimonies about the practical benefits—physical, psychological, and economic—of breaking the smoking habit. You can gather this testimony from friends and acquaintances who were once heavy smokers but who broke the habit.

You have approached your writing assignment as a problem, and you discovered something to say by specifying and analyzing your special problem. Then, by rehearsing several possible solutions, you finally settled on a strategy that seemed likely to solve the problem. You know now where you have to go to find the material for your speech: to friends and acquaintances for their testimony about the practical advantages of breaking the cigarette habit. The final test of your strategy will, of course, be the effect of the speech on the audience.

●

The first draft as search and discovery

All of the systems reviewed so far may be considered part of the prewriting stage. But paradoxically, many writers find that the writing of even the first draft is still a part of the *pre*writing stage for them. For those writers, **the composing of a rough draft turns up additional material to be incorporated into the final product**. The writing of a sentence or a paragraph suggests to them other things that need to be put into the essay, matters that were not turned up by whatever system of search and discovery they may have used before they sat down to write. As one writer has said, "I don't know what I want to say until I have said it." And it is surprising how much additional material is turned up in the very act of writing.

Verbalizing your thoughts on paper may suggest a direction or a line of development that you did not foresee when you began to write. Robert M. Gorrell, a contemporary rhetorician, uses two terms to describe this phenomenon: **commitment** and **response**. In speaking about the development of a paragraph, he proposes that some sentence you write—often the topic sentence—sets up a commitment between you and your readers. If you are to deliver on that commitment, you must follow through on it. In a sense, you make a "promise" to your reader, and you must fulfill that promise.

Take a declarative sentence like this one: "In those circumstances, a concerned citizen has three courses of action open to him or her." The commitment and response implicit in that sentence should be obvious. Having made that declaration, you have committed yourself to *naming* three courses of action open to a concerned citizen. In addition, you may find that you are also committed to proving that those three courses of action are available to concerned citizens and to showing that other courses of action are not feasible or productive. Similarly, larger units of the discourse—a cluster of related paragraphs, for instance—may establish a commitment that you have to meet. In defending an idea, for instance, you may feel that your next step should be a rebuttal of possible counterarguments or the removal of possible suspicions that you are prejudiced or have a vested interest.

Once you actually begin writing, you may find that the development of your essay gathers its own momentum. You begin to see many directions that your essay might take. After a

Finding Something To Say

while, so many of these may present themselves to you that you will have to pause and gain control once again of your movement. Some directions may take you too far afield, and if you follow them, you may get lost; consequently, the bonanza of things to say that you discovered in the act of writing may prove to be more of a disadvantage than an advantage. But at least you will have overcome any inertia and have discovered more than enough to say.

If the use of some of the systems of search and discovery reviewed in this chapter does not turn up ample material for a writing assignment, don't despair. **Try sitting down at your desk or typewriter and begin to write**. You may be pleasantly surprised, as other writers have been, to find that the minimal material you discovered begins to blossom and ramify. One word will generate another word; one sentence will generate another sentence; one paragraph will generate another paragraph. You may soon find yourself in the happy position of having to *cut* material rather than having to pad it out!

Chapter 4
Selecting and Organizing
What You Have Discovered

Discovering something to say about a subject is often the most difficult and the most crucial stage in the writing process. The various systems of search and discovery discussed in the previous chapter may help you in this stage. But once you have discovered something to say, you are faced with the next stage in the writing process: *selecting and organizing what you have discovered.* It is here that you first begin to give some shape and form to your discourse. You have to make some decisions about what you want to include in your paper and about the order in which you will arrange the parts.

In making selections from the material available, you will derive some help from the same set of considerations that you used in fixing on a subject in Chapter 2:

1 **The number of words you are allotted.**
2 **The purpose of your writing.**
3 **The occasion of your writing.**
4 **The nature of the audience for whom you are writing.**

Selecting and Organizing

5 The extent and depth of your knowledge of the subject (to which might be added here the amount of material you were able to gather in the discovery stage).

6 The thesis or central point you want to make about the subject.

You already put some limits on your treatment when you used these considerations to fix the subject you were going to write about. But some, if not all, of them will come into play again when you decide which of the available materials you will use and which you will discard. Your allotted **wordage**, for instance, may show that although you have enough material to treat five aspects of your subject, you have space to treat only three. You will then have to decide which three they will be. In making that decision, you might derive help from some of the other criteria, such as your **purpose** or the **occasion** or the **audience** for whom you are writing. Considering **audience**, for instance, you might make your choice simply on the grounds of which three of the five available aspects are likely to be most interesting or most impressive to your readers. Or a consideration of your **purpose** might help you make your choice. If your purpose is to win acceptance of your point of view on a controversial subject, you will tend to exclude material that is mainly explanatory and use only the material that presents arguments.

Of the six considerations, however, the one that will invariably come into play in helping you make selections from the available material is the sixth: the **thesis** or *central point* you want to make about the subject you are writing about. While some of the considerations will not always be helpful, a **consideration of your thesis or central point will almost always guide you in the selection process.** If, for instance, your subject were "the energy crisis," a thesis like "With the current high cost of oil and gas, environmentalists may have to relax the pollution standards they insist on for coal as a source of energy'' would guide you in choosing, from the available material, which facts, statistics, and arguments would be most relevant to the development of that subject. That thesis might make you decide to include, for instance, material you discovered about the current prices of domestic and imported oil, estimates of the future price of oil, the comparative costs of oil and coal, figures showing the plentiful reserves of coal in this country—and to exclude the less relevant material about working-conditions in the mines, the hazards of lung disease for miners, the politics of the coal-mining unions, the increasing educational opportunities for middle-class children in Arab lands, the sharp rise in sales of Cadillacs and Mercedes-Benzes in Arab oil-producing countries. Some of this latter material might be usable if you were allotted 10,000 words to argue your case, but it becomes dispensable when you are confined to 1200 words, and your thesis will help you discriminate the more usable from the more dispensable material.

Rhetoric is the art of making judicious choices. One of the choices to be made in the writing process is the choice of material that has been turned up by the discovery process. Considerations like the six outlined above should help you make judicious choices.

The next judicious choice you have to make is the choice of ways in which to arrange the material you have discovered and selected. **The proper arrangement of what you have to say can be of crucial importance for the effectiveness of your communication.** The wrong choice of order for the different parts of your writing could blur, if not completely obscure, the message you have to convey to your readers.

The basic structure of any extended piece of writing is, as Aristotle pointed out in his *Poetics*, a beginning, a middle, and an end. That view of basic structure is philosophically sound,

Selecting and Organizing

but it is too general to be of much help to you when you have to make hard decisions about how to arrange the parts of your paper. You need more specific guidelines. The Aristotelian structure of beginning, middle, and end must become functional—that is, in terms of *what* must be done or *what* is typically done in each of the three basic parts of an extended discourse.

●

The beginning

A more common term for *beginning* is **introduction**, used for that section of a paper that leads into the main part (the middle). In his *Rhetoric*, Aristotle observes that an introduction is not an *essential* part of a persuasive oration. What is essential is that you state your case and then prove it. Get right to the point, Aristotle seems to be suggesting. Being a realist, however, Aristotle had to concede that readers or listeners cannot always be plunged abruptly into the main part; they have to be eased into it. Just as the orchestra at an opera or a musical plays a prelude or overture before the curtain goes up, writers often have to prepare their audience for what they are about to say. **An introduction thus *prepares* your audience to receive the message that will be delivered in the middle section of the paper.**

But what does that *preparation* entail? It all depends on a number of circumstances: on the nature of the subject and the extent of your readers' familiarity with it; on the attitude of your readers toward the subject; on their attitude toward you. Some subject matter would not require much preparation of the readers—a subject, for instance, that has been much discussed or that has figured prominently in the news. Other subject matter, because of its complexity or its unfamiliarity, might require much preparation. You might have to establish the importance of the subject or give some background information about it. You might have to define some key terms. You might want to state at the outset what point you intend to make about the subject. And the introduction is often the place where you announce what the thesis or central point of your paper is.

The presumed attitude of your readers toward the subject or toward you also requires some attention before you launch into the middle section. If your readers harbor some hostility toward the subject or some hostility toward you, you will have to spend some time allaying that hostility. You may have to establish your credentials to talk about the subject or at least reveal your concern about it. As Aristotle put it in his *Rhetoric*, you may have to spend some time in your introduction rendering your audience *attentive* (disposed to listen to you), *benevolent* (well-wishing toward you), and *docile* (willing to be instructed or persuaded by you). In short, **you will have to put your audience in the right frame of mind to receive your message.**

How much space you can devote to this preparation of your audience will depend partly on how much wordage you are allotted. If you are limited to 500–800 words for the entire essay, you may be able to devote only 150 or even fewer words to orienting and disposing your audience. In that case, you will have to practice extreme economy. For a longer paper, you will be able—in fact, you may be obliged—to devote several hundred words, spread out over three or four paragraphs, to the introduction.

●
The middle

Once you have *introduced* yourself and your subject, you have to settle down to the development of your subject. You are

Selecting and Organizing

ready to get into the "heart of the matter," into the core of your paper. Here you will have to make the most crucial, and sometimes the most difficult, decisions about the order of the parts. Because an introduction is usually short, it does not have many parts that require some "most effective" order, even if you have some minor decisions to make within it, such as whether you will establish your credentials first and then inform your reader about the subject and thesis to be developed—or adopt the reverse order. However, even in a paper as short as 800–1000 words, **the middle section may have three, four, or five major divisions that will require a "best" order for maximum effectiveness.**

Some kinds of writing have a natural order, requiring no deliberation. For instance, narratives of an event and expositions of a process naturally fall into a *chronological* sequence: first this happened, then this happened, and then that happened; or, in the case of an exposition of a process, first you do this, then you do this, and then you do that. It is true that sometimes in reporting events or in storytelling, we open with something that happened further ahead in time and then through flashbacks recount happenings that occurred previously. But most often, narratives have a strictly chronological order. So if you're writing a narrative or an exposition, you won't have to spend much time considering the order of the parts. **You simply have to make sure that all the necessary parts are there and that they are in the order in which they occurred.**

The difficult decisions about the most effective ordering of the parts will present themselves when you are dealing with those kinds of writing or those subjects that don't have a single, natural order but rather offer a number of different orders. When, for instance, you are writing an argumentative essay, you may have to decide whether you will first refute the opposing arguments and then present your own or adopt the reverse order; or you may have to decide whether to begin with your weakest argument and then present progressively stronger arguments or begin with the strongest and then follow with progressively weaker arguments. If your subject matter is "the causes of the American Civil War," you will have to make some decision about the order in which you discuss the various causes. Will you treat the economic causes first or the political causes? Will you treat the minor causes first or the major causes? Or will you treat the more familiar causes first and then the lesser-known?

Answers to these and similar questions will depend on such considerations as the occasion of your writing, the mood of your audience, the prevailing climate of opinion, the emphasis to be achieved by a climactic order or an anticlimactic order. Presenting the strongest argument first, for instance, will not always be the best order in all situations and for all audiences. Because **such decisions will always have to be made in relation to a particular situation or to a great many other circumstances**, it is impossible to lay down general principles that should prevail in all cases. What we can do, however, is set forth some of the common patterns of organization that are used in certain kinds of discourse. (See Fig. 4.1 for an outline of these patterns.)

Some Common Patterns of Organization

CHRONOLOGICAL SEQUENCE

Time commonly governs the order of the parts in narratives (first this happened, then this, then that, etc.), and in expositions of a process (first you do this, then this, then that, etc.).

FROM THE FAMILIAR TO THE UNFAMILIAR

Movement from the *more* familiar to the *less* is often used in explaining a new or complicated idea, issue, movement, etc.

SOME COMMON PATTERNS OF ORGANIZATION

CHRONOLOGICAL ORDER	FAMILIAR TO UNFAMILIAR ORDER	WHOLE TO PART (OR REVERSE)
—In **narrative** prose, takes events in order of **time.** In description of **process,** follows actual sequence.	—In **explanatory** prose, explains new, complex ideas, issues, etc. by moving from known to unknown.	—In **descriptive** prose, works from the smaller to the larger, from aspect to whole (or reverse), etc.

SPATIAL ORDER	CLIMACTIC ORDER	ANTICLIMACTIC ORDER
—In **descriptive** prose, follows a "natural" order, as from top to bottom, right to left, outside to inside, etc.	—In **narrative** and **argumentative** prose, takes matters in order of increasing importance or intensity.	—In **argumentative** and occasionally in **expository** prose, takes matters in order of decreasing importance or intensity.

CLEARING THE GROUND BEFORE (OR AFTER) BUILDING	LOGICAL ORDER	ASSOCIATIONAL ORDER
—In **expository** and **argumentative** prose, sets forth the inadequacies of previous accounts, explanations, etc. **or** refutes arguments of opponents **and then** sets forth own account, explanation, or argument.	—In **expository** and **argumentative** prose, employs **inductive** reasoning (from the particular to the general) or **deductive** reasoning (from the general to the specific) or **cause-to-effect** or **effect-to-cause** reasoning.	—In any prose where one thing, person, place, etc. "**naturally suggests**" (in the mind of the writer) some other person, place, thing. In **stream-of-consciousness** prose, follows mind's own erratic, illogical motions. In **episodic narrative** and in accounts of **personal experiences,** events follow one another in no discernible order.

Figure 4.1

Selecting and Organizing

Beginning with what is likely to be more familiar to readers helps to orient them and prepare them for the less familiar or the totally unfamiliar.

FROM THE WHOLE TO THE PART

Giving readers an *overview* of something before proceeding to the *parts* is common in descriptive writing, especially in descriptions of a physical object or a scene. If, for instance, you were describing a historic battlefield, it might help to orient your readers by presenting the layout of the battlefield from a bird's-eye view. Sometimes, but perhaps less often, the reverse order—from part to whole—will be the best one to follow.

THE SPATIAL SEQUENCE

Like the chronological sequence, the spatial sequence is *a linear or one-after-the-other pattern that begins at some point and proceeds in natural spatial sequences such as from top to bottom, from left to right, in a circle, around the four sides of a square.* In describing a room in an art museum, for instance, you might begin by relating what you see as you stand in the entryway of the room, then describe what you see as you walk up the left-hand side, then describe what you see along the back wall, then describe what you see as you walk down the right-hand side of the room. Of course, you could reverse that order and walk up the right-hand side first and then come back down the left-hand side. The important thing would simply be to adhere to a natural spatial order and not violate it by shifting from right to left to right.

THE CLIMACTIC ORDER

This pattern, common in narrative writing, arranges the parts in an order of *increasing importance or intensity*. We speak of a story as "building toward a climax"—that is, the incidents are arranged so that the reader becomes increasingly excited or fascinated until the story reaches the height of intensity. But the climactic order is often used also in argumentative writing, where the arguments are arranged in sequence from the weaker to the stronger. As an argumentative writer, you decide to use this order because you want to leave the audience with your strongest argument ringing in their ears.

THE ANTICLIMACTIC ORDER

This order is the reverse of the previous one. *It proceeds from the strongest to the weakest.* Narrative writing almost never uses this order, but argumentative writing and occasionally expository writing sometimes follow it. As an argumentative writer, you might conclude that you would win greater acceptance of your weaker arguments if you presented your strongest argument first.

THE PATTERN OF "CLEARING THE GROUND" BEFORE (OR AFTER) "BUILDING"

In expository writing, this pattern takes the form of *first pointing out the shortcomings of previous explanations* of something before presenting the preferred explanation. In argumentative writing, it takes the form of *first refuting the arguments of your opponents* before presenting your own. Sometimes, however, it is strategically advisable to reverse this pattern and to do the "building" before the "demolishing."

THE LOGICAL ORDER

This is often the natural order to follow in expository and argumentative writing. It can take a variety of forms. Two basic

Selecting and Organizing

logical patterns are the **inductive** order and the **deductive** order. In the inductive order, you proceed from a series of *particulars* to a *generalization* (for instance, describing conditions in the ghettos of some of the major cities and then making some generalization about those conditions). In the deductive order, you begin with a *generalization* and then examine a series of *particulars* that support the generalization. For instance, you might begin with the generalization that "the miserable conditions existing in many urban ghettos are dehumanizing" and then present a number of examples of this dehumanizing process. Two other basic logical patterns are **effect-to-cause** and **cause-to-effect.** For instance, an essay might begin with portraits of a number of mentally disturbed children (the effects) and then proceed to seek out the causes of those pathologies. The cause-to-effect order would simply reverse that sequence.

THE ASSOCIATIONAL ORDER

In some people's view, this order is "no order at all." Although it has the appearance of being chaotic or, at best, arbitrary, it has a "logic" of its own: it follows the sequence that naturally *suggests* itself to you, the writer. One thing follows another because it is *associated* in your mind—but not necessarily in your audience's mind—with what has just been mentioned or discussed.

An extreme form of the associational order is the so-called stream-of-consciousness technique devised by such fiction writers as James Joyce and Virginia Woolf. This technique tries to duplicate the ways in which the mind often moves. If you could observe your own mind, you would discover that it rarely "thinks" in the neat, orderly ways outlined above. It often moves in fits and starts, in stop-and-go patterns. It begins a line of reasoning or reflecting, then suddenly and inexplicably shoots off on a tangent. That tangent may in turn shoot off on another tangent. After entertaining that tangent for a few seconds, the mind might return to the original line of reasoning or reflecting and pursue that line; but it might also never return to the original line and instead end up "miles" away from the starting point.

Stream-of-consciousness is an extreme example of associational order. Less extreme instances include episodic narratives (the incidents follow no noticeable principle of order, not even the usual chronological order) and accounts of personal experiences (the events are so arranged simply because one event suggested another that was part of the total experience but that did not necessarily follow the first in the actual experience). *Associations of things in your mind dictate the ordering of the parts*.

However, you cannot always justify the apparent chaos of your paper by saying, "I'm using an associational order here." There will be occasions when the associational order will not be the appropriate or effective one, and on those occasions it will justifiably be judged as chaotic.

Plotting an Outline

After finding and selecting your material and deciding to arrange it according to one of the patterns outlined above, you may want to *plot* that order in an *outline*—a device that you are probably familiar with and that you may have been required to include in papers you wrote for class. The standard format of the major divisions of a paper resembles the outline shown in Figure 4.2.

Selecting and Organizing

Introduction: [followed by some statement of what you will do in this introductory section]

I [followed by a phrase or a complete sentence that indicates the main topic dealt with in this section]

II [followed by a phrase or a sentence, grammatically parallel with the phrase or sentence above, that indicates the main topic dealt with in this section]

III [followed by a parallel phrase or sentence that indicates the main topic covered in this section]

Conclusion: [you might state here what your major conclusion is from the study presented in the roman-numeral divisions of the paper]

Figure 4.2

Note that the introduction and the conclusion in Figure 4.2 are not preceded by roman numerals; the roman-numeral divisions outline only the middle section of your paper. Sometimes you may be required to preface the entire outline with a thesis statement, in a format like this:

THESIS: Stricter laws on the possession and use of marijuana are not likely to cure the drug problem.

Sometimes you have such a clear mental preview of the parts of the paper that you can prepare a more detailed outline, with two or three levels of subdivisions under the roman-numeral divisions. See Figure 4.3 for the format of a detailed outline (each of the divisions and subdivisions in Figure 4.3 would be followed by a sentence or phrase or word that indicated the main topic in that part). But many writers confess that they cannot prepare a detailed formal outline *before* they

Introduction:
 I.
   A.
      1.
      2.
      3.
   B.
      1.
      2.
            a.
            b.
   C.
      1.
      2.
 II.
   A.
   B.
   C.
   D.
 III.
   A.
      1.
      2.
   B.
      1.
      2.

Conclusion:

(One caution about the format of the outline: if you make any division in your outline, you must have *at least two parts.* Division implies a "breaking into parts," and if you have only one part, no division has been made.)

Figure 4.3

Selecting and Organizing

write their paper. (In fact, many outlines are put together *after* the paper is written.)

Writers who have difficulty preparing a formal outline often find it helpful to sketch notes for themselves about how their paper is going to proceed. Such notes might look like this:

> Introduction:
> a brief review of the literature on this subject, followed by a statement of the problem that persists after all this investigation and an indication of how I propose to deal with the problem.

—What the previous investigators have failed to notice. The hidden causes that have escaped the attention of other investigators. Why the apparent causes don't get us to the heart of the problem.

—Jacob Miller's hang-up on "ethnic origins."

—The dead end that Susan Black reached when she pursued "economic predeterminers."

—The explosion of Pierre LeClerc's "social implosion" theory.

—The do-gooders.

—The ultraconservatives.

—The clergy, of all faiths, either barking up the wrong tree or just barking.

—Why has no one thought of looking at the psychological traumas of unemployment? Mental depression. Schizophrenia. Loss of dignity. Marital tensions. Alcoholic "solace". Withdrawing into a shell. Male menopause.

—Back to the womb. At least back to the childhood environment.

Someone picking up these notes wouldn't find them very revealing. (Is this writer investigating the possible causes of the current unemployment or the reasons for the prevalence of mental illness in our society?) Unlike the formal outline, which can be revealing to readers even before they read a paper, a set of loose notes like these is meaningful only to the writer. The writer knows what they mean. They suggest what is going to be covered in the paper and the probable order in which the points are going to be covered. In short, they indicate the stages of the development of the paper.

Somewhere between the detailed formal outline and the set of loose notes is the system that plots the organization of the paper in **blocks**. The size of the blocks might indicate to the writer the relative length of that part of the paper. (See Fig. 4.4 for an example of the block system.)

Some writers find it even more helpful to put blocks within blocks. These blocks-within-a-block (represented by a slight indentation; see Fig. 4.5) show the number of paragraphs in the larger block, and each of them has a note indicating what is covered in that paragraph.

These are some of the systems of plotting the organization of the middle section of a paper that have worked for some writers. You might try these systems to find out whether they are helpful to you in organizing your papers.

Other writers, however, are incapable of such systematic planning. When they sit down to write, they have some general idea of the points they want to cover and perhaps a clear idea of how they are going to begin; but they trust that *the writing itself* will suggest the order in which to take up their points. This "playing it by ear" might be the procedure used by writers who find that the first draft is still part of the discovery process for them. **Each writer must find, through trial and error, the system of organization that works best for him or her.** Try one or all of these systems, and see which works best for you.

Figure 4.4

Introduction

one paragraph

First major division of paper

two paragraphs

Second major division of paper

three paragraphs

Third major division of paper

two paragraphs

Conclusion

one long paragraph (100-150 words)

SECOND MAJOR SECTION OF THE PAPER

Figure 4.5

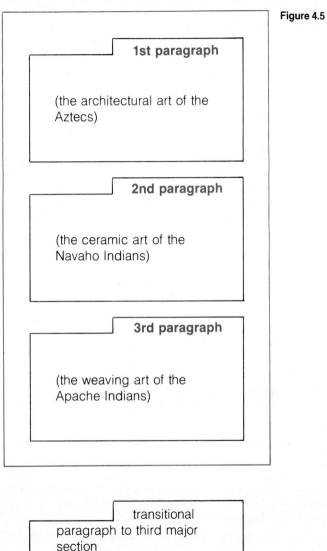

1st paragraph

(the architectural art of the Aztecs)

2nd paragraph

(the ceramic art of the Navaho Indians)

3rd paragraph

(the weaving art of the Apache Indians)

transitional paragraph to third major section

Selecting and Organizing

●

The end

The more common term for that part of a paper that Aristotle called the *end* is **conclusion**. Just as Aristotle denied that a beginning or introduction was essential, so he denied that a conclusion was essential. But he was realist enough to concede that audiences expected and appreciated having an essay rounded off with a concluding section. Listeners and readers often feel uncomfortable when a speech or an essay comes to an abrupt halt. **They want at least a few parting words that will wrap up the discussion.** Presenting a conclusion is, at least, a courtesy to the audience, much like saying farewell when you take leave of friends or acquaintances. Moreover, a conclusion can render a valuable service for the audience, satisfying them that a discussion has been brought full circle.

What do you ordinarily do in a conclusion? Recall Aristotle's saying that the function of an introduction is to render the audience *attentive, benevolent*, and *docile*. But as the end of an essay approaches, you hardly need to make your readers *attentive* any longer. In fact, if they have not already left you by that point, the mere announcement or hint that you are concluding your essay serves to perk them up and revive their attentiveness. Notice the almost palpable sigh of relief you hear when a speaker says, "In conclusion. . . ." You sit up straight in your seat and pay special attention to what (you hope) will be only two or three more minutes of speech.

There is also not much need at the end of an essay to render your audience *docile*—that is, willing to be instructed or persuaded by you. It was important to put your audience in that mood at the beginning, but by the time you reach the conclusion, you have very little instructing or persuading left to do. But you do want to make your audience receptive to a summary of the main points that you made in the middle section of your paper. Your audience will be receptive if in the conclusion you **touch on only the *highlights* of the points made at length in the middle section** and if you **keep the summary as *brief* as possible.** Any unnecessarily elaborate rehashing of the points will weary and perhaps alienate your readers.

There may be a need at the end of a paper—perhaps more than at the beginning—to render the audience *benevolent* toward you. It is especially important to make this effort if you have been espousing an unpopular cause, if you have had to bruise their feelings in any way, or if you have had to discredit anything that they favor. Some conciliatory words, some generous gesture toward your opponents, some acknowledgment of the "right" on the other side of the issue—overtures like these at the end of your paper will help to confirm or regain your readers' benevolent attitude.

Another way to secure that benevolent attitude is to make an *emotional* appeal to your audience. On certain occasions, orators are inclined to pull out all the emotional stops in the concluding part of their speech. Their sentences shower fire and bombast; figures of speech begin to cascade one after the other; explicit or subtle appeals to emotions of sympathy, fear, or anger begin to appear.

In the written medium, however, emotional appeals are not likely to be as blatant as they are in oratory, particularly oratory on occasions of crisis, such as wartime, or of social importance, such as election time. **The written medium demands a tighter rein on emotional appeals.** But restrained emotional touches are still common in some kinds of writing, especially in argumentation where you are trying to move your audience to action. Arguments mainly influence the intellect; emotional appeals mainly influence the will. An au-

Selecting and Organizing

dience could be intellectually convinced that it should do something—like donating blood to the Red Cross—and still not be moved to action. In that situation, the will of the audience needs to be moved, and the best way to move the will is through the emotions. (A military or football band is an example of this.) In addition, emotional appeals, if skillfully managed, can also dispose an audience to feel *benevolent* toward a speaker or writer. And while it is sometimes necessary to secure that attitude at the beginning of an essay, it can also be necessary, or at least advisable, to secure or reinforce a benevolent attitude in the conclusion.

Another thing that is commonly done in the conclusion is to remind the readers of the importance and the larger dimensions of your subject. If you have done your job properly in the introductory and middle sections, the importance of what you have been discussing should be obvious, but it doesn't hurt to underscore that importance at the end. You can reinforce the audience's sense of that importance by putting the topic or issue in some larger context. You might, for instance, say something like, "The adoption of this policy will restore confidence and lead to a revitalization of faith in the economy." By thus enlarging the dimensions of the subject, you at least reassure your audience that it has not been a waste of their time to listen to you.

Not every piece of writing needs an extensive conclusion, but if it does need to be *concluded* rather than just "ended," it will require more than two or three sentences. *You will have to compose at least a substantial paragraph.* Here in summary outline are some of the things that are customarily done in the conclusion and that you may also have to do—not all of them always, but certainly some of them sometimes:

1 **Recapitulate or summarize the main points you have made in the middle section of your paper.**

2 **Make your readers well disposed toward you.**

3 **Make some kind of emotional appeal to your readers.**

4 **Emphasize the crucial importance or the larger dimensions of what you have been talking about.**

The functions of the three-part structure of beginning, middle, and end can be summarized in a bit of advice that is sometimes given to speakers: "**Tell them what you're *going* to tell them. *Tell* them. And then tell them what you've *told* them.**"

Chapter 5
Expressing What You Have Discovered, Selected, and Arranged

After the stage of prewriting, you are faced with the task of *putting words on paper*—of verbalizing what you have discovered, selected, and arranged. For you, as for many other writers, this part of the writing process may be the most difficult. But if you have been conscientious in the prewriting process, you will find that the actual writing is easier—although it may never become altogether *easy.* The writing becomes easier because you know what you want to say and because you have enough skill in the use of your native language to convey your thoughts to other speakers of the same language. You may not always be able to write clearly, economically, and gracefully, but with your basic ability you can convey the substance of your message. What every serious writer seeks to improve is the effectiveness of written expression—its clarity, conciseness, brevity, and gracefulness.

●
Words and the structure of sentences

At a very early age, you acquired a basic competence in speaking your native language. You were in command of a minimal vocabulary and of most, if not all, of the basic sentence structures, and you could understand many more words and structures than you yourself used. From that point on, your style matured through your acquiring a larger vocabulary and learning how to use a wider range of sentence structures.

What you *know*, perhaps subconsciously, is that the English sentence is basically a two-part structure, consisting of a subject and a predicate verb. Minimally, this structure can consist of a single word in each position, as in the sentence

Birds sing.

More often, however, the subject-verb structure consists of a cluster of words, in both positions, as in the sentence

The shiny red apples pleased me very much.

A child first utters isolated words—*mama, doggie, ball*. Next, the child begins to form phrases—"red ball," "doggie hungry." Finally, the child forms the minimal, two-part structures like those in the sentences above. The maturing of style comes when the child learns how to expand and vary the minimal structures.

By an almost miraculous process, we eventually learn how to expand the minimal sentence

Birds sing

into a sentence like

Expressing What You Have Put Together

The huddled gray birds sing forlornly in the bare branches of the tree.

This latter sentence is the result of **embedding**, a process of combining several minimal sentences into a single sentence:

The birds sing.
The birds are gray.
The birds are huddled.
The birds sing forlornly.
The birds sing in the bare branches of the tree.

By deleting repeated words ("the birds," for instance) and rearranging the remaining words, a writer combines all of the meaning contained in the series of sentences into the single sentence "The huddled gray birds sing forlornly in the bare branches of the tree."

Because you can do this kind of deleting, rearranging, and combining, you have the basic competence to express what you want to say. But some writers are better at this process than others, partly because they have practiced more and partly because they have acquired a larger vocabulary and a wider range of sentence patterns. In speaking, you can often get by with imprecise diction and with sprawling, awkwardly constructed sentences. **In writing, however, you need more exact words and tighter, neater sentences**. But you can't produce what you don't have in the first place. You can't come up with alternative words if those words are not part of your vocabulary. You won't come up with alternative sentence structures if those structures are not part of your equipment. Rhetoric is an art of making choices, but you can't make choices if you haven't things to choose between.

Your vocabulary will expand as you gain new experiences; you unconsciously absorb new words. But you can also make conscious efforts to expand your vocabulary. One way is systematically to study lists of new words. In his *Autobiography*, Malcolm X tells us that while he was in prison, he prepared himself to become a writer by systematically copying out the definitions of words in a dictionary that he had in his cell.

Studying word lists is one way to expand vocabulary, but it is not the ideal way, because by that method, you learn words in isolation. A much better way is to **look up the meaning of any unfamiliar word that you encounter in your reading or listening.** Thumbing through a dictionary each time you meet an unfamiliar word is a nuisance, but a necessary one if you want to speed up expansion of your vocabulary.

However, it is not enough for you to look up the meanings of unfamiliar words in a dictionary. **New words can be made part of your working vocabulary only if you make a deliberate effort to use them in sentences you write.** At first, you may use the new words awkwardly or inappropriately, but you will eventually gain a more finely tuned sense of their shades of meaning, and then they will become a permanent part of your vocabulary, ready for use when needed.

The advice given here is about all that a text on writing can produce to help you add to your stock of words so that you can make choices from among alternatives. However, a text can do more than merely give advice when it comes to expanding your stock of alternative *sentence structures.* It can present some exercises that will acquaint you with a variety of sentence patterns. You may not want to use all the structures that you have practiced, but you will at least be able to produce them if they serve your purpose.

The following are some exercises that can acquaint you with a variety of sentence patterns and perhaps add to your repertory.

Expressing What You Have Put Together

●

Copying passages of prose

Copying passages of prose may seem a simpleminded exercise just because it is so simple, but it can pay big dividends if engaged in conscientiously. The system consists in taking a short passage of prose that you admire and copying it by hand. The mere act of writing out the sentences that someone else has written can reveal structures that only the most careful reading might show. **Copying passages makes you pay close attention to how a writer has put words together and can acquaint you with sentence patterns that might never otherwise occur to you.**

In order to see how this system works, write out the following paragraph:

> It is time for the baby's birthday party: a white cake, strawberry-marshmallow ice cream, a bottle of champagne saved from another party. In the evening, after she has gone to sleep, I kneel beside the crib and touch her face, where it is pressed against the slats, with mine. She is an open and trusting child, unprepared for and unaccustomed to the ambushes of family life, and perhaps it is just as well that I can offer her little of that life. I would like to give her more. I would like to promise her that she will grow up with a sense of her cousins and of rivers and of great-grandmother's teacups, would like to pledge her a picnic on a river with fried chicken and her hair uncombed, would like to give her *home* for her birthday, but we live differently now, and I can promise her nothing like that. I give her a xylophone and a sundress from Madeira, and promise to tell her a funny story (Joan Didion, "On Going Home," in *Slouching Towards Bethlehem* [New York: Farrar, Straus & Giroux, 1967]).

● Copying Passages of Prose

Here are some features of the passage that you may have noted and that you may want to make part of your skills:

1 **The specific, concrete wording:** *a white cake, straw-berry-marshmallow ice cream, a bottle of champagne; crib, face, slats; cousins, rivers, great-grandmother's teacups; fried chicken, hair uncombed; xylophone, sundress from Madeira.*

2 **The large number of one-syllable words** (130 of the 170 words).

3 **Variety of sentence length:** the number of words in the six sentences is 22, 27, 33, 7, 63, 18 (an average of 29 per sentence). You wouldn't gain so specific an idea of the variations in length from merely copying the passage; you have to do some counting. Even without counting, however, everyone who copied the passage would note the dramatic difference in length between the fourth and fifth sentences.

4 **Variety of ways of beginning sentences:** although four of the six sentences begin with the subject followed immediately by the verb (*She is. . . , I would like. . . , I would like. . . , I give. . .*), there is some variety. The first sentence begins with what is called an **impersonal structure** (*It is. . .*). There is another impersonal structure at the beginning of the second clause of the third sentence (*it is just as well that. . .*). The second sentence begins with a prepositional phrase (*In the evening*), followed by an adverb clause (*after she. . .*).

5 **Variety of grammatical types of sentence:** no two consecutive sentences are of the same grammatical type. But this fact alone does not entirely reveal the variety. These six sentences have nine independent clauses and four subordinate clauses, and in three of the sentences, the predicate verb is compounded.

6 **Some notable sentence patterns:** (*a*) the adverb clause in the second member of a compound predicate ("and touch

her face, *where it is pressed against the slats, with mine*");
(*b*) the two parallel phrases placed after the noun that the
pair modifies ("She is an open and trusting child, *unprepared
for and unaccustomed to the ambushes* of family life"); (*c*)
the three parallel verb-phrase structures beginning with the
same words ("I *would like to promise her. . . , would like to
pledge her. . . , would like to give her. . .*"); (*d*) the three
parallel phrases ("*of her cousins* and *of rivers* and *of great-
grandmother's teacups*").

You may have been struck by some other features in this
passage of 170 words. But in whatever passage you copy, you
will usually find some feature, either of vocabulary or of
sentence structure, that strikes your attention. Later, you will be
surprised at how often some feature noted in the act of copying
appears in your own writing.

One of the side-benefits of the copy exercise is that you can
learn spelling and punctuation by doing it.

Some Advice about the Copy Exercise

1 **Don't spend more than fifteen or twenty minutes at any
one time on the copy exercise.** When your attention
wanders, you will only be copying words. It is more fruitful to
spend ten minutes a day over a period of several weeks than
to spend thirty minutes a day for only a few weeks.

2 **Don't concentrate on a single author; copy passages
from a variety of authors.** The object is not to acquire
someone else's style but to acquaint yourself with the variety
of vocabulary and sentence pattern that professional writers
employ. Concentrate on contemporary writers, especially
those that you admire; but you may also profit by occasionally copying a passage written by an eighteenth- or nineteenth-
century writer.

3 **Choose your passages from a variety of sources**—
newspapers, magazines, books, collections of essays, ads,
business and promotional letters, even some of your textbooks.

4 **Read the passage all the way through** both *before* and
after you copy it, to get a sense of the whole.

●
Imitating sentence patterns

This exercise consists of writing out a single sentence, composed by someone else, analyzing its structure, and then
writing a sentence of your own on the pattern of that sentence.
You must be able to distinguish various kinds of grammatical
structures, even if you cannot label them properly. **Your own
sentence need not have the same number of words as the
model sentence, but it should have the same pattern.** For
instance, if a sentence begins with a participial phrase, your
sentence should begin with one; if the main verb of the
sentence is a transitive verb followed by an object, your
sentence should use a transitive verb rather than an intransitive
verb or a linking verb.

Here are some examples of analyses and imitations of
sentence patterns:

Expressing What You Have Put Together

MODEL

We don't encourage animals to come into the house, but they get in once in a while, particularly the cosset lamb, who trotted through this living room not five minutes ago looking for an eight-ounce bottle (E. B. White, "A Shepherd's Life").

ANALYSIS

This sentence consists of two independent clauses and of an adjective clause in the second independent clause. You should observe at least that much of the pattern in the sentence you write, but you may also want to include a participial phrase like the one that concludes White's sentence (*looking for an eight-ounce bottle*).

IMITATION

The police will not allow outsiders to walk across the picket lines, but children stray into the lines occasionally, especially bewildered five-year-olds, who weave in and out of the lines searching for their mothers.

MODEL

How beautiful he was, with his olive-tinted flesh and dark gold ringlets, his eyes of mingled blue and brown, his perfect limbs, and the soft voluptuous roll which the blood of Africa had moulded into his features (W. E. B. DuBois, "Of the Passing of the First-Born").

ANALYSIS

This sentence begins with the main clause that notes, in a general way, the beauty of the new-born child and then spells out, in a series of prepositional phrases, the particular features that contribute to his beauty. In your own sentence, you might want to employ more phrases than the model sentence does.

IMITATION

How noisy it was, with the scarlet-coated brass band and the bright, ornate steam-calliope, the cages of roaring lions and tigers, the jingling tambourines, the honking horns, the exploding firecrackers, and the comic old-fashioned automobiles that the clowns maneuvered in circles with exaggerated backfirings.

Expressing What You Have Put Together

MODEL

If it is not perfect, it is not love, and if it is not love, it is bound to be hate sooner or later (Katherine Anne Porter, "The Necessary Enemy").

ANALYSIS

This is a balanced sentence: the two sentences on both sides of the conjunction *and* have the same grammatical structure—an adverb clause followed by the main clause.

IMITATION

When you are happy, you are a gentleman, but when you are a gentleman, you are a bore.

MODEL

From the age of six onward, I constantly polished the enamel with peanut brittle, massaged the incisors twice daily with lollipops, and chewed taffy and chocolate-covered caramels faithfully to exercise the gums (S. J. Perelman, "Dental or Mental, I Say It's Spinach").

ANALYSIS

Try analyzing the structure of the sentence yourself.

IMITATION

After the beginning of the year, his girl friend promptly returned his engagement ring with an ironic thank-you note, canceled three appointments with her hairdresser, and resumed her tennis lessons avidly to improve her game.

Expressing What You Have Put Together

MODEL

Four steps past the turnstiles, everybody is already backed up haunch to paunch for the climb up the ramp and the stairs to the surface, a great funnel of flesh, wool, felt, leather, rubber and steaming alumicron, with the blood squeezing through everybody's old sclerotic arteries in hopped-up spurts from too much coffee and the effort of surfacing from the subway at the rush hours (Tom Wolfe, "A Sunday Kind of Love").

ANALYSIS

Try analyzing the structure yourself.

IMITATION

Try writing a sentence of your own on the pattern of the model.

From these examples, you should have an idea of how this exercise works. In order to expand your own range of sentence patterns, you should choose the kinds of sentences that you like but do not normally write. If you exercise yourself in this way, you will soon be using some of the unusual patterns in your own writing.

Combining and rearranging sentences

In the copy exercise, you merely reproduced a passage of prose, noting unusual features of vocabulary and structure that

● Combining and Rearranging Sentences

you might be able to use. In the previous exercise, you took a single sentence, analyzed its structure, and tried to write a sentence on the same pattern. In the exercise that follows, you are asked to combine and/or rearrange groups of whole sentences according to specific directions.

We will begin with some simple exercises in combining and rearranging and move to progressively more complex combinations and rearrangements.

I. BASE SENTENCES

1   I tried to discuss religion with the villagers.
2   I found the villagers reluctant to discuss religion with strangers.

A. DIRECTIONS

Combine sentences (1) and (2) into a single sentence by the conjunction **but**.

RESULT

I tried to discuss religion with the villagers, but I found the villagers reluctant to discuss religion with strangers.

To avoid the repetition of **villagers** and **religion**, you could rewrite the sentence in this way:

I tried to discuss religion with the villagers, but I found them reluctant to discuss the subject with strangers.

B. DIRECTIONS

Take the same two sentences and combine them into a single sentence with two verbs joined by the conjunction **but**.

Expressing What You Have Put Together

RESULT

I tried to discuss religion with the villagers but found them reluctant to discuss the subject with strangers.

After repeated practice of this kind, you will find that you can combine two sentences into a simple sentence with a compound predicate verb only when both sentences have the same subject. If sentence (1) had the subject **I** and sentence (2) had the subject **he**, a simple sentence with a compound predicate would be impossible. Instead of using the noun **subject** here as a substitute for **religion**, you could use the pronoun **it**.

C. DIRECTIONS

Take the same two sentences and combine them by converting sentence (1) to a dependent clause beginning with the subordinating conjunction **when**.

RESULT

When I tried to discuss religion with the villagers, I found them reluctant to discuss it with strangers.

The positions of the **when** clause and the main clause can be reversed, but the words **religion** and **villagers** will also have to be transferred from the *when* clause to the main clause:

I found the villagers reluctant to discuss religion with strangers when I tried to discuss it with them.

D. DIRECTIONS

Combine the same two sentences by turning sentence (1) into a phrase, using the *-ing* form of *try*.

● Combining and Rearranging Sentences

RESULT

Trying to discuss religion with the villagers, I found them reluctant to discuss it with strangers.

REMINDER

You will discover a variety of ways in which sentences can be combined and/or rearranged, but you will also find that not all resultant sentences will be equally good stylistically. Faced with a number of *possible* options, you will have to choose the best, or at least the better, option.

II. BASE SENTENCES

1 Craig Beard won the state lottery.

2 Craig Beard is a carpenter.

3 Craig Beard is an electrician.

A. DIRECTIONS

a convert sentence (1) to the passive voice, making **the state lottery** the subject.

b convert sentence (2) to a clause beginning with **who**.

c convert sentence (3) to an adjective clause beginning with **who**.

d combine the two **who** clauses.

e combine all the converted sentences into a single sentence.

RESULTS

a The state lottery was won by Craig Beard. (passive voice)

b who is a carpenter (*clause with* **who**)

Expressing What You Have Put Together

c who is an electrician (*clause with* **who**)

d who is a carpenter and an electrician (*combining adjective clauses*)

e **The state lottery was won by Craig Beard, who is a carpenter and an electrician.** (*combining all converted sentences*)

B. DIRECTIONS

a Using the same three sentences, make no change in sentence (1).

b reduce sentence (2) to an appositive.

c reduce sentence (3) to an appositive.

d combine the appositives with sentence (1) to form a single sentence.

RESULTS

a Craig Beard won the state lottery. (*no change*)

b a carpenter (*appositive*)

c an electrician (*appositive*)

d **Craig Beard, a carpenter and an electrician, won the state lottery.** (*combining and rearranging converted sentences*)

III. BASE SENTENCES

1 The team of engineers uses sophisticated electronic equipment.

2 The team inspects power-plant boilers.

3 The team inspects power-plant smokestacks.

● Combining and Rearranging Sentences

A. DIRECTIONS

a leave sentence (1) unchanged.

b change the verb in sentence (2) to the infinitive form (**to** . . .)

c change the verb in sentence (3) to the infinitive form (**to** . . .)

d combine the two infinitives into a single infinitive phrase.

e combine all the converted sentences into a single sentence.

RESULTS

a The team of engineers uses sophisticated electronic equipment. (*no change*)

b to inspect power-plant boilers (*infinitive form*)

c to inspect power-plant smokestacks (*infinitive form*)

d to inspect power-plant boilers and smokestacks (*combining infinitives*)

e **The team of engineers uses sophisticated electronic equipment to inspect power-plant boilers and smoke-stacks.** (*combining converted sentences*)

IV. BASE SENTENCES

1 Maggie Miller wrote the manifesto.

2 Maggie Miller was one of the leaders of the committee.

3 Maggie Miller said [*SOMETHING*].

4 The time has come for a revolution.

A. DIRECTIONS

a convert sentence (1) to the passive voice, making **manifesto** the subject.

b reduce sentence (2) to an appositive phrase.

Expressing What You Have Put Together

c convert sentence (3) to a dependent clause beginning with **who**.

d convert sentence (4) to a dependent clause beginning with **that**.

e combine all four converted sentences into a single sentence, substituting the converted sentence (4) for the [*SOMETHING*] in converted sentence (3).

RESULTS

a The manifesto was written by Maggie Miller. (*passive voice*)

b one of the leaders of the committee (*appositive phrase*)

c who said [*SOMETHING*] (*adjective clause*)

d that the time has come for a revolution (*noun clause*)

e **The manifesto was written by Maggie Miller, one of the leaders of the committee, who said that the time has come for a revolution.** (*combining all converted sentences*)

V. BASE SENTENCES

1 They intended [*SOMETHING*].

2 They buy groceries.

3 They came home from work.

4 They saw the rain.

5 The rain was falling.

6 The rain was heavy.

7 The rain was cold.

8 They decided [*SOMETHING*].

9 They take a taxi.

10 The taxi was standing on the corner.

● Combining and Rearranging Sentences

A. DIRECTIONS

a leave sentence (1) unchanged.

b reduce sentence (2) to the infinitive form (**to** . . .)

c convert sentence (3) to a dependent clause beginning with **when**.

d convert sentence (4) to a dependent clause beginning with **when**.

e reduce sentence (5) to a participle.

f reduce sentence (6) to an adjective.

g reduce sentence (7) to an adjective.

h leave sentence (8) unchanged.

i convert sentence (9) to the infinitive form (**to** . . .)

j convert sentence (10) to a dependent clause beginning with **which**.

k combine all of these transformed sentences into a single compound-complex sentence joined by **but**, substituting the infinitive phrase in (b) for the [*SOMETHING*] in (1) and substituting the infinitive phrase in (i) for the [*SOMETHING*] in (8).

RESULT*

They intended to buy groceries when they came home from work, but when they saw the heavy, cold rain falling, they decided to take a taxi, which was standing on the corner.

---

* (a) through (*j*) as combined in (*k*).

Expressing What You Have Put Together

Exercise in combining and rearranging

Now that you have seen several examples of combining and rearranging groups of sentences, try to combine and/or re-arrange each of the following groups of base sentences into a single sentence. If you see more than one way of combining and rearranging, write out all the alternatives you can devise.

A (1) Primitive societies depend on human memory for the retention of knowledge.
  (2) Primitive societies depend on the human voice for the transmission of knowledge.

B (1) Undercoating does two things.
  (2) Undercoating prevents rust.
  (3) Undercoating deadens sound.

C (1) The decisive event may have been the oil embargo.
  (2) The oil embargo began about 1973.

D (1) Some of the guests were uncomfortable.
  (2) Some of the guests were restless.
  (3) Others enjoyed the chitchat.
  (4) Others enjoyed the gossip.

E (1) The polls tell us [SOMETHING].
  (2) The American people want honesty in government.
  (3) The American people want a reduction in federal spending.

F (1) He walked cautiously.
  (2) He skirted the rain puddles.
  (3) He slipped on a banana peel.

G (1) One of the eight bodies was found near a culvert.
  (2) The culvert was in a farm community near Philadelphia.
  (3) The body was identified as that of the wife of one of the three men.

(4) The three men are being held in the county jail.

H (1) I was leaving the party.
(2) I heard the host say [*SOMETHING*].
(3) Everyone should drive carefully.

I (1) This week we received a letter from a friend.
(2) Our friend is a close observer of the national scene.
(3) Our friend monitors violations of regulations.
(4) The regulations govern environmental pollution.

J (1) This country is like an addict.
(2) An addict can't kick his drug habit.
(3) This country still finds itself dependent on the importation of foreign oil.

●
Varying sentence patterns

A variation on the exercise in the previous section is to take a sentence and try to express the same meaning in a variety of other ways—by changing some of the words or by altering the order of words or by using different grammatical structures. Take the following sentence, for instance:

They refused to attend the concert, for they thought that the price of admission was exorbitant.

Here are some other ways to express approximately the same meaning:

1 They refused to attend the concert because they thought that the price of admission was exorbitant.

2 Because they thought that the price of admission was exorbitant, they refused to attend the concert.

3 The reason they refused to attend the concert was that the price of admission was exorbitant.

Expressing What You Have Put Together

4 The reason they gave for refusing to attend the concert was that the price of admission was exorbitant.

5 Their reason for refusing to attend the concert was simple: the price of admission was exorbitant.

6 Thinking that the price of admission was exorbitant, they refused to attend the concert.

7 They registered their objection to what they regarded as an exorbitant price of admission by refusing to attend the concert.

8 The allegedly exorbitant price of admission made them refuse to attend the concert.

9 "We refuse to attend the concert because we think the price of admission is exorbitant."

10 The price of admission struck them as being exorbitant, so they refused to attend the concert.

11 Since they thought the price of admission was exorbitant, they refused to attend the concert.

●

Exercise in varying patterns

See in how many different ways you can express the meaning of the following sentences:

1 Many of the assembled stories, of course, can be dated quite definitely, but all of them were recited for live audiences by traveling bards for at least a hundred years before they were written down.

2 Those who are genuinely concerned about the energy shortage, about environmental pollution, and about worldwide malnutrition will be following with great interest the

astronomers' studies of the sources of energy in interstellar space.

3 As inheritors of the past, we must both respect and ignore our heritage if we are to make significant advances.

4 It should be conceded that subjecting these problems to the scrutiny of concerned citizens may result in more confusion than enlightenment for the community.

5 There are, according to my judgment, three conflicting stories in the defendant's testimony, including the story about his visit to a friend's house on the night of the murder.

6 She was perturbed by the indifference of the committee to the plight of the refugees, but she felt that she would only jeopardize the relief program if she openly criticized the committee.

7 The supervisors had to decide whether the workers staged the walkout in deliberate defiance of the injunction from the State Supreme Court.

8 If we are to understand the dilemmas that our forefathers confronted, we must do more than just read history books; we must read the newspapers, broadsides, pamphlets, and manifestos published between 1776 and 1783.

9 While searching in the library for some information about sunspots, I discovered a fascinating book about Unidentified Flying Objects.

10 Founded by missionaries, who were primarily interested in spreading the gospel among the heathen, the Institute has served the people well, bringing medical relief to thousands who might otherwise have died.

Regular practice in some or all of the exercises set forth in the previous sections will build up a store of words and sentence structures to be used in your own writing. What you derive from

Expressing What You Have Put Together

these exercises may become a permanent part of your own style.

●
Figures of speech

An expanded vocabulary and range of sentence patterns are not the only resources that make writing easier and more effective. Suitable use of figures of speech can make your prose lively and clear. But in order to use them, you must increase your awareness of the great variety of figures of speech.

Figurative language is an integral part of everyone's speech. Not only do you use hundreds of figures of speech in your own talking and writing—probably unconsciously—but you have even invented some of your own.

Basically, **a figure of speech is the use of a word in a *transferred* sense. It departs from the common literal meaning of a word and gives the word another meaning.** When we say, "The runner was a bolt of lightning," we obviously do not mean to say that the runner is literally a bolt of lightning. What we want to convey is a notion of the runner's amazing speed. We *could* say, "The runner is amazingly fast," and frequently of course we use such literal language. But we convey the same meaning with greater vividness by using the metaphor of a *bolt of lightning*. **Metaphor** is one of several figures of speech that are based on **analogy:** *something is like something else.* When we use a **simile**, we point out the analogy by actually using the words **like** or **as**: "the runner was like a bolt of lightning." By dropping the **like** or the **as** in a metaphor, we *imply* the analogy.

Everyone's speech or writing contains numerous **dead metaphors** or **submerged metaphors**—*figures that have* *been used so often that we no longer think of them as being used in a transferred sense and instead use them quite literally.* Words and phrases like "skyscraper," "leg of a table," "bulldozer," "eye of the storm," "mouth of the river," "glowing words," "stonefaced," "turtleneck sweaters," "ashen complexion" are examples of dead or submerged metaphors.

There is nothing wrong with using dead metaphors; in fact, use of them is inevitable, because they have become a regular and serviceable part of the vocabulary. *But be on guard against the use of* **trite metaphors.** There is a difference between dead or submerged metaphors and trite or tired metaphors, although the line between them is sometimes thin. Dead metaphors have been used so often that they have become an indispensable part of the language. *Tired metaphors, on the other hand, have been used so often that we are weary of them and would like to see them go away.* There is a significant difference between expressions like "skyscraper" and "the mouth of the river" and expressions like "a beacon of hope" and "a tower of strength." The first two are so apt that it would be hard to find alternative words or phrases to replace them. The latter two expressions are so stale that we wish they would disappear from the language.

Another kind of figurative language that you should avoid is the **mixed metaphor.** *A mixed metaphor results from joining, in one and the same unit of speech, two or more comparisons that clash because their imagery is different.* We mix metaphors when we write, for example, "Now that he's back in the saddle, everything will be smooth sailing." Besides being *trite*, the two metaphors *clash*: one uses the imagery of horsemanship, the other that of sailing. Unmixing might yield "Now that he's at the rudder, everything will be smooth sailing." We can shift metaphors as we move from one part of our paper to another or even from one sentence to another, but we

Expressing What You Have Put Together

should not mix *clashing images* in the same expression. Trite metaphors creep into our writing when we unthinkingly use an expression that has been left ringing in our ears from frequent repetition; mixed metaphors come from a conscious but careless effort to "tone up" our writing.

Some of the freshest and most startling figures of speech are those that appear unbidden, in a sudden flash, as we write. No one can account for those sudden, apt, vivid images, but they do occur. Spontaneity, however, is not their only source. Writers tell us that some of their best metaphors have resulted from a conscious effort on their part to invent a figurative way of saying what they wanted to say. Both the spontaneous metaphor and the deliberate metaphor must, however, be used with care—care that the spontaneous metaphor is not trite and that the deliberate metaphor is not mixed.

One final bit of advice: **it is better to try using figurative language and make mistakes than not to dare use it at all.** A clumsy or a stale or an inappropriate figure of speech is evidence that the writer is at least moving toward the creation of word-pictures.

Let us summarize the points that have been made about figurative language:

☐ **Figures of speech are not mere decoration; they are an integral and indispensable part of everyone's language.**

☐ **Figures of speech enliven prose by expressing things in vivid, concrete ways.**

☐ **You must sensitize yourself to language so that you can avoid both trite and mixed figures of speech.**

☐ **Apt, vivid figures of speech can come to you spontaneously or can be produced deliberately.**

Some Common Figures of Speech

☐ **It is better to risk making mistakes in the use of figures of speech than not to attempt figures of speech at all.**

●

Some common figures of speech

Here are definitions and illustrations of some of the common figures of speech.

METAPHOR

Suggests **a comparison between two things of different nature that nevertheless have something in common.**

The colorful display was a **magnet** for all the buyers in the room. (*here the metaphor is in the noun*)

He **knifed** his way through the dense crowd of shoppers. (*here the metaphor is in the verb*)

His **snail's-paced** crawl toward the sensitive bomb held the onlookers in suspense. (*here the metaphor is in the adjective*)

SIMILE

Directly states **a comparison between two things of different nature that nevertheless have something in common.**

He raced for the goal-line **like an antelope**. (*the sentence "He raced for the goal-line like O. J. Simpson" would be a simple comparison, not a simile, because the things being compared both have the same nature—they are both human*)

Expressing What You Have Put Together

Her eyes were as inert **as stone.**

Silence hung in the room **like a ball of lead.**

SYNECDOCHE

A part stands for the whole.

Male teenagers often get caught up in a love affair with their **wheels.** (*here* **wheels** *stands for the entire car or motorcycle*)

Give us this day our daily **bread.** (*here* **bread** *stands for food in general*)

The buccaneers raised their **steel** with a resounding shout. (*here* **steel** *stands for the whole sword*)

METONYMY

A thing stands for the person, position, or state of affairs that uses it.

They dedicated their **pens** to the cause of peace. (*here* **pens** *stands for writing talent*)

The people maintain an unshakable loyalty to the **crown.** (*here* **crown** *stands for the king or queen or for royalty in general*)

The women exchanged their **typewriters** for the **key to the executive washroom.** (*here* **typewriters** *stands for jobs as secretaries, and* **key to the executive washroom** *stands for positions as business executives*)

PUNS

A play on words, such as repeating a word in two different senses or using words that sound alike but have different meaning.

He was always **game** for any **game.**

That huckster has had **lots** of experience selling **lots** to senior citizens.

If you feel **alone**, come to us for **a loan.**

While the **sun** shines, his prodigal **son** makes hay.

PERIPHRASIS

Substitutes a descriptive word or phrase for a proper name or substitutes a proper name for a quality associated with that name.

The **little old lady from Dubuque** wouldn't approve this movie (*here* **little old lady from Dubuque** *stands for any prim and proper lady from small-town America*)

The **Human Backboard** won her match in straight sets. (*here* **Human Backboard** *refers to a tennis player, like Chris Evert, who relentlessly returns the ball over the net*)

They tried to fight **Jim Crow** with legislation. (*here* **Jim Crow** *refers to racial discrimination against blacks*)

What are you going to do about the **Archie Bunkers** in the electorate? (*here* **Archie Bunkers** *refers to the kind of bigoted middle-class citizens like the character in the TV show* All in the Family)

PERSONIFICATION

Assigns human qualities or abilities to abstractions or to inanimate objects.

His naivete would make **stones weep.**

The thatch-roofed cottages in the valley seemed **to be asleep.**

Expressing What You Have Put Together

Integrity **thumbs its nose** at pomposity.

While **vigilance nodded, rapacity rampaged** through the streets.

HYPERBOLE

Exaggerates for the purpose of emphasis or heightened effect.

No sooner had I thrown the hamburger away than a **million** flies swarmed over it.

My son's friends tracked a **ton** of mud through my clean kitchen.

Her sunny smile would **melt ice.**

I was so embarrassed that I felt about **as big as a peppercorn.**

LITOTES

Understates or downplays for the purpose of emphasis or heightened effect.

She lives in New York City, which, you might say, has a **few** people in it.

"It's only a **slight wound**," he said, showing me the stump of his leg.

He was a **bit annoyed** about the vandals having set fire to his garage.

You can be sure we were **not unhappy** to see the village after six days of trudging through the waist-high snow.

OXYMORON

Couples two contradictory terms.

He was a **cheerful pessimist** about his chances.

They were stunned by the **loud silence** that greeted their performance.

She revelled in her **luxurious** poverty.

Ralph proclaimed his **wholehearted indifference** to the project.

IRONY

A word intended to convey a meaning just the opposite of its ordinary or literal meaning.

"Do I love him? Who wouldn't **love** a cheat, a liar, and a scoundrel?"

Robbing a widow of her life savings was certainly a **noble** act.

It was one of those **glorious** days—overcast skies, a cutting wind, and sub-zero temperatures.

She wanted him to buy one of those **modest** cars, like a Cadillac or a Mercedes.

You needn't know the names or the definitions of figures of speech to be able to use them in your writing. In fact, you have used dozens of figures already without being aware that you were using them and without knowing what to call them. If, however, you are aware of the various figures of speech, it is probable that you will consciously use them if you see that they serve your purpose. Being able to create fresh figures of your own may also keep you from resorting to trite figures.

●

Some special artistic patterns

The purpose of the imitative exercises presented earlier in this chapter was to make you aware of some patterns of phrasing

Expressing What You Have Put Together

that are available in the English language but that you may not have used in your own writing. In this section you will meet some special artistic patterns that almost never occur in writing unless the writer makes a conscious decision to use them. They are unusual patterns that, like figures of speech, create *special* effects.

tricolon
- isocolon,
anaphora

When Winston Churchill said in one of his famous speeches during World War II, ''We shall fight on the beaches, we shall fight on the landing-grounds, we shall fight in the fields and in the streets, we shall fight in the hills,'' he was speaking on a special occasion for a special purpose with a special effect. He was addressing the people of Great Britain at a time during the war when their fortunes seemed to be at rock bottom. Hitler's armies had rolled over all opposition in the first nine months of the war, and in May of 1940, the Dutch and the Belgian armies had surrendered to the Germans, leaving the British people in a very precarious position. The speech that Churchill delivered on June 4, 1940 rallied the spirits and the resolve of the British people. The sentence quoted above occurred in that famous rallying speech. By phrasing his message in a series of parallel clauses, all beginning with the same words (''we shall fight''), Churchill drew special attention to this part of his message. The drum-roll of that repeated pattern conveyed the firm determination that it was intended to convey. If sentence after sentence of the *entire* speech had begun with the same words, the pattern would soon have grown monotonous and ultimately ridiculous. But used in the right place at the right time, an artistic pattern like that can produce a stunning effect.

There are two things one needs to learn about these artistic patterns: (1) *what* they are, and (2) *when* they should be used. You can very quickly learn what the special patterns are, and you will be introduced to some of them below. A sense of when they can be used appropriately and effectively will develop with your growth in the use of language.

● Some Special Artistic Patterns

Here are definitions and illustrations of some of the special artistic patterns (many of these are based on the principles of parallelism and repetition):

(A) PARALLEL PATTERN

Stringing together a series (three or more) of grammatically similar phrases or clauses.

As Abraham Lincoln said, what this country needs is a government of the people, by the people, and for the people. (*a series of prepositional phrases*) *tricolon* *epistrophe*

We will achieve this kind of government when our legislative bodies are representative of all segments of society, when elected officials are responsive to the needs and desires of their constituencies, and when the laws truly promote the welfare of all the citizens. (*a series of adverb clauses*)

By electing intelligent and dedicated men and women, by insisting on honesty and integrity, by establishing an effective system of checks and balances, and by maintaining a free and vigilant press, we can achieve this kind of government.

(B) REPETITIVE INITIAL PATTERN

Repeating two or more words at the beginning of successive phrases or clauses. *name?*

We must strive relentlessly to foster honest values, to foster honest goals, and to foster honest responsibilities. (*a series of infinitive phrases beginning with the same group of words*)

Why should we promote the interests of unscrupulous mountebanks? Why should we promote the aspirations of

Expressing What You Have Put Together

impractical visionaries? Why should we promote the schemes of self-aggrandizing entrepreneurs? (*a succession of parallel clauses beginning with the same words*)

(C) REPETITIVE ENDING PATTERNS

Repeating two or more words at the end of successive phrases and clauses.

Nations assume the burdens of responsibility, special-interest groups extoll the burdens of responsibility, and individuals avoid the burdens of responsibility.

(D) ANTITHETICAL PATTERNS

Joining contrasting ideas in a pair of grammatically similar phrases and clauses.

We advocate social justice, yet we tolerate racial discrimination; we praise merit, yet we reward mediocrity, we preach integrity, yet we practice duplicity.

(E) REVERSED PATTERNS

Reversing the normal order of words in a sentence.

name?

Harmony they planted; discord they reaped.

A reliable, affectionate, mild-mannered son he was not.

The struggle, the heartache, the disappointment I cannot claim to be familiar with.

(F) CRISSCROSS PATTERNS

Reversing grammatical structures in successive

chiasmus **clauses.**

He praises his enemies, but his friends he maligns.

I know what they want; what they would settle for I can't imagine.

(G) CLIMACTIC PATTERNS

Arranging a series of words, phrases, or clauses in an order of increasing importance.

name?

Her way of life was expensive, pointless, and utterly ruthless.

He wanted to educate his children, serve his country, and satisfy his God.

This law should meet with your approval because it is simple, because it is enforceable, and because it is just.

(H) ALLITERATIVE PATTERNS

Repeating the initial consonant(s) in two or more adjacent words.

Brainless brawn can break the bravado of brittle men.
Try a tasty, tempting tart today.

Although the alliterative pattern is effective occasionally as an attention-getting device or or a humorous effect, writers should use it sparingly. The alliterative pattern is especially conspicuous, but all of the special artistic patterns outlined in this section should be used only occasionally, as when you want to create a special effect or to draw unusual attention to what you have written.

●

Paragraphing

After the sentence, the paragraph is the next largest unit in a piece of writing. It is a collection of related sentences. Groups

Expressing What You Have Put Together

of paragraphs, in turn, mark off still larger units in this development.

A good way to regard the paragraph is as a form of visual punctuation marking off stages in the development of thought. By using the visual device of *indentation*, you indicate the breaks and shifts in the development of your thought. You thereby make it easier for your reader to follow and understand you. To demonstrate this, simply imagine yourself reading a text that had no paragraph indentations at all. As a reader, you would have to work much harder to follow that text. **Indentation is to a text what punctuation marks are to a sentence.**

Your own individual way of putting thoughts together and developing them from sentence to sentence within any paragraph reveals a pattern. *Look for this pattern in your writing.* It will reveal itself in the *length* of your average paragraph, and this in turn will govern the *number* of paragraphs that occur in your writing. Your own "style" of paragraphing will be influenced partly by the kind of writing you are doing and partly by the subjects you are writing about. If you were writing an instruction manual for assembling an electronic computer, your paragraphs might be only two sentences long—one "paragraph" for each stage of the assembly. If, on the other hand, you were explaining a political concept, you might have to string together six, eight, ten sentences— enough sentences to make the concept clear to your readers. Occasionally, you might use a one-sentence paragraph to emphasize a point or to signal a transition to the next major section of your paper. Despite these variations in length, however, the collection of paragraphs in your paper will reveal an *average* length that is characteristic of your writing.

Now let us look at some of the principles governing the construction of paragraphs.

Unity

We defined the paragraph as a *collection of related sentences.* One of the principles that helps to relate the sentences in a paragraph is the principle of unity. **A unified paragraph is one in which all of the sentences are talking about the same topic.** The four sentences in the following paragraph seem not to be talking about the same topic:

> A chemist is interested in the atomic weights of the elements in a substance. When she heard the explosion, she ran to the telephone to call the police. The cost of education in these inflationary times puts some segments of our population at an extreme disadvantage. Automobiles have begun to roll off the assembly line once again.

Admittedly, this is an extreme example of a disunified paragraph. A more usual kind of breakdown in unity is the one in which the first three or four sentences of a paragraph deal with the same topic, but then suddenly and without warning, a sentence occurs that introduces another topic. The following paragraph is an instance of this disunity:

> Bluegrass is a distinct kind of country-and-western music. Associated with the Appalachian regions of the country, it has its roots in the folk culture of the rural people who inhabit the hills and the mountains of these regions. The instruments that are featured in this kind of music are the acoustic guitar, the banjo, the fiddle, the dobro, and the autoharp. The fast-paced, rippling melodies issuing from those instruments are often more important than the lyrics. Nashville is now the capital of the country-and-western industry. Big-name performers can be seen

every day driving up to the plush recording studios in their Cadillacs and Continentals.

The first four sentences of this paragraph deal with some of the characteristics of bluegrass music. But with the appearance of the fifth and sixth sentences, a new topic is introduced. Nashville, of course, has some connection with bluegrass music, but the fifth and sixth sentences do not talk about that connection. Instead, they introduce the notion of Nashville being the capital of country-and-western music, of which bluegrass is only a part. The writer should have begun a new paragraph with the fifth sentence.

Associate unity with *one*. **Each paragraph should deal with only one topic.** Be vigilant. *If you detect that a sentence in a paragraph you wrote shifts to a discussion different from the topic you started out with, either drop that sentence or begin a new paragraph.* See section **50** in the handbook for further discussion of paragraph unity.

Coherence

Coherence is another principle that governs the relationship of sentences in a paragraph. It is the principle that ensures the "hanging-together" of all the sentences in a paragraph. Unity also contributes to the "hanging-together" of sentences in a paragraph, but conceivably, a paragraph could be unified and still not be coherent. Coherence governs the *logical and connected flow* of sentences, whereas unity governs the *logical wholeness* of the group of sentences. **A *unified* paragraph keeps the focus on a *single topic*; a *coherent* paragraph makes it easy for the reader to *move from sentence to sentence.***

Here are some of the devices that help the reader sense the interconnections between the sentences of a paragraph:

(A) LOGICAL BRIDGES

1 **The carry-over of the same idea or topic from sentence to sentence.**
2 **Parallel structure of successive sentences.**

(B) VERBAL BRIDGES

1 **Repetition of key words in several of the sentences.**
2 **Use of synonymous words in successive sentences.**
3 **Use of pronouns referring to nouns in previous sentences.**
4 **Use of coordinating conjunctions and conjunctive adverbs.**

Even more than pronouns and repeated and synonymous words, coordinating conjunctions and conjunctive adverbs explicitly tie sentences together and indicate the kind of relationships that exist between sentences. Here is a list of some of the commonly used conjunctions and conjunctive adverbs arranged in categories that indicate the kind of relationships they establish:

(C) ADDITIVE

and / also / besides / moreover / furthermore / in addition / not only . . . but also / both . . . and / first, second . . . finally.

(D) OPPOSING

but / yet / however / rather / nevertheless / instead / on the contrary / on the other hand.

Expressing What You Have Put Together

(E) ALTERNATIVE

or / either . . . or / nor / neither . . . nor.

(F) TEMPORAL

then / next / afterwards / previously / now / meanwhile / subsequently / later / thereafter / henceforth.

(G) CAUSAL

for / so / / therefore / thus / consequently / hence / accordingly / as a result / otherwise / perhaps / indeed / surely / clearly.

Observe the use of some of these linking devices in a coherent paragraph:

> The flexibility of a racquet—that is, the amount of "give" in the frame—is important to your game. You can test the flex of a racquet by clamping the handle to the edge of a table with one hand and then pressing down on the end of the frame with the other. Metal racquets are generally more flexible than wood racquets. The more flexible a racquet is, the more power it will add to your shots by its greater whiplash action during a swing. But it provides that extra power at the expense of control. Stiffer racquets thus offer more control, although they can subject your arm muscles to damaging vibrations if you have tennis elbow (Jeffrey Bairstow, "Which Racquet Is Right for Your Game?" *Tennis*, 11 [January 1976], 21–22).

Analysis of the coherence devices in this paragraph:

LOGICAL BRIDGES

1 Every sentence in the paragraph is dealing in some way with the "topic" of the paragraph—the flexibility of tennis racquets. The frequent occurrence of comparative phrases—**more flexible, more power, greater whiplash action, extra power, more control, stiffer racquet**—indicates that the major means of development in the paragraph is **comparison and contrast.**

2 There are no instances in this paragraph of the use of parallel structures in successive sentences to promote coherence.

VERBAL BRIDGES

1 Repetition of key words in several of the sentences—**flexible, racquet, power, control, frame.**

2 Use of synonomous words in successive sentences—**flexibility:** *flex, amount of 'give';* **greater power:** *extra power;* antonym of **flexible:** *stiffer.*

3 Use of pronouns—**racquet:** *it;* **racquets:** *they;* **one hand:** *other;* **you,** *your.*

4 Use of coordinating conjunctions and conjunctive adverbs—**But, thus, then, that is.**

Since coherence is vital to intelligibility, you should never relax in the pursuit of this skill. Another benefit of the copy exercise recommended earlier in this chapter is that you can learn how practiced writers make their prose "hang together." For further discussion and illustration of paragraph coherence, see section **51** in the handbook.

●
Adequate development

No definite rule can be established to help you determine whether a paragraph is adequately developed. A paragraph must be as long as it needs to be, but that is not saying much. Judgments about adequate development must always be made in relation to *particular* paragraphs. Although we cannot specify in the abstract how many sentences a paragraph must have to be adequately developed, we can say that **usually—but only usually—the topic of a paragraph cannot be adequately developed with only one or two sentences.** Most readers would sense that the following two-sentence paragraph, for instance, was not adequately developed:

> There are several questions we must ask when we are buying a new or a used car. Are we getting true value for our money?

Readers readily sense the inadequacy of development here because the first sentence mentions "several questions," and the second sentence poses only *one* question. What are some of the other questions that must be asked?

Even where the inadequacy of development is not as obvious as it was in the paragraph quoted above, most readers can tell when a paragraph does not give them all that they expected or all that they needed to know. They may not be able to specify what is missing; nevertheless, they are quite sure that they have been "cheated" by the skimpy paragraph. Although some paragraphs give readers "too much" or, at least, more than is needed, the more common fault is that paragraphs give readers "too little."

Although no definite rules can be laid down about the adequate development of paragraphs, two practical bits of advice can be given:

☐ **Look carefully at all one-sentence, two-sentence, and even three-sentence paragraphs that you find in your paper.** (Do those paragraphs say all that you could say or all that you *should* say on the topic of the paragraph?) **Most of the time you will find that those thin paragraphs need to be fleshed out with a few more sentences.**

☐ **Use the "topic sentence" of your paragraph as a gauge to test whether the paragraph you wrote is adequately developed. This is the commitment-and-response test.** (What did the topic sentence of your paragraph *commit* you to do? Do the other sentences in the paragraph totally or at least *sufficiently* deliver on that commitment?)

Finally, remember that there are some legitimate uses of one- and two-sentence paragraphs:

1 **For dialogue:** a new paragraph must be started each time the speaker changes, even if the speaker utters only one sentence or a fragment of a sentence or only a single word.

2 **For emphasis:** an important idea can be given great prominence by being set off in a paragraph by itself. A listing of important points, for instance, might be laid out in a sequence of one-sentence paragraphs.

3 **For transition:** a one- or two-sentence paragraph can sometimes be used effectively to signal the shift from one section of a paper to the next section—e.g. "Now let us consider the disadvantages of this system."

4 **For newspaper copy:** journalists are encouraged to break up their copy into one- and two-sentence paragraphs so that their paragraphs won't appear to be formidably dense when they are printed in the narrow columns of the newspaper.

Expressing What You Have Put Together

●

Topic sentences

A topic sentence is a sentence that indicates, in a general way, what idea or thesis or subject the paragraph is dealing with. A recent study of paragraphs from some of the nation's most famous newspapers and magazines revealed that professional writers frequently do not include in their paragraphs a sentence that could be regarded as the topic sentence. The absence of a topic sentence, however, does not mean that their paragraphs do not have a central *idea* or *thesis*; it simply means that sometimes writers do not explicitly indicate what the central idea or thesis is but instead allow the reader to infer the topic of the paragraph. In fact, paragraphs of narrative prose and of descriptive prose frequently do *not* have topic sentences.

Nevertheless, a close study of published prose also reveals that many paragraphs do have a topic sentence, and **beginning writers should include a topic sentence somewhere in their paragraphs.** The presence of a topic sentence can serve as a guideline to ensure the unity, coherence, and adequate development of the paragraph by suggesting to the writer how that unit of the paper might be developed.

Although experienced writers probably do not consciously formulate a topic sentence and then go on to develop it, beginners should try to do so. After a while, the formulation and development of topic sentences will become as instinctive for them as for experienced writers. As models for the formulation of topic sentences, here are some randomly selected sentences from contemporary prose:

1 Aerosols, in fact, may have a slight edge over other hazards when it comes to danger potential.

2 For some time now, the Boy Scouts have been going to considerable lengths to modernize their image.

3 The toy business has been expanding despite the decline in the birthrate.

4 Social Security is not a pension plan; it is an income-transfer plan.

5 More than most businesses, florist shops are constantly adjusting to new—and unusual—market conditions.

6 In contrast with what I saw years ago, I was struck by the earnest, stolid attitude of the ordinary people on the streets and in the restaurants and department stores of Peking.

7 The field of astronomy is in the midst of what is often called its "golden age."

8 The first version provides two criteria that the critic may use in determining whether a given work justly belongs to science or to literature.

9 Unlike many modern stories for children, fairy tales present evil as being no less omnipresent than virtue.

10 If there is any one major question posed by the CIA's behavior in Laos and elsewhere, it is that the CIA may have reached the point at which it has itself become a threat to our national security.

See the section on Methods of Development below for suggestions about how some of these topic sentences might be developed.

Although topic sentences theoretically can—and actually do—occur anywhere in the paragraph, *they most often occur first, if they occur at all.* **It will definitely be helpful to you to begin most of your paragraphs with the topic sentence.** Placed in that initial position, it will trigger the development and suggest the direction that the development must take.

Here is a summary of the points made about topic sentences:

☐ **Not all paragraphs have a clear-cut topic sentence;**

sometimes the topic of a paragraph is *implied* rather than stated.

☐ However, many paragraphs do have an explicit topic sentence.

☐ You should make it a practice consciously to formulate a topic sentence for your paragraphs.

☐ Although the topic sentence can occur anywhere in the paragraph—at the beginning, at the end, or somewhere in the middle—you should begin most of your paragraphs with the topic sentence.

●

Methods of development

Just as experienced writers probably do not *consciously* formulate a topic sentence for their paragraphs, they also probably do not *consciously* decide how they will develop their paragraphs. Most professional writers just put down one sentence after the other, without any preconceived plan, but because of frequent practice in writing, their paragraphs are usually unified, coherent, and adequately developed. And although they may not have paused to ask themselves *how* they would develop a particular paragraph, their method of development seems to be not only appropriate but inevitable

But when you closely study the paragraphs of published prose, you discover that the paragraphs *were* developed by one or another of the methods recommended in chapter 2 for discovering something to say about a subject. There are only a limited number of ways in which the human mind operates. So when you face the task of writing a sentence or a paragraph or a whole essay, you go about it in one or another of these set ways.

Here, from section **52** of the handbook, is a list of the common ways in which writers develop their paragraphs—develop, that is, the implied central idea or the clearly stated topic sentence:

☐ **They present examples or illustrations of what they are discussing.**

☐ **They cite data—facts, statistics, evidence, details, precedents—that corroborate or confirm what they are discussing.**

☐ **They quote, paraphrase, or summarize the testimony of others about what they are discussing.**

☐ **They relate an anecdote that has some bearing on what they are discussing.**

☐ **They define terms connected with what they are discussing.**

☐ **They compare or contrast what they are discussing with something else—usually something familiar to the readers—and point out similarities or differences.**

☐ **They explore the causes or reasons for the phenomenon or situation they are discussing.**

☐ **They point out the effects or consequences of the phenomenon or situation they are discussing.**

☐ **They explain how something operates.**

☐ **They describe the person, place, or thing they are discussing.**

117

Expressing What You Have Put Together

A consideration of the topic sentence will often suggest not only the direction that the paragraph might take but also one or more ways to develop the paragraph. Let us look at some of the topic sentences listed on p. 114 and see how they might suggest possible lines of development:

Aerosols, in fact, may have a slight edge over other hazards when it comes to danger potential.
Possible lines of development:

1 Cite some examples of the hazards of aerosol-spray cans.
2 Compare aerosol-spray cans with other common household hazards and show how aerosols are potentially more dangerous.

Social Security is not a pension plan; it is an income-transfer plan.
Possible lines of development:

1 Define *pension plan* and *income-transfer plan.*
2 Compare the Social Security system with a regular pension plan and show how it differs.

The toy business has been expanding despite the decline in the birthrate.
Possible lines of development:

1 Cite some statistics to confirm the decline in the birthrate and the increasing sales of toys.
2 Explore the causes or reasons for the expansion of the toy business despite the declining birthrate.

In contrast with what I saw years ago, I was struck by the earnest, stolid attitude of the ordinary people on the streets and in the restaurants and department stores of Peking.
Possible lines of development:

1 Describe the current behavior of the Chinese people observed in public places in Peking.

2 Contrast their current behavior with their behavior several years ago.

For some time now, the Boy Scouts have been going to considerable lengths to modernize their image.
Possible lines of development:

1 Describe the dress and the demeanor of the "new" Boy Scouts.

2 Quote some comments about the changing image of the Boy Scouts.

The first version provides two criteria which the critic may use in determining whether a given work justly belongs to science or to literature.
Possible lines of development:

1 Specify the two criteria and show how they operate to discriminate types of literary texts.

2 Point out the beneficial effects of adopting this set of criteria.

As you can see from these examples, careful consideration of the topic sentence can suggest not only *what* you are obliged

Expressing What You Have Put Together

to do in the paragraph but also *how* you might go about doing what you have to do. This is another instance of the commitment-and-response approach. **Discover what your topic sentence commits you to do, and then make a decision about the kind of response that will best fulfill your commitment.**

One of the benefits of the copy exercise recommended earlier in this chapter is that it reveals how professional writers structure and develop their paragraphs. Among other things, you can learn how to pick out the topic sentence—if the paragraph has one—and see the variety of positions that the topic sentence can occupy in a paragraph; finally, you can become acquainted with the variety of ways of developing topic sentences. From observations based on copying, you discover the *choices* of means available for structuring and developing paragraphs. Discovery of the variety of ways of writing paragraphs may eventually make this task less of a mechanical exercise and more of an art. Then you will have acquired a *style.*

Chapter 6
Putting It All Together

Having reviewed the several steps involved in the writing process, you will now see what it is like to run through the whole sequence, from original assignment to final product, and see how all our theory works out in practice. By taking an assignment and running it through the stages of

1 **settling on a subject**
2 **deciding on a thesis**
3 **discovering something to say on the subject**
4 **selecting from what you have found**
5 **organizing what you have selected**
6 **writing the first draft**
7 **revising the first draft**
8 **writing the final draft**

you will realize the series of *choices* you have to make at every stage. In facing and making those choices, you will become aware, in a concrete way, of what the art of rhetoric is all about.

Putting It All Together

●
Assignment

As you saw in Chapter 2, most of the time when you have to write something, you do so in response to an assignment. Your assignment to write something will usually designate the general subject and the length of the paper. You may be allowed to decide *what aspect* of the general subject to treat and *how to treat it*.

Let us suppose that in a sociology class you are assigned to review a continuing series on television and to write a 1200–1500-word paper on the social implications of that series. There is the general assignment: the subject that you are to deal with and the length of the paper are set for you. What is left to your decision is the particular series that you will review and write about—and of course dozens of subsequent decisions.

From among the continuing TV series, you can make a choice of talk shows, game shows, news broadcasts, situation comedies, detective dramas, etc. About any one of those, you might be able to write an interesting and significant paper. But recently, you have become hooked on watching some of the daytime soap operas. Almost despite yourself, you, like millions of other viewers, have been fascinated by these slow-paced, crisis-packed domestic dramas. And yet you think you can still be somewhat objective in evaluating the social significance of these sometimes tawdry tales of American life. So you make your first decision: you are going to review and write about daytime soap operas.

●
Settling on a subject

Having decided on the particular kind of television series to write about, you now have to make some further decisions that will narrow your subject to manageable size. You have only 1200–1500 words in which to treat your subject. Having to put 1200–1500 words together might chill you at first, but when you stop to think about it, an allotment of 1200–1500 words really doesn't give you very much room in which to work—somewhere between four and six double-spaced typed pages. So you conclude that while you may be able to say something in general about soap operas, you will have to concentrate on a *single* soap opera, preferably one that is fairly representative.

You are faced then with another decision: *which* soap opera to focus on. From the three or four that you have regularly watched, you decide to concentrate on *Days of Our Lives*, an hour-long NBC soap opera that deals, in a rather daring way, with some of the controversial social issues of the day. You realize that there is something arbitrary about that choice, because you could just as easily write about *All My Children* or *General Hospital*. But you make this choice anyway, perhaps for the simple reason that *Days of Our Lives* is the soap opera that most captures your interest.

●
Deciding on a thesis

You have chosen a particular soap opera for your paper, and yet you feel that you still have some further narrowing to do if you are to treat your subject adequately in 1200–1500 words. There are many *aspects* of this soap opera that you could deal with—the kinds of characters that figure in the drama, the quality of the acting, the pace of the show, the kinds of social issues dealt with. Which of these—or others—will you carve out of the larger subject to deal with?

You sense that you might be better able to make that decision if you could formulate a *thesis* for your paper. Sometimes, writers are not able to formulate a thesis until they have ex-

Putting It All Together

plored the subject. But you are familiar enough now with soap operas in general, and with *Days of Our Lives* in particular, to formulate at least a *tentative* thesis. You might decide later to modify or refine or even change it, but you are prepared at this point to attempt a thesis—one that might help you decide which aspect of *Days of Our Lives* to treat in 1200–1500 words.

You know that **a thesis should be formulated in a single declarative sentence**—basically, a sentence in which something about the subject is asserted or denied, a sentence like "War is hell" or "An increase in taxes will not by itself solve the problem of welfare."

What thesis sentence could you formulate about soap operas in general or about *Days of Our Lives* in particular? Your sociology teacher specified that your paper should deal with the *social* implications of some television series. That specification considerably narrows the range of your choices. The specified length of the paper also sets some limits for the choice of a thesis. Some theses that you can think of in connection with this soap opera would need at least 10,000 words for adequate treatment.

With those considerations in mind, you make a stab at formulating a thesis sentence. What has particularly intrigued you as you watched *Days of Our Lives* from day to day is the way in which men and women experience seemingly endless conflicts based on blind sexual desire. On the surface, the conflicts revolve around such situations as a crumbling marriage, an interracial romance, a miscarriage, someone's wavering faith, a decision about artificial insemination. But at the root of most of these situations, one can detect impetuous sexual motivation. One could view this drama as a good example of the old wisdom that when men and women don't come together out of love and respect for each other, they get burned. This last sentence has the air and ingredients of a thesis sentence. You decide on it as the tentative thesis for your paper, which you formulate in these terms:

> **Soap operas, like *Days of Our Lives*, show that sex without genuine love, mutual respect, and firm commitment leads to frustration, exploitation, and unhappiness.**

That thesis sentence may later have to be rephrased, but at this point it can at least give a tighter focus to your subject. For one thing, it will guide you in selecting those features, incidents, and situations that are pertinent to the aspect that you have decided to write about.

●
Discovering something to say: research

Having settled on a narrowed subject and on a thesis, you are faced now with the task of discovering something to say. Your thesis commits you to presenting some evidence that soap operas in general and *Days of Our Lives* in particular demonstrate the misfortunes that arise when unbridled passions rule the mind. *The chief source of material to develop that thesis will be some firsthand research.* This means watching several of the shows and taking notes about episodes that manifest the unbridled sexual motivations of the characters. Of course, you have watched several of the shows already, and you remember several previous episodes that will be pertinent to your thesis. Watching a few additional shows will provide you with some more material and, more importantly, may confirm the continuing sexual orientation of the dramatic conflicts.

To provide a context for your discussion, you might want to give your readers some background information about soap

Putting It All Together

operas in general and about *Days of Our Lives* in particular. To gather that kind of information, you will have to do some outside reading, but not much, because background information will be only a small part of your 1200–1500-word paper. You might be able to get by with reading only a half-dozen or so authoritative articles.

A good source for finding magazine articles is the *Reader's Guide to Periodical Literature*. Consulting some installments of this reference work, you discover these promising articles on soap operas:

Edith Efron, "The Soaps—anything but 99 44/100 Percent Pure," *TV Guide*, March 13, 1965.

"Sex and Suffering in the Afternoon," *Time*, January 12, 1976.

Bebe Moore Campbell, "Hooked on Soaps," *Essence*, November, 1978.

Tania Modleski, "The Search for Tomorrow in Today's Soap Operas," *Film Quarterly*, Fall, 1979.

Ellen Torgerson, "Don't You Just Want to Scratch Their Eyes Out?" *TV Guide*, July, 1979.

"Season of the Nightsoaps," *Time*, February 9, 1981.

"Rich Man, Pitch Man," *Newsweek*, February 9, 1981.

When you mention to your former English teacher that you are writing a paper on soap operas for your sociology class, he calls your attention to Dennis Porter's article "Soap Time: Thoughts on a Commodity Art Form" in the April 1977 issue of *College English* and lends you a copy of an anthology that reprints a portion of the classic article on radio soap operas that James Thurber wrote for the *New Yorker* magazine in 1948. Consulting the card catalogue in the library under the subject heading "Soap Operas," you discover the titles of two books: Madeleine Edmondson and David Rounds, *From Mary*

Noble to Mary Hartman: The Complete Soap Opera Book (New York: Stein & Day, 1976) and Kathryn Weibel, *Mirror, Mirror: Images of Women Reflected in Popular Culture* (New York: Anchor Books, 1977). A friend of yours shows you her collection of fan magazines about soap operas with titles like *Daytime TV, Soap Operas, Daytime Digest*. With those available published sources, you are assured that you will be able to supplement what you already know about soap operas from having watched them for several years.

●
Finding something to say: recall

To orient your readers to the particular soap opera of your choice, you can rely mainly on your memory of the show to supply you with some data. (Where your memory does not supply you with the needed information about the show, you can probably get that information from the articles and digests.) In stimulating your memory to recover this kind of background information about the show, you might make use of the journalistic formula of **who, what, when, where, how,** and **why** or Kenneth Burke's pentad of **act, agent, agency, scene,** and **purpose**. The classical topic of **definition** suggests that you ought to provide your readers with a definition of the soap opera. Your definition will be based on conclusions drawn from your experience with soap operas. Since your thesis commits you to demonstrating that there seems to be some connection between the characters' actions and their sexual drives, the classical topic of **cause-and-effect** or **antecedent-consequence** may be relevant in your search for something to say about your subject. The topic of **testimony** should also be useful. It would certainly strengthen your case if you could find some quotations by experts—psychologists, for instance—

Putting It All Together

confirming your thesis. But since you already know much about your subject, perhaps the best system to use in this case would be **brainstorming**, reinforced perhaps by some quiet **meditation** on the subject.

At least you now know how to gather something to say on your subject: you must do some brainstorming and meditating; you must do some reading; you must make use of those systems (the journalistic formula, the Burkeian pentad, or the classical topics) most likely to yield some material; and you must watch, and take notes on, some of the episodes of *Days of Our Lives*.

●

Your subject "notebook"

Let us suppose that over a week's time you do all of the above things and that you end up with a collection of random notes like the following:

Some notes about soap operas in general

More than 20 million Americans watch one or more daytime serials regularly or occasionally.

Mainly watched by housewives, senior citizens, college students, and the unemployed.

Thirteen soap operas now on the networks, beginning about 11:00 A.M. and running until 4:00 in the afternoon.

More revenue from daytime serials than for many prime-time regular series shows. According to January 12, 1976 cover story in *Time*, an hour-long evening show costs at least $250,000 to produce but brings in ad revenue of only $400,000, whereas while it costs NBC $170,000 to produce five days of *Days of Our Lives*, those five showings bring in $600,000 of ad revenue. (Inflation has certainly increased those costs and incomes since 1976.)

The majority of the soap operas have been expanded to hour-long shows. *Search for Tomorrow*, the oldest TV soap opera, began as a black-and-white, 15-minute show back on September 3, 1951.

At some periods in the afternoon, three different soap operas will be running concurrently, but the most popular of these three often commands as many as ten million viewers in that time slot.

Consistently rated among the most popular daytime serials are *General Hospital, All My Children, One Life to Live, Days of Our Lives*.

There are now four nighttime soaps: *Dynasty, Flamingo Road, Knots Landing*, and *Dallas*. The last three are all produced by Lorimar Productions, described as "TV's hottest film factory."

The major script-writers earn annual salaries ranging from $100,000 to $250,000. Irna Phillips, a writer of soap operas for over 40 years before her death in 1973 at age 70, was the author of *Days of Our Lives, As the World Turns*, and *Another World*. Agnes Nixon, another successful soap-opera writer, is the author of *One Life to Live* and *All My Children*.

Several monthly magazines about soap-opera personalities are published—e.g. *TV Picture Life, Soap Opera, Daytime Stars, Daytime TV, Daytime Digest*. Some of these have press runs exceeding 400,000 copies.

Several prominent people watch soap operas regularly—e.g. Supreme Court Justice Thurgood Marshall, entertainer Sammy Davis, Jr., former governor John Connolly, artist Andy Warhol, literary critic Leslie Fiedler.

Soap operas are very popular with college students. Some students arrange their class schedules so that they won't miss their favorite show. Several students rush back to the dormitory or to the Student Union between classes to catch their favorite daytime serial on TV.

Some data about *Days of Our Lives*

An hour-long show produced by NBC. Year after year, it rates as one of the most popular soap operas on TV.

Originally featured the drama in the lives of four generations of the Horton family in the small town of Salem. In recent years, the Hortons have not been as prominent on the show as they once were.

Almost 30 actors appear in episodes at some time or other during the year.

Susan Seaforth has played the role of the trouble-making Julie on the show for more than a dozen years. In 1974, in real life, Susan married Bill Hayes, who plays Doug Williams, a character who was once married to Julie's mother on the show.

Dr. Neil Curtis is another long-time character on the show. Over the years, he has been married and divorced several times.

Driven into a convent several years ago as the result of a traumatic incident involving her brother Mickey Horton, Marie Horton plays a part in the drama now as a nun who has been assigned to her hometown of Salem.

Some ideas generated by the use of one or other of the discovery systems

Definition: Soap operas are serial dramatizations of domestic conflicts involving married and unmarried men and women. Soap operas derive their name from the fact that in the early days most of them were sponsored by manufacturers of soaps and detergents.

● Your Subject "Notebook"

Some characteristics of soap operas: The focal characters are usually women, young or middle-aged. Young or middle-aged men, usually of the professional class (doctors, lawyers) also figure in these dramas, often as the complicating factors in the story. But audiences are more interested in what happens to the women. From time to time, new characters are added to the show, and some of the long-time characters disappear from the show either temporarily or permanently.

Soap operas present a constant round of marital infidelities, seductions, fornications, divorces, remarriages, pregnancies, abortions, torrid embraces, secret rendezvous, rivalries, intrigues, broken homes.

The action of the plots is slow-paced and protracted. A simple incident is often strung out over several days. Between Monday and Friday of any week, the plot may have advanced very little.

Five or six plots, involving different characters, are often interwoven in a single show. The scenes tend to be short, and shifts are made from scene to scene abruptly. On hour-long shows, the "story" is interrupted every nine minutes for a series of 30-second commercials. Proportions: about 45 minutes of story to 15 minutes of commercials in each hour period.

Complications are constantly and often artificially introduced into the stories. A show usually ends on a note of high tension for one or more groups of characters, and the Friday show usually ends with a "cliff-hanger" in order to entice the audience to tune in on Monday after the long weekend.

Comparison with other kinds of popular dramatizations, like westerns, detective stories, situation comedies: Soap operas are *like* these other forms in that they tend to be melodramatic. Melodramas are sensational, not very believable, have superficial characters, and are often very sentimental. They *differ* from the other forms mainly in the kinds of incidents and characters portrayed. Westerns deal mainly

131

with physical conflicts between "good guys" and "bad guys." Detective stories deal with the solving of a crime and the catching of the criminal(s). Situation comedies are *like* soap operas in that they deal with the day-to-day conflicts in family life, but they *differ* in that the conflicts are exploited for comedy rather than for the disruptive effect on the family.

Cause-and-effect (or antecedent-consequence): Most of the conflicts in the lives of the characters are produced by something that has a sexual basis. There is a continual succession of marriages, divorces, affairs, remarriages, adulteries, pregnancies, abortions.

Serious illnesses and accidents are frequently complicating factors in the lives of the characters. Frequently these are artificial means of breaking deadlocked plots. The death or terminal illness of some character often frees another character to pursue a romantic interest. A favorite such device is amnesia, often the result of a fall.

Reasons (cause-and-effect) for the appeal of these melodramas

Vicarious sexual interest in one or more of the characters.

Relief from the monotony of the viewers' humdrum lives.

Audience identification: sometimes the situations are so much like the experiences of the TV audience that the viewers can get pleasure or comfort from watching others cope with similar problems. Sometimes the situations are so different that viewers can vicariously enjoy experiences that they never had themselves but that they are curious about.

Feelings of smugness or superiority in the audience.

Feelings of satisfaction from seeing nasty characters get put down. Feelings of satisfaction from seeing a sympathetic character get a well-deserved reward.

The natural human appetite for stories.

● Your Subject "Notebook"

Pertinent quotations from articles and from authorities

Edith Efron, "The Soaps—Anything but 99 44/100 Percent Pure," *TV Guide*, March 13, 1965: "Folks squawking about cheap nighttime sex should hearken to the sickly sexuality of daytime soap opera. *Love of Life* details frank affairs between married women and men; *Search for Tomorrow* has a single girl in an affair with a married man, result: pregnancy; *The Secret Storm* has another single girl expecting a married man's child."

"The fundamental theme of soap operas is the male-female relationship."

"The act of searching for a partner goes on constantly in the world of soap opera. . . . This all-consuming, single-minded search for a mate is an absolute good in the soap-opera syndrome. Morality—and domestic conflict—emerge from how the search is conducted. Accordingly, there is sex as approached by good people, and sex as it is approached by villains."

Frank Dodge, producer of *Search for Tomorrow*: "These shows are a recognition of existing emotions and problems. It's not collusion but a logical coincidence that adultery, illegitimate children, and abortions are appearing on many shows. If you read the papers about what's going on in the suburbs—well, it's more startling than what's shown on the air." (quoted in the Efron article)

Dr. Harold Greenwald, of the National Psychological Association for Psychoanalysis and the supervising psychologist of the Community Guidance Service in New York: "They're realistic. . . . They're reflecting the changes taking place in our society. There are fewer taboos. The age of sexual activity in the middle classes has dropped, and it has increased in frequency. There is more infidelity. These plays reflect these problems." (quoted in Efron)

133

Putting It All Together

Betty Friedan, author of *The Feminine Mystique*: "The image of woman that emerges in these soap operas is precisely what I've called 'The Feminine Mystique.' The women are childish and dependent; the men are degraded because they relate to women who are childish and dependent; and the view of sex that emerges is sick." (quoted in Efron)

Edith Efron: "On the basis of these comments, one can certainly conclude that all this sex-based human wretchedness is on the air because it exists in society. And the producers' claims that this is dramatic 'realism' appear to have some validity."

James Thurber, "Ivorytown, Rinsoville, Anacinburg, and Crisco Corners," *The New Yorker*, copyright 1948 (reprinted in *Writing Prose: Techniques and Purposes*, ed. Thomas S. Kane and Leonard J. Peters, 2nd edition (New York: Oxford University Press, 1964), pp. 445–456. "Thus, a soap opera is an endless sequence of narratives whose only cohesive element is the eternal presence of its bedevilled and beleaguered principal characters."

"Time in a soap opera is now an amazing technique of slow motion. It took one male character in a soap opera three days to get an answer to the simple question 'Where have you been?' If, in *When a Girl Marries*, you missed an automobile accident that occurred on a Monday broadcast, you could pick it up the following Thursday and find the leading woman character still unconscious and her husband still moaning over her beside the wrecked car."

"As for the sexual aspect of daytime morality, a man who had a lot to do with serials in the nineteen-thirties assures me that at that time there were 'hot clinches' burning up and down the daytime dial . . . there has been a profound cooling off, for my persistent eavesdropping has detected nothing but coy and impregnable chastity in the good women."

" 'Emotional understanding,' a term I have heard on serials several times, seems to be the official circumlocution for the awful world 'sex.' "

Dennis Porter, "Soap Time: Thoughts on a Commodity Art Form," *College English*, April 1977, 782–788: "And soap opera is, in effect, unique to the extent that it is the only genre in any medium whose duration year after year is coextensive with that of the calendar year. Soap opera has its rhythms, its weddings, births and even deaths as well as its Labor Days, Thanksgivings, Christmases, and New Year celebrations."

"It is, of course, no accident if most of the principal characters are of an age and physique that connote non- problematic sexual pleasure for the viewer, since the great majority of 'problems' on which soap opera chooses to focus are erotically centered. They concern courtship and marriage, adultery and divorce, pregnancies—wanted, unwanted, or merely desired—and the whole range of emotions that are traditionally invoked in any representation of intimate relations."

Kathryn Weibel, *Mirror, Mirror: Images of Women Reflected in Popular Culture* (New York: Anchor Books, 1977): Some of the most frequent themes in the soap operas: the evil woman; the great sacrifice; the winning back of an estranged lover/spouse; marrying her for her money, respectability, etc.; the unwed mother; deceptions about the paternity of children; career vs. housewife; the alcoholic woman (and occasionally man).

Bebe Moore Campbell, "Hooked on Soaps," *Essence*, November 1978, 100–103: "A soap opera without a bitch is a soap opera that doesn't get watched. The more hateful the bitch, the better. Erica of 'All My Children' is a classic. If you want to hear some hairy rap, just listen to a bunch of women discussing Erica."

Tania Modleski, "The Search for Tomorrow in Today's Soap Operas: Notes on a Feminine Narrative Form," *Film Quarterly*, Fall 1979, 12–21: "As a rule, only those issues which can be tolerated and ultimately pardoned are introduced on soaps. The list includes careers for women, abortions, premarital and extramarital sex, alcoholism, divorce, mental and even physical cruelty."

"If soaps refuse to allow us to condemn most characters and actions until all the evidence is in (and of course it never is), there is one character whom we are allowed to hate unreservedly: the villainess, the negative image of the spectator's ideal self. Although much of the suffering on soap operas is presented as unavoidable, the surplus suffering is often the fault of the villainess who tries to make things happen and control events better than the subject/spectator can."

Ellen Torgerson, "Don't You Just Want to Scratch Their Eyes Out?" *TV Guide*, July 7, 1979, 10–13: "Of course, there wouldn't be half so much fun to the soaps without the machinations of the clever, devious, manipulative, seductive, egocentric, everlastingly bad women like Lisa [Coleman, of *As the World Turns*], Linda [Phillips Anderson, of *Days of Our Lives*], and Erica [Kane Martin Brent, of *All My Children*]. Nothing exciting would ever happen in soapland sans these ladies, all so smoothly skilled in making trouble, setting teeth on edge and planning ever more deliciously depraved acts. After all, Medea, Becky Sharp, and Scarlett O'Hara are far more interesting than the goody-gumdrop, tremulous-lower-lip types June Allyson was always portraying."

●

Selecting and arranging your material

You now have material for your paper, but obviously you have more than you can use. You will have to do some *selecting*, and after you have selected the material, you will have to decide how you are going to *organize* it. Recall from Chapter 4 that what can help you in making the selection is consideration of such things as the specified **length** of the paper, the **occasion** and **purpose** of your paper, the **audience** for the paper, and, above all, the **thesis** of the paper.

● Selecting and Arranging Your Material

☐ **The specified length of the paper is 1200–1500 words.**
The specified length of the paper will be a major factor in the selection process. In your case, you have to work within 1200–1500 words—a relatively short paper—and the four or five pages will quickly fill up. You will have to tightly control the material you incorporate into your paper.

☐ **The occasion of the paper is an assignment for a sociology class.**

☐ **The purpose of the paper is to point out the social implications of some continuing show on television.**

☐ **The audience for the paper will be your sociology teacher, but your teacher may ask you to show or read your paper to your classmates.**

These last three considerations will help you somewhat in deciding which material to select. They will help you at least on the basis of whether the material fits the assignment or the purpose or the interests of your audience.

However, the consideration that will be *most* helpful in the selection process is the thesis you have decided on for your paper:

> **Soap operas *like* Days of Our Lives *show that sex without genuine love, mutual respect, and firm commitment leads to frustration, exploitation, and unhappiness.***

Since you have decided to demonstrate that thesis by citing examples from a single, typical soap opera,

1 You will concentrate on the material having to do with the soap opera *Days of Our Lives,*

2 You will concentrate on the material connected with that show that best exemplifies the impetuous sexual motivation of the characters' actions.

Putting It All Together

In the preliminary part of your paper, you will have to say something about soap operas *in general*, just to provide a context for the more particular discussion. So you will be able to use *some* of the material that doesn't deal specifically with *Days of Our Lives* or with the sex-conflict basis of the actions of the show. How much of this *general* material you will be able to use will be dictated mainly by the limitations on the length of your paper.

So the next decision you have to make is how much of your paper will be devoted to preliminary, background material about soap operas. And with that decision, you are into the next stage—the stage in which you make decisions about the organization of your paper. At this point, any decisions you make about organization must involve guesswork and cannot be final; still, you make these rough estimates:

1½ pages—introduction

(background information about soap operas in general and *DOL* in particular)

2 pages—development of your thesis

1 page—conclusion

(summary remarks about the social implications of soap operas)

You decide that your next step will be to make some rough notes of what will go into each of these three sections and of the order in which you will take up the various points. Later, you may be able to turn these rough notes into a formal outline or a block outline. In making these rough notes, you will be accomplishing two things: (1) selecting from your available material in the light of earlier considerations of length, occasion, purpose, audience, and thesis; (2) organizing—at least tentatively—what you select. Since you already have a *full* set of notes, you decide that here you will jot down *very brief* notes that can refer you to the fuller set.

1½ pages—introduction and general background information

Audience of 20 million.

Mainly housewives, senior citizens, unemployed men, students.

Prominent people who watch: Thurgood Marshall, Sammy Davis, Jr., John Connolly, Andy Warhol, Leslie Fiedler.

Extremely lucrative. Evening show costs $250,000 to produce but only $400,000 in ad revenue. DOL $170,000 to produce five shows but $600,000 in ad revenue.

Salaries of script-writers—$100,000 to $250,000. Salaries for performers—$35,000.

Magazine side-industry. Circulation of 380,000.

Viewer-appeal: satisfies appetite for stories, escape, audience identification, vicarious sexual titillation.

Sexual implications of soap operas, using *DOL* as typical example, will be pursued.

Thesis: Soap operas, like *Days of Our Lives*, show that sex without genuine love, mutual respect, and firm commitment leads to frustration, exploitation, and unhappiness.

2 pages—body of paper (development of thesis)

General information about *DOL*: 1 hour, produced by NBC, high ratings, more than two dozen actors involved in the show during the year.

Julie Anderson's frustrated love for Doug Williams, her deceased mother's husband.

Putting It All Together

Doug Williams and the artificial-insemination program.

Julie's son David goes to live with a black family, falls in love with their daughter Valerie.

David's abandoned girl friend, Brooke. Her abortion and suicide attempt. Julie eventually marries and divorces Doug. Now married to a woman named Lee, Doug is again wooing Julie.

Dr. Neil Curtis another long-time member of the show, was once married to Phyllis Anderson but was involved in an affair with one of his patients, a wealthy, attractive widow named Amanda Howard, with whom a colleague, Dr. Greg Peters, was also in love.

Neil Curtis is now pleading with Liz Courtney to marry him, but she is reluctant because she feels that he has not been totally open with her.

Marie Horton, another long-time character, joined the convent several years ago when she discovered that the Korean War veteran who had been wooing her was her own brother Mickey, who had suffered from amnesia and had undergone extensive plastic surgery while being listed as "missing in action."

Assigned by her religious order to her hometown of Salem, Marie has been counseling Joshua Fallon, a handsome new character on the show. Joshua is attracted to her, and Marie wonders whether her religious vows are strong enough to help her resist her own interest in him.

1 page—conclusion (summary remarks about general social implications of all this display of sexual motivation).

Edith Efron quote about "searching for a partner" and "domestic conflict."

Dennis Porter quote about problems in soap operas being "erotically centered."

James Thurber quote about how moral soap operas were in the 1940s.

Dr. Harold Greenwald quote about soap operas being reflections of morals of society.

Dr. William Menaker quote about changing morals of society (quoted from Efron article).

Kathryn Weibel's list of frequent themes in soap operas.

Tania Modleski quote about role of villainess in soap operas.

Ellen Torgerson quote about wicked women in soap operas.

Frank Dodge quote about why shows are showing sex-based conflicts.

●
Making an outline

Now that you have a set of rough notes recorded in some kind of order and distributed according to the three main divisions of your paper—introduction, body, and conclusion—you decide to sharpen this arrangement of parts by making a more formal outline. Of the kinds of outlines discussed in Chapter 4, the one that you find it easiest to work with is the **paragraph outline**, arranged in blocks. So you decide to arrange your selected material in a sequence of blocked paragraphs, with some labeling that will indicate to you what is covered in each paragraph. Your block outline appears in Figure 6.1.

●
Writing the first draft

With your outline drawn up, you now have a map to follow. **It is important that you not feel locked in by the outline**—no matter how good it is. After you begin writing, you may discover

Putting It All Together

THE SOCIAL IMPLICATIONS OF SOAP OPERAS

INTRODUCTION 1½ pages

> The great popularity of soap operas.

> Soap operas very lucrative for the producers.

> Why soap operas are popular with viewers. Statement of thesis.

BODY 2 pages

> General information about *Days of Our Lives.*

> Past episodes of *Days of Our Lives* that illustrate the basis of the conflicts.

> Episodes involving long-time characters and new characters added to the show.

CONCLUSION 1 page

> Conclusion: summary remarks about the social implications of soap operas.

Figure 6.1

an unexpected detour that you have to take or a shortcut that did not appear on your map. **You must remain flexible at all stages of the writing process.** Your outline points you only in the general direction that you want to go and marks off only the main stages on the way. So if some convenient alternative shows up after you start out, you will be faced with another choice: whether to take that alternative or stick to the route you plotted in your outline.

Often, the first sentence of a paper is the hardest one to write. A blank sheet of paper is facing you, and you have to begin putting words down on that paper. What will that first sentence be? A well-thought-out first sentence can overcome paralysis, get you on your way, and launch a series of other sentences. So it would be well if you could conceive of such an initial sentence. But if after racking your brains you can't come up with one, the next best thing is to **put down the first relevant sentence that occurs to you.** Sometimes, just the act of putting some words on paper breaks the logjam. You may later decide to scrap your first sentence, but at least it has served its purpose: it has given you a shove in the direction you want to go. Once you are in motion, don't stop, because if you do, you will just have to overcome the inertia once more. Hang on to the momentum and keep going forward.

Let's see if you can come up with a well-thought-out first sentence rather than rely on a haphazard one. A sentence that immediately grabs the reader's interest or attention is often a good one to begin with. Sometimes, a **provocative question** will hook the reader's attention:

Is it true that today's college student is barely literate?

Sometimes, a sentence that poses a **critical situation** will gain attention:

Nuclear power plants can save us or doom us.

143

Putting It All Together

Sometimes a sentence that stresses the **importance or uniqueness of the subject** you are going to talk about will hook the reader:

Since total disarmament of the major nations of the world is improbable, an effective program of arms control is the only measure that can prevent an end-of-the-world global war.

But note the *sometimes* repeated in the previous paragraph. An initial sentence does not always have to be dramatic. Sometimes, a very quiet, unpretentious sentence will do. What is important is that the first sentence lead easily and naturally into the next one.

Now, after much thought, you come up with initial sentence for your paper:

Between the hours of 11:00 A.M. and 4:00 P.M., Monday through Friday, twenty million Americans sit down at their television sets and watch one or more of about a dozen soap operas now being broadcast on the networks.

With the inertia broken, you settle down to write the first draft of your paper. With all of its fumblings and strike-overs, the following represents the first draft of your paper on soap operas.

The Social Implications of Soap Operas

Between the hours of 11:00 a.m. and 4:00 p.m., Monday through Friday, some twenty million Americans sit down in front of their television sets and watch one or more of about a dozen soap operas now being broadcast on the networks. Who are these Americans who have the leisure and the desire to watch these melodramas about domestic life in small towns in America? Mainly they are housewives, senior citizens, the unemployed, and college students. Usually, they are not just drop-ins on the shows; they are regular, loyal watchers of the shows. They may knit or drink cokes or xxxxx munch pretzels or smoke cigarettes or do/exercises while they are watching, but for all their casualness they are following the story with great intensity. The characters portrayed in the dramas are familiar to them, sometimes more familiar than members of their own family, and often the viewers are vitally concerned about what happens to the characters. The viewers resent the frequent interruptions of the flow;of the story by the commercials, but very few of them will abandon their watching of a p̸y̸p̸d̸p̸d̸p̸ show before it is completed.

What is the reason for the appeal of soap operas for many Americans/ Iṣ is easy to understand the appeal from the standpoint of the producers. Soap operas d̸p̸d̸ constitute a very lucrative business. In a X̸X̸X̸X̸X̸X̸ cáver story i̸p̸ T̸i̸p̸d̸ about soap/ operas (January 12, 1976), _Time_ magazine pointed out that while it costs NBC $170,000 to produce the five days of <u>Days of Our Lives</u>, those five showings bring in $600,000 of ad revenue. The major script-writers earn annual salaries ranging from $100,000 to $250,000. Many of the actors earn as much as $35,000. You can be sure that in the years since 1976, inflation has substantially increased those costs, salaries, and ad revenues.

Putting It All Together

                                        T
Although the financial rewards explain the appeal of soap operas

for the producers. But what accounts for the appeal of soap operas

for the potential viewers? The simplest explanation is that soap operas

appeal to the natural human appetite for stories. But why do soap operas

attracts larger audiences than do other kinds of popular dramas, like

                                              permit
Westerns and detective stories? For one thing, they inxine more audience

identification. Sometimes the situations are so much like the experiences

of the TV audience that the viewers can derive pleasure and comfort from

watching others cope with similar problems. On the other hand, the

situations are sometimes so different from the humdrum experiences lives

of most people that viewers can participate vicariously in experiences that

they have never had themselves but that they are curious about. Because

of their close identification with the characters on the show, viewers

can get more satisfaction from seeing a nasty characters get their

comeuppance or sympathetic characters getting their deserve reward.

But we should not underestimate the appeal of the subtle or blatant

sexual titillation of the shows. The conflict in soap is ultimately

based on the romantic entanglements between male and female characters.

It is this sexual orientation of the soap operas that I would like to

discuss. I contend that soap operas show that sex without genuine love,

mutual respect, and firm commitment leads to frustration, exploitation,

and unhappiness. I can best demonstrate this thesis by considering a

soap opera that is typical of the shows, <u>Days</u> <u>of</u> <u>our</u> <u>Lives</u>.

    <u>Days</u> <u>of</u> <u>Our</u> <u>Lives</u> is an hour-long, daytime TV show that deals with

centers on the troubled lives of four generation of the Horton family

and the other men and women who become involved with that family. After

more than fifteen years on the air, the relationships of the twenty-five

or so characters who appear on the show during the course of a year may

become so hopelessly scrambled by a succession of courtships, marriages,

-3-

divorces, affairs, and remarriages that a chart made of these relationships would be as complicated as the circuit design for a solid-state television set.

Many of the situations that have been dramatized in past shows and that continue to spark the drama in the lives of the intermeshed characters illustrate the sexual bases of this domestic melodrama. Julie, one of the long-time leading characters on the show, had already been married and divorced twice when she became enamored of Doug Williams, a handsome older man who had been married to Julie's mother, now dead. While Julie was trying to lure Doug into a marriage with her, he participated in an artificial-insemination program so that his child by Julie's mother would have a playmate, and unbeknownst to him, his housekeeper has arranged to be the child's mother. Meanwhile, Julie's son David by a previous marriage went to live with the Grants, a black family, and fell in love with their daughter Valerie. His abandoned girlfriend, Brooke, tried to commet suicide after she had had an abortion to get rid of David's child, After a series of frustrations, Doug eventually marries Julie. But in soapland, marriages are seldom "until death do us part." After divorcing Julie, Doug marries a woman named Lee. Lee develops an illness that confines her to a wheelchair, and she resorts to that pscholsomatic paralysis as a way of retaining the attention and affections of her husband, who has begun to woo Julie again.

Dr. Neil Curtis is another of the continuing characters on the show whose libido keeps messing up his life and the lives of several people associated with him. While he was married to a character named Phyllis Anderson, he was involved in an affair with one of his patients, a wealthy widow named Amanda Howard. That affair frustrated the aspirations of his colleague Dr. Greg Peters, who was madly in love with Amanda and wanted to marry her. Although Dr. Curtis's "rovingeye" seems to destine him to be an unfaithful spouse, five years later, he is pursuing still another beautiful

Putting It All Together

young woman, Liz Courtney, and pleading with her to marry him. We can understand the reluctance of this woman to enter into a liaison with this man who "keeps secrets from her."

As veteran soap-opera fans know, long-time characters, for one reason or another, drop out of the show either permanently or temporarily, and new characters are introduced. The new characters are usually young men and women, in the age bracket between 25 and 35 years, and invariably, they are physically attractive and incurably amorous. Before long, they are romantically involved with one or more of the other characters in the show, and the romantic entanglements become so complicated and traumatic that the happiness of several clusters of people is seriously threatened. A good example of the intersecting lives of old and new characters in _Days of Our Lives_ is is the developing relationship between Marie Horton and several of the young, beautiful characters who have been added to the show. Many years ago, Maximilian a veteran of the Korea War who had suffered from amnesia and had undergone extensive plastic surgery came to Salem and fell in love with Marie Horton. When Marie eventually learned that the man in love with her was her own brother Mickey, who had been listed as"missing in action," she was so upset that she joined the convent. Having dropped out of sight for a long while, she is back on the show now, with only a short veil to distinguish her as a member of a religious order of nuns. She has been counselling Joshua Fallon, one of the new characters, who has fallen in love with one of the new women on the show, Jessica Blake, who has taken a fancy to Joshua's look-alike, Tod Chandler, another new comer on the show. But the most titillating aspect of these enmeshed relationships is the not-too-subtle suggestion that Joshua is falling in love with Marie and that Marie is wondering whether her religious vows are strong enough to withstand her gorwing interest in Joshua.

-5-

                    like
                         e
    Conflicts ~~of~~ this~~e~~ are typical not only of <u>Days</u> <u>of</u> <u>Our</u> <u>Lives</u> but also
of most of the daytime soap operas. If one looks only at the surface of
                    dramatic
many of the ~~episodes~~ conflicts, one can posit jealousy, rivalry, misunderstanding, selfishness, or resentment as the motive power for the actions
of the characters, but if one looks deeper, one can detect that sexual
instincts are the mainspring of the actions. All of the characters in
some way and to some degree and to some degree seem to be motivated by
their libido. As Dennis Porter said, "It is, of course, no accident if
most of the principal characters are of an age and physique that connote
non-problematic sex~~x~~ual pleasure [prowess?] for the viewer, since the
great majority of 'problems' on which soap opera chooses to focus are
erotically centered." <u>Time</u> magazine entitled its cover story on soap
operas "Sex and Suffering in the Afternoon." And one gets the impression
that if it weren't for the sex~~x~~ there would be no suffering. In 1965,
in an article in <u>TV</u> <u>Guide</u> entitled "The Soaps--Anything but 99 44/100
Percent Pure," Edith Efron remarked that the them of nine out of ten
daytime shows was "the mating-marital-reproductive cycle set against a
domestic backgrlund. . . . This all-consuming, single-minded search for
a mate is an absolute in the soap-opera syndrome. Morality--and dramatic
conflict--emerge from how the search is conducted."

    Apparently, the sexual undertones of the soap operas on radio were
not as blatant as they are on television today. In the article "Ivorytown,
Rinsoville, Anacinburg, and Crisco Corners" that he wrote about radio
soap operas in 1948 for the <u>New</u> <u>Yorker</u>, James Thurber remarked about
"the coy and impregnable chastity" of the characters on these shows.
Edith Efron quoted some prominent psychologists to back up her claim
that this"sex-based human wretchedness is on the air because it exists in
society." Dr. Harold Greenwal, the supervising psychologist of the

Putting It All Together

Community Guidance Service in New York City, maintains that soap operas "reflect the changes taking place in our society. There are fewer taboos. The age of sexual activity in the middle classes has dropped, and it has increased in frequency. There is more infidelity. These plays reflect these problems." Dr. William Menaker, Professor of Clinical Psychology at New York University, says, "Increasing frankness in dealing with these problems isn't a symptom of moral decay but rather reflects the confused values of a transitional period of sociosexual change." These soap operas seem to be reflecting the increasing public frankness about sexual matters and the growing rejection of society's taboos about sex. The implications of what we are seeing portrayed on the television screen are that there is more unbridled sex in our society and consequently more frustration, exploitation, and unhappiness. If he were alive today, Dr. Sigmund Freud might say, "I told you so."

In her book _Mirror, Mirror: Images of Women Reflected in Popular Culture_ (New York: Anchor Books, 1977), Kathryn Weibel lists some of the most frequent themes in the soap operas: the evil woman, the great sacrifice, the winning back of an estranged lover-spouse, marrying her for her money, respectability, etc., the unwed mother, deceptions about the paternity of children, career vs housewife, the alcoholic woman (and occasionally men). What is notable about this list is the number of these themes that are sexually rooted. Even the theme of the evil woman, which is a sine qua non of the soap opera is rooted in the sexual instincts. As Tania Modleski observed in her article "The Search for Tomorrow in Today's Soap Operas," which appeared in the Fall, 1979 issue of _Film Quarterly_, "Although much of the suffering on soap operas is presented as unavoidable, the surplus suffering is often the fault of the villainess, who tries to tries to make things happen and control events better than the subject/spectator can." The villainess makes things happen and controls events

150

-7-

mainly by playing the role of the siren. As Ellen Torgerson said in her
article "Don't You Just Want to Scratch Their Eyes Out?" in the July 7,
1979 issue of <u>TV Guide</u>, "Of course, there wouldn't be half so much fun
to the soaps without the machinations of the clever, devious, manipulative,
seductive, egocentric, everlastingly bad women like Lisa [on <u>As the World
Turns</u>], Linda [on <u>Days of Our Lives</u>], and Erica [on <u>All My Children</u>]."
It takes a lot of suds to clean up all the dirt stirred up by the
manipulative sex that prevails in soapland.

Putting It All Together

Revising and polishing the rough draft

You have the first draft of your paper written now, and if time permits, you can put it aside for a day or two and then come back to it to revise and polish it. In the **revision**, you may have to do some cutting or some expanding or some shifting. In **polishing** the essay, you may be able to smooth out the phrasing, tighten up some of the sentences, substitute more precise wording. Writing the first draft is usually the hardest part; revising and polishing that draft can actually be enjoyable. Let us look at the first draft again and make notes of the changes you may want to make in the next draft.

Get more precise title
Possibilities: Sex in Soap Operas
The Sexual Basis of the Conflicts in Soap Operas

The Social Implications of Soap Operas

(EST)

Between the hours of 11:00 a.m. and 4:00 p.m., Monday through

Friday, some twenty million Americans sit down in front of their

to
television sets ~~and~~ watch one or more of about a dozen soap operas

The size of the audience
now being broadcast on the networks. ~~Who are these Americans who~~
is even more remarkable when one considers that the only
~~have the leisure and the desire to watch these melodramas about~~
people who have the leisure to watch these shows during the daytime,
~~domestic life in small towns in America? Mainly they~~are housewives,
Because of
⟩ senior citizens, ~~the unemployed,~~ and college students. ~~Usually, they~~
this huge and loyal audience, soap operas have become a very
~~are not just drop-ins on the shows; they are regular, loyal watchers~~
lucrative business for their producers.
of the shows. / They may knit or drink cokes or xxxxx munch pretzels
physical
or smoke cigarettes or do/exercises while they are watching, but for

Cut   all their casualness they are following the story with great intensity.

The characters portrayed in the dramas are familiar to them, sometimes

more familiar than members of their own family, and often the viewers

are vitally concerned about what happens to the characters. The viewers

resent the frequent interruptions of the flow; of the story by the com-

mercials, but very few of them will abandon their watching of a p̶r̶o̶g̶r̶a̶m̶

show before it is completed.

What is the reason for the appeal of soap operas for many Americans/

It is easy to understand the appeal from the standpoint of the producers. /

Soap operas a̶r̶e̶ constitute a very lucrative business. / In a x̶x̶x̶x̶x̶x̶ cover

story i̶n̶ T̶i̶m̶e̶ about soap/ operas (January 12, 1976), Time magazine pointed

out that while it costs NBC $170,000 to produce the five days of Days of
each week   *that it*
Our Lives, those five showings bring in $600,000 of ad revenue; The major
and that
script-writers earn annual salaries ranging from $100,000 to $250,000;
m
M̶any of the actors earn as much as $35,000. You can be sure that in the

years since 1976, inflation has substantially increased those costs, salaries,

and ad revenues.

Putting It All Together

-2-

New ¶ / Although intellectuals tend to look down their
~~the financial rewards explain the appeal of soap operas~~
noses at the taste of the millions of people who watch these
~~for the producers. But what accounts for the appeal of soap operas~~
soap operas daily, and to disparage the commercialism of the
~~for the producers viewers? The simplest explanation is that soap operas~~
sponsors, soap operas represent a cultural phenomenon that
~~appeal to the natural human appetite for stories. But why do soap operas~~
are not likely to disappear from the American scene. What
~~attracts larger audiences than do other kinds of popular dramas, like~~
are the social implications of this phenomenon Permit One doesn't
~~Westerns and detective stories? For one thing, they more audience~~
have to watch many soap operas to become aware that most of the
~~identification. Sometimes the situations are so much like the experiences~~
dramatic conflicts presented on the "Soaps" are based ultimately
~~of the TV audience that the viewers can derive pleasure and comfort from~~
on the romantic entanglements between the male and female
~~watching others cope with similar problems. On the other hand, the~~
characters. In 1965, in an article in TV Guide entitled "The Soaps
~~situations are sometimes so different from the humdrum lives~~
anything but 99 44/100 Percent Pure," Edith Efron remarked that
~~of most people that viewers can participate vicariously in experiences that~~
the theme of nine out of ten daytime shows was "the mating
~~they have never had themselves but that they are curious about. Because~~
of the genital reproductive cycle set against a domestic
~~of their close identification with the characters on the show, viewers~~
background... This all-consuming, single-minded search
~~can get more satisfaction from seeing a nasty characters get their~~
for a mate is an absolute in the soap opera syndrome.
~~comeuppance or sympathetic characters getting their deserve reward.~~
~~But we should not underestimate the appeal of the subtle or blatant~~
search is conducted."
~~sexual titillation of the shows. The conflict in soap is ultimately~~

based on the romantic entanglements between male and female characters.

New ¶ It is this sexual orientation of the soap operas that I would like to

discuss. I contend that soap operas show that sex without genuine love,

mutual respect, and firm commitment leads to frustration, exploitation,
from several
~~shows~~ and unhappiness. I can ~~best demonstrate~~ could support this thesis by ~~considering a~~ citing incidents *(drop the adjectives)*
now being
broadcast, but
soap opera that is typical of the shows, Days of our Lives. produced by NBC,
in the interest
of brevity, I
Days of Our Lives is an hour-long, daytime TV show that ~~deals with~~
will confine
my attention to ~~the~~ centers on the troubled lives of four generations of the Horton family After

more than fifteen years on the air, the relationships of the twenty-five
have
or so characters who appear on the show during the course of a year ~~may~~
and intertwined
become so hopelessly scrambled by a succession of courtships, marriages,

154

-3-

divorces, affairs, and remarriages that a chart made of these relationships *of*
would be as complicated as the circuit design for a solid-state television
set.

Many of the situations that have been dramatized in past shows and that
continue to spark the drama in the lives of the intermeshed characters illustrate the sexual bases of this domestic melodrama. Julie, one of the ~~long-time~~ *veteran*
leading characters on the show, had already been married and divorced twice
when she became enamored of Doug Williams, a handsome older man who had been
married to Julie's mother, now dead. While Julie was trying to lure Doug
into a marriage with her, he participated in an artificial-insemination
program so that his child by Julie's mother would have a playmate, and
unbeknownst to him, his housekeeper ~~has~~ arranged to be the child's mother. *secretly*
Meanwhile, Julie's son David by a previous marriage went to live with the
Grants, a black family, and fell in love with their daughter Valerie. His
abandoned girlfriend, Brooke, tried to commit suicide after she had had an *i*
abortion to get rid of David's child, After a series of frustrations, Doug
eventually marries Julie. But in soapland, marriages are seldom "until *sealed*
death do us part." After divorcing Julie, Doug marries a woman named Lee.
Lee develops an illness that confines her to a wheelchair, and she resorts
to that pscholsomatic paralysis as a way of retaining the attention and *y*
affections of her husband, who has begun to woo Julie again.

Dr. Neil Curtis is another of the continuing characters on the show whose
libido keeps messing up his life and the lives of several people associated
with him. While he was married to a character named Phyllis Anderson, he
was involved in an affair with one of his patients, a wealthy widow named
Amanda Howard. That affair frustrated the aspirations of his colleague
Dr. Greg Peters, who was madly in love with Amanda and wanted to marry
her. Although Dr. Curtis's "rovingeye" seems to destine him be an *to*
unfaithful spouse, five years later, he is pursuing still another beautiful

Putting It All Together

young woman, Liz Courtney, and pleading with her to marry him. We can

understand the reluctance of this woman to enter into a liaison with

this man who "keeps secrets from her."

As ~~veteran~~ regular soap-opera fans know, some long-time characters, for one reason

or another, drop out of the show either permanently or temporarily, and

new characters are introduced. The new characters are usually young

men and women, in the age bracket between 25 and 35 years, and invariably,

they are physically attractive and incurably amorous. Before long, ~~they~~ these new characters

are romantically involved with one or more of the other characters in the

show, and the romantic entanglements become so complicated and traumatic

that the happiness of several clusters of people is seriously threatened.

[new ¶] A good example of the intersecting lives of old and new characters in Days

of Our Lives is ~~is~~ the developing relationship between Marie Horton and

several of the young, beautiful characters who have been added to the show.

Many years ago, ~~Maxie Maxiam~~ a veteran of the Korean War who had ~~suffered~~ been inflicted

~~from~~ with amnesia and had undergone extensive plastic surgery came to Salem

and fell in love with Marie Horton. When Marie eventually learned that

the man in love with her was her own brother Mickey, who had been listed

as "missing in action," she was so upset that she joined the convent.

~~Having~~ After dropped~~ped~~ ing out of sight for a long while, she is back on the show

now, with only a short veil to distinguish her as a member of a religious

order of nuns. She has been counselling Joshua Fallon, one of the new

characters, who has fallen in love with one of the new women on the show,

Jessica Blake, who has taken a fancy to Joshua's look-alike, Tod Chandler,

another new comer on the show. But the most titillating aspect of these

enmeshed relationships is the not-too-subtle suggestion that Joshua is

falling in love with Marie and that Marie is wondering whether her religious

vows are strong enough to withstand her growing interest in Joshua.

-5-

like
Conflicts of thise are typical not only of <u>Days of Our Lives</u> but also
other
of most of the daytime soap operas. If one looks only at the surface of
dramatic
many of the episodes conflicts, one can posit jealousy, rivalry, misunder-

standing, selfishness, or resentment as the motive power for the actions

of the characters, but if one looks deeper, one can detect that sexual

instincts are the mainspring of the actions. All of the characters in

some way and to some degree and to some degree seem to be motivated by

in the april 1977 issue of College English,
their libido. As Dennis Porter said, "It is, of course, no accident if

most of the principal characters are of an age and physique that connote
sexual
non-problematic sexual pleasure [prowess?] for the viewer, since the

great majority of 'problems' on which soap opera chooses to focus are

erotically centered." <u>Time</u> magazine entitled its cover story on soap

operas "Sex and Suffering in the Afternoon." And one gets the impression

that if it weren't for the sex there would be no suffering. In 1965,

Transfer this quotation to first paragraph on P. 2

in an article in <u>TV Guide</u> entitled "The Soaps--Anything but 99 44/100

Percent Pure," Edith Efron remarked that the them of nine out of ten

daytime shows was "the mating-marital-reproductive cycle set against a

domestic backgrlund. . . . This all-consuming, single-minded search for

a mate is an absolute in the soap-opera syndrome. Morality--and dramatic

conflict--emerge from how the search is conducted."

Cut

Apparently, the sexual undertones of the soap operas on radio were

not as blatant as they are on television today. In the article "Ivorytown,

Rinsoville, Anacinburg, and Crisco Corners" that he wrote about radio

soap operas in 1948 for the <u>New Yorker</u>, James Thurber remarked about

"the coy and impregnable chastity" of the characters on these shows.

Edith Efron quoted some prominent psychologists to back up her claim

that this "sex-based human wretchedness is on the air because it exists in

society." Dr. Harold Greenwal, the supervising psychologist of the

Putting It All Together

Cut

Community Guidance Service in New York City, maintains that soap operas "reflect the changes taking place in our society. There are fewer taboos. The age of sexual activity in the middle classes has dropped, and it has increased in frequency. There is more infidelity. These plays reflect these problems." Dr. William Menaker, Professor of Clinical Psychology at New York University, says, "Increasing frankness in dealing with these problems isn't a symptom of moral decay but rather reflects the confused values of a transitional period of sociosexual change." These soap operas seem to be reflecting the increasing public frankness about sexual matters and the growing rejection of society's taboos about sex. The implications of what we are seeing portrayed on the television screen are that there is more unbridled sex in our society and consequently more frustration, exploitation, and unhappiness. If he were alive today, Dr. Sigmund Freud might say, "I told you so."

In her book <u>Mirror, Mirror: Images of Women Reflected in Popular Culture</u> (New York: Anchor Books, 1977), Kathryn Weibel lists some of the most frequent themes in the soap operas: the evil woman, the great sacrifice, the winning back of an estranged lover-~~spouse~~ *spouse*, marrying her for her money, respectability, etc., the unwed mother, deceptions about the paternity of children, career vs housewife, the alcoholic woman (and occasionally men). What is notable about this list is the number of these themes that are sexually rooted. Even the theme of the evil woman, which is a <u>sine qua non</u> of the soap opera is rooted in the sexual instincts. As Tania Modleski observed in her article "The Search for Tomorrow in Today's Soap Operas," which appeared in the Fall, 1979 issue of <u>Film Quarterly</u>, "Although much of the suffering on soap operas is presented as unavoidable, the surplus suffering is often the fault of the villainess, who tries to ~~tries to~~ make things happen and control events better than the subject/spectator can." The villainess makes things happen and controls events

-7-

mainly by playing the role of the siren. As Ellen Torgerson said in her
article "Don't You Just Want to Scratch Their Eyes Out?" in the July 7,
1979 issue of TV Guide, "Of course, there wouldn't be half so much fun
to the soaps without the machinations of the clever, devious, manipulative,
seductive, egocentric, everlastingly bad women like Lisa [on As the World
Turns], Linda [on Days of Our Lives], and Erica [on All My Children]."
It takes a lot of suds to clean up all the dirt stirred up up by the
manipulative sex that prevails in soapland.

add these two paragraphs for a new conclusion

Most social critics view soap operas as being accurate reflections
of many of the moral and psychological ills of contemporary society.
Some of these ills are due to "sick sex." The sex is sick, not because
sex in itself is evil or dirty but because, as exemplified in these
daytime serials, it is compulsive, unbridled, and selfish. It clearly
lacks appropriate restraints and real commitment and mutual respect on
the part of the men and women involved in these human dramas.

Meanwhile, the portrayal of the troubled lives of the more than
300 characters that figure in all the daytime serials continues to
provide titillating excitement for millions of daily viewers. On the
night of November 21, 1980, when it was revealed who shot the despicable
J.R. Ewing, Dallas, the first prime-time soap opera, drew the largest
audience, up to that time, that had ever watched a regularly scheduled
television show. It is unlikely that even satirical parodies of soap
operas such as Mary Hartman, Mary Hartman and Soap will discourage many
viewers from tuning in tomorrow to find out how the characters on their
favorite soap opera fared since yesterday. We can endure misery--if we can
experience it vicariously.

Putting It All Together

As is clear from the notes written on the first draft, you saw that it was taking you too long to get into the main part of your paper. Your introduction took up as many paragraphs (three) as the body of the essay did. When one has turned up a lot of interesting material on a subject, one is tempted to include it all in the paper. When you made your rough outline, you should have noticed that your introduction was taking up a disproportionate amount of space, but it was only after you had written your first draft that you saw that the "tail was wagging the dog." Then **you recognized the need to condense the introductory section so that you could get down to the main point of your paper sooner.**

Cutting out big chunks from the introduction not only will get you into the main part of your paper sooner but will bring the paper as a whole down below the specified maximum length of 1500 words. (The first draft ran to about 1650 words.) **You also made some readjustments in the arrangement of the paper.** You saw, for instance, that a quotation from the conclusion would be more effective if shifted to the introduction. Knowing that you are not obliged to keep the paragraph divisions used in your rough outline, **you also saw the possibility of breaking up some of the long paragraphs** in the body of the paper into shorter paragraphs. And **you saw the need to round off your conclusion by adding a few more sentences** at the end.

When you type up another draft from your annotated first draft, you may discover the need for further additions, subtractions, rearrangements, and revisions. If this second draft gets to be too messy because of those further changes, you will have to type up a third and final draft. That third draft, however, may not be the final one. The *final* draft of a paper is the one that represents your best efforts under the circumstances.

●
Writing the final draft

Here is the draft that you finally turned in to your sociology teacher.

The Sexual Basis of the Conflicts in Soap Operas

Between the hours of 11:00 a.m. and 4:00 p.m. (EST), Monday through Friday, some twenty million Americans sit down in front of their television sets to watch one or more of about a dozen soap operas being broadcast on the networks. The size of that audience is even more remarkable when one considers that the only people who have the leisure to watch these shows during the daytime are housewives, the unemployed, senior citizens, and college students. Because of this huge and loyal audience, soap operas have become a very lucrative business for their producers. In a cover story about soap operas (January 12, 1976), *Time* magazine pointed out that while it costs NBC $170,000 to produce the five days of Days of Our Lives each week, those five showings of the popular soap opera bring in $600,000 of ad revenue, that the major script-writers earn salaries ranging from $100,000 to $250,000, and that many of the actors earn as much as $35,000 per season. You can be sure that in the years since 1976, inflation has substantially increased those costs, salaries, and ad revenues.

Although intellectuals tend to look down their noses at the millions of people who watch these shows regularly and to disparage the commercialism of the sponsors, soap operas represent a cultural phenomenon that is not likely to disappear from the American scene. What are the social implications of this phenomenon? One doesn't have to watch many soap operas to become aware that most of the dramatic conflicts presented in these shows are based ultimately on the romantic entanglements between the male and female characters. In 1965, in an article in TV Guide entitled "The Soaps--Anything but 99 44/100 Percent Pure," Edith Efron remarked that the theme of nine out of ten daytime serials was "the mating-marital-reproductive cycle set against a domestic background. . . . This all-consuming, single-minded search for a mate is an absolute

---

Putting It All Together

in the soap-opera syndrome. Morality--and dramatic conflict--emerge from how the search is conducted."

It is this sexual orientation of the soap operas that I would like to discuss. I contend that soap operas show that sex without love, respect, and commitment leads to frustration, exploitation, and unhappiness. I could support this thesis by citing incidents from several shows now being broadcast, but in the interest of brevity, I will confine my attention to one typical soap opera, Days of Our Lives.

Days of Our Lives, an hour-long, daytime TV show produced by NBC, centers on the troubled lives of four generations of the Horton family and the other men and women who become involved with that family. After more than fifteen years on the air, the relationships among the twenty-five or so characters who appear on the show during the course of a year have become so hopelessly scrambled and intertwined by a succession of courtships, marriages, divorces, affairs, and remarriages that a chart made of those relationships would be as complicated as the circuit design for a solid-state television set.

Many of the situations that have been dramatized in past shows and that continue to spark the drama in the lives of the intermeshed characters illustrate the sexual bases of this domestic melodrama. Julie, one of the veteran leading characters on the show, had already been married and divorced twice when she became enamored of Doug Williams, a handsome older man who had been married to Julie's mother, now dead. While Julie was trying to lure Doug into a marriage with her, he participated in an artificial-insemination program so that his child by Julie's mother would have a playmate, and unbeknownst to him, his housekeeper arranged to be the child's mother. Meanwhile, Julie's son David by a previous marriage went to live with the Grants, a black family, and fell in love with their

-3-

daughter Valerie. His abandoned girlfriend, Brooke, tried to commit suicide after she had had an abortion to get rid of David's child. After a series of frustrations, Doug eventually marries Julie. But in Soapland, marriages are seldom sealed "until death do us part." In due course, Doug divorces Julie and marries a Southern woman named Lee. Lee develops an illness that confines her to a wheelchair, and she resorts to that psychosomatic paralysis as a way of retaining the attention and affections of her husband, who has begun to woo Julie again.

Dr. Neil Curtis is another continuing character on the show whose libido keeps messing up his life and the lives of several people associated with him. While he was married to a character named Phyllis Anderson, he was involved in an affair with one of his patients, a wealthy widow named Amanda Howard. That affair frustrated the aspirations of his colleague Dr. Greg Peters, who was madly in love with Amanda and wanted to marry her. Although Dr. Curtis's "roving eye" seems to destine him to be an unfaithful spouse, five years later, he is pursuing still another beautiful young woman, Liz Courtney, desperately pleading with her to marry him. We can understand Liz's reluctance to enter into a union with this man who "keeps secrets from her."

As regular soap-opera fans know, some long-time characters, for one reason or another, drop out of the show either permanently or temporarily, and new characters are periodically introduced. The new characters are usually young men and women, in the age bracket between 25 and 35 years, and invariably, they are physically attractive and incurably amorous. Before long, these new characters are romantically involved with one or more of the other characters, and these romantic entanglements become so tortuous and traumatic that the happiness of several clusters of people is seriously threatened.

A good example of the intersecting lives of old and new characters

Putting It All Together

in <u>Days</u> <u>of</u> <u>Our</u> <u>Lives</u> is the developing relationship between Marie Horton and several of the young, beautiful characters who have been added to the show. Many years ago, a veteran of the Korean War who had been inflicted with amnesia and had undergone extensive plastic surgery came to Salem, the mythical town in which the show takes place, and fell in love with Marie. When Marie eventually learned that the man in love with her was her own brother Mickey, who had been listed as "missing in action," she was so upset that she joined the convent. After dropping out of sight for a long while, she is back on the show, with only a short veil to distinguish her as a member of a religious order of nuns. She has been counselling Joshua Fallon, one of the new characters, who has fallen in love with one of the new women on the show, Jessica Blake, who has taken a fancy to Joshua's look-alike, Tod Chandler, another newcomer on the show. But the most titillating aspect of these enmeshed relationships is the not-too-subtle suggestion that Joshua is falling in love with Marie and that Marie is wondering whether her religious vows are strong enough to withstand her growing interest in Joshua.

Conflicts like these are typical not only of <u>Days</u> <u>of</u> <u>Our</u> <u>Lives</u> but also of most of the other daytime soap operas. If one looks at the surface of many of the dramatic conflicts, one can posit jealousy, rivalry, misunderstanding, selfishness, or resentment as the motive power for the actions of the characters, but if one looks deeper, one can detect that sexual instincts are the mainspring of the actions. All of the characters in some way and to some degree seem to be motivated by their libido. As Dennis Porter said in the April 1977 issue of <u>College</u> <u>English</u>, "It is, of course, no accident if most of the principal characters are of an age and physique that connote non-problematic sexual pleasure for the viewer, since the great majority of 'problems' on which soap opera chooses to

focus are erotically centered." _Time_ magazine entitled its cover story
on soap operas "Sex and Suffering in the Afternoon," and one gets the
impression that if it were not for the sex there would be no suffering.

In her book _Mirror, Mirror: Images of Women Reflected in Popular
Culture_ (New York: Anchor Books, 1977), Kathryn Weibel lists some of
the most frequent themes in the soap operas: the evil woman, the great
sacrifice, the winning back of an estranged lover-spouse, marrying her
for her money, respectability, etc., the unwed mother, deceptions about
the paternity of children, career vs. housewife, the alcoholic woman
(sometimes the alcoholic man). What is notable about this list is the
number of these themes that are sexually rooted. Even the theme of
the evil woman, which is a _sine qua non_ of the soap opera, is rooted in
the sexual instincts. As Tania Modleski observed in her article "The
Search for Tomorrow in Today's Soap Operas," which appeared in the Fall
1979 issue of _Film Quarterly_, "Although much of the suffering on soap
operas is presented as unavoidable, the surplus suffering is often the
fault of the villainess, who tries to make things happen and control
events better than the subject/spectator can." The villainess makes
things happen and controls events mainly by playing the role of the
siren. As Ellen Torgerson said in her article "Don't You Just Want
to Scratch Their Eyes Out?" in the July 7, 1979 issue of _TV Guide_,
"Of course, there wouldn't be half so much fun to the soaps without
the machinations of the clever, devious, manipulative, seductive,
egocentric, everlastingly bad women like Lisa [on _As The World Turns_],
Linda [on _Days of Our Lives_], and Erica [on _All My Children_]." It
takes a lot of suds to clean up all the dirt stirred up by the manipulative sex that prevails in Soapland.

Most social critics view soap operas as being accurate reflections
of many of the moral and psychological ills of contemporary society.

Putting It All Together

Some of these ills are due to "sick sex." The sex is sick, not because sex in itself is evil or dirty but because, as exemplified in these daytime serials, it is compulsive, unbridled, and selfish. It clearly lacks appropriate restraints and real commitment and mutual respect on the part of the men and women involved in these human dramas.

Meanwhile, the portrayal of the troubled lives of the more than 300 characters that figure in all the daytime serials continues to provide titillating excitement for millions of daily viewers. On the night of November 21, 1980, when it was revealed who shot the despicable oil baron J.R. Ewing, <u>Dallas</u>, the first prime-time soap opera, drew the largest audience, up to that time, that had ever watched a regular series on television. It is unlikely that even satirical parodies of soap operas such as <u>Mary Hartman</u>, <u>Mary Hartman</u> and <u>Soap</u> will discourage many viewers from tuning in tomorrow to find out how the characters on their favorite soap opera fared since yesterday. We can endure misery--if we can experience it vicariously.

●
Summary

In "Putting It All Together," you have gone through the following series of steps:

(1) GETTING THE ASSIGNMENT

It is important that you pay close attention to, and clearly understand, the assignment. If there is something about the assignment that you do not understand, ask for a clarification.

(2) SETTLING ON A SUBJECT

Although the general subject may be assigned, you will usually have some choice of the part or aspect of that general subject to write about. It is important that you narrow the subject to fit the length, occasion, purpose, audience, and thesis.

(3) DECIDING ON A THESIS

Sometimes you may not be able to formulate a precise thesis until after you have gone through the search process. But even a tentatively formulated thesis at the outset will guide you in what to look for in your search for something to say.

(4) DISCOVERING SOMETHING TO SAY

Discovering something to say is the most important step in the composition process. If you engage conscientiously in this step, your paper will almost write itself later on.

Putting It All Together

(5) SELECTING AND ARRANGING THE MATERIAL

Because the previous step will usually turn up more material than you can use in your paper, you will have to select the material you are going to use and make some decisions about organizing the material that you have selected.

(6) MAKING AN OUTLINE

You will frequently find it helpful to draw up some kind of outline before you begin to write your paper.

(7) WRITING THE FIRST DRAFT

In writing the first draft, you should not be concerned about the correctness of your grammar, punctuation, spelling, and style. It is more important at this stage to get your thoughts written out.

(8) REVISING AND POLISHING THE FIRST DRAFT

After you have written the first draft, you can come back to it and correct the faulty grammar, punctuation, spelling, and style, and you can cut or expand or shift passages.

(9) WRITING THE FINAL DRAFT

The final draft is the one that you submit. It may represent the second or the third or the twelfth rewriting of the paper. But it should be as well wrought and as flawless as time and your talents permit.

What has been displayed in this chapter is the process that one writer went through in doing an assigned paper on a specified topic. The process and the product would vary, slightly or considerably, from writer to writer. The process exhibited in this chapter is linear and sequential—that is, a process in which the nine steps outlined above are supposed to follow one after the other, in the same order every time. But you must not get the impression that the series of steps laid out in this chapter represents the one and only way to write a paper. For you and for many other writers, the process may involve different steps in a different order. Your practice, for instance, may be that instead of moving steadily forward from one step to another in the order outlined above, you constantly loop back to an earlier step and then move forward again—a spiral or recursive process rather than a straight-ahead linear process. As you gain more practice in writing, your writing habits may change; you may shorten or even omit some of the steps and discover new ones. But during your training as a writer, you may find the sequence outlined in this chapter—or some modification of it—extremely helpful to you. This sequence of steps can at least serve you until you have devised your own method of composing.

Chapter 7
Writing the Various Forms
of Discourse

In the previous chapters, after looking at the process that many writers go through in writing a piece of discourse, we saw an illustration of this process, from original assignment to final product. In this chapter, we will consider the process of writing as it applies to the common, primitive forms of discourse. Then in Chapter 8, we will look at the process as it applies to three special writing assignments.

First of all, the term *discourse* in this book refers to *any piece of writing that presents an extended, continuous, structured discussion of a subject*. There have been many attempts throughout history to classify the various kinds of discourse. The classification used in this chapter is a familiar one, often attributed to the nineteenth-century rhetorician Alexander Bain: **narration, description, exposition,** and **argumentation.**

Although each of these forms will be explained at length in its own section of this chapter, we might look at brief definitions of these four types here:

● Writing the Various Forms of Discourse

NARRATION

Narration is that form of discourse that tells a story or gives an account of an event.

DESCRIPTION

Description is that form of discourse that presents a verbal picture of a person, a place, a thing, or a scene.

EXPOSITION

Exposition is that form of discourse that informs, explains, or instructs.

ARGUMENTATION

Argumentation is that form of discourse that attempts to persuade an audience to adopt a certain position or to act in a certain way.

Rarely will you find pure examples of these forms. Most of the time, examples present a mixture of two or more of the forms of discourse. A particular example of *exposition*, for instance, might make use of *description* and *narration* to accomplish its main purpose of explaining something to someone. Usually, however, a piece of discourse, whatever the extent of the mixture of forms, can be classified as *primarily* one of them. For example, although there are instances of exposition and narration in the paper on soap operas in the previous chapter, that paper can be classified as primarily *argumentative* because the author's main purpose was to persuade the readers to accept the chosen thesis:

Writing the Various Forms of Discourse

Soap operas show that sex without love, respect, and commitment leads to frustration, exploitation, and unhappiness.

Another alleged shortcoming of the four-part classification used in this chapter is that the labels designate the *products* of writing rather than the *process* of writing. Indeed, most of the time, we apply those labels to pieces of prose that have already been composed. Many of the anthologies of prose used in Freshman English classes, for instance, group the essays under the heads of Exposition, Description, Narration, and Argumentation.

But these labels can also be used when the *process* of writing is being considered. One way in which they can be used as part of the process is to *indicate the general objective of a writing assignment*. A teacher might say, "For your next assignment, I want you to write an exposition of how the annual Pro Football draft of college players works." By specifying a piece of exposition, the teacher would not only be initiating the writing process but also putting fences around the assignment by designating the *subject* (the professional-football draft) and the *form* (a piece of exposition). In this case, the teacher would have contributed to the writing process by making two of the decisions that the students themselves would have had to make if the choice of a subject and a form had been left to them. When professional writers are not actually commissioned by the editor of a magazine or newspaper to write an article on a specified topic, they must themselves select the subject of the article and decide how to treat it—that is, whether they are going to write a short story about the subject (*narration*) or write an informative article about the subject (*description, exposition*) or write an *argumentative* article calling for some action by the readers in regard to the subject.

So the four forms of discourse are not just tags for finished products; they can play a part in the process of writing. Moreover, **each of the four forms has its own set of strategies that the writer resorts to in the process of writing**. Some of the *invention techniques*, for instance, are more productive for exposition than for the other three forms. Likewise, some patterns of *organization* and some devices of *style* seem to be more suitable for one form of discourse than for the others.

Although there are other serviceable ways of classifying the kinds of discourse, the labels *narration, description, exposition,* and *argumentation* will be used throughout this chapter to designate four common and distinct kinds of formal writing. These are primitive forms of discourse—"primitive" in the sense that they are ultimate, basic forms. Although the edges of these categories sometimes overlap, these forms are broadly discriminating, and they are exhaustive, in the sense that all instances of formal discourse can be fitted into one or other of these categories.

Let us now look more particularly at each of these forms of discourse.

●
Narration

The definition of narration bears repeating:

Narration is that form of discourse which tells a story or gives an account of an event. Narrative discourse may be the most primitive of the forms of discourse. Storytelling goes back to the infancy of civilizations, and it is still very much with us. At a very young age, soon after they have gained some mastery of their native language, children manifest an appetite for the orally delivered fictional tale. Ancient bards composed and recited

Writing the Various Forms of Discourse

for live audiences narratives like the *Iliad* and the *Odyssey* long before the written form of a given language existed. Probably the first extended and connected piece of discourse that most of us ever uttered was a form of narration. Narration comes so naturally to us that we hardly need to be schooled in how to do it. But there is an art, a rhetoric, of narration.

Narration comes in two main varieties: the *fictional* and the *factual*.

> *Fictional narratives* **are stories created out of the imagination of the author.**
> *Factual narratives* **are accounts of real-life happenings.**

Some of the familiar types of fictional narrative are the *fable*, the *fairy tale,* the *legend*, the *epic*, the *short story*, the *novel*. Fictional narration will not be dealt with in this chapter. In the next chapter, in the section dealing with Writing about Literature, the craft of fictional storytelling will be dealt with.

In this chapter, we will deal only with factual narrative—a retelling of an event that has actually taken place. We will treat of two species of factual narration: the **personal narrative** and the **public narrative**.

Personal narrative

A personal narrative is an account of an event from the first-person point of view. The first-person pronoun *I* is very prominent in such accounts. The *I* could be the focal character of the narrative as well as being the one who reports the event, or the *I* could be merely the reporter of the event. Some of the common types of personal narratives are *diaries, journals, memoirs, eye-witness adventure stories, autobiographical anecdotes*.

Public narrative

The so-called public narrative is the reporting of an event that actually occurred, but **in this kind of account, the reporter suppresses all references to himself or herself and focuses attention on the event itself and the persons involved in it.** Although readers of public narrative are aware that an event is being related to them, they are not made conscious that a narrator stands between them and the event, because the narrator never mentions himself or herself and certainly never uses the pronoun *I*. The most common instance of public narrative is the newsstory found in a daily newspaper or in a weekly news magazine like *Time* or *Newsweek*. But any account of a historical event ("historical" in the sense of *something that happened in time and space*) told from an *omniscient* or an *objective* point of view (see the discussion of these two points of view in the writing-about-literature section of the next chapter) can be classified as a public narrative.

The Rhetoric of Narrative Discourse

(1) SEARCH AND DISCOVERY

Personal narrative

In order to find something to say in a personal narrative, you can rely mainly on *memory*. Since you are recounting an event or episode in which you yourself were involved, you have only to resort to your memory to recover the details of the "happening." This is one reason why many people find personal narrative the easiest kind of writing to do. Of the informal methods of search and discovery mentioned in Chapter 3, *meditation* is the one that fits best with the exercise of the memory. In an atmosphere free of distractions, you can activate your memory to recollect the details of the event that you are going to recount.

If you want to give some structure to your meditation, the formal method of search and discovery that will serve you well is the *journalistic formula* or the variation of that, *Burke's pentad.* So instead of just allowing the memory to search aimlessly, you can give specific directions to the memory by asking questions like these:

> **What happened?**
> **Who was involved in the happening?**
> **How did it happen?**
> **Why did it happen?**
> **When and where did it happen?**

As your memory begins to collect the details relevant to the *who, what, when, where, how,* and *why,* you may want to jot down some notes, in the form of single words or short phrases or even complete sentences. You will find notes of that sort very helpful when you emerge from your period of meditation.

Public narrative

In order to find something to say in a public narrative, you may have to rely primarily on *observation.* Usually when you are asked to write a public narrative, you have not been, or you will not be, an active participant in the event you recount; instead, you play the role of a reporter or just a spectator. Your memory will play some part in retrieving details about the event, but your activated powers of observation will play a still greater part. You will have to attune your senses of sight, hearing, touch, taste, and smell so that they will be keenly receptive to the details of the happening. Furthermore, your mood at the moment and your attitude toward the event will influence what you perceive. Despite the differences in yield caused by such circumstances, however, at least the general details of the event will impinge on the consciousness of almost any observer of the scene.

Today's reporters record the details of an event on film or on videotape or on audiotape. Deprived of those recording devices, almost every reporter scribbles notes in a notebook. However, if you are asked to recount an event that you were not previously commissioned to witness, you will have to rely on your memory to retrieve the details of that event. The journalistic formula of *who, what, when, where, how* may help you to recall and organize the pertinent details of the event.

(2) SELECTING AND ORGANIZING THE DETAILS OF A NARRATIVE

Selecting

Whether you have relied primarily on memory or on observation to find material for your narrative, **you will invariably end up with more material than you can or should use.** The recording of an event on film is inclusive and undiscriminating, because the camera records everything that it is pointed at. For that reason, TV stations have to edit the films they take of public events. Written recordings of events have to be even more severely edited than films are. Like film editors, writers must lop off long stretches of an event, but even within particular scenes of an event, writers must be *selective* of details.

The selection of narrative material can be guided by the set of general considerations used in Chapter 2 to help you fix on a subject and again in Chapter 4 to help you select from what your system of search and discovery had turned up:

Writing the Various Forms of Discourse

1 **The number of words you are allotted.**
2 **The purpose of your writing.**
3 **The occasion of your writing.**
4 **The nature of the audience for whom you are writing.**
5 **The extent and depth of your knowledge of the subject (to which might be added here the amount of material you were able to gather in the discovery stage).**
6 **The thesis or central point you want to make about the subject.**

These general considerations, however, can be supplemented with some others that are more specifically related to narrative discourse. For instance, the sixth consideration—*the thesis or central point you want to make about the subject*—could be supplemented with questions such as "Which incidents connected with the event should be omitted because they would be likely to blur the vividness or the point of the narrative?" or "Do I need to start at the beginning of the event as I experienced it in order for my account to have the effect I want it to have?" The fourth consideration—*the nature of the audience for whom you are writing*—could be supplemented with more pointed questions such as "What aspects of the event are my teenage readers more likely to be interested in?" or "Would my audience of senior citizens be likely to think that this particular episode was as funny as I think it is?" The second general consideration—*the purpose of your writing*—could be tempered by the further consideration of whether your primary intention was to *entertain* your readers rather than *inform* them about the state of a situation. The third consideration—*the occasion of your writing*—could be sharpened by the further consideration that you were writing to *honor* rather than merely *describe* someone.

Organizing: Chronology

Once you have made some decisions about *what* to tell and *how much* to tell, you have the problem of organizing what you have selected. Fortunately, a narrative is probably the mode of discourse that is easiest to organize, because there is such a limited number of ways in which a story can be told. **Chronology is the main principle governing the organization of a narrative.** The natural order in which to arrange the incidents in a fictional story or a factual event is the order in which the string of incidents happened. The incidents or happenings are strung one after another like beads on a string:

$$\text{1st} \rightarrow \text{2nd} \rightarrow \text{3rd} \rightarrow \text{4th} \ldots \rightarrow \text{conclusion}$$

There are two common variations on this straight sequence. One of those variations is to start out with some incident that occurred somewhere between the beginning and the end of the event, then to go back to the beginning (sometimes called a *flashback*) and pick up the incidents that occurred earlier, and then to resume the narrative from where you started and carry the story through to its conclusion. That pattern would look like this:

$$\text{3rd} \rightarrow \text{1st} \rightarrow \text{2nd} \rightarrow \text{4th} \rightarrow \text{5th} \ldots \rightarrow \text{conclusion}$$

Another variation is to start with an event that actually occurred toward the end of the story and then flashback to the beginning and bring the story up to where you began and then bring the story to a concluson. Television dramas, for instance, sometimes start out with a climactic event (for example, a convicted murderer being marched off to be executed), because the network wants to "hook" the viewers and keep them from

Writing the Various Forms of Discourse

switching channels, and then pick up the story at its beginning and carry it forward to its conclusion, in a pattern like this:

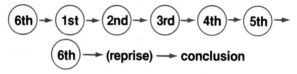

There are other variations—for example, an alternating back-and-forth movement—but the three patterns outlined above are the most common ones. *Time* is the common element in all three of them, and the differences in the patterns involve variations of the normal linear sequence.

Organizing: Cause & effect

Time is the most important element involved in the relationship between incidents, but it is not the only relationship. *Cause-and-effect* is another kind of relationship that prevails between incidents. One incident may be placed after another one not only because it *occurred after* the other one but also because it was *caused by* the previous event. The most artistic and satisfying plots in fictional stories are those in which the sequence of episodes is governed by a cause-and-effect relationship: *incident 1 causes incident 2; incident 2 in turn causes incident 3; incident 3 then causes incident 4; and so on and so on.* An incident that serves as the cause of another incident must actually occur *before* the other one, but in written accounts of events, you can vary this cause-and-effect order too. The arrangement pointed out earlier under Chronology, in which the narrative starts out with an incident that actually occurred toward the end of the event, is an arrangement that begins with an *effect* (the murderer being led off to execution) and then goes back to expose the cause or causes of that effect.

Basically, then, you will organize your narrative according to the principle of time—first this happened, then this happened, then this happened. If you depart from that natural and usual order, you do so for a calculated purpose. You may alter the normal order

1 because you want to attract and hold your readers by starting out with the most exciting incident in the story;

2 because you want to intensify the suspense in your narrative account;

3 because you want to give increased emphasis to some incident by putting it in a spot outside the actual sequence.

Otherwise, you will organize your narrative in the order in which the series of incidents actually happened.

(3) METHODS OF PRESENTING A STORY OR AN EVENT

There are two basic ways of presenting a story or an event: **showing** and **telling**.

Showing is the dramatic way of relating a story—the way we are accustomed to on the stage, in movies, or on television. The story or event is "acted out" before our eyes, without our being conscious of a narrator standing between us and the action.

Telling is the oldest method, the method used by the ancient bards to present their epic tales, but it is still a method often used today. Whenever we are conscious of someone serving as the medium through whom the action of the story or event is coming to us, we are being exposed to the *telling* method of presenting a narrative.

Once you become aware of these two ways of presenting a narrative, you will find if easy to detect the differences between

Writing the Various Forms of Discourse

them. Dialogue, for instance, is usually a sign of showing rather than of telling.

TELLING

The candidate asserted firmly that he would not run for office in the fall.

SHOWING

Senator Johnson pounded his fist on the podium and shouted, "I swear to you that I absolutely, positively, will not run for public office in November."

Note the difference in the way a character's emotional reaction is represented in the following example:

TELLING

I was scared out of my wits when I heard the noise from the upstairs bedroom.

SHOWING

I heard the chains clanking in the upstairs bedroom. Instantly, my blood froze in my veins; my heart began to pound furiously inside my rib cage; the tiny hairs on the back of my neck bristled. I tried to move my feet, but I could not budge: my shoes were nailed to the wooden floor.

In both cases, we the readers get the idea that the character was frightened by the noise from the upstairs bedroom, but in the first case, we are *told* that the person was frightened, and in the second case, we deduce that the person was frightened from what we are *shown*, and we can relive the experience with the writer.

Both *showing* and *telling* are legitimate ways of presenting a narrative. As the writer, you will have to decide which of them is better in a particular case. In personal narratives, most writers tend to resort to *telling*. But *showing* will often be the more effective way of presenting even a personal narrative. The illustrative passages above about the frightening noise are both instances of personal narrative (the *I* here is the intermediary between us and the incident), but the writer of the second passage chose to *dramatize* (show) the *I*'s emotional reaction rather than just *tell* us what that reaction was. On the other hand, *telling* may sometimes be the more appropriate way to present a public narrative.

One of the advantages of the *telling* method is that it is a quicker way to present a story. It usually takes fewer words to tell a story than to dramatize it. So there will be times when it will be necessary or advisable for you to resort to telling—for instance, when you have been allotted only a limited number of words for the whole discourse, and you merely want to let your readers know what happened.

Showing or dramatizing an event, however, is usually a more vivid, a more affecting way in which to present a narrative. It invites readers to share in the experience, to feel the happening on their pulses, to participate vicariously in the event. So if you are not severely limited in the number of words you can expend and if you want to evoke a strong emotional response from your readers or if you want to induce your readers to relive the experience with you, employ the *showing* method.

One final word of caution: **there is a greater chance that your narrative will be dull and unimpressive for your readers if you _tell_ your story than if you _show_ it.**

Writing the Various Forms of Discourse

(4) THE STYLE OF NARRATIVE DISCOURSE

It is questionable whether there is any one style that is most appropriate for narrative discourse. Narratives have been written in styles ranging from formal to informal, from intimate to impersonal, from extravagantly figurative to severely literal. As with any other kind of discourse, the most appropriate style for a particular piece of narrative discourse must be judged in relation to the nature of the event being narrated, the occasion, the audience, the desired effect, the personality of the writer. But we can point to some stylistic characteristics that are frequently, if not invariably, found in narrative discourses:

1 The style is likely to be relaxed and conversational rather than stiff and formal.

2 The style tends to be unobtrusive: it concentrates the audience's attention on the story rather than on itself.

3 Since narratives deal with actions, verbs—especially active verbs—play a prominent part in the presentation of the narrative.

4 Specific, concrete, sensory words are especially prominent in narratives managed by *showing* rather than by *telling*.

5 Highly emotional diction will appear in both personal narratives and public narratives but usually will be more prominent in personal narratives.

6 Since time is such an important element in narratives, adverbs denoting or connoting time will be especially prevalent in this kind of discourse—for example, *once upon a time, afterwards, yesterday, first, secondly, formerly, now, then, later, meanwhile.*

7 In scenes depicting rapid action, the sentences tend to be short.

8 The paragraphs in narrative discourse tend to be shorter than those in the other kinds of discourse. (Remember that

in passages of dialogue, a new paragraph begins each time the speaker changes.)

9 The pronoun *I* will be especially prominent in personal narratives. If the narrator tends to take the audience into his or her confidence, the pronoun *you* will be prominent too.

10 If the narrative is told rather than shown, the rhythm of the prose will tend to approximate the rhythm of casual speech.

None of the characteristics listed above is absolute. You can readily find examples of narratives that depart from any or all of those characteristics.

●

Description

Description is that form of discourse which presents a verbal picture of a person, a place, a thing, or a scene—an image in the mind of the listener or reader. The image conjured up is probably only a dim approximation of what is being described, but sometimes we have to settle for verbal representations of absent persons, places, things, or scenes.

Extended pieces of descriptive discourse are very rare. And they seldom exist for their own sake. Descriptive passages are usually a part of an expository, a narrative, or an argumentative discourse. Although the ordinary person does not have much occasion to write descriptions, descriptive writing does play a part in the affairs of everyday life. Examples of descriptive writing commonly appear in travelogues, in mail-order catalogues, in real-estate brochures, in reports of various kinds, and in advertisements. (Descriptive passages are very common in novels and short stories too, but in this chapter, we will not be concerned with description as it figures in fiction.) Even in cases where there is a photograph or drawing or painting of a person, place, thing, or scene, a description in words is often appended. The verbal description can sometimes convey information that the pictorial medium cannot or does not supply.

The Rhetoric of Descriptive Discourse

(1) SEARCH AND DISCOVERY

The material for a piece of descriptive writing will come mainly from *observation*. Since description always deals with concrete matters that exist outside of you, you must turn your attention outward in order to discover details that can be incorporated into the picture that you want to convey to others. But even this deliberate act of the will does not guarantee that you will perceive important details. Some people do a better job of observing than others do—perhaps because they have trained themselves to observe keenly. One of the side benefits of having to write descriptions is that your powers of observation are refined by your being in a situation where you have to exercise them.

Observation, then, is the inventional procedure that serves you best when you are writing descriptive discourse. The other inventional procedures outlined in Chapter 3 are not readily adaptable to this kind of discourse. But some of the topical questions about physical objects might be useful, such as:

---

1 **What are the physical characteristics of the object (shape, dimensions, materials, etc.)?**
2 **What sort of structure does it have?**
3 **What other object is it similar to?**
4 **How does it differ from things that resemble it?**

What questions like these do in the process of search and discovery is focus your attention on significant features of the object being described.

(2) SELECTING AND ORGANIZING THE DETAILS OF A DESCRIPTION

Like most techniques of search and discovery, observation will supply you with more data than you can use in your description. You need some criteria to help you select and organize the details that you have observed about the object you are going to describe.

Selecting: Dominant impression

Dominant impression is a principle that can help you select and focus details. Dominant impression is comparable to a thesis statement as a device to give shape and focus to a discourse. **You have to ask yourself what *dominant impression* of the person, place, thing, or scene you want to convey to your readers.** In describing a person, for instance, do you want to convey a favorable or an unfavorable impression of that person? If you wanted to convey a favorable impression of a man, for instance, you would select a different set of details if you decided to emphasize his mental prowess rather than his good looks.

Edgar Allan Poe made great use of dominant impression as a way of focusing his own compositions. As he tells us in an essay entitled "The Philosophy of Composition," he would decide what effect or impression he wanted to create with whatever he was writing, and having made that decision, he saw to it that everything he selected contributed to the establishment and maintenance of that impression or effect. If

Writing the Various Forms of Discourse

he wanted to create an impression of dread—as he so often did in his stories—he made sure that every detail he chose contributed to that note of dread. There would be no cheerful passages in the composition to offset that dominant note of dread.

The principle of dominant impression will help you not only to select pertinent and unifying details but also to reduce the number of details included in your picture. **An overabundance of detail tends to obscure rather than clarify a picture.** Excessive detail can be even more obfuscating in the verbal medium than in the visual medium. Since it is harder in the first place to paint a picture with words than it is with visual images, you just compound the difficulty by multiplying words. Skill in writing description is dependent partly on keenness of observation and partly on the choice of a few significant details. The choice of a single highly suggestive and representative detail might do more to conjure up the picture for readers than a half-dozen authentic but indiscriminate details. Too few details will leave the picture dim; too many details confuse the picture. You must develop a sense for "just enough" detail.

Organizing: The spatial frame

After selection of details, the next task you face is organizing the description. Whereas narration is organized primarily in the dimension of time, **description is organized primarily in the dimension of *space*.** So you will have to adopt some spatial principles to help you arrange your description.

One spatial decision you have to make is the choice of a physical point of view in relation to whatever you are describing. In describing a place, for instance, you have to decide, first of all, where you are standing in relation to the place you are describing, and secondly, whether your point of view will be stationary or mobile. The position you assume in relation to what is described will determine what you perceive and may determine the order in which you report details. For instance, if you were describing a building, you could not mention the fire escapes at the back of the building if you had indicated or implied at the beginning that you were standing in front of the building. If it were clear that you were walking through or around the building, you might eventually be able to describe the fire escapes at the back, but to be consistent with your roving point of view, you would have to describe different parts of the building in the order in which you came upon them.

Organizing: The time frame

Time will have some effect on your point of view, especially in relation to places and scenes. It can make a difference in what you see and report if your viewing is done at noontime or at twilight, in the wintertime or in the springtime, on a calm day or on a stormy day. Even the appearance of a person or a thing could change at different times of the day or at different seasons.

Organizing: Order of details

You have to decide on the order in which you will report the details of what you are describing. Here are some possible patterns that might help you organize your description:

1 **First give an overview of the person, place, thing, or scene and then focus on individual parts.**

2 **Report the major details first, then the minor details.**

3 **Report the familiar details first, then the strange and exotic details.**

Writing the Various Forms of Discourse

---

4 **Describe from top to bottom or from bottom to top; from left to right or from right to left.**

5 **In a roving point of view, report details in the order in which they come into your range of view.**

---

(3) METHODS OF PRESENTING A VERBAL PICTURE

The patterns of order just outlined will have a great influence on how the verbal picture is presented to readers. The determining factor in descriptive writing is a spatial one. *Fundamentally, you must decide where you will begin your description, then where you will go, and ultimately where you will terminate your description.*

But another consideration that influences your method of presenting the verbal picture is whether you keep yourself out of the description or color your description with your comments about what you are describing. Just as there is a distinction between *personal narrative* and *public narrative*, so there is a distinction between **personal description** and **public description.**

Public description

In writing a public description, you try to be as objective and noncommittal as you can. You do not intrude your voice into the description. You are like a movie camera, recording only what you can see and hear. (A movie camera, of course, can be made to editorialize on what it records, but that editorializing is done so subtly that it is almost unnoticeable.)

Personal description

In a personal description, you do project your own voice into the presentation. You want your readers to know how you feel about the person, place, thing, or scene you are describing. Sometimes you introduce your editorial commentary into the description simply by your choice of words. To write "The walls were painted pink" is to write an objective, noncommittal description. But you can change that *public* description into a *personal* description simply by adding one word: "The walls were painted a bilious pink." Here the word *bilious* betrays your attitude about what you are describing. You are not just presenting the "facts" about the place you are describing; you are presenting the "facts" plus your opinion of the "facts."

There are other ways, of course, in which you can introduce your presence into the description. You can be explicit about letting your readers know that you are present in the scene you are describing. The presence of the describer is revealed by such touches as "As I passed from the bedroom into the dimly lit hallway, I noticed . . ." or "To confirm her suspicion that the portrait was done in acrylic paints rather than oils, she lightly scratched a corner of the painting with her fingernail."

Description in a larger setting

Earlier, we observed that descriptive writing seldom exists for its own sake. Most of the time, it is part of one of the other three forms of discourse. *The purpose that the description serves in the larger discourse is another consideration that will help to determine how the verbal picture should be presented.* In a story, for instance, if the primary purpose of a description of a person were to give readers a mental picture of what a particular character looked like, you would probably paint the picture with noncommittal details. However, if the primary purpose were to influence the readers' reactions to a particular character, you would color the description with words or details that had favorable or unfavorable connotations.

Thus in a courtroom trial—which is essentially an argumentative situation—the prosecuting attorney might present a vivid description of a brutal murder because he wanted to arouse a strong emotional reaction against the defendant among the members of the jury. *Frequently, however, such descriptions will have a greater emotional impact if they are presented objectively than if they are colored with the feelings of the describer.*

Knowing that many readers are impatient with lengthy descriptions that interrupt the story, not a few writers of fiction will present descriptions of persons, places, or scenes not in one long set piece but in sentences scattered throughout the story. Writers of factual discourses of various kinds might also find it more appropriate or effective to present descriptive details in much the same way rather than in one long set piece. The particular situation will dictate which of these two strategies it would be better for the writer to adopt.

As we have already noted, the secret of good description lies in knowing what details and how many details to include. But knowing *what* and *how much* to include is more a matter of instinct than of cultivated skill. Consequently, no practical advice can be given to help you acquire this ability. All that can be done in a practical way is to remember that *multiplying details does not necessarily make the picture more vivid.*

(4) THE STYLE OF DESCRIPTIVE DISCOURSE

Of all the forms of discourse, descriptive writing is the one associated in most people's minds with a highly ornate style.

● Description

Whether descriptive writing deserves that reputation is debatable; nevertheless, the impression exists and persists. Another impression that exists is that descriptive writing relies heavily on adjectives—"flowery adjectives" is the term one often hears. Another prevailing impression is that description is inevitably boring and dispensable. Despite these impressions, the fact is that not all descriptive writing is highly ornate, heavily adjectival, and essentially boring. There is no reason in the nature of this kind of writing that description should be characterized by any of these qualities.

It is concrete

A safer generalization about the style of descriptive discourse is that this kind of writing—when it is well done—is likely to make heavy use of specific, concrete, sensory diction. That kind of diction is essential in a mode of discourse in which you are trying to conjure up a picture with mere words. **You have to resort to words that are likely to create pictures or images in readers' minds.** Thus the skillful writer of description is inclined to use a specific word like *elm* rather than a general word like *tree*, a concrete world like *gold* rather than the abstract word *wealth*, and a sensory word like *a burning forehead* rather than a word like *fever*. If adjectives must be used, the skillful writer tends to resort to those that appeal to one of the senses:

SIGHT: *red* (any color word), *flickering, crooked, dark, swollen*
HEARING: *hissing, plangent, rackety, shrill, guttural*
TOUCH: *smooth, rigid, gritty, moist, frosty*
SMELL: *acrid, musky, putrid, aromatic, smoky*
TASTE: *tart, sweet, spicy, biting, salty*

Writing the Various Forms of Discourse

It can be figurative

The descriptive writer is also likely to make frequent use of figures of speech. Figures of speech are not peculiar to description, of course, but they are very common in this kind of writing because they are by their very nature pictorial expressions. Moreover, many of the figures of speech help readers to "see" what they do not actually see. Because metaphor and simile, for instance, are built on the principle of analogy, they can, by comparing something unfamiliar to something familiar, help readers visualize the unfamiliar thing. When Richard Selzer, the surgeon, wanted to give his readers some idea of the appearance and the position of the human liver, he used a series of metaphors and similes:

> Let us celebrate that great maroon snail, whose smooth back nestles in the dome of the diaphragm, beneath the lattice of the rib cage, like some blind wise slave, crouching above its colleague viscera, secret, resourceful, instinctive
>
> from *Mortal Lessons*

In personal descriptions, figures of speech also help writers convey to their readers what their attitude is toward what they are describing. An author's attitude toward the sound of an automobile engine would obviously be different if she wrote "The engine snorted like an asthmatic pig" instead of "The engine purred like a contented kitten." Consult the section Some Common Figures of Speech in Chapter 5 to see which of the tropes would be especially useful in helping you convey *a picture* of what you are describing and which ones would be useful for conveying *your attitude* toward what you are describing.

Purple prose

It is not difficult to find examples of excessively ornate descriptive writing. A term that is sometimes used to label that kind of writing is "purple prose." For some strange reason, beginning writers are prone to slip into that kind of prose when they have to describe something. Purple prose is easy to recognize. For one thing, it is usually dripping with mellifluous adjectives. Although such prose is easy to recognize, the danger is that inexperienced writers are likely to think that it is admirable and therefore worthy of being imitated.

Descriptive writing, however, does not have to be done in the florid style. In fact, description is often more effective if done in a subdued, plain style. When you gain sufficient command of diction to be able to choose apt, precise words, you will be able to evoke vivid pictures with language that does not call attention to itself. Next to poetry, description is probably the kind of writing that requires the greatest command of vocabulary. Until your reservoir of words is well stocked, you may have to resort frequently to a thesaurus, the kind of reference book that supplies writers with copious lists of synonyms. But resort to a thesaurus can be dangerous too: until you learn to be discriminating in the choice of available words, you can easily slip into "purple prose."

●

Exposition

Exposition is that form of discourse which informs, explains, or instructs. That kind of utilitarian prose is a very common form of writing in the workaday world. Once you finish school, you may have little or no occasion to write a narration

Writing the Various Forms of Discourse

or a description, but if you have to do any formal writing at all in connection with your vocation in life, you will certainly have to write some exposition. If you can do this kind of writing at least competently, you will enjoy a considerable advantage in your chosen field.

The place where most people encounter expository discourse regularly and frequently is the daily newspaper. The newsstory is a classic instance of that species of expository prose which imparts information to readers. But the newspaper also contains examples of other kinds of expository prose—that which tries to explain something to readers and that which tries to instruct readers about something.

People encounter expository prose in other places too—in reports, instruction manuals, encyclopedias, textbooks, business letters. The set of written directions accompanying the furniture or appliance that you buy at a department store is another common example of expository prose. Most of the writing that appears on the back of a box of breakfast cereal can be classified as exposition. Most of the prose in college catalogues is expository. We will explore the rhetoric of this familiar kind of writing.

The Rhetoric of Expository Discourse

(1) SEARCH AND DISCOVERY

You saw in the previous section that descriptive writing deals with concrete phenomena that exist in the world outside yourself—persons, places, things, and scenes. Just as there can be descriptions of persons, places, things, and scenes, there can also be *expositions* of them. A biographical sketch, for instance, gives *information* about a person; an article on psychology might present an *explanation* of a person's behavior; a medical treatise might provide some illuminating *instruction* about a person's physical mechanism. But in addition to expositions of persons, places, things, and scenes, there can be expositions of processes, events, movements, concepts, ideologies. The great range and variety of expository discourses necessitate a corresponding range and variety of methods, approaches, and strategies.

You saw that *observation* is the most useful way of discovering something to say in a descriptive piece of writing. *But virtually all of the formal and informal methods of discovery mentioned in Chapter 3 are useful in helping you to gather something to say in a piece of expository writing.* Some of the methods, however, will be more productive for some subjects than for others.

Observation, for instance, will be a more fruitful method of invention for an exposition of a process (for example, how a particular machine works) than for an exposition of a concept (for example, the notion of reciprocal trade). On the other hand, the *classical topics* will yield more material for an exposition of the notion of reciprocal trade than they will for an exposition of how an internal-combustion engine works. The *journalistic formula* of *who, what, when, where, how* will work better for an exposition of how a bill works its way through the congressional process than for an exposition of the term *metastasis*. Reading a number of scholarly interpretations of a particular passage in the Bible will probably do more to help you compose a plausible explanation of that passage than any amount of brainstorming or meditation.

The point is that while all of the methods of search and discovery outlined in Chapter 3 are potentially useful when you are faced with writing exposition, you will usually have to exercise some discretion in choosing the method that will be most productive for the particular kind of exposition you have to write. The advantage of being familiar with several methods of search and discovery is not only that you are more likely to find a method that fits your temperament but also that you may increase your chances of finding one that is especially productive for a particular kind of exposition.

Whenever you are given an expository assignment, you may at first have to run your finger down the list of search-and-discovery procedures outlined in Chapter 3 and try to judge which one is likely to work best for you with that particular assignment. After some practice in systematically running through the whole list, you may develop a knack for deciding immediately which method or methods will be best.

(2) SELECTING AND ORGANIZING THE DETAILS OF AN EXPOSITION

Again, the six considerations first introduced in chapter 2 to help you fix on a subject and repeated earlier in this chapter in connection with narration and description will be helpful criteria for guiding your selection of the material turned up by whatever inventional system you used:

1 **The number of words you are allotted.**
2 **The purpose of your writing.**
3 **The occasion of your writing.**
4 **The nature of the audience for whom you are writing.**
5 **The extent and depth of your knowledge of the subject (supplemented by whatever you were able to turn up on the subject by the inventional system you used).**
6 **The thesis or central point you want to make about the subject.**

Of those six considerations, the second and the fourth will be especially helpful in guiding your selection of material for an exposition. If your purpose is primarily to *inform* your audience, you will make some selections that differ from those you would make if your purpose were to *instruct* your audience. Whether your primary purpose is information, explanation, or instruction, the nature of your audience will also have a bearing on what you need to include in your exposition. **You will have to estimate as accurately as you can what your audience can be presumed to know about the subject you are writing about and what you will need to mention or elaborate on.**

You will not necessarily omit everything that your audience can be presumed to know already. You might in some cases want to include some familiar material just to assure your audience that they are not wandering through completely foreign territory. One of the other considerations, however, like the number of words you are allotted for this piece of writing, might make it necessary for you to cut some material, and in an expository discourse, it makes sense to cut what you think most of your audience is likely to know already about the subject. Redundancy—that is, including more than enough—can serve as a reinforcing device in expository writing, but redundancy is expendable if you are not granted the luxury of indulging in a leisurely, expansive explanation of something.

We saw in the previous sections that there are a limited number of ways in which to organize a piece of narrative or descriptive discourse. *Time* is the element that mainly determines the order of the parts in a narrative discourse, and *space* is the main determining element in descriptive writing. But expository discourse lends itself to a variety of organizing principles.

For an exposition of a process—of how to do or make something or how a system or a mechanism works—the organizing element is the same one that operates in a narrative,

Writing the Various Forms of Discourse

time. Essentially, the pattern for such an exposition is the temporal sequence of the various steps in the process: first you do this, then you do this, and then you do this. The exposition of a simple process, like changing a flat tire on an automobile, would observe the same order that one would actually follow in changing the tire. Even an exposition of how a machine works would observe the chronological order—for example, when that lever is depressed, a mixture of air and gasoline is injected into the chamber, and then. . . .

Expositions that provide a definition or explanation of a fairly complex concept or movement could be organized in a variety of ways. For instance, the exposition of a movement, such as the development of liberalism in the nineteenth century, could be organized *chronologically*, from its beginnings early in the century through the successive steps during the rest of the century. Or it could be organized *thematically*, according to the types of liberalism that developed concurrently during the century—for example, political liberalism, social liberalism, religious liberalism. Or it could be organized according to a *cause-and-effect* pattern—for example, starting out with the establishment of the cause or causes of the growth of liberalism and then tracing out the effects of the cause or causes as they manifested themselves in the political, social, and cultural arenas.

Figure 4.1 in Chapter 4 outlines some of the other patterns of organization that might help you arrange the parts of your expository discourse. For most attempts at explanation or instruction, a good strategy is to start out with what is relatively familiar to the audience and *move to the progressively less familiar* aspects. Or you could move *from the whole to the parts* (from the integrated view of the subject to an analysis of the constituent parts) or *from the particular to the general* (the inductive order) or *from the general to the particular* (the deductive order). For most types of exposition, you could observe the *clearing-the-ground-before-building* principle of organization— pointing out previous instances of misinformation or inadequate explanation before presenting your own exposition of the subject. Extremely skillful writers might be able to employ the *associational order* for their expositions, but this principle of arrangement is not particularly suited to expository discourse because the very arbitrariness of the sequence in which things are discussed tends to keep readers disoriented. When readers are seeking to learn something, they value an orderly presentation. The associational order works best with some kinds of narratives—for example, episodic tales, anecdotes, reminiscences, accounts of dreams—but it does not usually work well with expository discourse.

(3) METHODS OF PRESENTING EXPOSITIONS

Utilizing readers' strengths

The best way for you to discover effective methods of presenting an exposition is to **try to imagine the writer/reader relationship in a situation where one party is dependent on the other party for information, explanation, or instruction.** Presumably, the writer in such a situation knows something that the reader does not know but wants or needs to know. (An obvious exception to that situation is an academic examination, where the writer/student usually does not know as much about the subject as the reader/teacher does.) What do you as the writer do to render the reader as knowledgeable as yourself about a particular subject? For one thing, you must realize (1) that you share a large stock of knowledge and values with your readers and (2) that your readers probably know more about some subjects (other than the one being discussed at the moment) than you do. That realization suggests one strategy

Writing the Various Forms of Discourse

that you can use: taking advantage of both the common and the special knowledge that exists in this relationship in order to help transfer to your readers information about the subject being discussed. For example, if you are aware that your readers know a great deal about automobiles (maybe even more than you know), you might use an analogy drawn from automobile lore to help you explain a concept that you are trying to convey to those readers. In short, take advantage of your readers' strengths—if you can determine what they are.

Furnishing context & orientation

For another thing, you must realize that in some instances—especially in those involving explanation or instruction—it is not simply a matter of *telling* your readers something. In areas that are new and strange to readers, you may first have to **provide readers with a context, a background, an orientation.** Readers can feel lost and bewildered when they venture into the study of a new discipline. Readers, for example who take up the study of philosophy for the first time must become acclimated to the new territory before they can feel comfortable in it. It is not just a matter of their becoming accustomed to new concepts and new terminology; it is also a matter of their adjusting their perspectives and mindset. In short, what they need to do is learn how to look at, and talk about, things in the way a philosopher does. Likewise, when they take up the study of a totally different discipline, such as physics, they have to learn how to look at, and talk about, things in the way a physicist does. For this reason, expositions of technical matters for a mass audience are much more difficult to write than expositions of the same matter for an audience of one's peers. The most difficult rhetorical lesson for many writers to learn is the need to adapt their message to the capacities of various audiences. That skill is absolutely crucial for success in expository writing.

Knowing your audience

What all of this discussion comes down to ultimately is that for purposes of communication, a knowledge of the audience can be as important as knowledge of the subject. You have perhaps had experience of people who were acknowledged experts in their field who nevertheless failed to communicate their knowledge to others because they did not make the necessary adjustments for talking with people who were something less than experts. *Your mastery of the rhetoric of expository discourse depends crucially on your realization of the disparities in the levels of knowledge that exist among people and on your ability to adjust the level of your exposition to the capacities of the particular audience that you are trying to communicate with.*

Aside from the general considerations of the writer/reader relationships involved in the process of exposition, what more specific strategies can you resort to when faced with the task of conveying information, explanation, or instruction in writing to an audience of readers? Here are some practical suggestions:

1 **Ask yourself what you found especially difficult to understand when *you* were first introduced to the idea or concept you are writing about and touch on those points in your exposition.**

2 **Ask yourself what a person who was relatively uninformed about the subject you are writing about would need to know in order to become reasonably**

well informed and then answer your own questions in your exposition. (For example, readers who were uninformed about a particular event would need answers to the who, what, when, where, why, how questions.)

3 **Quote someone to verify the information you are dispensing or to clarify what you are trying to explain.**

4 **Draw an analogy between what you are trying to explain and something that most of your readers are likely to be familiar with.**

5 **Present two or more different explanations of especially difficult concepts, so that if one explanation is not clear to some readers, one of the other explanations may be.**

6 **Repeat an explanation you have given.** (Sometimes it is effective to put the repeated explanation not right after the first explanation but in a different place, such as near the end or even in the conclusion.)

7 **Present some examples of what you have been trying to explain, or start out with a series of examples and then proceed to your explanation.**

8 **Tell a story or an anecdote that will illustrate the point you are trying to explain.**

9 **Quote a dictionary definition of what you are trying to explain, or present an extended definition that you yourself have composed in language that could be understood by an ordinary literate person.**

10 **Define any technical terminology that you may have to use.**

11 **Supplement your verbal exposition with a picture or a sketch or a chart or a graph, if the subject you are**

> **writing about lends itself to such graphic presentation.**
>
> 12 **For all assignments in exposition, keep in mind Aristotle's wise observation: "Our discussion will be adequate if it has as much clearness as the subject matter admits of, for precision is not to be sought for alike in all discussions."**
>
> Nichomachean Ethics, trans. W. D. Ross

(4) THE STYLE OF EXPOSITORY DISCOURSE

Clarity

The prime virtue of the style of a piece of writing in which the author's intention is to convey information, explanation, or instruction to readers would seem to be *clarity*. A style that is difficult for readers to process will not readily communicate its message. But this demand for a clear style carries with it two qualifications: (1) we should not expect that all subjects can be rendered equally clear; (2) we should be aware that a style which is clear for one set of readers may be muddy for another set of readers. In short, clarity of style is relative.

With that admonition in mind, we would not expect that a philosophical discussion of *substance and accidents* could be as easily rendered in a clear style as a discussion of the economic law of *supply and demand*, nor would we expect an exposition of nuclear fission written for a professional journal read by physicists to be written in a style that could be readily comprehended by the ordinary literate lay-person. *What we have a right to expect is that an exposition of nuclear fission for a beginning course in college physics be written as simply and as clearly as it can be written for its intended audience.*

Writing the Various Forms of Discourse

Readability

There are formulas for measuring the readability of prose. Most of these formulas are constructed on an absolute scale. That is, the same formula is applied to prose of any kind on any subject, and the formula is supposed to measure the level of difficulty of the prose, usually in terms of the grade-level (e.g. the sixth-grade level, the twelfth-grade level). Publishers have used one or other of these formulas to determine the grade-level at which a textbook is written.

A widely used readability formula is the one that Rudolf Flesch devised back in 1949 for his book *The Art of Readable Writing*. Actually, Flesch devised two formulas, one for measuring the degree of interest of a piece of prose, the other for measuring the degree of difficulty. For his ease-of-reading formula, Flesch looked at two features of the prose: (1) the average number of words per sentence (calculated by dividing the total number of words in the passage by the total number of sentences) and (2) the average number of syllables in 100 consecutive words. The first criterion measured the length of sentences; the second measured the length of words. Flesch's thesis was that prose became more difficult to read in proportion to the length of the sentences and the length of the words. According to Flesch's scale, a piece of prose that averaged eleven words per sentence and 168 syllables per 100 words (or 1.68 syllables per word) was rated as "fairly difficult" prose; a piece of prose averaging twenty words per sentence and 179 syllables per 100 words (or 1.79 syllables per word) was rated as "difficult" prose.

One might question a particular rating in Flesch's formula or in any of the other readability formulas, but the lesson for the writer—especially for the writer of expository prose—is that a preponderance of long sentences and of polysyllabic words (like *preponderance* and *polysyllabic*) may, and often does, increase the difficulty that readers have in comprehending a piece of prose. When a difficult style is added to complexity of subject matter, the problems for readers are compounded. Expository writers should not for that reason cultivate a style on the level of a Dick-and-Jane reader, but *they should strive to facilitate the reading of their prose by carefully choosing their words and structuring their sentences so that it can be handled by the readers to whom it is directed.*

Rules, conventions, characteristics

As E. D. Hirsch, Jr., pointed out in his book *The Philosophy of Composition* (Chicago: University of Chicago Press, 1977), the appearance of the same or similar maxims about good writing in handbook after handbook indicates that certain practices usually, if not always, produce easily readable prose. He concedes that every stylistic rule is open to exceptions: ''The accurate form of all such maxims is: 'Do *X*, unless you have weighty reasons for not doing *X*.' The point in giving the rule is that doing *X* will be better than not doing *X*—most of the time.''

Most of the time, then, you can ensure that your expository prose will be easily readable by observing maxims like the following:

---

1 **Use familiar and appropriate words.**

2 **Keep related words together.**

3 **Avoid ambiguous words and structures.**

4 **Omit unnecessary words.**

5 **Make clear the connections between sentences.**

6 **Vary the length and structure of your sentences.**

In the section on Style in the handbook part of this book, all these maxims (stated in slightly different words) are discussed at some length.

Writing the Various Forms of Discourse

The principal key to achieving a lucid style is a constant awareness of audience. Pronouns, for instance, are often misused, simply because writers lose sight of their readers. Writers themselves always know what the pronoun they use refers to in a particular sentence, and it is natural for them to presume that their readers also know what the pronoun refers to. But writers often fail to provide the grammatical or lexical signals that link the pronoun to its antecedent (the noun to which it refers), and as a result, there is at least a momentary, and sometimes a serious, breakdown in communication. The careless handling of pronouns is just one instance of unclear writing that is due to writers' losing sight of their readers.

In some kinds of expository writing—for example, scientific writing, technical reports, newsstories—the use of emotional language and figures of speech is supposed to be avoided or kept to a minimum, and the voice of the writer is supposed to be suppressed. The theory behind these conventions is that in extremely objective kinds of expository writing, the focus should be kept on the subject and that any intrusion of personal, emotive, or figurative language tends to distract the attention of readers from the subject being discussed.

One manifestation of this theory is the widespread proscription of the pronouns *I* and *you* in theses, dissertations, and technical reports. This ban has been somewhat relaxed in recent years, but you will still find many situations where the use of the first-person and second-person pronouns is discouraged if not forbidden. And it must be conceded that in some situations, an indulgence in personal, emotive, and figurative language will defeat rather than promote the achievement of your purpose.

Because expository writing ranges from the very formal, highly technical kind of scientific writing to the informal, relaxed, colloquial kind of journalistic writing, some of the stylistic characteristics listed below are likely to be more prominent in some kinds of expository writing than in other kinds. One of the skills that writers eventually acquire with practice is the ability to adapt their style to fit the genre, the occasion, the purpose, the subject matter, the audience, etc.

Some characteristics of the expository style (with exceptions, of course):

1 A predominance of declarative sentences (that is, sentences that make statements rather than ask questions or give commands).

2 A prevalence of sentences that observe the normal word order of the English sentence—subject/verb/complement—rather than sentences that begin with long introductory phrases or clauses or sentences with inverted structures (for example: *The high voltage we could not turn off immediately*).

3 Very few, if any, compound sentences joined with semicolons.

4 Frequent use of passive verbs, partly because of the emphasis on the impersonal style.

5 Tendency to rely on the *denotations* rather than the *connotations* of words.

6 Sparing use of adjectives and adverbs, especially of adjectives and adverbs that represent judgments or opinions rather than objective fact ("the *red* barn" but not "the *ugly* barn").

7 Many new words or old words with new meanings.

8 Likelihood of some jargon (that is, terminology peculiar to certain professions and occupations).

Writing the Various Forms of Discourse

9 More use of concrete diction than of abstract diction, especially in examples of informative writing.

10 Some traces of humor and irony in some kinds of journalistic writing.

●

Argumentation

Argumentation is that form of discourse in which the writer attempts to persuade an audience to adopt a certain position and/or to act in a certain way. The objectives of argumentative discourse can be spelled out more particularly than they are in this general definition. We can say that this kind of writing tries to achieve one or more of the following objectives:

1 to reinforce the readers' present position.

2 to persuade readers to modify their present position.

3 to persuade readers to reject their present position.

4 to persuade readers to reject their present position and to adopt another one.

5 to persuade readers to act in a certain way.

6 to dissuade readers from acting in a certain way.

Argumentation may be the most prevalent form of discourse in the day-to-day world. Some people would nominate exposition as the predominant form, but those who contend that argumentation is predominant argue that in a certain sense, all four of the forms of discourse considered in this chapter are fundamentally persuasive, because ultimately all of them seek to win the acceptance of readers. Argumentation is also the mode that is most likely to use all three of the other modes in order to accomplish its overall objective of persuading an audience. It is not uncommon in a piece of argumentative discourse for the writer to incorporate a narrative, a description, and an exposition in order to effect his or her principal purpose.

But whether or not argumentation is the most common and the most inclusive of the forms, there is no disputing the fact that it is a very common and useful mode of discourse in contemporary society. If the majority of literate citizens are not frequently required to write persuasive discourses, they are certainly *exposed* frequently to persuasive discourses, such as political speeches, flyers from political candidates, sermons, appeals from charitable organizations, sales letters, promotion letters, public-relations brochures, proposals, editorials. The most pervasive and constant form of persuasive discourse in modern life, however, is the ad or commercial. Most ads and commercials reach people through such media as television, radio, magazines, newspapers, and billboards. Although the advertising message is frequently transmitted in pictures, it is a rare advertisement or commercial that is not accompanied also with a verbal text, either spoken or printed. There is a *writer* behind almost every ad.

Advertisements are perfect examples of the kind of discourse we are calling argumentation. The ultimate purpose of every ad or commercial is to induce people to buy a product or a service. In other words, advertisers seek to influence the actions of a group of people. They try to get people to buy what the advertising copy is selling. Sometimes before people can be moved to the action of buying, their attitude toward the product or service being sold must be reinforced or changed. Customers must be persuaded that the proferred service or product is necessary or useful or in some way beneficial. In short, it must be made to appear *desirable*.

Writing the Various Forms of Discourse

In pursuit of this goal, writers of advertising copy are usually very skillful rhetoricians. Whether they are always ethical in the means they employ to entice buyers is a matter that will not be discussed here. But because advertising is such an inescapable phenomenon in our daily lives, we can look to it for some valuable lessons in how to compose a discourse that will influence readers to think or act in a certain way.

The Rhetoric of Argumentative Discourse

(1) SEARCH AND DISCOVERY

The so-called *classical topics* were designed specifically for persuasive oratory. Rhetoricians like Aristotle, Cicero, and Quintilian fashioned them to aid speakers in finding arguments or ''proofs'' that would affect the thinking or the actions of a listening audience. As we saw in Chapter 3, which reviewed various invention systems, four common topics were designated as a means of finding something to say for any kind of writing assignment: *definition* (''What is it?''); *comparison* (''What is it like or unlike?''); *relationship* (''What caused it?''); *testimony* (''What is said about it?''). These same topics can be very helpful to writers in discovering at least the *kind* of arguments that will be effective in a particular case.

Definition

For instance, if you were trying to persuade a group of readers that jogging was a health-preserving exercise, you might find that *definition* was a fruitful source of arguments. You might find it necessary to define *jogging* and *health-preserving exercise*. If you had been involved in jogging yourself, it might seem to you that these terms were self-explanatory. But to the group of readers that you were trying to persuade, these terms might not be self-explanatory. So you would have to give your readers some explanation of these terms. (Definition is basically a form of exposition.) However, your definitions of the key terms in the proposition that you were arguing—"Jogging is a health-preserving exercise"— might not be serving just an expository function; they could also be having a persuasive impact on your readers. Sometimes the mere clarification of what something is removes people's fear or dislike of it and consequently disposes them to accept the "something." For some people, *exercise* is not an appealing word, and when *health-preserving* is joined to it, the term could be quite intimidating for those people. But if you explained what you meant by the term, you might leave your readers saying, "Well, if that's all you mean by *health-preserving exercise*, jogging doesn't seem to be as formidable as I thought it was, and maybe I should consider taking it up." In that case, definition would have modified those readers' attitudes toward jogging and disposed them to act in the way you wanted them to act— namely, to take up jogging.

Comparison

In your efforts to clarify what jogging was and what was involved in it, you would likely be led into the use of another of the classical topics, *comparison*. By comparing jogging to other athletic activities, like sprinting, racing, walking, you would not only be defining what jogging was but you would also be removing any uncertainties or allaying any fears that your readers might have by showing them what jogging was like and what it was unlike. Or the comparison could lead to a differentiation not of kind but of degree: jogging is a faster pace than the one involved in walking and a slower pace than the one involved in

Writing the Various Forms of Discourse

the 1500-meter run. Comparison, like definition, could help to familiarize your audience with what you are talking about (thereby performing an expository function), and that familiarization in turn could pave the way ultimately to persuasion.

Relationship

Another of the classical topics that could suggest a line of development for your argumentative discourse on jogging is *relationship*. Since you would be trying to convince your audience that jogging was health-preserving, you would have to establish that there was a cause-and-effect relationship between jogging and health, and you would have to refute the counterarguments that jogging can induce injury to one's back, knees, and ankles.

Testimony

This thesis also calls for proof by resort to the classical topic of *testimony*. You would certainly want to quote some doctors, coaches, athletes, and well-known joggers who testify to the health-preserving benefits of jogging and can counteract the adverse testimony of others who contend that jogging is injurious to health. Of course, in order to find pertinent quotations, you might have to do some research in the form of reading, and to find the pertinent reading material, you would have to know where to find and how to use the appropriate reference tools in the library. (See the section in the next chapter on the use of the library.)

The point of all this discussion on finding pertinent and persuasive arguments for a paper on the alleged health-preserving properties of jogging is *that since the classical topics were originally designed as inventional devices for persuasive speeches, they can always be resorted to when you are faced with the task of finding something to say in an argumentative discourse.*

Topical questions

Some of the other inventional devices outlined in Chapter 3 might be easier and more fruitful for you to use in discovering suitable and effective "proofs" for an argumentative discourse. The *topical questions*, for instance, work well for some people. For an argumentative paper on the thesis that "jogging is a health-preserving exercise," this set of topical questions from Chapter 3 might be especially productive:

ABOUT PROPOSITIONS (statement to be proved or disproved)

1 **What must be established before the reader will believe it?**

2 **What are the meanings of key words in the proposition?**

3 **By what kinds of evidence or argument can the proposition be proved or disproved?**

4 **What counterarguments must be confronted and refuted?**

5 **What are the practical consequences of the proposition?**

The journalistic formula

Although the *journalistic formula* outlined in Chapter 3 is especially useful for narratives and for expositions of processes, it can sometimes be helpful too for suggesting effective lines of development in an argumentative discourse. Questions

Writing the Various Forms of Discourse

like *who*? *what*? *when*? *where*? from the journalistic formula could suggest some fruitful lines of development in a paper arguing for the health-preserving benefits of jogging. Take just the *who* question for instance. It could suggest that one part of your argumentative paper should deal with just who could be benefited by jogging and who could not be benefited. Thus people with a history of heart trouble or of chronic back-pains are said to be more harmed than helped by jogging, yet middle-aged men and women who were very athletic when they were teenagers and who recently quit smoking and are now dieting are thought to be candidates for physical benefits from a regimen of jogging. And in further pursuit of the **who** question, you could make the point that even people who had suffered heart attacks could, with the advice and supervision of a physician, be considered potential beneficiaries of jogging. Certainly the *why* and the *how* questions from the journalistic formula could suggest many lines of argument for the thesis that jogging is a health-preserving sport.

Problem-solving

Problem-solving is always a possibility as a source of arguments. There is usually a problem implicit in any situation where you are faced with having to prove something or convince someone. The procedures outlined in chapter 3 for solving a problem can usually be applied to a situation where you have to write a paper that will prove something or convince someone of something. Recall what those procedures are:

---

1 **Specify what the problem is.**
2 **Analyze the problem ("What do I know for sure? What is the unknown?").**

---

3 **Formulate one or more hypotheses about the unknown.**
4 **Test the hypotheses.**

Just going through those four steps mentally can yield the substance and the structure of your paper.

Pinpointing the problem is the most crucial step in the use of the problem-solving procedure for generating material for an argumentative paper. In the case of the sample topic on jogging that we have been looking at, there are a number of potential problems in connection with trying to convince readers that jogging can be good for their health. Depending on the particular audience you were addressing—or on your own assessment of the situation—here are some of the problems you might face in dealing with this topic:

1 How to overcome the antipathy that many people have to strenuous exercise.
2 How to counteract the reports that many people have heard about the danger to the jogger's body.
3 How to counteract the reports many people have heard about the boredom of jogging.
4 How to lure people away from their commitment to other participant sports.
5 How to allay many people's apprehensions about the hazards of weather for joggers—heat, cold, rain, snow, sleet, ice.

As you can see, the particular problem that a particular writer would face in dealing with this topic would vary from audience to audience. What might be a problem with one audience (e.g. a group of high-school athletes) might not be a problem with

Writing the Various Forms of Discourse

another audience (e.g. a group of middle-aged executives in business). It is important that you get to know as much as possible about the audience so that you can pinpoint what the special problem might be with that particular audience.

What all the sample problems listed above have in common is that they represent possible negative attitudes that the audience may have toward jogging. If you were the writer in this case, you might conclude that the special problem centered on how to overcome such negative attitudes. As a result, you might further conclude that before you could present your own arguments in favor of jogging, you had to overcome these negative attitudes. When you proceeded to the next step of posing one or more hypotheses for solving the major problem, you might tentatively decide that you would have to say something about each of the five "problems" listed in the previous paragraph. So then as a result of resorting to the problem-solving technique, you would have discovered what you had to do and the order in which you had to do it in *this particular* argumentative paper for *this particular* group of readers. Now all you would have to do before you could begin writing is think up convincing "answers" for the five (or more) "problems" that you listed. But if you were an experienced and dedicated jogger, you might conjure up what you considered plausible and convincing answers from your own resources, and you could supplement your own arguments with testimony from others.

First draft as source

Finally, you should not underestimate the value of writing the first draft as a way of generating ideas for an argumentative paper. Writing the first draft can be a fruitful discovery procedure for any of the four forms of discourse dealt with in this chapter, but for some reason, it is an especially fruitful procedure for argumentative discourse. Putting your ideas, your arguments, down on paper makes you see, as you often cannot see before you start writing, what is adequate and what is inadequate for your purpose, what you must do to strengthen your case, what structure you must adopt to present your case most effectively, what opposing views you need to refute, what set of values shared by you and your readers you need to emphasize, what fears you need to allay. *If your recourse to the other systems of search and discovery does not turn up enough "proofs" for you argumentative paper on a particular topic, try writing the first draft.* You may find that just the physical act of putting words down on a piece of paper serves to break the psychological block that has been frustrating you.

(2) SELECTING AND ORGANIZING THE DETAILS OF AN ARGUMENTATIVE DISCOURSE

Many of the principles discussed in Chapter 4 will be useful to you in selecting and organizing the material you have discovered for your argumentative paper. The same set of criteria outlined at the beginning of that chapter will certainly be helpful to you in selecting your "proofs":

1 **The allotted wordage.**
2 **Your purpose.**
3 **The occasion.**
4 **The nature of the audience.**
5 **The amount of material gathered.**
6 **The thesis you are trying to prove.**

For organizing your argumentative paper, you may find the traditional *formal outline* to be the most helpful device. Or you

Writing the Various Forms of Discourse

may find useful the more informal *scratch outline* or *block outline* discussed in Chapter 4. The nine *Common Patterns of Organization* presented in that chapter may also be helpful to you. Of those nine patterns, the three that most often have a bearing on the organization of an argumentative paper are the *Logical Order*, the *Climactic Order*, and the *Clearing the Ground Before (or After) Building Order* (see the discussion of these in Chapter 4).

Classical rhetoric, however, developed a pattern for organizing a speech that may be useful to you in organizing the argumentative paper you are writing. The number of parts specified for a classical oration varied slightly from rhetorician to rhetorician, but the general pattern was fairly standard. Here is a common pattern, with modern terms used to designate the parts:

> 1 **The Introduction**
> 2 **The Statement of the Issue**
> 3 **The Proof of the Case**
> 4 **The Refutation of the Opposing Case**
> 5 **The Conclusion**

In Chapter 4, we saw that Aristotle had maintained that every piece of extended, connected discourse should have a *Beginning*, a *Middle*, and an *End*. In the pattern of a classical oration, the Introduction was the *Beginning*; the Statement of the Issue, the Proof of the Case, and the Refutation of the Opposing Case constituted the *Middle*; and the Conclusion was the *End*. We will look at each of these parts in some detail in order to discover the possible usefulness of this pattern for organizing a piece of argumentative prose.

1. Introduction

The Greek rhetoricians often called this part of an oration the *prooemium* (from a phrase meaning "before the song"), and the Latin rhetoricians called this part the *exordium* (from a verb meaning "to begin the web"). The implication behind both terms is the notion of establishing a basis for what follows. As we saw in Chapter 4, **the function of the Introduction is to prepare the readers to receive the message that will be delivered in the middle section of the paper.** The preparation that needs to be done for an argumentative discourse, however, is often more complex and elaborate than it is for the other forms of discourse. While some of the following things sometimes need to be done in narration, description, and exposition, most, if not all, of these preparations are usually necessary in argumentation:

> 1 **Reveal the thesis you are going to argue** (sometimes, however, if you are arguing for an unpopular case, you may find it advisable to conceal your thesis until later in the discourse).
>
> 2 **Define some of your key terms** (if they are strange terms for the audience or if they are familiar terms that you will be using in a special sense).
>
> 3 **Establish your credentials with the audience** (especially if you are unknown to the audience or if you are discussing something that requires some expertise).
>
> 4 **Put your audience in a receptive mood** (especially if the audience is likely to be hostile to you or if you are arguing for an unpopular thesis).

Obviously, *what* you must do and *how much* you must do in the Introduction to an argumentative discourse will depend on the particular rhetorical situation in which you find yourself. There are situations where you need to devote only a single paragraph of three or four sentences to prepare your audience for the subsequent argument. There are other situations where you will have to devote several pages to conditioning your audience.

2. The statement of the issue

In a fairly short paper (3–6 pages), this section might be combined with the Introduction, for its function is, like that of the Introduction, to orient the readers. But in longer, more complex papers, **a separate section might be needed to inform the readers about what is going to be argued in the main part of the paper.** Because of its informative function, this section is fundamentally expository. Usually, no arguing goes on in this section. As the writer, you are simply giving readers more specific information about the case you are going to argue than you gave them in the Introduction.

If you had announced your thesis in the Introduction, you would have let your readers know in a *general* way what you were going to argue. Now, however, you want to give your readers more *specific* background information about what is involved in the controversy you are going to deal with in your paper. One thing you might do in this section to provide your readers with this background is to *give a short history* of the controversy. Another thing you can do is to *list the main issues* that you are going to deal with and maybe *indicate the order* in which you are going to deal with those issues.

The two qualities that should characterize this section are brevity and clarity. Since the primary function of this section is to give your readers the necessary background information about what is going to be discussed in the main part of the paper, it is important that your exposition here be crystal-clear. You do not want to confuse your readers; you want to orient them. And since this section is just another preliminary for the main business of the paper, you should strive to keep it as succinct as you can make it. Take as much space as you need to provide your readers with an adequate background, but do not clutter up this section with superfluous, irrelevant information. It would be difficult to imagine a situation which would require that this section be longer than the argumentative part of the paper.

3. The proof of the case

This section constitutes the heart of the argumentative paper. **In this section, you present the positive arguments that you have selected from the set of arguments that your search-and-discovery process turned up.** In the two previous sections of your paper, you may have stated or implied what your thesis is (a proposition like "Jogging is a health-preserving sport"), and you may have given your readers the necessary background information about this issue. Now you must prove your case. You must convince your readers to accept, and maybe to act upon, the thesis you have proposed.

One of the crucial decisions you will have to make in this section is how to organize the presentation of your arguments. For this task, you can draw upon the decisions about order that you may have made before you began to write. You may have sketched out the order in the form of a *formal outline* or a *block outline* or a simple *listing of steps*.

For example, say that you had selected five arguments to demonstrate your thesis. Here are some questions that you might ask yourself to help you decide the best way to marshal these arguments:

Writing the Various Forms of Discourse

1 Should I put my strong arguments first and then present my weaker arguments, or should I adopt the opposite order, from the weaker to the stronger?

2 Should I first present the arguments that my readers are likely to be familiar with and then present the less familiar arguments—or vice versa?

3 Should I first present the arguments that my readers are likely to be more open to and then present the arguments that they are likely to be more hostile to—or vice versa?

4 Should I adopt an alternating pattern of strong and weak arguments—and end with my strongest argument?

Answers to questions of that sort will vary as the circumstances vary—the subject, the occasion, the purpose, the audience, the mood or personality of the writer. In isolation from a specific case, no hard-and-fast rules can be laid down.

4. The refutation of the opposing case

Having argued positively in support of your own case in the previous section, **you now try to knock the props out from under the opposing arguments.** Here you are arguing negatively; in the previous section you were arguing positively. Demonstrating your thesis can be effected by either confirming your own case or refuting the opposing case or by a combination of confirming and refuting.

So far, we have presumed that the best order for the argumentation is to confirm your own case and then refute the opposing case. But there will be circumstances when the more effective order will be to refute the opposing case first and then present your own case. Recall that one of the common patterns of organization is the one labeled in this book as *Clearing the Ground Before Building*. There will be times when the arguments in support of your contention will get a more receptive hearing from your readers if you first clear the ground of contrary arguments. Usually—but not always of course—it will be a wise strategy for you to demolish these opposing arguments first, especially if they are likely to be more familiar or acceptable to your readers than your own arguments.

5. The conclusion

Buried in the origin of the word *conclusion* is the Latin verb *claudere*, meaning "to shut," the implicit image of which is a closing door or gate. Think of the Conclusion as that part which "closes down" a discourse. That closing serves to terminate the discussion. You could just *stop*, but just as there is an uneasiness about plunging right into the heart of a discussion without any preparation of the readers, so there is a natural uneasiness about closing down the discussion abruptly. An Introduction is a preparation for discussion; a Conclusion is a preparation for silence.

We can repeat here what was said in Chapter 4 about The End or The Conclusion of a discourse. What can be done—what may have to be done—in the Conclusion is one or more of the following:

---

1 **Recapitulate or summarize the main points you have made in the middle section of your paper.**
2 **Make your readers well disposed toward you.**
3 **Make some kind of emotional appeal to your readers.**
4 **Emphasize the crucial importance or the larger dimensions of what you have been talking about.**

Another image that gives us an idea of the function of the Conclusion is the metaphor of "closing the circle." (Recall the title of the popular folk song, "Will the Circle Be Unbroken?") No matter how persuasively you have presented your arguments in the body of your argumentative paper, **you will leave your readers uneasy and unsatisfied if you do not bring the discussion full circle.** Again, what you have to do in the Conclusion and how long you need to make the Conclusion will depend on the situation peculiar to the particular argumentative discourse.

(3) METHODS OF PRESENTING AN ARGUMENTATIVE DISCOURSE

Aristotle maintained that there were three methods of persuasion: (1) appealing to the audience's reason (*logos*); appealing to the audience's emotions (*pathos*); (3) exerting the appeal of the speaker's or writer's character (*ethos*). It is conceivable that you might persuade an audience by relying on only one of these methods of appeal, but it is more likely that you would succeed by relying on some combination of these appeals. One of the appeals might predominate, but in most cases, all three appeals would play a part in effecting persuasion. We will look in some detail at each of these three methods of persuasion.

The rational appeal

There are two basic ways in which you can appeal to reason: **induction** and **deduction**. These two methods work in opposite directions. ***Induction* moves from a consideration of particulars to a generalization or a conclusion. *Deduction* moves from a generalization to a particular and then to a conclusion.**

In *inductive reasoning*, common sense tells you that the more particulars of the same kind that you consider, the stronger—that is, the more valid—your generalization will be. A generalization, for instance, that a certain make of automobile is susceptible to a dangerous breakdown of the steering mechanism is stronger—and therefore more convincing to an audience—if the generalization is based on the discovery of that defect in 187 automobiles of that make rather than in only nineteen. (The audience might regard the breakdowns in only nineteen cars as being just the normal number of such breakdowns in any make of automobile.) Common sense can also serve you in assessing the validity of *deductive reasoning*. You seldom, if ever, encounter deductive reasoning in the form of a full syllogism like the following:

All sports that contribute to cardiovascular development are health-preserving sports.

Jogging is a sport that contributes to cardiovascular development.

Therefore, jogging is a health-preserving sport.

Ordinary citizens, confronted with a deductive argument of that sort, would perhaps respond, ''Well, it sounds okay,'' because they might sense instinctively that the reasoning was valid (they would probably say ''logical'' instead of ''valid''). And by all the formal rules of *logic*, the argument presented in that syllogism *is* valid. If they still did not accept the conclusion that jogging was a health-preserving sport, it would be because they rejected the *truth* of one or other or both of the propositions (called *premises* in logic) preceding the conclusion. But *truth* and *validity* are distinct qualities in reasoning. Truth concerns the *content* of the argument (*is the proposition true or false*?). Validity concerns the *form* of the argument (*was the argument conducted in a logical way*?)

The average person is more likely to encounter deductive reasoning in the form of the **enthymeme**, often called an ''abbreviated syllogism'' because *the conclusion and only one of* *the propositions are stated; the other proposition or premise is left unstated.* The enthymeme form of the syllogistic argument above might be phrased like this:

> Jogging is healthy because it promotes cardiovascular development.

The person who enunciates that argument in that way makes a *claim* (another term for *generalization* or *conclusion*) and then supplies a *reason* or *warrant* (two alternative terms for *premise*) for making that claim. The people who hear or read that enthymeme are expected to supply subconsciously the proposition implicit in that argument: *anything that promotes cardiovascular development is healthy*. They are also expected to subscribe unhesitatingly to the proposition they themselves supply. Because the listeners/readers have, in a sense, participated in the making of the argument, they may be more inclined to be persuaded by it.

It is usually more difficult to detect the fallacy in an enthymeme than in a syllogism, partly because with the enthymeme, one may first have to reconstruct the full syllogistic argument before determining whether the reasoning is valid and the premises are true. But common sense can usually detect at least the most flagrant instances of fallacious reasoning. Even without knowing the rules of a valid syllogism, you can sense that something is wrong with the reasoning in statements like "He must be a jogger because he looks so healthy" or "Yesterday I saw her wearing a pair of running shoes, so she is undoubtedly a jogger."

The same common sense that helps you detect fallacious reasoning should guide you in constructing arguments that will not shock other people's common sense. Short of taking a formal course in logic, you can develop a "rhetoric of good reasons" to guide you in appealing to the reason of your readers. Ultimately, what any kind of rhetoric must rely on to persuade others is a set of *good reasons*. Rhetoric deals with only the *probable* areas of human affairs, and in those areas, scientific proof is often not available. **To persuade others about the probability of something happening, you have to offer good reasons for agreeing with the thesis being argued.**

What do we mean by "good reasons"? We could substitute a number of adjectives for the broad term *good*, each of which would suggest something of what is implicit in the expression "good reasons": *true, valid, sound, realistic, plausible, sensible, just, justifiable, legitimate, pertinent, compelling*. All of us have an instinct for recognizing good reasons in a particular situation. In appealing to the reason (*logos*) of our readers in an argumentative discourse, we must rely on that instinct.

The emotional appeal

What about the appeal to our readers' emotions? First of all, we must rid ourselves of the widespread notion that all appeals to emotions are illegitimate. Appeals to emotions can be inappropriate or overdone, but they are not necessarily illegitimate. In fact, there are situations when we are motivated to do good things more by appeals to our emotions than by appeals to our reason. Appeals to the emotions work mainly on the will. We could be convinced intellectually that it was a good thing to give a pint of our blood to the Red Cross, but the appropriate emotion might have to be stirred to get us to actually give a pint.

Aristotle devoted the major portion of Book II of his *Rhetoric* to analyzing pairs of opposing emotions—for example, anger and mildness, fear and confidence, shame and shamelessness—considering in each case the circumstances in which the emotion is felt, the persons toward whom the emotion is

Writing the Various Forms of Discourse

felt, and the things that arouse or dampen the emotion. You do not have to be a trained psychologist to be able to wield emotions in persuasive discourse. You have experienced emotions yourself, and you have stirred emotions in others; you know, partly from instinct and partly from experience, the intricate mechanism of emotional response. Just as you can often rely on common sense to guide you in constructing rational appeals, so you can rely on your instincts and experiences to guide you in making appropriate emotional appeals as part of the persuasive process.

Your own instincts and experience tell you that you cannot command someone to feel a particular emotion. You cannot say to someone, "Be happy," and expect that person to feel happy. The way to get somebody to feel happy is to *paint a vivid and believable picture* of some person or situation that is likely to arouse happiness in normal human beings.

Emotions can also be subtly aroused by *stylistic means* —mainly by the choice of words and by the rhythms of sentences. Words should be carefully chosen for their emotional connotations. It makes a difference in the emotional impact of a statement whether you call someone "the accused" or "a delinquent" or "a lawbreaker" or "a criminal" or "a thug." If you do not have a rich vocabulary at your command, you can resort to a thesaurus to find synonymous words with the appropriate connotations for the favorable or unfavorable emotional reaction you want to arouse in your readers toward what you are writing about.

Arousing emotions by the *sound effects* of your sentences is a strategy that applies mainly to persuasive discourses delivered in the oral medium, but skillfully constructed sentences can also exert an emotional effect even in the silent medium of print. Developing an ear for the sound and rhythm of sentences is a very sophisticated skill—one of the verbal skills that most writers acquire only after years of practice and that some tone-deaf writers never acquire. The following famous sentence was originally delivered orally by Winston Churchill in a speech to the British House of Commons in June 1940 after the retreat at Dunkirk, but even when you read it today in print, you can be affected emotionally, not only by what is said but also by *how* it is said (see the analysis of this sentence in the section on Some Special Artistic Patterns in Chap. 5):

> We shall go on to the end, we shall fight in France, we shall fight on the seas and oceans, we shall fight with growing confidence and growing strength in the air, we shall defend our Island, whatever the cost may be, we shall fight on the beaches, we shall fight on the landing grounds, we shall fight in the fields and in the streets, we shall fight in the hills; we shall never surrender.

It is not enough, however, to know how to arouse emotions. *You must also develop a sense for judging when an emotional appeal is appropriate and how intense the emotional appeal should be.* One of the reasons for the rather prevalent suspicion about emotional appeals is that some people have resorted to this kind of appeal inappropriately and extravagantly. When you want your readers to make judgments coolly and rationally, you should not be trying to whip up their emotions. And when it is appropriate to stir your readers' emotions, you should not risk spoiling the effect of your emotional appeal by overdoing it. Knowing *when* and *how much* is a delicate skill, which you will have to learn because it cannot be readily taught. One principle about the emotional appeal, however, that can be laid down is that *usually* **you should withhold an emotional appeal until your case has been established by appeals to the readers' reason.** Then the emotional appeal can reinforce, rather than interfere with, the effect of the rational appeal. Especially if you want to persuade your readers to *do* something or to *act* in a certain way, it is advisable to insert the emotional appeal toward the end of the discourse.

The ethical appeal

The ethical appeal, the third of the methods of persuasion that Aristotle talked about, is often the most effective of the appeals. If readers do not respect and trust the writer, they are not going to be persuaded by that writer, no matter how skillful he or she is in managing the appeals to reason and to the emotions. Aristotle maintained that the *ethos* of speakers and writers would be persuasive if the audience perceived them to be persons of *good sense, good moral character,* and *goodwill*.

In argumentative discourse, perhaps more than in any of the other forms, **it is crucial that you come across to your readers as a person of intelligence, integrity, and benevolence—in short, as a person that they can respect and trust.** You might get by sometimes by just *appearing* to be that kind of person, but you would be on the safe side if you actually *were* that kind of person. Remember the old saying: "You can fool some of the people all of the time, all of the people some of the time, but not all of the people all of the time."

How do you become a person of good sense (intelligence), good moral character (integrity), and goodwill (benevolence)? It is not the province of rhetoric to make you that kind of person. Other agencies in our society are charged with that responsibility—the family, religion, the schools. The responsibility of rhetoric is to make you aware of the importance and the potency of the ethical appeal and suggest ways in which you can project an image that can elicit the respect and trust of your readers.

Sometimes in order to establish your *ethos* with your audience, you can explicitly present your credentials to your readers. Often in the Introduction of a discourse, writers give their readers information about themselves—their education, their occupation, their experiences, their interests, their values, their affiliations, etc. It is possible to present your credentials without creating the impression that you are bragging. To say "I always excelled in mathematics in school" might come across to an audience as boasting, but to say "I never received a final grade of less than A-minus in any math course I took in school" is likely to be accepted by an audience as just a sober statement of fact. The general principle to observe in presenting your credentials is this: *let the facts, not your claims, certify your credentials.*

There are other, more subtle, more indirect ways of projecting a favorable image of yourself to your readers. Some of those ways will involve *what* you say in the discourse, and others will involve *how* you say what you say. Your readers will be favorably impressed if what you say shows clearly that you speak with authority because you are knowledgeable about your subject and that the information or judgment you are conveying is accurate, fair, balanced, and thoughtful.

The *what* begins to blend with the *how* when readers begin to make judgments about your sincerity, your confidence, your modesty, your considerateness, your consistency, your altruism, your fairmindedness. If you resort to appeals to reason, readers will expect you to speak truthfully and logically. If you resort to emotional appeals, readers will expect you to be appropriately restrained. Any noticeable extravagance in your efforts to elicit an emotional response from your readers is likely to damage your *ethos*.

Your ethical appeal can also be exerted by your prose style. Style is so subtle in its appeal that many readers are not aware

Writing the Various Forms of Discourse

that part of the favorable impression they get about the writer has been conveyed by the skill with which the writer handles the language. One notion about style that has prevailed down through the ages is that style mirrors the character or the personality of the speaker or writer. Another way to phrase that notion is to say that you express yourself the way you do because of the kind of person you are. You may try to affect a particular kind of style, but if that style does not fit your personality, your readers will eventually see through your mask and will reject your message because they perceive you as a phony.

You should not underestimate the extent to which correct grammar, spelling, mechanics, and punctuation influence readers' estimate of your *ethos*. Because readers expect correctness in these surface features of the written language, they are shocked when they encounter errors in grammar, spelling, mechanics, and punctuation in your writing, and as a result they lose a measure of their confidence in you. For this reason, you cannot afford to be careless or indifferent about these matters. You must also be aware that even a sloppy paper or careless handwriting can diminish readers' respect for you as a writer. And if you lose that respect, you lose a great deal of your effectiveness in persuading your readers.

(4) THE STYLE OF ARGUMENTATIVE DISCOURSE

Argumentative writing probably lends itself to a greater range and variety of styles than do the other three kinds of writing treated in this chapter. Even in the same piece of persuasive prose, writers might have occasion to range from the plainest of styles to the most ornate. The Latin rhetoricians preached that speakers and writers had to be in command of at least three levels of style: (1) the low or plain style, (2) the middle or moderate style, and (3) the high or eloquent style. The plain style was most appropriate when your purpose was to instruct (*docēre*) your readers or to prove (*probare*) something to your readers. The middle or moderate style was most appropriate when your purpose was mainly to please (*delectare*) your readers. And the high or eloquent style was most appropriate when your main purpose was to arouse (*movēre*) your readers to action. Another way in which the three styles were equated was the following: (1) the low style for the rational appeal, (2) the middle style for the ethical appeal, (3) the high style for the emotional appeal.

Versatility

Whether writers must be in command of three styles or six styles or eight styles is a moot question. The main point is that *all writers must have some versatility in style so that they can make the necessary adjustments to fit various audiences, subject matters, occasions, and kinds of discourse.* Argumentative discourse especially seems to encourage writers to "sing" in a variety of keys, since it is the most audience-oriented of the forms of writing. For instance, you would have to make some adjustments in the level and tone of your style if the piece of argumentation that you originally wrote for an audience of college students had to be revised to appeal to a group of state legislators. A proposal that was going to be judged for funding by a board of electrical engineers could be written in a more technical style than if it was going to be judged by the Board of Directors. The more homogeneous your group of readers is, the easier it is to settle on a style that will fit the audience. The larger your audience is, the more likely it is that the audience will be heterogeneous, and the harder it will be to find a style that will fit the full range of readers. **When in doubt, use the plain style.**

Writing the Various Forms of Discourse

Exposition, description, narration

Argumentative discourse is also the kind of writing that is most likely to make use of exposition, description, and narration in various sections of the discourse. Those sections are therefore likely to exhibit many of the stylistic features that we have pointed out earlier as being characteristic of exposition, description, and narration. So when you are incorporating one or other of these three in your argumentative paper, you may find it helpful to review the sections of this chapter that deal with the styles peculiar to these forms.

Emotion

Since, as we have seen, emotion plays a legitimate part in argumentative discourse, we are likely to find in this kind of discourse those stylistic devices that stir emotions. Words are very likely to be chosen primarily for their connotative value—favorable connotations when you are talking about things or situations or persons that you want your readers to be well disposed toward and unfavorable connotations when you are trying to elicit antagonistic reactions. Figures of speech and special artistic patterns of sentences (see Chap. 5) usually play a prominent part in argumentative discourse, not only because they enliven the prose and therefore catch the attention of readers but also because of the emotional impact of this kind of language. Unusually skillful writers will exert some of their emotional appeal through the rhythm of their sentences, and to achieve those affective kinds of rhythms, they will deliberately use such devices as parallel structures, repetitive patterns, series of triplets, lots of polysyllabic words made up of pleasant-sounding combinations of consonants and vowels.

"I" & "you"

Because of the close writer/reader relationships in argumentative discourse, the pronouns *I* and *you* are likely to occur frequently. Since the ethical appeal plays such an important part in argumentative discourse, we are not surprised by the intrusions of the author's voice and personality into the discourse. So we do not resent the frequent occurrence of *I*, and we are perhaps flattered by the frequent occurrence of *you*. The bond between the writer and the readers is finally cemented when the writer starts to use the pronoun *we*. The *we* signals the writer's assurance of having achieved identification with the audience. When that kind of community has been achieved, readers no longer resent the frequent intrusion of the imperative mood of the verb—"Do this, do that," "Vote for me," "Pass this tax levy," "Buy this product."

Because argumentative discourse demands so much stylistic finesse and versatility, the writer who is effective in this mode of discourse usually has the stylistic resourcefulness to operate successfully in the three other modes.

Chapter 8
Special Kinds of Writing Assignments

This chapter will deal with the rhetoric of three special kinds of writing assignments—writing about *literature*, writing *essay examinations*, and writing *reports*. Like the four kinds of writing dealt with in the previous chapter, these also involve the processes of **finding, selecting, arranging,** and **expressing.** What makes them "special" is either that they deal with a particular kind of subject-matter or that they follow certain conventions of style and form.

Whole courses are devoted to two of these kinds of writing—writing about literature and writing reports—and this little book cannot deal with all of their details and technicalities. However, it will show the highlights of these special kinds of writing assignments. In connection with writing about literature, it will explain some of the techniques of fiction, drama, and poetry and suggest questions you can ask yourself as you search for something to say about a literary text. In connection with writing essay examinations, it will give practical advice about how to improve your performance in this kind of writing under pressure. And in connection with writing reports, it will discuss some of the special considerations governing this kind of writing and will discuss the parts and organization of a typical formal report.

● Writing about literature

In a literature course, you will certainly be asked to write papers about literary texts that you have read—poems, plays, essays, short stories, novels. The course will acquaint you with various ways of reading and discussing literary texts. Some of the classroom discussions will deal with the **content** of the text—*what is said? what is implied? what happens? what does it mean? is it worth our attention?* Other discussions will be concerned with the **form** of the text—*what type of literature are we dealing with?* (poem? play? short story? novel? essay?); if a *poem*, for instance, *what kind of poem?* (lyric? epic? narrative? descriptive? didactic? satirical?); if a *lyric* poem, for instance, *what special form of lyric?* (sonnet? ode? ottava rima?); *what special verse form is the lyric written in?* (iambic pentameter? blank verse? free verse?).

Whether you talk about the content or the form, your principal reference will be the text itself. You can supplement what the text tells you with what your other reading or experience tells you about the history of the text, about the type of literature, about the author, about the period when the text was written, about the original audience.

Classroom lectures and discussions are designed to teach you how to read, understand, appreciate, and evaluate a literary text. But eventually, you will be asked to write out your response to a literary text. You will not be expected—in fact,

Special Kinds of Writing Assignments

you may be forbidden—to do any research (that is, to read what others have said about the text). (That kind of response to a literary text will be dealt with in the next chapter, in the section on writing the research paper.) Instead, you will be expected to present, in a well-organized essay, your *own* response out of your *own* literary awareness. You will be asked to give the kind of response—but more fully and more coherently—that you give to a friend who asks you, "How did you like the movie last night?" Your immediate response to that question might be, "It was great." But then you might go on to tell your friend what the movie was about or to comment on the unusual way in which the movie was put together or on some of the special effects created by the photography or on the acting or on the theme of the movie.

In writing about literature, you will be engaged in one or more of the following activities:

☐ **analyzing the work**

☐ **interpreting the work**

☐ **evaluating the work**

In **analyzing the work,** you will be answering one or both of these general questions: *what is the work about? how is the work put together?* In **interpreting the work,** you will be answering these general questions: *what did the author mean? what does the work mean to you?* In **evaluating the work,** you will be answering one or both of these general questions: *how well did the author accomplish what he or she set out to do? was the work worth your time and attention?*

A series of questions will be given in this section, questions that could give you some ideas of what to say in a paper about a literary text. You might be able to write a 3–4-page paper in response to a single question. Or you might make use of five or six (or more) questions in writing your paper. You might find that some questions yield more material when applied to one kind of literary work (a short story, for instance) than they do when applied to other kinds. Or you might find that it is easier for you to write in response to questions about the *what* of a work (the content) than it is to write about the *how* of the work (the form). Use the questions that work best for *you*. Eventually, you may be able to invent questions that work better for you than any of those in the text. Whatever questions you use, think of them as devices to help you *find something to say* about a literary text.

●
Analyzing a literary work

General Questions to Be Answered in *Analyzing a Literary Work*
What is the work about? (content) and/or
How is the work put together? (form)

What kind of work is it?

One way to respond to that question is to **classify the work according to its literary type:** *poem, short story, novel, essay, play.* But once you determine the general type, you may want to **classify it more particularly.** For instance, if you are dealing with a novel, you may want to indicate what kind of novel it is: a detective story (Agatha Christie's *Who Murdered Roger Ackroyd?*), an adventure story (Mark Twain's *Huckleberry Finn*), a ghost story (Henry James's *The Turn of the Screw*), a war story (Ernest Hemingway's *A Farewell to Arms*), a political novel (George Orwell's *1984*), a social novel (John Steinbeck's

Special Kinds of Writing Assignments

The Grapes of Wrath), a novel about "growing up" (J. D. Salinger's *Catcher in the Rye*).

If you are dealing with a poem, you may want to indicate whether it is a narrative poem (an epic like Homer's *Iliad* or a ballad like "Bonnie Barbara Allan") or a didactic poem (a poem that "teaches," like Alexander Pope's *An Essay on Criticism* or Karl Shapiro's *Essay on Rime*) or a descriptive poem (a poem that pictures a scene, like Matthew Arnold's "Dover Beach"), a satirical poem (John Dryden's "MacFlecknoe"), a poem of social protest (William Blake's "The Chimney Sweeper" or Allan Ginsberg's "Howl"), a lyric poem (any one of a wide variety of poems in which the "voice" in the poem gives vent to thoughts or emotions about an intense personal experience).

If you are dealing with a play, you may want to say whether it is a tragedy (Shakespeare's *Hamlet* or Arthur Miller's *Death of a Salesman*), a comedy (Oliver Goldsmith's *She Stoops to Conquer* or Eugene O'Neill's *Ah, Wilderness!*), or a historical play (Shakespeare's *Richard III* or Robert Sherwood's *Abe Lincoln in Illinois*).

There are, of course, more types of poems, plays, and fiction than are named above, and there are many variations of the types that are named. Your literature courses will acquaint you with these additional types and variations.

What happens or what is said?

If you are dealing with a short story, novel, play, or narrative poem, one way to respond to this question is to give a **summary of the plot.** The *plot* is the sequence of actions or events in a story—first this happened, then this happened, then this happened, etc. If you ever wrote a school "book report," one of the things you may have been asked to do, in order to prove that you read the book, was to retell the story in your own words. In college, a paper in which you gave only a summary of the plot would probably be unacceptable. But you might be allowed to give a *brief* summary of what happened as the basis for your discussion of some other aspect of the work. And you certainly would be allowed to cite incidents from the story as examples of, or support for, some point you were making about it.

If you are dealing with a poem other than a narrative poem, you can't respond to this question by summarizing the plot, because there is no plot to summarize. What you do in that case is talk about the "what is said" part of the question. You **paraphrase** the poem—that is, you tell *in your own words* what the poet said in the verse lines. Let's look at a short poem, a sonnet by John Keats, and then at a paraphrase of it:

On First Looking into Chapman's Homer

Much have I travell'd in the realms of gold,
And many goodly states and kingdoms seen;
Round many western islands have I been
Which bards in fealty to Apollo hold.
Oft of one wide expanse had I been told
That deep-brow'd Homer ruled as his demesne;
Yet did I never breathe its pure serene
Till I heard Chapman speak out loud and bold:
Then felt I like some watcher of the skies
When a new planet swims into his ken;
Or like Cortez when with eagle eyes
He star'd at the Pacific—and all his men
Look'd at each other with a wild surmise—
Silent, upon a peak in Darien.

Special Kinds of Writing Assignments

PARAPHRASE

In this sonnet, the poet tells us how he felt when he read Homer's *Odyssey* for the first time in Chapman's English translation. He could have told us how he felt in straight-forward literal language ("I was excited, awestruck"), but instead he tells us how he felt by using the two metaphors of *travel* and *discovery*. In the first eight lines, under the metaphor of travel, he tells us that he had read many of the Greek and Roman poets in translation but because he couldn't read Greek, he never read Homer's epic until he came across Chapman's translation. In the last six lines, using the metaphor of discovery, he tells us what the effect of that experience was. It was like the excitement that an astronomer feels when he sees a new planet through his telescope. It was like the astonishment that Cortez (actually it was Balboa) and his men felt when they stood on a mountain in Mexico and caught their first glimpse of the Pacific ocean.

What is the source of conflict?

The basic element in all story-telling—what holds our attention and keeps us turning the pages—is **conflict.** Conflict results from some kind of problem, struggle, or tension facing the characters in the short story, the novel, or the play. The conflict may take the form of physical action (a fight, a shoot-out, a race, a journey). Or it may take the form of a verbal contest between two or more characters (an argument, a clash of opinions or ideologies, a debate about values). Or it could take the form of some kind of psychological struggle (a character debating with himself or herself about a crucial decision, a character struggling to solve some kind of problem or mystery). **Whatever form the conflict takes, it is basically a struggle**

between two forces, and the more nearly the opposing forces are equal, the greater the drama, the more eager we are to read on in order to find out how the struggle comes out.

Conflict is an element you discuss when you are dealing with fiction and drama, but in dealing with some poems, you could talk about how the speaker in the poem resolved the psychological or spiritual *tension* he or she was experiencing.

What kind of characters appear?

You could write an entire paper in response to this question. Often it is the characters, rather than the plot, that most interest us. If a storyteller is especially skillful, the characters become even more *real* to us than people we know in our daily lives, and we can talk about them as though they were *real* people. They are men or women, young or old, noble or base, aggressive or timid, likable or unappealing, intelligent or stupid. We can picture what they look like, how they dress, how they carry themselves. We hear their voices and what they say, and sometimes we are even allowed inside their heads to find out what they are thinking. We care about what happens to them. If they are sympathetic characters, we want to see them succeed or survive; if they are "wicked" characters, we want to see them defeated, shamed, or routed.

Such an infinite number of things could be said about characters in a story, a play, or even a poem that it is hardly necessary to suggest specific aspects that could be discussed. *Just talk about characters as you would about people in real life.*

How does the author characterize the people in the work?

Special Kinds of Writing Assignments

We spoke in the previous section about how lifelike people in stories become for us. How does an author create lifelike people and give us an idea of what kind of people they are? Here are the principal means of characterization:

☐ **By actions**—*what people do and how they do it.*

☐ **By speech**—*what people say and how they say it.*

☐ **By description**—their *physical appearance* (facial features, weight, height, stature, carriage) and their *manner of dress.*

☐ **By testimony**—*what others say about a person.*

☐ **By thoughts**—*what a person thinks and feels* (all those *interior* reactions that reveal so much about a person—speculations, dreams, rationalization, reveries, emotions, etc.).

☐ **By exposition**—*a summary sketch by the author.*

An author may use all of these means to give us an idea of what kind of people the characters are, but he or she will probably use two or three of them more than others.

What is the setting?

Every story is acted out in a particular place and time. You may want to talk about that setting, either for its own sake or for its function in the story. You may find the setting interesting for its own sake because it transports you to a faraway place and a long-ago time; or you may find the setting interesting simply because it is familiar and contemporary. In either case, the author's descriptions help you to visualize the scene.

But sometimes you are interested in the setting because it plays an important part in the drama of a story. The setting becomes more than just a place and time in which the action occurs; it becomes **atmosphere,** helping to set the mood and the tension in the story. Recall how important setting and atmosphere are in a ghost story or an adventure story. Setting and atmosphere usually play a dominant role, for instance, in the stories of Edgar Allan Poe and Joseph Conrad. In the following description of a bridal chamber in Poe's story "Ligeia," the reader gets not only a vivid picture of the setting and atmosphere but also a strong sense that something tragic will happen in that room (as indeed it does later in the story):

> The room lay in a high turret of the castellated abbey, was pentagonal in shape, and of capacious size. Occupying the whole southern face of the pentagon was the sole window—an immense sheet of unbroken glass from Venice —a single pane, and tinted of a leaden hue, so that the rays of either the sun or moon passing through it fell with a ghastly lustre on the objects within. Over the upper portion of this huge window extended the trellis-work of an aged vine, which clambered up the massy walls of the turret. The ceiling, of gloomy-looking oak, was excessively lofty, vaulted, and elaborately fretted with the wildest and most grotesque specimens of a semi-Gothic, semi-Druidical device. From out the most central recess of this melancholy vaulting depended, by a single chain of gold with long links, a huge censer of the same metal, Saracenic in pattern, and with many perforations so contrived that there writhed in and out of them, as if endued with a serpent vitality, a continual succession of parti-colored fires.

Descriptions of setting can also tell us something about the characters. A messy room, for instance, tells us something about the habits of the occupant of that room; a room with floor-to-ceiling bookshelves laden with leather-bound volumes tells us something about the interests of the occupant of that room.

Special Kinds of Writing Assignments

The next time you see a movie or a television drama, make a special effort to study the setting. Try to figure out what part that setting is playing in the drama you are watching and what that setting tells you about the characters associated with it.

What is the style of the work?

Although you may not have paid much attention to the *style* of a literary work, the style does exert a subtle influence on you. If you have ever remarked about the style, you may have said things like the following.

The author's style is easy to understand.

The sentences flow smoothly and gracefully.

I felt the power of the author's style.

She uses lots of short, vivid, sensory words.

Metaphors keep tumbling at you so fast you can't absorb them all.

I was so bored by the heavy, plodding sentences that I skipped over dozens of pages at a time.

Except for the two statements that mention *words* and *metaphors*, the statements are rather general and impressionistic. In your paper, you may want to give only your general impressions of the author's style, but if you want to be more specific in your commentary on the style, you can do some counting and tabulating of features like the following:

☐ **The average sentence length in number of words**
(you get this average by dividing the total number of words by the total number of sentences; if, for instance, you counted 150 sentences and found a total of 3678 words, you would have an average sentence-length of 24.5 words per sentence).

☐ **The average paragraph length, figured either in average number of words per paragraph or in average number of sentences per paragraph**

(if there were 20 paragraphs in the 3678-word sample, you would have an average of 183.9 words per paragraph and an average of 7.5 sentences per paragraph).

☐ **The percentage of single-syllable words in a 200-word sample**

(you get this average by dividing the total number of single-syllable words by 200; if you found 136 single-syllable words in 200 words, the percentage would be 68%).

☐ **The number or percentage of nouns and pronouns in a 200-word sample**

(you could also determine the number and percentage of verbs, adjectives, and adverbs in the same 200-word sample, although it might be more significant to determine the relative proportions of active verbs and passive verbs or of concrete nouns and abstract nouns).

☐ **The number and kinds of figures of speech in a selected passage**

(see the list and definitions of figures of speech in Chapter 5).

There are some finer points of style that you might look at, like sentence rhythms, parallel structures, symbols, imagery, but the five features listed above are the easier features to find and catalogue, *if* you want to say something specific about an author's style in a short story, novel, play, or poem.

How is the work organized and structured?

As we saw in the discussion of nonfictional narratives in the previous chapter, the basic organizing principle in fictional nar-

Special Kinds of Writing Assignments

ratives (short stories, novels, plays, narrative poems) is **time** (*chronology*)—first this happened, then this happened, then that happened; in other words, the incidents in a story are arranged in the order in which they happened. But sometimes stories depart from a straight time-sequence. An author may halt the forward movement of the story to give us a **flashback**—something that took place before the time when the story begins. Or the author may give us a **foreshadowing**—a hint of something that will happen later in the story.

The basic structure of a story follows this pattern:

1 **Posing the basic conflict of the story.**

2 **Complicating or intensifying the basic conflict**—making the situation get worse.

3 **Reaching the climax**—the point of highest dramatic intensity in the story, the point in the story where the conflict is finally resolved.

4 **Winding down the story**—usually very short, sometimes called the *anticlimax* or *denouement* ("the unknotting").

But some stories depart from this basic structure. A story might begin with the "end," for instance—a man being stood up before a firing squad—and then it would go back to the "beginning" to show you the sequence of events that brought the man to that critical moment. Television dramas often begin with an exciting incident that occurs later on in the story; the TV producers want to "hook" the viewers and prevent them from turning to another channel.

A number of typographical devices are used to mark off the parts of literary works. Novels are likely to be broken up into chapters. The parts of short stories are sometimes marked with roman numerals (I, II, III, etc.) or simply with extra space on the page between parts. Plays are usually marked off into Acts and Scenes (often with two or more scenes in each act). Poems are often marked off in stanzas—groupings of lines with extra space between each group. The thought structure of a sonnet, a fourteen-line poem, often observes one of these patterns:

1 The **Italian** or **Petrarchan sonnet:** a two-part structure composed of the first eight lines, called the *octave*, and the concluding six lines, called the *sestet*. (John Keats's "On First Looking into Chapman's Homer" has this structure.)

2 The **Shakespearean** or **Elizabethan sonnet:** a structure of *three quatrains* (three groups of four lines) and a *concluding couplet* (a group of two lines).

There are many other stanzaic patterns, which you will meet in literature courses that study poetry.

You probably won't feel the need to comment on the organization and structure of a narrative unless the story presents interesting variations of the basic time-sequence. There are some other interesting variations of structure besides *flashbacks* and *foreshadowing*. Sometimes a novel that involves several groups or families of interrelated people will use an **alternating** or **interweaving** pattern—one chapter will present an incident involving one group, the next chapter the second group, the next chapter the third group, and then the next chapter will resume the story of the first group, etc. Sometimes authors interrupt the forward movement of the novel by throwing in an *interchapter* every now and then—a chapter that deals with something other than the story. In *Tom Jones*, Henry Fielding has interchapters that deal with the art of fiction; in *Moby Dick*, Herman Melville frequently interrupts his narrative with interchapters dealing with whales and the whaling in-

Special Kinds of Writing Assignments

dustry; in *The Grapes of Wrath*, John Steinbeck throws in inter-chapters that deal with the larger social implications of the poverty of the sharecroppers during the dust-bowl years in the 1930s. It is variations like these that you may want to comment on in your paper.

What is the point of view from which the story is told?

The point of view is the consciousness, the filter, through which the events in a story come through to the reader. Another way to get at the point of view is to ask yourself "Who is telling the story?" or "Through whose eyes do we see the action of the story?" Point of view is a factor only in short stories, novels, and narrative poems. There is no point of view involved in a play, a movie, or a television drama, because there is no one standing between us, the viewers, and the events being acted out.

There are four points of view from which a story can be told—two of them *interior* points of view, two of them *exterior* points of view:

(1) INTERIOR (told by a character *in* the story)

(A) First-Person Point of View

This is the easiest of the points of view to distinguish. It is a major or minor character in the story who is referred to in the narrative parts (that is, the non-dialogue parts) of the story by the pronoun *I* (hence the term *first-person*). This first-person narrator can report anything that the *I* can see or hear or know, can give us the *I*'s thoughts, but cannot give us the thoughts or inward reactions of any other characters in the story.

Here is an example of the first-person point of view. The *I* (*me*) here is Huck Finn, the hero of Mark Twain's novel *Huckleberry Finn*:

> After supper she got out her book and learned me about Moses and the Bulrushers, and I was in a sweat to find out all about him; but by and by, she let it out that Moses had been dead a considerable long time; so then I didn't care no more about him, because I don't take no stock in dead people.
>
> Pretty soon I wanted to smoke, and asked the widow to let me. But she wouldn't. She said it was a mean practice and wasn't clean, and I must try to not do it any more. That is just the way with some people. They get down on a thing when they don't know nothing about it. Here she was a-bothering about Moses, which was no kin to her, and no use to anybody, being gone, you see, yet finding a power of fault with me for doing a thing that had some good in it. And she took snuff, too; of course that was all right, because she done it herself.

(B) Third-Person Point of View

This is a major or minor character in the story, who is referred to, in the narrative parts of the story, by his or her name (James Stokes, Nancy Reems) or by the pronoun *he* or *she* (hence the term *third-person*). This narrator can report anything that he or she can see or hear or know, can give us his or her thoughts, but cannot give us the thoughts or inward reactions of any other characters in the story.

In the following example of the third-person point of view, the *he* (*his, him*) is a high-school boy named William, who is the main character of John Updike's short story "A Sense of Shelter":

Special Kinds of Writing Assignments

> When he emerged into the hall it was not empty: one girl
> walked down its varnished perspective toward him, Mary
> Landis, in a heavy brown coat, with a scarf on her head
> and books in her arms. Her locker was up here, on the
> second floor of the annex. His own was in the annex base-
> ment. A ticking sensation that existed neither in the
> medium of sound nor of light crowded against his throat.
> She flipped the scarf back from her hair and in a conversa-
> tional voice that carried well down the clean planes of the
> hall said, "Hi, Billy." The name came from way back,
> when they were both children, and made him feel small
> but brave.

> [From *Pigeon Feathers and Other Stories* (New York: Alfred A.
> Knopf, 1962), pp. 94–95]

(2) EXTERIOR (told from a consciousness or vantage-point *outside* the story)

(A) Omniscient Point of View

This is an all-knowing, godlike consciousness outside the
story that is unlimited in what it can report. In addition to being
able to tell us anything that is taking place or has taken place,
the omniscient narrator can give us the thoughts and inward
reactions of all of the characters but may choose to give us the
thoughts and reactions of only one of them. If the thoughts of
more than one character are exposed, you know for sure that
the story is being told from the omniscient point of view.

If the thoughts of only one character are exposed, you can
distinguish the omniscient point of view by noting whether you
are given information that a first-person or third-person narrator
could not or would not give you. For instance, if a story is being
told by a first-person or third-person narrator, you will not get a

description of the physical appearance of that narrator (unless he or she is looking in a mirror and reporting the image seen there). So if you get a physical description of a character in addition to an exposure of his or her thoughts or if you get some information that the narrator would not or could not supply, you know that the story is being told by an omniscient narrator.

In the following example of the omniscient point of view, from Edith Wharton's short story "Roman Fever," note the information or commentary we get about the two women from some *outside* source ("the two ladies, who had been intimate since childhood"; "Mrs. Ansley was much less articulate than her friend") and the exposure of the thoughts of *both* women:

> Mrs. Slade drew her lids together in retrospect; and for a few moments the two ladies, who had been intimate since childhood, reflected how little they knew each other. Each one, of course, had a label ready to attach to the other's name; Mrs. Delphin Slade, for instance, would have told herself, or any one who asked her, that Mrs. Horace Ansley, twenty-five years ago, had been exquisitely lovely—no, you wouldn't believe it, would you? . . . though, of course, still charming, distinguished. . . . Mrs. Ansley was much less articulate than her friend, and her mental portrait of Mrs. Slade was slighter, and drawn with fainter touches. "Alida Slade's awfully brilliant; but not as brilliant as she thinks," would have summed it up; though she would have added, for the enlightenment of strangers, that Mrs. Slade had been an extremely dashing girl; much more so than her daughter, who was pretty, of course, and clever in a way, but had none of her mother's—well, "vividness," someone had once called it.
>
> [from *The World Over* (New York: D. Appleton-Century, 1936), p. 219]

Special Kinds of Writing Assignments

(B) Objective or "Camera-eye" Point of View

Think of this point of view as a motion-picture camera equipped to record sound. This point of view is restricted to reporting only what can be recorded on film and on sound-tape. It cannot, and does not, report the thoughts of any of the characters. The camera-eye point of view relays to the reader only what is done or said or can be seen, without any commentary or background information.

Outside of the script for a play or a movie, it is difficult to find a *pure* example of the objective or camera-eye point of view. Occasionally, authors will use the objective point of view in parts of their story but then shift to one of the other three points of view. In the first half of his long short story "Big Boy Leaves Home," Richard Wright uses the objective point of view, but after Big Boy kills the white man at the swimming-hole, Wright shifts to the third-person point of view of Big Boy. Most of Ernest Hemingway's famous short story, "The Killers," is told from the objective point of view, but after the scene shifts from Henry's lunchroom to Ole Anderson's rooming-house, we see and hear things from Nick Adams's point of view, although the story continues to be told largely through dialogue.

The objective point of view that we observe in these paragraphs of George Milburn's novel *Catalogue* prevails throughout the story:

> The sun was blistering the sanded green paint on the M. K. & T. railway station. A gray farm wagon drawn by two mousy mules turned up the dust-cushioned road and came gritting along the graveled platform. It stopped on the shady east side of the depot. The driver eased his blue hulk to the ground and went into the waiting room for Whites.
>
> He gaped a moment at the empty slat benches. Flies droned against the paint-sealed windows. There was a

muffled chatter of telegraph in the room beyond. The ticket window was shut; so he lumbered on through to the sunny side of the station. He went round and stuck his head in at the Negro waiting room, off which the office door opened.

"Hello, Mr. Conklin! Hello!" he bawled.

[from *Catalogue* (New York: Harcourt, Brace, 1936), pp. 194–195]

Why did the author choose this point of view from which to tell the story?

The previous question could be answered in a single sentence—e.g. "Mark Twain tells his story from the first-person point of view of the main character, Huck Finn." A more important question and one that would take you at least a full paragraph to answer adequately is the question "Why did the author choose this particular point of view for his story?"

The choice of point of view determines not only *what* can be narrated to us but also *what effect* the story could have on us. A change in point of view could result in a different story and a different effect. Some authors have experimented with telling the same story from a variety of points of view. In *The Sound and the Fury*, for instance, William Faulkner tells the same story four times, each time from the perspective of a different character in the story—Benjy, Quentin, Jason, and Dilsey.

Perhaps the most important decision that a fiction writer makes is the choice of point of view, because that point of view determines what can, and what cannot, be told to us and what effect the story could have upon us. A detective story, for instance, cannot be told from the omniscient point of view, because an all-knowing narrator would know "whodunit" right from the outset and could not withhold that information from the reader. Detective stories are usually told from the

Special Kinds of Writing Assignments

third-person or the first-person point of view, and that first-person or third-person narrator is usually the detective who is trying to solve the mystery. Detective stories can also be told—and sometimes have been told—from the objective or camera-eye point of view. (In that case, the story would be told in much the same manner as it is told in a movie or in a television drama.)

An author will choose the omniscient narrator when the drama of his story depends on the exposure of the thoughts of more than one character, because omniscience is the *only* point of view that allows the thoughts of more than one character to be exposed. Or an author might choose the omniscient point of view if it is necessary to supply vital background information about characters or situations that could not or would not come naturally from a character within the story.

An author who has a tale of strange and exotic adventure to tell will often choose the first-person point of view, because readers more easily believe a tale of adventure told by an eyewitness. An author who wants to gain some distancing from the intensely personal tone of the I point of view will adopt the third-person point of view. An author who wants to tell a story from a completely impersonal point of view, without any interpretive or influencing commentary by a narrator will adopt the objective point of view.

One of the ways in which to approach the answer to the question "Why did the author choose this point of view from which to tell this story?" is to **imagine what the story and its effect might have been if the author had told the story from one of the other three points of view.**

A word needs to be said here about the *psychological viewpoint* of the narrator. Sometimes the narrator in the story gives the events *as* they are happening or *shortly after* they happened; at other times, the narrator presents episodes from a perspective many years removed from the time when they actually took place. In a story about childhood, for instance, it makes a big difference whether the story is being told as the child is experiencing it or whether it is being told by an adult looking back on an experience he or she had as a child. A child and an adult are bound to have different perspectives on what happened, and this *difference in perspective* can make a profound difference in what is reported to the readers and in the effect the narrative has on them.

●

Interpreting a literary work

General Questions to Be Answered in *Interpreting a Literary Work*

What did the *author* mean? (*objective* interpretation) and/or

What did the work mean to *you*? (*subjective* interpretation)

The *analysis* of a literary work tries to discover *what is there*—either in the content or in the form. The *interpretation* of a literary work seeks to discover the *meaning or significance of what is there*. Obviously, analysis must precede interpretation. You don't have to analyze the work *totally* before you can proceed to interpretation, but at least you must first discover that portion of the work that you are going to interpret.

Sometimes when you are assigned to write a paper on a literary text, you are not expected to analyze the work—at least not in the paper itself—but instead you are asked to interpret the work or a part of the work. What you are being asked to do is explain *what the author meant* (**objective interpretation**) and/or *what the work means to you* (**subjective interpretation**). The two meanings do not *necessarily* differ; the meaning

Special Kinds of Writing Assignments

you derive from the work could be the same meaning that the author intended.

But usually when you are asked to discuss what the work means to you, you are being asked to discuss a different kind of meaning from the meaning of the text itself. You are being asked for your *personal response* to the work: how the work relates to your life, your experiences, your views, your values. Presumably, there is one *objective* meaning to the text—or at least the author intended one meaning—and we should be able to discover what that one meaning is. But there could be as many *subjective* meanings as there are readers of the text, because the significance of a work for various readers will differ because of different experiences, education, attitudes, values, etc. For that reason, the subjective interpretations cannot be judged *right* or *wrong* or *good, better, best;* they can only be viewed as *different.*

In order to focus your interpretation, the teacher, in making the assignment, may pose a question (or questions) to guide you. Listed below are some typical questions that could guide you in writing an interpretive paper on a short story, novel, play, or poem. These questions cannot be easily separated into those that are concerned with the Author's Meaning (objective) and those that are concerned with the Meaning to You (subjective). There is a sense, of course, in which all interpretation can be said to be subjective, because it represents what *you* think the words mean. But some interpretations will appear to be more objective than others because they are self-evident or because the author has been explicit about the meaning or because there is clear evidence in the text to support a particular interpretation. Whenever a critic has to *argue* that a particular interpretation is likely or tenable, we are probably getting a relatively subjective interpretation. Whether the answers to any of the following questions are objective or subjective will largely depend on how much indisputable evidence can be ad-duced from the text to support the interpretation. If the interpretation is mainly expository, it is probably objective; if the interpretation is mainly argumentative, it is probably subjective.

Some of the questions, especially those mentioning characters and incidents, apply only to narratives (short stories, novels, and plays). Regard the parentheses in some of the questions as *blanks* in which could be put the names of particular characters, incidents, objects, etc.

What is the theme of the work?

As in the case of expository and argumentative writing, so too does imaginative writing have a theme. This theme may not be formally stated in the work, as it often is in expository or argumentative writing, but it is there just the same. **You may have to deduce the theme from the work.** This theme enunciates a supposed "truth about life" that the reader has learned from reading the literary work. The theme, for instance, of a story about young love might be this: "When two people are head over heels in love, they are not likely to heed the advice of parents, relatives, or friends"; or it might be this: "A man in love will strive relentlessly to overcome every obstacle that separates him from his loved one." Those are only two of dozens of themes that a story about young love could have. Think of the theme as a general statement about the *meaning* or *significance* of a work.

In what way is (a particular incident or passage) related to the theme of the work?

If a theme is a summary statement of what the parts of a work add up to, individual incidents or passages should be

Special Kinds of Writing Assignments

somehow related to that theme. If, for instance, a story about young love had as its theme, "When two people are head over heels in love with one another, they are not likely to heed the advice of parents, relatives, and friends," a particular incident in that story could be a concrete illustration of two young lovers ignoring the advice of the girl's father. Other incidents or passages in the story could be illustrations of the same theme but in a different way.

What did (a particular character) mean when he/she said, "(quotation of the statement)."

Sometimes you will be asked to interpret the meaning of a particular sentence or sentences. Usually, it will be a passage in which the meaning is not apparent but which has an important bearing on the theme or on the relationships of the characters or on the course of the action. You will have to derive the meaning from the context—who was saying what to whom for what purpose?

What is the symbolism of (a particular event or object in the work)?

Sometimes an author intends certain events or objects to have a larger meaning than their surface meaning. For instance, a ticking clock that keeps getting mentioned at crucial moments in a story could become something more than just a ticking clock: it could symbolize that time is running out for a particular character and could foreshadow the death of that character. There's danger, of course, in "symbol-hunting." Readers on the lookout for symbols begin to see symbols everywhere—even when an author didn't intend any symbolism. But an author who intends something to be symbolic usually gives us hints, such as frequent occurrence or unusual prominence of the symbolic event or object.

What patterns do you find in the (incidents, characters, diction, figures of speech)?

Sometimes authors deliberately arrange various elements in patterns or motifs. For instance, they might set up incidents in the story in a counterpointing pattern: scenes of hope alternating with scenes of despair; scenes of hectic urban life alternating with scenes of placid rural life. Characters too fall into balancing groups: male and female, achievers and failures, idealists and pessimists, intellectuals and nonintellectuals, and (the common grouping in westerns) "good guys" and "bad guys" or "white hats" and "black hats." Patterns or motifs of language frequently appear in literary texts—the images of disease in *Hamlet*; the variations on the words *nothing* and *nature* in *King Lear*; the motif of *light* in Wordsworth's "Ode on Intimations of Immortality" (*glory, sunshine, starry, gleam, radiance, moon, splendor*). It is usually easier to find and demonstrate patterns of this kind than to detect and interpret symbols.

How is the ending of the work related to other parts of the work?

What this question is asking you to do is to show that the ending follows naturally, plausibly, or inevitably from the other events in the work. Sometimes we are left unsatisfied with the ending of a story because it seems arbitrary, contrived, unexpected. In other stories, even in those that end unhappily (like

Special Kinds of Writing Assignments

the tragic death of Cordelia in *King Lear*), we are satisfied because the story ended in the way that the previous incidents dictated that it *must* end.

Why did (a particular character) do what he/she did?

This question concerns motivation. When we observe characters in action in a story, we are interested not only in what they do and how they do it but also in *why* they do what they do. Were they motivated by some circumstance? by what some other character did? by some trait in their character? Because the motivation of a character is not always made apparent by the author, we have to arrive at the motivation by interpretation of character and situation. We must be satisfied that the motivation we discover through interpretation is psychologically sound—that is, that it gives a plausible explanation for the character's doing what he or she does.

What kind of person is (a particular character in a story or the persona that speaks in a poem)?

In the section on analyzing a literary work, we saw the various ways by which an author characterizes the people who appear in the work—by **action, speech, description, thoughts,** and **exposition.** We form our idea of what kind of person the character is from whichever of those means the author uses. One way to answer this question is to write a character sketch that summarizes the traits of that "created" person. It is a bit more difficult to get an idea of the persona that speaks in a poem, because our only source of information about the speaker in a poem is what the speaker says in the poem. We gain our notion of the persona from *what* he or she says and *how* he or she says it. We formulate our image of the persona from the views, values, tone, and attitude revealed through his or her speech.

What attitude does the narrator have toward (a particular character) and how is this attitude revealed?

Usually, the attitude that the narrator has toward a particular character is the attitude that the author of the story wants the reader to have too. But sometimes the attitude of the narrator may differ from the reader's. The narrator may admire a character that the reader despises; or the narrator may despise a character that the reader admires. Usually, when there is that kind of difference in attitude, we can be sure that the author planned it that way. The author deliberately tells the story through the eyes of an obviously **unreliable narrator** so that the reader will form an attitude toward the character that is quite the opposite of the narrator's.

A good example of this unreliable narrator is the gabby small-town barber in Ring Lardner's short story "Haircut." The story is one long, uninterrupted monologue in which the barber tells a stranger who comes to his shop about Jim Kendall, a salesman who had lost his job for incompetence and ended up being murdered by the town's idiot boy. It is obvious from the tales the barber tells that he considered Jim to be the funniest man he had ever met. But we the readers cringe at the tales of the cruel, "sick" jokes that Jim played on his family, friends, strangers, and the idiot boy. The barber's admiration for Jim constantly clashes with our disgust. The author intended that our reaction to Jim be the natural one and that the barber's

Special Kinds of Writing Assignments

reaction be an *un*natural one. Ring Lardner reveals his attitude toward Jim Kendall through the outrageousness of his narrator's admiration for the man.

Of course, in most instances, the narrator's attitude toward some character in the story will be the same as ours. But we must be aware that in those cases our attitude toward the character, whether favorable or unfavorable, has been subtly influenced by the narrator. The narrator shapes our attitude by the things he or she chooses to tell us about the character, by the comments made about the character, by the reactions of other characters toward the character. If we trust the narrator, we will accept his or her estimate of the character.

● Evaluating a literary work

> General Questions to Be Answered in *Evaluating a Literary Work*
> **How well does the author accomplish what he or she set out to do?** and/or
> **Was the work worth your time and attention?**

Once you have *exposed* what is in the text through analysis and once you have *discovered* the meaning of the text through interpretation, you can legitimately proceed to *evaluate* the text—that is, express your estimate of the author's accomplishment and your personal reaction to the text. You have progressed from the most objective part of the process, the analysis, to the most personal part, the evaluation. In evaluating the text, you will be expressing your *opinion*, and your opinion is likely to be a mixture of your *taste* and your *judgment*. Your taste reflects your *personal preferences*; your judgment reflects your *reasoned estimate.* For instance, you might not like a particular novel simply because you don't like tales of violence. In that case, your evaluation is based mainly on your taste. But if you said that you didn't like a particular novel because the characters were not believable people, your estimate would probably be based on a reasoned judgment. Of course, you are still expressing an opinion (other readers may find the characters perfectly believable), but at least you could present some arguments to support your opinion.

Here are some questions that can guide you in evaluating the literary text. They are divided into two main groups: *questions about the author's accomplishment* and *questions about your personal reactions.*

● Questions about the author's accomplishment

Was the work true-to-life?

We expect a literary work to reflect life as we know it. We can, of course, read stories set in a distant time or place, or we can read fantasies (fairy tales, science fiction) and still find them true-to-life if they are consistent with the conditions that the author has set up. If we feel that that a story violates the author's own terms, we reject it as being "untrue" or "unrealistic." We are willing to accept Superman's being able to roll a 1000-pound boulder up a steep hill in order to let it roll down on his pursuers, but we are not willing to accept that same action in a western where the "good guy" is trying to escape from the "bad guys."

Special Kinds of Writing Assignments

Was the action plausible?

This question is similar to the previous one. But the previous question is concerned with what is *possible;* this question is concerned with what is *probable*. There is a subtle but real difference between the possible and the probable. The possible refers to what *could* happen; the probable refers to what is *likely* to happen. Strange things happen occasionally, and because they are strange, they usually merit a story in the newspaper. Somebody falls out of a five-story window and escapes with only a bruised shoulder. It is *possible* for a person to survive a fall like that, but it is not *probable*. In at least nine cases out of ten, the person would be killed.

One of the ways in which fiction differs from real life is that events have to be made to seem probable, plausible. The reader must be made to feel that something happened because of something that took place previously or because of the nature of the characters or circumstances involved. Things that happen by chance are possible but not probable. Those stories are most satisfying where we feel that there is a cause-and-effect relationship between events: what happened in this scene *caused* what happened in the next scene. When we point out that an event is not plausible or probable, we are pointing out a serious flaw in the author's art.

Were the characters believable and consistent?

This question too is concerned with the true-to-life, but it is concerned with characters rather than with actions. When we ask whether a character is *believable,* we are asking whether that character behaves as a person of that nature could be expected to behave. Strange as a character may be, we still expect him or her to be recognizably human. A character will strike us as being recognizably human when his or her thoughts, words, and actions seem to be properly and plausibly motivated. If we can't figure out *why* a character did, said, or thought something or if the reason given is an unlikely explanation, the character will cease to be believable to us.

We also expect characters in novels, short stories, and plays to be *consistent*. In real life, of course, all of us occasionally behave inconsistently, but except for those occasional lapses, we behave most of the time in a fairly predictable way. And we expect characters in fiction to be more consistent than people in real life. Once the author has clearly established what kind of person a character is, we expect that character to behave consistently with the traits that have been fixed. If a person has been shown throughout the story to be very tightfisted in spending money, we don't expect that character suddenly to turn into a wild spender—not unless we are given some good reason for the sudden, surprising change.

It is surprising how often a negative estimate of an author's accomplishment is prompted by his or her failure to create believable, consistent characters.

Was the author's style clear and pleasing?

The danger with this question is that your answer to it could be purely a matter of taste. You may not like an author whose style demands close attention. In order to justify your displeasure, you could accuse the author of having a heavy, plodding style, when really what you should be saying is that you don't like any style that is so packed with meaning that you have to pay close attention to every sentence. Your judgment that the style was heavy and plodding would be more impressive if you could show that the author uses an unusually

Special Kinds of Writing Assignments

high percentage of difficult, abstract words, that he writes sentences that are unusually long and involved, that he does not vary the length or pace of his sentences, that he spins out sentence after sentence about a relatively minor point. All those charges might still not add up to a "heavy, plodding style," but at least you are presenting some concrete evidence of what *you* think constitutes a heavy, plodding style.

The important point here is that you cannot get by with mere assertions, favorable or unfavorable, about the clarity and attractiveness of an author's style. You must back up your assertions with some specific evidence from the text. If that evidence is convincing, you will have made a responsible judgment about the failure of the author's style.

What changes would improve the work?

Obviously, if the author is deficient in any of the matters raised by the previous four questions, the right changes made in those matters would improve the work. But you might be able to suggest other changes too that would improve the work:

☐ **Use a different point of view to tell the story.**

☐ **Add a scene or character to take care of a "missing link" in the story.**

☐ **Shift a scene from its present position to a later position to delay the climax and intensify the suspense.**

☐ **Cut out some material that is unnecessary and that slows the pace of the story.**

☐ **Correct errors of fact in the story (e.g. kinds of climate and terrain used in a travel story).**

● Questions about Your Personal Reactions

☐ **(if you are dealing with a poem) Substitute less hackneyed images or use a more appropriate verse form.**

Suggesting changes is a form of evaluating a work, because the suggestions imply that the author made the *wrong choices*. But you should be aware that the danger in such suggestions is that you may be proposing to the author the kind of work you think should have been written, instead of suggesting how the work might have been improved.

● Questions about your personal reactions

Did the work capture and hold your interest?

This is an important question to ask about any literary work. The answer to that question represents, of course, only *one* reader's response to the work, and it may be based solely on the reader's taste. But if we are convinced that the critic has given a careful and sensitive reading to the text, we do pay attention to such individual responses. The evaluations of reviewers of new books in the mass media have some influence on sales, and often we are moved to read a work simply on the recommendation of a friend. You can strengthen your answer to this question by explaining *why* the work captured and held your interest.

How does the work compare with other literary works you have read or with some movie, play, or television drama you have seen?

Special Kinds of Writing Assignments

Comparison is another way of evaluating work. In the act of comparing, you point out *similarities* and *differences*, and eventually you make judgments about which is *better*. Sometimes, you have the opportunity to compare a work produced in two different media. For instance, you might compare the novel *Jaws* with the movie made from the novel. You probably liked one version better than the other, and you could write a whole paper in which you give the reasons for your preference. You should make allowances, however, for the different media. Some things can be done in the written medium (for instance, reproducing the thoughts of characters) that cannot be done in a pictorial medium. On the other hand, the pictorial medium can present some scenes more dramatically and vividly than written words can. Allowances must also be made for the fact that you may be more familiar with one medium than with another.

Do you agree or disagree with what other critics have said about the work?

Other critics' judgments about a work can serve as a springboard for your own evaluation. If you have done a careful job of analyzing and interpreting the work, you should be able to state the grounds for your agreement or disagreement with other critics. But remember that you cannot just assert your contrary judgments. You have to present arguments to support your judgments.

If you were writing a review of the work for a newspaper, what would you say to encourage others to read or not read the work?

● Questions about Your Personal Reactions

This question suggests a good way in which you might approach the writing of a short paper on a literary work. It offers you a wide range of things that you could talk about—the plot, the characters, the theme, the ideas, the style. Knowing the audience for, say, a college newspaper, you can concentrate on those aspects of the work that are likely to interest such readers and that are most likely to induce them to read (or not read) the work.

What have you learned from reading this work that could make your life better or different?

We read literature mainly to be entertained. But there is a *teaching* function to literature also. Frequently, literature gives us a taste of experiences that we might never have in real life. It can transport us imaginatively to distant times and places; it can introduce us to types of people that we never meet in real life; it can plunge us into experiences that are much more exciting than our humdrum lives. In short, literature can extend our range of experiences. And the sensitivity of the author's vision can make us *see* more, *realize* more, even in the familiar experiences of our lives. Whether we are aware of it or not, the reading of literature can affect our lives, for better or for worse. You could write an entire paper in which you talk about how a particular work has affected you.

The sets of questions grouped under *Analyzing Literature, Interpreting Literature*, and *Evaluating Literature* are intended to suggest, but not exhaust, the things you might say in a paper you are asked to write about a literary text. Your paper might deal with all three processes of analysis, interpretation, and evaluation, but it might confine itself to only one of those proc-

Special Kinds of Writing Assignments

esses. The advantage of writing about literature is that you have a definite subject to write about. All the material you need is right there in the words of the text. The questions are intended as a device to *discover* what is there to talk about in your paper.

● Writing essay examinations

Throughout your college years, you can hardly escape from having to write examinations. Many examinations, of course, simply require you to blacken spaces, fill in blanks, or put down the numbers of correct answers. But inevitably you will take some examinations in which you have to write out your answers in sentences, paragraphs, or essays. This kind of single-draft writing is done under pressure—the pressure of having to present "correct" answers within a time limit. This writing is more than a display of the knowledge you have acquired and retained; it is *also* a display of your ability to recall, select, organize, and express that knowledge.

You should develop some proficiency in this kind of writing-under-pressure, not only because it will help you get passing grades but also because much of the writing you will have to do in real life will be single-draft prose that has to meet a deadline. Leisure for extensive revising and rewriting of that kind of prose is a luxury that few people can afford. At best, the only reworking that a lot of written prose gets in the business and professional world is the retyping that an assistant does of a rough draft. Improving your ability to write essay examinations will prepare you for some of the writing you will have to do in connection with your job.

It is not likely that you have had any formal training in how to write examinations. You are merely thrown into a situation of having to take an essay examination and are expected to know how to perform. If you have learned how to perform passably well in such situations, you have learned mainly from repeated trial-and-error. There are a few bits of advice, however, that might help you perform better than you do if you merely muddle through. (But never forget: *there is no substitute for knowing the answer to the question.*)

(1) BE SURE YOU UNDERSTAND THE QUESTION BEFORE YOU BEGIN TO WRITE

You are inviting disaster if you begin to write *before you have a clear understanding of what the question is getting at.* **Really read the question.** If you don't completely understand what the examiner wants from you, the reason may be (1) that your grasp of the subject covered by the question is so weak that you can't even make sense of the question, much less answer it or (2) that your reading ability is so deficient that you read words without really understanding what they are saying or (3) that the question is vaguely or ambiguously phrased. It may be too late to do anything about the first condition, but you certainly can do something about the second or third condition: you can ask the examiner to clarify the question. Don't set out blindly; make sure that you're heading in the right direction *before* you start to write.

(2) ONCE YOU UNDERSTAND THE QUESTION, MAKE SURE THAT YOU ANSWER *THAT* QUESTION AND NOT SOME OTHER, IMAGINED, QUESTION

The chief cause for failure on written examinations—or at least for the loss of points on a question—is *not meeting the question head-on.* If you are not sure about the answer to the

Special Kinds of Writing Assignments

question, it is natural for you—and maybe wise—to say everything you know about the subject, even though much of what you say is not entirely relevant to the answer. But if you really know the answer, you should aim directly at the bullseye.

Look for certain key words in the question to help you keep your answer on target—words like **who, what, when, where, why, how** or words like **explain, define, identify, enumerate, cite, discuss, account for, trace, compare, contrast, relate, support, refute.** Words like those point you to the core of the question. A question like ''Who was mainly responsible for getting the Constitution adopted in New York state in 1789?'' is asking you to name the *person* or *group of persons* responsible for that event; any information about *what* was responsible (that is, the *causes*) is beside the point and will not gain you any credits for your answer. The word **explain** gives you a lot of room for your answer, but your explanation had better concentrate on the specified subject (e.g. ''the economic situation at the outbreak of the Civil War'') and not some imagined or wished-for subject (e.g. ''the prevailing mood of the slaves at the outbreak of the Civil War''). If you're asked to **compare and contrast** persons, events, situations, etc., you had better concentrate in your answer on the *similarities* (the **compare** part of the question) and the *differences* (the **contrast** part of the question).

(3)   SPEND SOME TIME PLANNING YOUR ANSWER

One way to ensure that you will keep your answer on target is to *spend a few moments planning your answer*. If you're allotted ten minutes for answering a question, you might do well to spend two or three of those minutes scribbling a few notes in the margin about the points you want to cover in your answer. Your answer may end up being shorter than it might have been if you had spent the full ten minutes writing. But it may prove to be more compact, more pertinent, and better organized as a result of your planning than if you had launched into your answer aimlessly. Some kind of sketchy outline is even more important when the question demands a well-developed essay rather than merely a 100-word paragraph.

(4) DEVELOP YOUR ANSWER ADEQUATELY

If failure to meet a question head-on is the chief reason for loss of points in an essay examination, *failure to develop an answer adequately or fully* is the next most common reason. This is a trickier pitfall for you, because "adequate development" is a relative matter. But sometimes the examiner gives you some helpful hints about what would constitute an adequately developed answer. If you must answer a question in *one sentence*, you have a definite guideline: a single, well-phrased sentence, if it hits the nail on the head, will constitute an adequate answer.

"In a paragraph of 100–150 words, explain why . . ."—if a question is phrased in that way, you have an idea of *how much* you must write to answer the question adequately. Sometimes the examiner will specify the amount of *time* you should devote to a question. If you are allotted twenty minutes for an answer, three sentences probably won't be enough to provide an adequate answer to the question. Sometimes the examiner suggests how much you should develop your answer by the number of *points* assigned to a question. A question assigned a value of twenty-five points is obviously going to require a more fully developed answer than a question assigned only five points.

But when hints of this kind are not supplied by the examiner, you will have to rely on your own sense of what constitutes an adequate answer. Just as the topic sentence of a paragraph suggests how much development a writer commits himself to, so the question asked in an examination may suggest how much development there must be in the answer. The question "Cite and discuss five causes for the decline of the dollar on the world market in recent years" offers some suggestions of what will be an adequate answer. Citing and discussing only *three* causes is going to lose you some points; citing five causes but not *discussing* them is going to lose you some points. Those who give essay examinations continually get answers in which everything that is said is true and relevant but in which not *enough* is said.

(5)   DON'T PAD YOUR ANSWER

Padding an answer is the opposite of shortchanging it. To say too much is probably better than saying too little, but the ideal is to say just enough. Students turn to padding either when they want to display everything they know about a subject or when they are not sure enough of the answer they are writing. The student may be thinking, "I'm really going to show everything I know on this one" or "Maybe if I keep piling on sentences, I'll come up with what the teacher is looking for." Both are cases of faking it. Most teachers can see through this kind of thing, and they are most likely to be annoyed than impressed by the extra reading they have to do. *There's a time to be expansive and a time to be brief.*

Examples of essay answers

Here are some illustrations of adequate and inadequate one-paragraph answers to a question in an American history examination:

● Examples of Essay Answers

QUESTION

What weaknesses in the Articles of Confederation, which were adopted by the Continental Congress in 1777, led to the movement in the 1780s to replace the Articles with the Constitution? (150–200 words, 15 points)

Essentially, this is a *why* question (why did something happen?) that should be answered with an *enumeration of reasons or causes* (in this case, an enumeration of the **weaknesses**). Here is an answer that would probably rate the full number of points allotted to this question:

The basic weakness of the Articles of Confederation was that they allowed the thirteen colonies to retain too much sovereignty and independence and didn't grant the Continental Congress enough power to conduct national and international affairs. All the other weaknesses stemmed from this basic one. The Articles set up only one legislative body and did not make provisions for a President, a Cabinet, or a Court to execute and supervise the laws passed by this body. Each state, depending on its population, sent anywhere from two to seven representatives to the Congress, but each state, regardless of size, was entitled to only one vote. Furthermore, this single arm of the central government could not levy taxes (it could only *request* each state to pay its fair share of the national budget), and it could not collect import duties, regulate commerce, or establish a national currency. As a result, the Confederation could not pay its heavy debts to France and Holland, could not negotiate vital trade agreements with Great Britain, could not maintain a national army or navy, and had no clout in dealing either with its own colonies or with foreign nations. The Articles of Confederation established an alliance of thirteen colonies but not a nation of *united* states.

The following answer is true *as far as it goes*, but it is not sufficiently developed, and does not specify enough of the weaknesses, to merit the full allotment of points:

> The Articles of Confederation allowed the colonies to be more concerned about their own welfare than about the interests of the nation as a whole. The states were determined not to let "big government" rule them. We see this same selfishness today in all the hullabaloo about states' rights. You can't run a government if all the parties go their own way. Everybody must unite and bear the burden together. Some of the Founders saw the weaknesses of the Articles right from the start, but they were powerless to overcome the opposition of the states'-rights advocates. Eventually, they saw that the only way to get rid of those weaknesses was to scrap the Articles of Confederation and replace them with a truly federal constitution.

Either because the following student didn't read the question carefully enough or because she didn't know, or couldn't recall, enough details about the Articles of Confederation, she wrote a padded answer, filled with a lot of irrelevant material, and never did meet the question head-on:

> It was a crucial time in the history of our country. After a hard war with the well-trained British redcoats, the colonists had won their freedom and were proud that their ragtail armies had beat the "superior" British troops. But all their blood, sweat, and tears would have been in vain if they couldn't create a government that was better than the one they had broken away from. So they commissioned some of the best minds in the country to set up the Articles of Confederation—men like James Madison of Virginia,

Ben Franklin of Pennsylvania, and Alexander Hamilton of New York. It was quite a challenge, but these men came up with a system of government that was as good as it could be under the circumstances. Sure, it had its weaknesses, but what government doesn't? Do you think we have a *perfect* government right now, even under the Constitution? Any government made up of humans is bound to have flaws in it. But at least it can be said that the Founders were smart enough to see the weaknesses in the Articles and tried to do something about correcting them. So they wrote our famous Constitution. They set up a system of checks and balances, safeguarded by the Bill of Rights and a workable system of passing amendments, like the Equal Rights Amendment we're trying to pass right now. So the thirteen original colonies were finally united, and except for the temporary split during the Civil War and the rebellion of young people during the Vietnam War, they have remained united. Our weaknesses were turned into strengths.

Writing an essay examination is much like other kinds of writing. You have to find something to say (in this case, the precise answer to a specific question), you have to select and arrange what your memory dredges up from what you have learned, and you have to express what you have recalled in well-chosen words and well-fashioned sentences. The major difference, of course, is that the whole process of finding, planning, and expressing has to be speeded up. Observing the following bits of advice, however, might improve the writing you do under the pressure of this situation:

> **1 Read the question carefully.**
> **2 Answer the question asked.**

Special Kinds of Writing Assignments

> 3 **Plan your answer.**
> 4 **Develop your answer sufficiently.**
> 5 **Avoid padding your answer.**

None of that advice will do you any good, of course, if you don't *know* the answer.

● Report writing

Report writing is one of the commonest forms of writing that people have to do in the business and professional world. In fact, it would be safe to say that if you have to do any writing in connection with your job, you will most likely have to write reports of some kind. And it isn't just people in high-level positions who have to write reports; many salespersons, police officers, clerks, nurses, and supervisors have to write reports every day as part of their jobs.

Since you have probably given oral or written reports in school, the form is not totally unfamiliar to you. But as you progress through college, the reports you are called upon to give will increase in number, length, and complexity. The practice you get in writing reports in school will prepare you to do this kind of writing later on in your job.

The principles governing report writing do not differ basically from those that govern other kinds of expository and persuasive writing. A report is an act of communication—someone saying something to someone else for a specific purpose. All the steps of the process that were discussed in the previous chapters—**finding, selecting, organizing,** and **expressing**—play a part in the writing of reports. What you need to become aware of is some of the special considerations and special formats of report writing.

●
Special considerations

Types of Reports

There is a great variety of reports, and you may have heard of some of them: accident reports, sales reports, annual reports, research reports, progress reports; reports of events, meetings, trips, investigations, surveys, polls, case studies; feasibility reports, evaluation reports, justification reports, problem-solving reports. For the sake of convenience, the several kinds could be classified into two general types: the **informative** and the **persuasive.**

INFORMATIVE REPORTS

The main function of *informative* reports is to record and convey to interested parties details about what happened, what was done, or what was discovered. In short, they record and share information. Someone may later do something *with* or *about* the information. For instance, an accident report that a police officer submits to the Accident Bureau may later serve as the basis of a lawsuit filed by one of the parties involved. But the primary purpose of an informative report is to gather, record, and transmit the "facts" about something. News stories, for instance, are basically informative reports. We read them to satisfy our curiosity about what happened, but most of the tiime, we don't do anything *with* or *about* the information we read in the newspaper.

Special Kinds of Writing Assignments

PERSUASIVE REPORTS

The main purpose of *persuasive* reports, on the other hand, is to get someone to *do* something—to lead to action. Persuasive reports contain information too—lots of it—but the information is there not only for the enlightenment of the reader, as it is in an informative report, but also for *action* by the reader. Whether its intent is to solve a problem, propose a policy, or recommend a product, the goal of the persuasive report is to move the reader to action based on the information presented and analyzed in the report. For instance, the writer of an evaluation report about various sources of energy may recommend that a manufacturing firm use a particular fuel for its main source of energy because her study has shown this fuel to be the cheapest and cleanest. **The persuasive report leads to *decision-making*.**

Your being able to classify your report as *informative* or *persuasive* will help you define your task.

Commissioning of Reports

Most of the time, reports are commissioned. Rarely does someone decide, on his or her own initiative, to write a report. One of the consequences of the fact that reports are usually commissioned is that several aspects of the writing assignments are often defined more sharply than they are in other writing assignments:

1 **A specific person or team of persons** is assigned to write the report.

2 **A definite audience** is designated for the report.

3 **A definite subject** is specified for the report.

4 **A clear purpose** is set for the report.

● Special Considerations

5 **A deadline** is set for the completion of the report.

These specifications clearly define the writer's task and help the writer focus the approach. Furthermore, the person or persons who commissioned the report know what to expect in the report. They cannot know ahead of time, of course, what the findings and recommendations of the report will be, but at least they know something about the subject, purpose, and scope of the report.

Problem and Purpose

More than any other elements, the statements of the problem and of the purpose define the goal of the report. What often prompts the commissioning of the report in the first place is some *problem*, some *unknown*, that needs to be solved. Solving the problem or the unknown becomes, in turn, the goal of the report. The following examples of problem/purpose show how these two elements sharply define the goal of the report:

PROBLEM

What has caused the breakdown and loss of efficiency in telephone communications between Plant *A* in one city and Plant *B* in a city fifty miles away?

PURPOSE

To find out what the snag in telephone communications is and, if the snag cannot be corrected easily and inexpensively, to find an alternative system of communication that will be an improvement over the present system.

Special Kinds of Writing Assignments

PROBLEM

Why has a 38% decline in the sales of Brand X Dog Food occurred in recent months?

PURPOSE

From a survey and evaluation of consumer response to the ten bestselling dog foods, to determine what may be lacking in the appeal of Brand X.

PROBLEM

Why has there been a ten-point decline in students' verbal scores this year when the average decine in the previous eleven years was only three points?

PURPOSE

To determine the cause or causes of the decline so that the nation's schools can take the necessary steps to stop the decline.

The answer to the problem has to be sought in some kind of research—an experiment, an investigation, a review of the literature on the subject. The report then will tell *what was done to find the answer* and *what the findings of the study were*, and if it is a *persuasive* report, it will recommend *what should be done to solve the problem.*

Completeness and Accuracy of the Report

A report must be as complete and as accurate as it needs to be. That truism may strike you as being so obvious that it hardly needs to be stated. But the general principle governing the length, fullness, and precision of a report cannot be stated in any other way. Each case must be judged on its own terms.

What mainly determines the length, fullness, and precision of the report is the complexity of the problem or the scope of the report. Some reports need to be only one or two pages long and can be presented in a letter or a memorandum. In order to respond to a questionnaire from the federal government about a company's Affirmative Action policy, the vice president of the company might ask the personnel manager to supply him with information about the number and percentage of women and ethnic minorities presently employed by the company. That information could be *completely* presented in a one-page letter. On the other hand, if the vice president of a company wanted to know what cost-accounting procedures were currently being used by the ten largest corporations in the country, the writer might need thirty or more pages in order to supply complete information.

The information supplied in a report should be as accurate as possible under the circumstances. Sometimes accurate information is not available. It may not be possible, for instance, to get accurate statistics about the number of auto thefts across the nation in a given year because an efficient system of reporting auto thefts has not yet been developed in some states. In that case, we have to settle for *approximate* figures. Fortunately, in many cases, round numbers will serve the purpose just as well as numbers figured out to three decimal points. We do expect the chemist to report the exact proportions of chemical elements used in an experiment. We expect the simple arithmetic of any calculations to be checked and double-checked. We expect conclusions to be drawn logically and responsibly from the data. We expect the names of persons, institutions, products, etc., to be accurate and correctly spelled.

Special Kinds of Writing Assignments

Decisions made on the basis of incomplete or inaccurate information *could* be disastrous. Perhaps the test of whether a report is complete and accurate enough is the readers' response to it. Do they feel that some important questions have been left unanswered? Do they have any doubts about the accuracy of the report?

The Intelligibility of the Report

Intelligibility is, of course, a relative term. A report that would be perfectly understandable to a group of specialists might not be clear to a general audience. Fortunately, the writer of a report has a more definite idea of the audience that will read the report than other kinds of writers do. Sometimes the report will be read by only *one* person, a person that the writer knows quite well, or it might be read only by the six electrical engineers in the company. Usually, the more limited and homogeneous the audience is, the easier it will be for the writer to make the report intelligible. The problem is complicated when one has to write a report for a large, mixed audience. A company's annual report, for instance, will be read not only by employees in various departments of the company but also by the stockholders. For that reason, the annual report must be written so that it will be understandable to all segments of that wide audience. The financial statement in that report cannot be presented in the same detail and complexity that a certified public accountant would require.

Intelligibility depends mainly on the language used and the level of technicality on which the subject is treated. Although even writers of reports intended primarily for experts are encouraged to avoid highly technical language wherever possible, they can use, and they may have to use, *some* technical language. In reports intended for a wider audience, however,

writers should try to explain difficult concepts or processes in ordinary language, and if they find it necessary to use some technical language, they have to define those words. And in their explanations, they should try to avoid the intricacies that would be understandable only to specialists.

The ideal for the writer is to treat the subject adequately enough to satisfy the experts and yet to use language that is simple and clear enough to be understood by ordinary, intelligent people. The writer has a right, of course, to expect the audience to make a reasonable effort to understand what has been written.

The Readability of the Report

The *readability* of the report is different from the *intelligibility*. Whereas *intelligibility* has to do with *how easy it is to understand the writing, readability* has to do with *how interesting or attractive the writing is*. Some writers have the knack of making reports on even the most complex and highly technical subjects exciting to read. That kind of readability is mainly a matter of **pacing**.

Pacing is a difficult quality to define, but you have probably experienced the effects of pacing while watching a movie or a play. If you found yourself growing impatient with the movement of the drama, the pacing was probably too slow. You very likely told your friends that the movie "dragged" or that it "took too long to get going." On the other hand, if you were bewildered by the movement, the pacing was probably too fast; you couldn't adjust yourself to the rapid movement and the quick changes.

Proper pacing is important in writing too, especially in a lengthy report. If the writer plods along at the same pace page after page, lingers over unimportant details, or becomes

Special Kinds of Writing Assignments

repetitious, you will soon become bored. On the other hand, if the writer rushes through the explanation of a complicated idea or process, doesn't provide helpful transitions between the parts of the report, doesn't pause occasionally to point out the significance or relevance of what has been talked about or if the organization is hopelessly scrambled, you will soon become confused.

Pacing is like timing in athletics. Some people seem to be born with a proper sense of pacing or timing. But if you were not born with that skill, you can improve it with practice and by observing and imitating those who do have it.

There are some physical devices also that can increase the readability of your writing. Leaving lots of white space on the page, marking the parts of the text with headings and subheadings, interspersing the text with charts and graphs and illustrations—typographical devices of this sort will help to make the reading of a long, complicated report less tedious. Even such a simple device as heavy black type produced by a fresh typewriter ribbon helps to make the text more attractive. You should not underestimate the effect of just the physical appearance of the page.

The Matter-of-Factness of the Report

Report writing should maintain an objective, impersonal tone. The writer may have to express opinions occasionally and present judgments about the "facts," but generally the readers of reports are more interested in the substance of the report than they are in the personality of the writer. **The writer should avoid exaggerated claims, highly emotional language, touches of humor, anecdotes (introduced for their own sake), sarcasm, gossip, wishful thinking, pet peeves— anything that shifts the attention of the reader from *what*** *is being said* to *who is saying it.* Metaphors are sometimes unavoidable—in fact, sometimes they really help the writer clarify a meaning or an explanation—but for the most part, *the writer of a report relies more on literal language than on figurative language.*

Because of the matter-of-fact tone that has to be maintained, the report writer finds it more difficult than other writers do to achieve the *readability* discussed in the previous section. But anybody who has read articles in the magazine *Scientific American* knows that readability can be achieved even in objective, impersonal writing.

Many of the considerations reviewed above are pertinent, of course, to other kinds of writing too. All writers, in some measure, have to strive to be complete and accurate and intelligible and readable, but the *combination* of considerations is especially important for report writers. Good report-writing is just as much of an art as good fiction-writing. Keeping these special considerations in mind can help the writer master this art.

● Special formats

The parts of a report

As was mentioned at the beginning of the section on report-writing, there are many kinds of reports, all of which can be classified as either *informative reports* or *persuasive reports*. There is also a great variety of formats for reports. Short, informal reports, for instance, are often presented in letters or memorandums or even on printed forms that leave blank

Special Kinds of Writing Assignments

spaces to be filled in. Long, formal reports usually follow a set pattern. If you are called upon to write reports in school or later in your job, you will often be given specific instructions about the format that you are to follow. In fact, many companies have prepared special manuals that give directions about the number and arrangement of the parts of different kinds of reports, and they keep a file of various reports that serve as models for the writer.

The following is the *typical* format of a full-fledged formal report. The number and order of the parts may vary slightly from company to company, but most long, formal reports follow this format:

1 **a letter of transmittal**
2 **a title page**
3 **a table of contents**
4 **a table of illustrations, tables, charts, and graphs**
5 **an abstract of the report**
6 **an introduction to the report**
7 **the body of the report**
8 **a list of conclusions**
9 **a list of recommendations**
10 **appendices**
11 **bibliography or list of references**
12 **index**

(1) LETTER OF TRANSMITTAL

The letter of transmittal, typed in the usual form of a business letter (see next chapter) and often very short, formally transmits the report to the interested parties. The body of the letter might say something like the following:

On February 6, 1981, the Board of Directors of Industrial Nucleonics commissioned me and five other members of the Engineering Department to make a feasibility study of converting from natural gas to electricity as the plant's main source of energy. I am now submitting copies of "A Report on the Advantages and Disadvantages of Electricity as the Main Source of Industrial Power" to the Board of Directors and the twelve Executive Officers of Industrial Nucleonics.

On behalf of the members of my staff, I apologize for the delay in the delivery of the report. But as you are aware, we were delayed for two weeks while the Commonwealth Electrical Company awaited a ruling from the U.S. Court of Appeals on its application for an increase in rates charged to industrial consumers of electrical energy. We could not complete our financial assessment of the project until Commonwealth got a ruling from the courts.

If my colleagues and I can be of further assistance to you, please do not hesitate to call on us.

Those who are not on the list of people scheduled to receive a copy of the report usually do not see this letter of transmittal. The copy they read may have all the other eleven parts but not this letter.

(2) TITLE PAGE

The title page contains at least two pieces of information: (1) the title or the subject of the report and (2) the names of the authors of the report. The amount of additional information included on the title page varies from company to company, but here is a list of other kinds of information often found on the title page:

Special Kinds of Writing Assignments

a the name of the person or agency to whom the report is addressed

b the date of the report

c the name of the agency that sponsored or funded the study (this could be the same as **a**)

d the code number of the report

e the publisher of the report

(3) TABLE OF CONTENTS

The table of contents lists the parts of the report, using the headings of major divisions and subdivisions and giving the page numbers of those sections.

(4) TABLE OF ILLUSTRATIONS, TABLES, CHARTS, AND GRAPHS

The table of illustrations, tables, charts, and graphs lists any visual material contained in the report. The items are usually numbered and labeled (e.g. *Figure 2, Classification of Workers according to Occupations*), and the page numbers where these items occur are given. Sometimes, especially when there are only one or two graphics, the items are listed in the table of contents rather than in a separate section.

(5) ABSTRACT

The abstract gives the reader a quick overview of the whole report. Because the abstract is not only an important part of a report but also an increasingly important form of writing aside from the report (especially in information-retrieval systems), it will be discussed at some length here.

Writing abstracts is something of an art, for it demands two skills: skill in reading and skill in writing. Unlike the other kinds of writing dealt with in this book, the abstract does not require the writer to find something to say. Instead, the writer takes what he or someone else has written and reproduces the substance of the text in a considerably shortened version. But that kind of abbreviation of the text is not as easy as it may appear. *One must be a skillful enough reader to be able to pick out the important points in a text and a skillful enough writer to set forth those important points in a coherent form and in a limited number of words.*

An abstract is in some ways like a sentence outline (see the form of an outline in Chap. 4). A sentence outline sets forth the major points (the roman-numeral divisions) of an essay or article and at least the first level of subordinate points (the capital-letter subdivisions). **The difference between an outline and an abstract is that whereas the outline is presented in the form of a *listing of points*, the abstract is written out in a *sequence of sentences*.** But if you are skillful enough to be able to construct a sentence outline of the main parts of a piece of extended prose, you should be able to pick out the main points that should go into the abstract.

Another way to approach the task of writing an abstract is to develop the skill of picking out the topic sentences of the paragraphs in the body of an essay. But a collection of *all* the topic sentences might make your abstract longer than it needs to be and might obscure the relationships and relative importance of the sentences. You might have to combine two or three topic sentences into a broader generalization and provide connecting links between sentences (see the discussion of connecting words in the section on coherence in Chap. 5).

Think of the process of abstracting as a distilling of the essence of a longer piece of prose. You need enough sentences to cover all the major points of the essay, but you

Special Kinds of Writing Assignments

have to boil away the supporting details of the longer version. What you are left with is a "concentrate" of the longer essay.

There are two kinds of abstracts: **descriptive** and **informative**. The *descriptive abstract*, which is usually quite short, merely indicates what *topics* or *areas* are covered in the longer text. The *informative abstract* actually *gives* readers the *main points* or *ideas* of the longer text. The difference between the two can be illustrated in the following sentences:

Descriptive

The major forms of literature produced in England in each of three consecutive centuries are discussed in this article.

Informative

In England, drama was the prevailing form of literature in the seventeenth century, the prose essay was the chief contribution of the eighteenth century, and the novel was the dominant form in the nineteenth century.

On pp. 297–299 you will see a descriptive abstract and an informative abstract of this chapter of the book.

Although you will find descriptive abstracts in some reports, you are more likely to find—especially in lengthy reports— informative abstracts, because the reader wants to get a preview of the main ideas presented in the report rather than merely an indication of the areas covered. As you will discover for yourself, the informative abstract is much harder to write than the descriptive abstract.

In preparing to write an abstract, either of a text you wrote or of a text someone else wrote, you might find these suggestions helpful:

1 **Read the text all the way through to get an overall view of it.**

2 **In a second reading of the text, make a checkmark in the margin opposite sentences or paragraphs that make what you think are major points.**

Aids that can guide you in picking out major ideas in a text: table of contents, introduction or preface, headings and subheadings in the text itself, summaries of sections, the conclusion of the whole text, italicized or boxed sentences and paragraphs.)

3 **After marking the main points, try making at least a rough outline of the text.**

4 **From the outline, decide how many points, and which ones, you should include in your abstract.**

(Sometimes a word limit is set for the abstract [e.g. 150 words or less]. If so, that limit will help you decide how many points, and which ones, you can include in your abstract.)

5 **Write the first draft of the abstract.**

(At this stage, don't worry about how many words you are using. Just get something down on paper.)

6 **Revise and trim the first draft, if necessary.**

(At this stage, see if you can supply linkages between the sentences to make the abstract read smoothly.)

7 **Write the final draft of the abstract.**

If you were to follow these suggestions in preparing to write an abstract of this chapter, for instance, you might write descriptive and informative abstracts like these:

Descriptive abstract

The three kinds of special writing assignments dealt with in this chapter are writing about literature, writing

Special Kinds of Writing Assignments

essay examinations, and writing reports. Sets of questions are proposed to help students generate ideas for an analysis, interpretation, or evaluation of fiction, drama, and poetry. Practical advice is given about how to write satisfactory answers in an essay examination. The special considerations and formats of informative and persuasive reports are discussed, and special attention is paid to the writing of descriptive and informative abstracts.

Informative abstract

In writing about literature, the student is involved in one or more of these acts: analyzing, interpreting, or evaluating. In an analysis of a literary text, the two general questions to be answered are (1) what is the work about? and (2) how is the work put together? In an interpretation of a literary text, the two general questions to be answered are (1) what did the author mean? and (2) what did the work mean to you? In an evaluation of a literary text, the two general questions to be answered are (1) how well did the author accomplish what he or she set out to do? and (2) was the work worth your time and attention? Sets of more particular questions can lead the student to more specific answers to these general questions.

In writing answers to essay-examination questions, the student should (1) read the questions carefully, (2) address the questions head-on, (3) plan the answers, (4) develop answers adequately, and (5) avoid padding answers. Examples of answers to an examination question in American history illustrate adequate and inadequate answers.

In writing both informative and persuasive reports, the student should give special consideration to the completeness, accuracy, intelligibility, readability, and objectivity of the report. The twelve parts of a typical formal report are (1) the letter of transmittal, (2) the title page, (3) the table of contents, (4) the table of illustrations, tables, charts, and graphs, (5) the abstract, (6) the introduction, (7) the body of the report, (8) the list of conclusions, (9) the list of recommendations, (10) the appendices, (11) the list of references, and (12) the index. Because of the importance of the abstract, both as a separate form and as a part of a report, procedures for writing descriptive and informative abstracts are discussed, and examples of descriptive and informative abstracts of this chapter of the book are presented.

In the next chapter, in the section on reference books, you will find descriptions of some of the collections of abstracts in the sciences and the humanities. You should consult some of these for further examples of abstracts—an increasingly important form of writing in the modern world.

(6) INTRODUCTION

The introduction to the report does not differ substantially from the introductions to other kinds of writing. In general, the introduction provides the preliminary information necessary for leading readers into the body of the report. It may define the scope and the purpose of the report, indicate the problem that prompted the report, explain the procedures and methodology of the study, and define some key terms. It varies in length from a single paragraph in short informal reports to several pages in long formal reports.

(7) BODY

The body of the report, like the body in other kinds of writing, is the longest part. It might occupy as much as 80 percent of the pages in a report. The body occupies such a large proportion of the report because it is in this section that the subject is treated in elaborate detail. The author (or authors) of the report may have to provide background information, describe procedures, summarize results, and present, analyze, interpret, and evaluate various kinds of supporting data. Some kinds of supporting data can be briefly presented in the form of illustrations, graphs, and statistical charts, but the discussion of those data may take up several paragraphs or several pages.

Because the body of the report is usually very long, the parts are marked with headings of various ranks. These headings serve a number of functions: (1) they alert the reader to the subject of that part; (2) they contribute to the readability of the report; (3) they help the reader see the relationships and relative rankings of the parts. The various ranks of heading are distinguished by different typography and different positions on the page.

EXAMPLES OF HEADINGS IN A REPORT

THIS IS A HEADING OF THE HIGHEST RANK

The text follows then, on a separate line and indented as here, and continues as a normal paragraph would.

This is a Heading of the Second Rank

The text follows then, on a separate line and indented as here, and continues as a normal paragraph would.

This is a heading of the third rank. The text follows then, on the same line as here, and continues as a normal paragraph would.

Figure 8.1

Headings of the highest rank (those that mark off major divisions) are *centered* on the page, *underlined*, and typed all in *capitals*. Headings of the second rank start at the *lefthand margin*, are *underlined* and *capitalized*, and occupy a *separate line* (above what follows). Headings of the next lowest rank are *underlined* but *do not occupy a separate line*, are *indented* from the lefthand margin (usually the same number of spaces as paragraph indentations), and are followed by a *period*. (See Fig. 8.1 for examples of the typography and positioning of the three ranked headings.)

(8) CONCLUSIONS

The conclusions summarize the findings of the study, research, or experiment. Here, the conclusions are placed right after the body of the report, where we normally expect to find them, but in some reports, the conclusions occur right after the introduction. The reason why the conclusions are sometimes placed earlier in the report is that for busy executives, who may be involved in decisions about the report, the conclusions and the part that follows (the recommendations) are the most important parts, and their reaction to the conclusions and recommendations may determine whether they go on to read all the details in the body of the report. (If the conclusions and recommendations were solidly negative, there would not be much point in the busy executive's going on to read the rest of the report.) But unless you are given specific instructions to place the conclusions right after the introduction, put them where the conclusions normally occur—right after the body of the report.

(9) RECOMMENDATIONS

The recommendations section usually occurs only in a persuasive report, the kind of report that calls for some action. This

Special Kinds of Writing Assignments

section presents the suggestions or proposals that the authors make as a result of the findings of the project. The authors might recommend, for instance, a change in company policy or the adoption of a more efficient procedure or the investment of money in some project or purchase. Sometimes the authors present a list of alternative recommendations, arranged in descending order of importance and numbered 1, 2, 3, etc. As was mentioned in the previous section (see #8), the conclusions and the recommendations are sometimes placed earlier in the report, right after the introduction and before the body of the report.

(10) APPENDICES

The appendices section contains all supporting material that does not fit conveniently or naturally in the body of the report— charts, graphs, tables of statistics, letters, affidavits, tabulations of surveys, etc. Sometimes material of that sort would distract readers from the flow of thought if it were inserted in the body of the report, and often that material is not needed ''right now'' to support a point being made. The author can say, in parentheses, ''(see Appendix B),'' and if readers want to consult that material right then, they can turn to Appendix B at the end of the report.

(11) REFERENCES

The list of references section corresponds to the bibliography page of a research paper. In this section, you should list all the written and published sources—if any—that you have consulted, cited, or quoted in the report—books, articles, pamphlets, monographs, brochures, letters, memorandums, and even other written reports.

(12) INDEX

The index section occurs only in lengthy, complex reports. Like the index of a book, it lists, in alphabetical order, key words or phrases, followed by page numbers where those terms appear. The table of contents, of course, lists the headings of major parts of the report, but sometimes readers want to track down the exact place in a long report where some term or idea or process is discussed, and only a detailed index can direct them to that place in the report.

It should be said once again that not all the parts reviewed in the previous pages appear in *every* long formal report, nor do they always occur in the order given above. These are typical parts of a report, listed in a typical order. If you are assigned to write a report, either by your teacher or by your employer, you will be given specific instructions about the format of the report, and you will probably have access to other written reports that can serve as a model for your own report.

Chapter 9
Writing Research Papers, Letters, Memorandums, and Résumés

The research paper, the memorandum, the résumé, and the letter are specialized forms of writing, to which we devote a separate chapter. In dealing with the research paper, we will concentrate on two concerns: (1) *gathering material* for the research paper; (2) the *format* of the research paper, including models for footnotes and bibliography. In dealing with the letter, the memorandum, and the résumé, we will be concerned only with the format.

●
Using the library

Unless your research paper is simply a report of a lab experiment, a questionnaire, or a series of interviews that you conducted, it will depend largely on your reading of books and articles. The main source of books and articles is the library—

either the public library or the college library. Perhaps the chief benefit that you derive from doing a research paper is that this exercise forces you to become acquainted with the library and its resources. Becoming aware of the wealth of knowledge stored in the library and getting to know *where* the various pockets of that wealth are located in the library and *how* to use them will be a valuable part of your general education.

The best way to get acquainted with the library is to visit it, to look around, to examine the card catalogue, to take some books down off the shelves and open them, and, above all, *to use it.* But if you want to speed up the getting-acquainted process, you can consult a book like Eugene P. Sheehy's *A Guide to Reference Books* (Chicago: American Library Association, 9th ed., 1980), which you can find on the reference shelves of the library. What follows is an introduction to a few general reference sources and some bibliographical sources, which would be both generally helpful in your pursuit of knowledge and particularly helpful to you in preparing to write a research paper.

General Reference Sources

(A) ENCYCLOPEDIAS

Multivolume encyclopedias are the most familiar and usually the most available source of information on a wide range of subjects. You are already aware that the material in an encyclopedia is arranged alphabetically, as a dictionary is. You also know that the treatment of topics in an encyclopedia varies in length from a few sentences to several pages. What you are probably not aware of is that often you can gather valuable additional information about your topic by consulting the *index volume*, which refers you to other entries where your topic is discussed. You should also be aware that many of the entries, especially the longer ones, list pertinent books and articles that you can consult for further information.

The encyclopedia is a good starting-point for a research project, but ordinarily it should not be the stopping-point. You will have to go on to more specialized reference sources. Here are three well-known multivolume encyclopedias and one very useful single-volume encyclopedia. All of them cover a wide range of subjects, are international in their scope, and cover all centuries, but each one is strong in a particular area. The first two publish yearbooks, which cover the main events and topics of the previous year.

> *Encyclopedia Americana* (Danbury, Conn.: Grolier Educational Corp., 1980). 30 volumes. Particularly useful for anything connected with the United States.

> *Encyclopaedia Britannica* (Chicago: Encyclopaedia Britannica Educational Corp., 1980). 30 volumes. Strong on both American and British topics.

> *Chambers's Encyclopedia* (Elmsford, N.Y.: Maxwell Scientific International, 1973). 15 volumes. Particularly strong on British topics.

> *The New Columbia Encyclopedia*, 4th edition (New York: Columbia University Press, 1975). One volume. More than 50,000 articles on the humanities, social sciences, life and physical sciences, and geography packed into 3052 pages.

(B) ALMANACS AND OTHER GENERAL SOURCES OF FACTS AND STATISTICS

You may not be able to afford a set of encyclopedias, but you certainly can afford to buy one of the annual paperback almanacs, a rich storehouse of factual and statistical information. The almanacs always retain the basic historical, geographical, social, political, and statistical information, but each year, they supply the pertinent factual and statistical information for the previous year. Here are the titles of two inexpensive paperback almanacs and the titles of two other sources of facts and statistics that can be found in the reference room of the library:

Information Please Almanac (New York: Simon and Schuster, 1947–   ). Published annually.

World Almanac (New York: Newspaper Enterprise Association, Inc., 1868–   ). Published annually.

Facts on File (New York: Facts on File, Inc., 1940–   ). Published weekly. A valuable source of information about the important events of the week.

U.S. Bureau of the Census: Statistical Abstract of the United States (Washington, D.C.: Government Printing Office, 1879–   ). Published annually. The most comprehensive source of statistical information about all aspects of American life.

(C) HANDBOOKS

Another source of general information about a particular field is the one-volume reference work that we will label *handbook*. Handbooks contain some of the same kinds of information supplied by multivolume encyclopedias, but the entries are shorter, and they are restricted to a special field, like literature or business. But precisely because they are restricted to a particular field, they often cover topics that are considered too minor or specialized for inclusion in a multivolume encyclopedia. In a handbook, you can expect to find these kinds of information about the field covered: definitions of key terms and concepts, identifications of allusions; accounts of historical or ideological movements; short biographical sketches; summaries of important books; bibliographies. Here is a list of a few important handbooks, one for each of seven different fields.

The Reader's Encyclopedia, ed. William R. Benet, 2nd ed. (New York: Crowell, 1965). A handbook of world literature.

Oxford Companion to the Theatre, ed. Phyllis Hartnoll, 3rd ed. (New York: Oxford University Press, 1967). A handy reference source for information about world drama, from its beginnings in ancient Greece.

Oxford Companion to Film, ed. Liz-Anne Bawden (New York: Oxford University Press, 1976). One of the many "Oxford Companions," about an art form that has become a prominent part of contemporary life.

Encyclopedia of Banking and Finance, ed. Ferdinand L. Garcia, 7th ed. (Boston: The Bankers Publishing Co., 1973). An invaluable one-volume reference work for anything connected with business.

The Concise Encyclopedia of Western Philosophy and Philosophers, ed. J. O. Urmson (New York: Hawthorn Books, 1960). Brief but authoritative information about philosophy and philosophers.

Dictionary of Education, ed. Carter V. Good, 3rd ed. (New York: McGraw-Hill, 1973). More than a dictionary, this reference work supplies the usual kind of handbook information about the field of professional education.

International Cyclopedia of Music and Musicians, ed. Bruce Bohle, 10th ed. (New York: Dodd, Mead, 1975). One of a number of very good one-volume handbooks on music.

(D) BIOGRAPHICAL DICTIONARIES

Encyclopedias and handbooks will provide you with brief biographical sketches of prominent men and women. But for fuller accounts of persons, both living and deceased, and for biographical sketches of less prominent people, you will have to go to the more specialized biographical dictionaries. Listed below are five of the best-known and most useful of these specialized biographical dictionaries.

Dictionary of National Biography (sometimes referred to as the *DNB*) (New York: Oxford University Press, 1921). 22 volumes (a reissue of the original 66-volume set published in 1885). Lives of about 18,000 *deceased* subjects of Great Britain and Commonwealth dependencies. Supplements bring the coverage up to 1960.

Who's Who (London: A & C Black, Ltd., 1849–   ). Published annually. Biographical information about distinguished *living* men and women of Great Britain.

Dictionary of American Biography (sometimes referred to as the *DAB*) (New York: Scribner's, 1927–1980). 16 volumes. The equivalent of the British *DNB*, this multivolume set gives the biographies of prominent and not-so-prominent *deceased* Americans.

Who's Who in America (Chicago: Marquis, 1899–   ). Published every second year. The equivalent of the British *Who's Who*, this reference source provides biographical information about notable *living* Americans.

International Who's Who (London: Europa Publications, 1935–   ). Published annually. Information about the lives of prominent *living* men and women of all nations.

Writing Research Papers, Letters, and Résumés

Bibliographical Sources

The reference works mentioned in the previous section can give you general information that could be useful for your personal enlightenment or for your classwork or even for your research paper. But since a research paper is usually written about a narrow topic in a specialized field, you will need more specific information than those general reference works can provide. You need to track down books and articles and monographs and pamphlets that deal more particularly with the topic of your paper. To track down that more specific material, you will have to turn to *bibliographical reference works*—works that list the authors, titles, and publication information of published books, articles, etc. Fortunately, there are a number of general and specialized bibliographical guides. A helpful guide to available bibliographies is the *Bibliographic Index* (New York: H. W. Wilson Co., 1937–   ). Supplements of this work are published every three months; and every four years, these quarterly supplements are gathered together and published in one volume. This guide to the bibliographies that have been published in books, pamphlets, periodicals, and bulletins is arranged alphabetically according to subject. If you were doing a research paper on the trucking industry and wanted to find out whether any bibliographies of this subject had been published, you could consult several volumes of the *Bibliographic Index* under the main subject-heading of *Transportation*. If you found a bibliography listed there on the trucking industry, you would then have to see whether the library had that bibliography, because it is *that* bibliography, and not the *Bibliographic Index* itself, that will give you the actual list of books and articles on the trucking industry.

Listed below are some general—and perhaps familiar—

guides to articles in periodicals (magazines and journals) and then a few specialized bibliographical guides.

(A) INDEXES TO PERIODICAL LITERATURE

Readers' Guide to Periodical Literature (H. W. Wilson Co, 1900–   ). Published every two weeks, with cumulations in a single volume every two years. Perhaps the most familiar of the general guides to articles appearing in American weekly, monthly, and quarterly magazines and journals, this reference work is arranged alphabetically according to author and subject.

International Index (New York: H. W. Wilson Co., 1907–   ), Volumes 1–18. Beginning with volume 19 in 1965, the title of this work was changed to *Social Sciences and Humanities Index*. Published every three months, with cumulations in a single volume every three years. It indexes, by author and by subject, articles appearing in some of the more learned American, as well as British and Canadian, periodicals.

Nineteenth Century Readers' Guide to Periodical Literature, 1890–1899. (New York: H. W. Wilson Co., 1944) 2 volumes. Indexes about fifty British and American periodicals published during the last ten years of the nineteenth century. The *Readers' Guide* picks up the coverage in the year 1900.

In the same section of the library in which you find these general guides to periodical literature, you will find specialized indexes to periodical literature in such fields as Art, Music, Business, Education, Psychology, Applied Science and Technology, Biology and Agriculture.

(B) SPECIALIZED BIBLIOGRAPHIES

In addition to the guides to periodical literature mentioned above, there are *specialized bibliographies* of the books, monographs, pamphlets, and bulletins published in most of the fields in the humanities, the social sciences, and the physical sciences. When you move into your area of specialization, you will be expected to become familiar with the bibliographical tools of that field. In addition to the standard bibliographies, sometimes occupying more than one volume, there are *annual bibliographies*, usually published in the scholarly journals, which list most of the books and articles published in the previous year. Scholars and graduate students consult these bibliographical sources when they are preparing to write books, articles, theses, and dissertations.

Listed below are three of the standard cumulated bibliographies in three different fields:

Cambridge Bibliography of English Literature, ed. F. W. Bateson (Cambridge: Cambridge University Press, 1957). 5 volumes.

Guide to Historical Literature, ed. George F. Howe and others (New York: Macmillan, 1961).

Sources of Business Information, ed. Edwin T. Coman, Jr., revised edition (Berkeley: University of California Press, 1964).

Abstracts

The general and specialized bibliographies mentioned above will enable you to compile a list of books and articles that might yield material for your research paper. The next step is to find some of those books and articles and read them.

In recent years, however, with the growth in the number of collections of abstracts in several fields, researchers have been able to get a *preview of the contents of books and articles* even before they get those publications in their own hands. After compiling your list of potentially useful books and articles, you might be able to save yourself some wasted motions by consulting the appropriate *collection of abstracts*. By reading a 150–200-word abstract of any of the books and articles on your list, you should be able to tell whether that book or article contains information pertinent to your paper. Most of the scholarly fields now publish annual collections of abstracts of books and articles published during the previous year. The sciences have been publishing abstracts for a number of years, and recently the humanities have begun to publish annual abstracts.

Listed below are some representative annual collections of abstracts in several fields. (Another benefit of looking at some of these collections of abstracts is that *you will find models for writing abstracts*, a form of writing discussed in the previous chapter. You can also use the collection of abstracts as a bibliographical source, since every abstract is headed with the name of the author, the title, and the publication information of the text being summarized.

Historical Abstracts 1775–1945 (Santa Barbara, Cal.: American Bibliographic Center, 1955–   ). Published quarterly. Abstracts articles, from some 1300 journals, on world history of the period from 1775 to 1945.

Journal of Economic Abstracts (Cambridge: Harvard University Press, 1963–   ). Published quarterly. Abstracts articles on various phases of economics from thirty-five periodicals published in various countries.

MLA Abstracts (New York: Modern Language Association, 1970–1975). Published annually. Abstracts of articles on the language and literature of America, Canada, Great Britain, and other European, Asian, and African countries.

Chemical Abstracts (Easton, Penn.: later Columbus, Ohio: American Chemical Society, 1907–   ). Published every two weeks. Abstracts articles from over 7000 periodicals published in more than ninety countries.

Sociological Abstracts (New York: Sociological Abstracts, Inc., 1952–   ). Published eight times a year. Abstracts books and articles published in a wide range of countries.

The Card Catalogue

The card catalogue—the rows of file-drawers in the library—is a valuable resource. Not only does it indicate whether the library has the particular book or periodical you are seeking and where in the library stacks the book or periodical can be found, but it is also another resource for compiling a bibliography for a research project. A library usually has at least three cards in the files for a single book—an *author* card (usually called the "main entry" card), a *title* card, and one or more *subject* cards. **It is the subject cards that give you the best leads on books pertinent to your research project.** Under the appropriate subject-heading will be grouped all the books that the library has on a particular subject. You can discover the "appropriate subject-heading" from looking at the Library of Congress card for a book that you *know* is pertinent to your study, because on every Library of Congress card, one or more subject-headings are suggested for a book.

Most libraries buy the printed cards prepared by a staff of classification experts at the Library of Congress in Washington, D.C. The Library of Congress (abbreviated L.C.) cards carry a lot of information. In Figure 9.1, four Library of Congress cards are displayed for a particular book, and the various parts of the card are tagged with letters of the alphabet. Here is the interpretation of those various lettered parts:

A The **name of the author** (last name first). This *author card* or *main entry card* will be found in the card catalogue in one of the drawers for the letter *S*.

B The **call number of the book**, typed in by the library staff. This is the number you must copy down if you want to find the book yourself in the stacks or if you want one of the library clerks to get the book for you.

C The **title of the book and publication information** about the book (i.e. the book was translated from Polish into English by J. Stadler; this is the first English edition of the book; the place of publication was Oxford, New York; the publisher was the Pergamon Press; and the date of publication was 1967).

D This entry supplies information about the **physical makeup of the book**: there are seven pages of introductory material and 323 pages of text; there are illustrations in the book; and the book measures 22 centimeters in height.

E This entry supplies some **additional information** about the book: the Polish title of the book and the fact that the book has a two-page bibliography.

F The two entries marked F, which were stamped on the card by the library staff, indicate that there are copies available in two locations—one in the Mathematics Department library, the other in the Commerce Department library.

G This entry carries four bits of information: (1) the **Library of Congress call number** (notice that this library has used this number as the call number for the book); (2) the suggested **Dewey Decimal call number** (the other classification

J ——————— MATHEMATICAL STATISTICS

MATHEMATICS

HB 74 **Sadowski, Wieslaw.**
M3 S31   Statistics for economists. Translated from the Polish by
1967   J. Stadler. [1st English ed.] Oxford, New York, Perga—

I ——————— ECONOMETRICS

MATHEMATICS

HB 74 **Sadowski, Wieslaw.**
M3 S31   Statistics for economists. Translated from the Polish by
1967   J. Stadler. [1st English ed.] Oxford, New York, Perga—

H ——————— Statistics for economists.

MATHEMATICS

HB 74 **Sadowski, Wieslaw.**
M3 S31   Statistics for economists. Translated from the Polish by
1967   J. Stadler [1st English ed.] Oxford, New York, Perga—

F ———

A ——— MATHEMATICS

HB 74 **Sadowski, Wieslaw.**
B ——— M3 S31 —— Statistics for economists. Translated from the Polish by
1967   J. Stadler [1st English ed.] Oxford, New York, Perga—
C ———   mon Press [1967]

D ——— vii, 323 p. illus. 22 cm.

E ——— Translation of Statystyka matematyezna.
Bibliography; p. 295P —296

F ——— COMMERCE

K ——— 1. Econometrics. 2. Mathematical statistics.   I. Title.

G ——— HB74.M3S213   1967   519'.024'33   OU 68–6 af
67–29914
Library of Congress   [10–2]

Figure 9.1

system used by some libraries); (3) the **order number** for the Library of Congress card; (4) a **code number**, typed in by the library staff, to indicate when the book was acquired by the library.

H The **title of the book**, typed in by the library staff on the *title card*. If you knew the title of the book but didn't know the author, you could find the book by looking for this title card in the card catalogue.

I The **subject-heading for the book**, typed in block capitals by the library staff on the first *subject card* for this book. Notice in K after the number 1 that *Econometrics* is the first subject-heading suggested by the Library of Congress staff.

J The **subject-heading for the book**, typed in block capitals by the library staff on the second *subject card* for this book. Notice in K after the number 2 that *Mathematical Statistics* is the second subject-heading suggested by the Library of Congress staff.

K This entry suggests two subject-headings for the subject cards and indicates that the book can also be filed under its title.

When you are compiling a bibliography for your research project, **the most important information for you to copy down from the L.C. card is the author, title, publication information, and call number of the book.** Of that information, the item most crucial for your gaining access to the book is the **call number**. That call number helps either you or the librarian to find the exact spot on the shelf where the book is stored.

In recent years, some college and university libraries have listed their holdings in a computer bank, and where such an accessing system is available, students do not have to consult the card catalogue even to discover the call numbers of books they want to get from the stacks. They can gain information about the location and availability of a book by going to a computer terminal and typing in the name of the author and/or the title of the book. Displayed on a television screen will be information at least about where the book is located in the library and whether the book has been checked out by someone else. In some cases, all the bibliographic information that can be found on an L.C. card will be displayed on the television screen.

Students should also be aware of another service that the card catalogue and the computer-accessing system can provide. Most of the time when students are faced with the task of writing a research paper, they do not know the authors and the titles of pertinent books. They can discover pertinent books by consulting the card catalogue or the computer under a subject heading that covers the subject of their research. But the key to discovering a list of books that would be useful for their research is getting the right subject heading. Looking for books under the wrong subject heading might yield the wrong kinds of books or no books at all.

The most helpful reference guide for finding the right subject heading is the two-volume *Library of Congress Subject Headings*, copies of which are readily available in almost every university or public library. Say that someone was assigned to do a research paper on the history of parochial schools in the United States and wanted to find what books the university library had on the subject. Before consulting the card catalogue or the computer under the heading of "parochial schools," the student would be well advised to look for that heading in one of the alphabetically arranged volumes of *Library of Congress Subject Headings*. There the student would discover that "parochial schools" is not one of the recommended headings but that the recommended heading for the library's holdings on this topic is "church schools." Also under this heading in the book, the student would find some *See also* references to related subjects, like "church and education," "private schools," and "religious education." By consulting the card catalogue or the computer under one of those headings, the student would get a list of all the books in that library on the subject of church-related schools.

Taking Notes: One Student's Project

After you have compiled a bibliography, you must then get your hands on the books and articles you have recorded in it, read that material, and take notes. Under the headings of Gathering Notes and Self-Contained Notecards on pp. 324–325, some practical advice is given about the process of note-taking.

Later on in this chapter, a research paper that Diana Ikenberry wrote on Nathaniel Hawthorne's short story "Young Goodman Brown" is printed. Diana began gathering her bibliography by looking at several of the annual bibliographies published in the scholarly journal *American Literature*. She checked the listings there of books and articles under the heading "Hawthorne" over a ten-year span. Since she couldn't tell from the titles of books listed there which books had sections (or whole chapters) on "Young Goodman Brown," she concentrated at first on those articles whose titles *did* indicate that they dealt specifically with "Young Goodman Brown."

Once she got her hands on some of these articles, she discovered, in footnotes, not only some leads on additional articles on "Young Goodman Brown" but also some leads on chapters in books that dealt specifically with "Young Goodman Brown." One of her most valuable finds was the discovery of a casebook on "Young Goodman Brown" edited by Thomas E. Connolly. This casebook carried the text of the short story and reprinted several of the critical articles that she had listed in her preliminary bibliography.

Once having gathered the books and articles she needed, she began taking notes on 3 × 5 notecards. Since she didn't know at this stage which material would be most useful to her when she came to write her paper, she took at least six times as many notes as she eventually used in the paper. Some of the material she paraphrased in her notecards; other material she copied down verbatim. In Figure 9.2, four of Diana's notecards are reproduced.

Card A represents a *verbatim quotation* from an article by Thomas F. Walsh, Jr. The way that Diana distinguishes notes copied verbatim from notes paraphrased is to enclose verbatim quotations in quotation marks and to leave paraphrased notes *without* quotation marks. Notice the page number between slashes (/335/) to indicate *where the quotation went over* to p. 335. Later, if she uses only part of the full quotation, she will know whether to cite one page or two pages in her footnote. On this and the other notecards, she uses a shorthand system for indicating the source of the note: the last name of the author of the article and the page number(s). On a separate notecard, she has recorded the full bibliographical information for the source. In the upper right-hand corner of each card, she has put the subject-heading she has made up for that note.

Card B represents a *verbatim quotation* from Hawthorne's short story. In a note at the bottom of the card, Diana indicates for her own information that the quotation occurred in the last paragraph of the story and that she, not Hawthorne, underlined some of the words in the quotation ("italics added")

Card C represents three *paraphrased notes* that Diana took from an article on Antinomianism. Even though these notes are set down in her own words, she has put down page numbers at the end of them, because if she uses some of those paraphrased notes in her paper, she may find it necessary to cite in an endnote her *authority* for the statements.

Card A

WALSH, pp 334-5   GOODMAN'S ANCESTORS

The facts concerning the persecution of the Quakers and the Indians, Goodman Brown must certainly have known before, although in the past he might never have allowed himself to think of them in relation to sin. But what is most interesting, of all those who are /335/ mentioned and revealed by the devil, his father and grandfather have in their history that which would make one suspect that they were of the devil's party.

Card B

Hawthorne, p. 21   EFFECT

"Be it so if you will; but, alas! it was a dream of evil omen for young Goodman Brown. A stern, a sad, a darkly meditative, a distrustful, if not a desperate man did he become from the night of the fearful dream."

(quotation from last paragraph of story. Italics added.)

Card C

> MATHEWS, pp. 73-74   ANTINOMIANISM
>
> Antinomianism – doctrine espoused by one group of Calvinists that salvation resulted from faith, not good works. (p. 73)
>
> Like other Antinomians of his day, Goodman Brown believed that if his faith was strong, no evil would be charged against him for his actions. (p. 74)
>
> Perry Miller has written about Antinomians in Massachusetts in his book "The New England Mind: The Seventeenth Century (Cambridge, Harvard Univ. Press, 1954), (p. 74)

Card D

> Connolly, p. 372   CALVINISTIC DOCTRINE
>
> "Calvinism teaches that man is innately depraved and that he can do nothing to merit salvation. He is saved only by the whim of God who selects some, through no deserts of their own, for heaven while the great mass of mankind is destined for hell."

Figure 9.2

● Format of the Research Paper

Card D represents a *verbatim quotation* from one of the articles that she later incorporated in full in her research paper.

The four notecards in Figure 9.2 represent the four kinds of notes that Diana took from her source material. They all have the virtue of being self-contained—that is, they contain all the information she will need to know if she uses the notes in her paper; she will not have to go back to the original source to recover any missing information. For that reason, they represent an ideal set of notes.

● Format of the research paper

General Instructions

A research paper reports the results of some investigation, experiment, interview, or reading that you have done. Some of the ordinary papers you write are also based on personal investigations, interviews, and reading, and when your paper is based on data derived from research you should acknowledge the source of the data. For instance, you can reveal the source of information or quotations by saying, right in the text of your paper, "Mr. Stanley Smith, the director of the Upward Bound project, with whom I talked last week, confirmed the rumor that . . ." or "James Reston said in his column in last Sunday's *New York Times* that . . ." Authors of research papers also use identifying lead-ins like those, but in addition, they supply—usually in endnotes—any further bibliographical information (such as the exact date of the newspaper they are quoting from and the number of the page from which the quotation was taken) that readers would need if they wanted to check the sources. By revealing this specific information about the source, authors enable readers to check whether they have been accurate or fair in their reporting, and they also enhance their credibility with readers.

In the pages that follow, we will present some advice about gathering and reporting material from outside sources, some models of note and bibliography forms, and a sample research paper. The instructor or the publication that you write for may prescribe a format that differs from the advice given here, but if no specific instructions are given, you can follow these suggestions and models with the assurance that they conform to the prevailing conventions for research papers written in most fields. The format for documenting references, citations, and quotations may differ slightly from discipline to discipline, but whether you are writing a research paper in the humanities or in the physical sciences or in the social sciences, the same kind of basic information about the sources is supplied in the documentation.

(A) GATHERING NOTES

If you do enough research, you will eventually discover a system of gathering notes that works best for you. Some people, for instance, just scribble their notes on full sheets of paper or in spiral notebooks. Others record their notes and quotations on 3×5 or 4×6 cards—*one* note or quotation to a card. The advantage of recording notes on separate cards is that later you can select and arrange the cards to suit the order in which you are going to use them in your paper. It is considerably more difficult to select and arrange notes if they are written out, one after the other, on full sheets of paper. You could, of course, cut out notes from the full sheets, but that activity involves you in an extra step.

(B) SELF-CONTAINED NOTECARDS

Each notecard should be self-contained—that is, it should contain all the information you would need to document that material properly if you used it in your paper. A notecard is self-contained if you never have to go back to the original source to recover any bit of information about the note. So each notecard should carry at least this much information:

1 The card should indicate whether the note is paraphrased or quoted verbatim. Don't trust your memory to be able to distinguish later whether a note is paraphrased or quoted.

2 If quoted material covers more than one page in the source from which it was copied, you should devise some system of indicating just where the quoted material went over to the next page. If later you use only part of that quotation, you have to know whether to cite one page (p. 189) or two pages (pp. 189–90) in the endnote. Some notation like **(→ p. 190)** inserted in the notecard after the last word on the page (in this case, after the last word on p. 189) in the original source will help you determine later whether you need to cite one page or two pages.

3 The notecard should contain all the bibliographical information needed to document the note in an endnote of your paper: name of the author, title of the book or article, publication information, and page numbers. If you are taking several notes from the same source, you can devise some shorthand system so that you do not have to write out all the bibliographical information on every notecard.

(C) WHAT NEEDS TO BE DOCUMENTED?

You will have to develop a sense for what needs to be documented with an endnote. Here are some guidelines to help you:

1 Ordinarily, every direct quotation should carry an endnote. However, if you were doing a research paper on, say, a novel, you could be

Writing Research Papers, Letters, and Résumés

spared having to document every quotation from the novel by using an endnote like this the *first time* you quoted from the novel:

> [8]John Steinbeck, <u>The Grapes of Wrath</u> (New York: Viking Press, 1939), p. 134. Hereafter all quotations from this first edition of the novel will be documented with a page number in parentheses immediately after the quotation.

2 Paraphrased material may or may not need an endnote. If the fact or information that you report in your own words is *generally known* by people knowledgeable on the subject, you probably need not document that paraphrased material. For instance, if you were writing a research paper on the assassination of Abraham Lincoln, you probably would not have to document your statement that John Wilkes Booth shot Lincoln in Ford's Theater in Washington in April of 1865, because that historical fact is common knowledge. But if one of the arguments in your paper concerned the *exact time of the day* when he was shot, you would have to document your statement that Lincoln was shot at 8:40 P.M. on the evening of April 14, 1865. When, however, you cannot resolve your doubt about whether paraphrased material needs to be documented with an endnote that reveals the source of the information, document it.

3 When you are summarizing, in your own words, a great deal of information that you have gathered from your reading, you can be spared having to document several sentences in that summary by putting an endnote number after the *first sentence* of the summary and using an endnote like this:

> [10]For the biographical information presented in this and the subsequent paragraph, I am indebted to Minnie M. Brashear, <u>Mark Twain: Son of Missouri</u> (Chapel Hill: University of

North Carolina Press, 1934), pp. 34-65, and
Gamaliel Bradford, "Mark Twain," <u>Atlantic
Monthly</u>, 125 (April 1920), 462-73.

(D) KEEP QUOTATIONS TO A MINIMUM

A research paper should not be just a pastiche of long quotations stitched together by an occasional comment or by a transitional sentence by the author of the paper. You should use your own words as much as possible, and when you do quote, you should keep the quotation brief. Often a quoted phrase or sentence will make a point more emphatically than a long quotation. You must learn to look for the phrase or sentence that represents the kernel of the quotation and to use that extract rather than the full quotation. Otherwise, the point you want to make with the quotation may be lost in all the verbiage. You will be more likely to keep your quotations short if you try to work most of them into the framework of your own sentence, like this:

Frank Ellis calls such an interpretation "the biographical fallacy, the assumption that an exact, one-to-one correspondence exists between the person who is imagined to be speaking the lines of the poem (the Spokesman) and the historical personage who is known to have written the poem."[12]

Writing Research Papers, Letters, and Résumés

However, when you find it difficult to present the essential point in a short extract, a long quotation (two sentences or more) may be necessary. Long quotations should be *inset* ten spaces from the left-hand margin, with *no quotation marks enclosing the quotation.* Although long quotations are usually *double-spaced,* some professors prefer that they be *single-spaced,* as in the following:

Frank Ellis offers this cogent argument to refute the charge that the Epitaph is not integrated with the rest of the poem:

> The evidence for this is said to lie in the fact that there are disparities between the two accounts that are given of the Stonecutter, one by the aged Swain and the other in Epitaph. But it has never been pointed out that these disparities are deliberate and dramatic. The illiterate old rustic is unsympathetic. His disapproval has been softened no doubt by death, but it is still apparent that to him the Stonecutter seemed lazy, queer, unsociable, and probably crazy. But the Epitaph enables the reader to see around this characterization. For the Spokesman, who composed the Epitaph, is an outlander, a fellow poeta ignotus, and therefore unsympathetic.[15]

(E). USE A LEAD-IN FOR ALL QUOTATIONS

Every direct quotation should be accompanied by a lead-in phrase or clause, which at least identifies by name the person who is about to speak. But it further aids coherence if the lead-in also points up the pertinence of the subsequent quotation to what you have been talking about or to what you are going to talk about. Here are some typical identifying and orienting lead-ins:

> Edmund Wilson countered this charge by saying that "there is never any reason for supposing that anybody but the governess sees the ghosts."
>
> "It apparently did not occur to any of Wilson's critics," says Oscar Cargill in defense of Wilson's interpretation, "that James might have an adequate motive for disguising his purpose in the tale."
>
> Robert Heilman has this to say about Wilson's interpretation of Henry James's haunting story:

(Following this last lead-in would be either a single sentence enclosed in quotation marks or a series of sentences inset and single-spaced, like the extended quotation in [D] above.)

(F) THE FORMAT OF ENDNOTES AND FOOTNOTES

The first line of every endnote is indented from the left-hand margin (usually the same number of spaces as paragraph indentations in the body of the paper), but any subsequent lines of the same endnote are brought out to the left-hand margin. The endnotes, which are double-spaced both *within* the endnote and *between* endnotes, appear at the end of the paper. If the notes appear at the bottom of the page on which the reference is made, they are called *footnotes*, and they are identical to endnotes in content and form, *except* that they are single-spaced *within* the footnote and double-spaced *between* footnotes. See MODEL FOOTNOTES (pp. 334–340) and the sample research paper (pp. 348–365) for models of notes.

(G) FORMS OF PRIMARY AND SECONDARY NOTES

A *primary* endnote or footnote form (that is, those giving full bibliographical information) must be used the *first time* a source is cited. Thereafter, that same source can be documented with a *secondary* endnote or footnote form (that is, a shortened form). See MODEL FOOTNOTES (pp. 334–340) and the sample research paper (pp. 348–365) for models of notes.

(H) THE FORMAT OF BIBLIOGRAPHICAL ENTRIES

Bibliographical entries are arranged alphabetically on separate pages at the end of the research paper. The list of entries is alphabetized according to the last name of the author (or, in the case of unsigned articles, according to the first significant word in the title). For that reason, the names of the authors are inverted in the bibliography—e.g. **Heilman, Robert.** The first line of each bibliographical entry begins at the left-hand margin, and any subsequent lines in that entry are indented (just the opposite of the format of endnotes). Bibliographical entries are single-spaced *within* the entry and double-spaced *between* entries. (If, however, the paper is being submitted for publication, the bibliographical entries are double-spaced both within the entry and between entries.) See MODELS FOR BIBLIOGRAPHY (pp. 341–342 and 343–347) for other differences between the format of endnotes and the format of bibliographical entries.

(l) ELLIPSIS PERIODS

Ellipsis periods (three spaced periods) are used to indicate that words or whole sentences have been omitted from a direct quotation:

```
The president said last week that "the Ameri-

can people . . . would not tolerate such vio-

lence."
```

(Note that there is a space between periods; wrong form: ...)

```
Philip Gove said in a letter to the New York

Times,

    The paragraph is, of course, a monstrosity,
    totally removed from possible occurrence in
    connection with any genuine attempt to use
    words in normally expected context. . . . A
    similar artificial monstrosity could be con-
    trived by jumbling together inappropriate
    words from formal literary language or from
    the Second Edition.
```

(The fourth period in this instance is the period used to mark the end of the sentence. Because of this period and the capital letter with which the next group of words begins, we know that at

least the end of the first sentence has been omitted and that possibly several sentences or paragraphs have been removed before the next sentence.)

Usually there is no need to put ellipsis periods at the beginning or end of a quotation, because the reader knows that the quotation has been extracted from a larger context. Reserve ellipsis periods for indicating omissions *within* quotations.

(J) SQUARE BRACKETS

Square brackets are used to enclose anything that the author of the research paper inserts into a direct quotation:

```
About this tendency to indulge in scatological
language, H. A. Taine wrote, "He [Swift] drags
poetry not only through the mud, but into the
filth; he rolls in it like a raging madman, he
enthrones himself in it, and bespatters all
passers-by."

The Senator was emphatic in stating his reac-
tion to the measure:  "This action by HEW
[ Health, Education, and Welfare ] will defi-
nitely not reverse the downward spiral [of
prices and wages] that has plagued us for the
last eight months."
```

We find this entry in the Japanese admiral's diary: "Promptly at 8:32 on Sunday morning of December 6 [sic], 1941, I dispatched the first wave of bombers for the raid on Perl Harber. [sic]."

(**Sic** *is a Latin adverb meaning "thus," "in this manner," and is used to let the reader know that the error in logic or fact or grammar or spelling in the quotation has been copied exactly as it was in the original source. It is italicized because it is a foreign word.*)

If your typewriter does not have keys that make square brackets, you will have to draw the brackets with a pen after you remove the paper from the typewriter, and so you should leave spaces for the brackets.

Format of the Research Paper: Model Footnotes

In research papers, documentation is usually in the form of endnotes which appear consecutively at the end of the paper, beginning on a new page titled "Notes." (See the endnotes for the sample research paper on pp. 348–365.) Documentation for dissertations, however, is usually in the form of footnotes, which appear on the bottom of the page on which the reference occurs. Some professors also prefer that you use footnotes in *research papers,* so it is best to ask which form your instructor requires. The only difference between endnotes and footnotes besides location is that footnotes are single-spaced *within* the footnote and double-spaced *between* footnotes, while endnotes are double-spaced *both within and between* endnotes. The notes below are in footnote-form.

The models presented for footnotes, endnotes, and bibliography (sections K–N) follow the forms prescribed in the *MLA Handbook* (New York: Modern Language Association, 1977).

(K) PRIMARY FOOTNOTES

(the first reference to a source)

(1) A single book by a single author:

> [14]Hozen Seki, <u>The Great Natural Way</u> (New York: American Buddhist Academy, 1976), p. 88.

8John W. Landon, Jesse Crawford: Poet of the Organ, Wizard of the Mighty Wurlitzer (Vestal, NY: The Vestal Press, 1974), pp. 75-76.

*(Notice that the first line of the footnote is indented and that subsequent lines of the footnote start at the left-hand margin. The **p.** is the abbreviation of **page; pp.** is the abbreviation of **pages**.)*

(2) A single book by more than one author:

12Paul A. Baran and Paul M. Sweezy, Monop-oly Capital (New York: Monthly Review Press, 1966), p. 392.

(3) A book of more than one volume:

13William Lee Hays and Robert L. Winkler, Statistics: Probability, Inference, and Deci-sion (New York: Holt, Rinehart & Winston, 1970), II, 137.

*(Whenever a volume number is cited [here the Roman numeral **II**], the abbreviation **p.** or **pp.** is not used in front of the page number.)*

(4) A book edited by one or more editors:

3Essays in American Economic History, ed. Alfred W. Coats and Ross M. Robertson (London: Edward Arnold, 1969), pp. 268-9.

> [9]The Letters of Jonathan Swift to Charles Ford, ed. David Nichol Smith (Oxford: Clarendon Press, 1935), p. 187.

(*Here the abbreviation* **ed.** *stands for* **edited by**.)

(5) An essay or a chapter by an author in an edited collection:

> [2]Martin J. Svaglic, "Classical Rhetoric and Victorian Prose," The Art of Victorian Prose, ed. George Levine and William Madden (New York: Oxford Univ. Press, 1968), pp. 268-70.

(6) A new edition of a book:

> [5]Oswald Doughty, A Victorian Romantic, Dante Gabriel Rossetti, 2nd ed. (London: Oxford Univ. Press, 1960), p. 35.

(*Here the abbreviation* **ed.** *stands for* **edition**.)

(7) A book that is part of a series:

> [26]William Heytesbury, Medieval Logic and the Rise of Mathematical Physics. University of Wisconsin Publications in Medieval Science, No. 3 (Madison: Univ. of Wisconsin Press, 1956), p. 97.

(*Here the abbreviation* **No.** *stands for* **Number**.)

(8) A book in a paperback series:

> [11]Edmund Wilson, <u>To the Finland Station</u>, Anchor Books (Garden City, NY: Doubleday, 1955), p. 130.

(9) A translation:

> [6]Fyodor Dostoevsky, <u>Crime and Punishment</u>, trans. Constance Garnett (New York: Heritage Press, 1938), p. 351.
>
> [7]Jacques Ellul, <u>A Critique of the New Commonplaces</u>, trans. Helen Weaver (New York: Knopf, 1968), pp. 139-40.

(*The abbreviation* **trans.** *stands for* **translated by**.)

(10) A signed and an unsigned article from an encyclopedia:

> [4]J. A. Ewing, "Steam-Engine and Other Heat-Engines," <u>Encyclopaedia Britannica</u>, 9th ed., XXII, 475-7.
>
> [10]"Dwarfed Trees," <u>Encyclopedia Americana</u>, 1948, IX, 445.

(*Since encyclopedias periodically undergo revision and updating, the particular edition consulted should be indicated by a date or a number. In the bibliography, unsigned articles are filed alphabetically according to the first significant word in the title— here* **Dwarfed**.)

Writing Research Papers, Letters, and Résumés

(11) An article from a journal:

> ^{12}Nelson Adkins, "Emerson and the Bardic Tradition," <u>PMLA</u>, 72 (1948), 665.
>
> ^{8}Theodore Otto Windt, Jr., "The Diatribe: Last Resort for Protest," <u>QJS</u>, 58 (1972), 9-10.

(*Well-known scholarly journals are commonly referred to by their abbreviated titles. Here* **PMLA** *stands for* **Publications of the Modern Language Association; QJS** *stands for* **Quarterly Journal of Speech**. *Volume numbers of journals are now designated by an Arabic number [here* **72** *and* **58**] *rather than, as formerly, by a Roman numeral. Because the volume number has been cited, the abbreviations* **p.** *and* **pp.** *are not used in front of the page numbers.*)

(12) An article in a popular magazine:

> ^{4}Robert J. Levin, "Sex, Morality, and Society," <u>Saturday Review</u>, 9 July 1966, p. 29.
>
> ^{7}Charles E. Silberman, "Technology Is Knocking on the Schoolhouse Door," <u>Fortune</u>, Aug. 1966, pp. 121-2.

(*Note that* **Saturday Review** *is a weekly magazine;* **Fortune** *is a monthly. Because no volume number is cited,* **p.** *and* **pp.** *are used in front of the page numbers.*)

(13) A signed and an unsigned article in a newspaper:

> [15]Art Gilman, "Altering U.S. Flag for Po-
> litical Causes Stirs a Legal Debate," Wall
> Street Journal, 12 June 1970, p. 1.
>
> [26]"Twin Games Bid: Wrestling, Judo," New
> York Times, 9 April 1972, Section 5, p. 15,
> cols. 4-6.

(*For editions of a newspaper with multiple sections, each with its own pagination, it is necessary to cite the section in addition to the page number. It is helpful also to give column numbers. Sometimes, if an article appeared in one edition of a newspaper but not in other editions, it is necessary to specify the particular edition of the newspaper—e.g.* **New York Times, Late City Ed., 4 Feb. 1972, p. 12, col. 1**.)

(14) A signed book review:

> [19]John F. Dalbor, rev. of Meaning and Mind:
> A Study in the Psychology of Language, by Rob-
> ert F. Terwilliger, Philosophy & Rhetoric, 5
> (1972), 60-61.
>
> [3]Brendan Gill, rev. of Ibsen, by Michael
> Meyer, New Yorker, 8 April 1972, p. 128.

(*The first review appeared in a scholarly journal; the second review appeared in a weekly magazine. The abbreviation* **rev.** *stands for* **review**.)

Writing Research Papers, Letters, and Résumés

(L) SECONDARY FOOTNOTES

(shortened forms after a source has once been given in full)

> ¹⁵Seki, p. 80.

(This is the shortened form of the first footnote given in (1) *under* PRIMARY FOOTNOTES.)

> ¹⁶Hays and Winkler, II, 140.

(This is the shortened form of the footnote given in (3) *under* PRIMARY FOOTNOTES.)

> ¹⁷Wilson, Finland Station, pp. 220-2.

(When more than one book or article by the same author has been cited in a paper, you must use an abbreviated title in addition to the surname of the author in order to identify the source. In footnote **17** *above,* **Finland Station** *is an abbreviated form of the full title,* **To the Finland Station.)**

> ¹⁸"Rendezvous with Ecology," p. 97.

(In the case of an anonymous article or book, the title or a shortened form of it must be used in subsequent references to that source.)

Format of the Research Paper: Models for Bibliography

The form of a bibliography entry differs in some ways from that of an endnote or a footnote reference. The following shows how the two forms handle a citation for the same book:

BIBLIOGRAPHY FORM

```
Ryan, Edwin.  A College Handbook to Newman.
    Washington, DC: Catholic Education Press,
    1930.
```

ENDNOTE AND FOOTNOTE FORM

```
    8
     Edwin Ryan, A College Handbook to
Newman (Washington, DC: Catholic Education
Press, 1930), p. 109.
```

The following lists, in parallel columns, point out the difference between the two forms:

BIBLIOGRAPHY	NOTE
(a) The first line begins at the left-hand margin, with all subsequent lines indented.	**(a)** The first line is indented, with all subsequent lines brought out to the left-hand margin.

BIBLIOGRAPHY	NOTE

(b) The name of the author is inverted (last name first) for purposes of alphabetizing the list of entries.

(b) The name of the author is set down in the normal order.

(c) The three main divisions (author, title, and publishing data) are separated by periods.

(c) The three main divisions (author, title, and publishing data) are separated by commas.

(d) Place of publication, name of the publisher, and publication date follow the title, without parentheses.

(d) Place of publication, name of the publisher, and publication date are enclosed in parentheses.

(e) The subtitle, if any, should be included in the citation. See (2) below.

(e) The subtitle, if any, may be omitted in the citation.

(f) There is no page reference unless the entry is for an article or part of a collection, in which case the full span of pages (first page and last page) is cited.

(f) Only a specific page reference is cited.

(M) CORRESPONDING BIBLIOGRAPHY FORMS FOR THE FOURTEEN MODEL FOOTNOTES

The bibliography entries are usually double-spaced both *within* the entry and *between* entries, as they are below and in the bibliography of the sample research paper (p. 348–365). However, some professors prefer that bibliography entries be single-spaced *within* the entry and double-spaced *between* entries, so it is best to find out which format your instructor requires.

(1) A single book by a single author:

```
Seki, Hozen.  The Great Natural Way. New York:

    American Buddhist Academy, 1976.

Landon, John W. Jesse Crawford: Poet of the

    Organ, Wizard of the Mighty Wurlitzer. Ves-

    tal, NY: The Vestal Press, 1974.
```

(2) A single book by more than one author:

```
Baran, Paul A., and Paul M. Sweezy.  Monopoly

    Capital: An Essay on American Economic and

    Social Order.  New York:  Monthly Review

    Press, 1966.
```

(*Only the name of the first author should be inverted. Notice that the subtitle, which was omitted in the footnote, is included here.*)

(3) A book of more than one volume:

```
Hays, William Lee, and Robert L. Winkler, Sta-

    tistics: Probability, Inference, and Deci-
```

```
sion. 2 vols. New York: Holt, Rinehart &

Winston, 1970.
```

(4) A book edited by one or more editors:

```
Essays in American Economic History. Ed.

    Alfred W. Coats and Ross M. Robertson. Lon-

    don: Edward Arnold, 1969.

The Letters of Jonathan Swift to Charles Ford.

    Ed. David Nichol Smith. Oxford: Clarendon

    Press, 1935.
```

(*In the bibliography, these books would be filed alphabetically according to the first significant word in the title—***Essays** *and* **Letters** *respectively.*)

(5) An essay or a chapter by an author in an edited collection:

```
Svaglic, Martin J. "Classical Rhetoric and Vic-

    torian Prose." The Art of Victorian Prose.

    Ed. George Levine and William Madden. New

    York: Oxford Univ. Press, 1968, pp. 268-88.
```

(*Because this essay is part of a collection, the full span of pages is cited in the bibliography.*)

(6) A new edition of a book:

```
Doughty, Oswald. A Victorian Romantic, Dante
    Gabriel Rossetti. 2nd ed. London: Oxford
    Univ. Press, 1960.
```

(7) A book that is part of a series:

```
Heytesbury, William. Medieval Logic and the
    Rise of Mathematical Physics. University of
    Wisconsin Publications in Medieval Science,
    No. 3. Madison: Univ. of Wisconsin Press,
    1956.
```

(8) A book in a paperback series:

```
Wilson, Edmund. To the Finland Station. Anchor
    Books. Garden City, NY: Doubleday, 1955.
```

(9) A translation:

```
Dostoevsky, Fyodor. Crime and Punishment.
    Trans. Constance Garnett. New York: Herit-
    age Press, 1938.
Ellul, Jacques. A Critique of the New Common-
    places. Trans. Helen Weaver. New York:
    Knopf, 1968.
```

Writing Research Papers, Letters, and Résumés

(10) A signed and an unsigned article from an encyclopedia:

```
Ewing, J. A. "Steam-Engine and Other Heat-
     Engines." Encyclopaedia Britannica. 9th ed.,
     XXII, 473-526.
"Dwarfed Trees." Encyclopedia Americana. 1948,
     IX, 445-46.
```

(Notice that the full span of pages of these articles is given.)

(11) An article from a journal:

```
Adkins, Nelson. "Emerson and the Bardic Tradi-
     tion." Publications of the Modern Language
     Association, 72 (1948), 662-7.
Windt, Theodore Otto, Jr. "The Diatribe: Last
     Resort for Protest." Quarterly Journal of
     Speech, 58 (1972), 1-14.
```

(Although in endnotes and footnotes well-known scholarly journals are commonly referred to by their abbreviated titles, it is advisable to give the full title in the bibliography.)

(12) An article in a popular magazine:

Levin, Robert J. "Sex, Morality, and Society."

Saturday Review, 9 July 1966, pp. 29-30.

Silberman, Charles E. "Technology Is Knocking

on the Schoolhouse Door." Fortune, Aug.

1966, pp. 120-25.

(13) A signed and an unsigned article in a newspaper:

Gilman, Art. "Altering U. S. Flag for Political

Causes Stirs a Legal Debate." Wall Street

Journal, 12 June 1970, p. 1.

"Twin Games Bid: Wrestling, Judo." New York

Times, 9 April 1972, Section 5, p. 15,

cols. 4-6.

(14) A signed book review:

Dalbor, John B. Review of Meaning and Mind: A

Study in the Psychology of Language, by

Robert F. Terwilliger. Philosophy & Rheto-

ric, 5 (1972), 60-61.

Gill, Brendan. Review of Ibsen, by Michael

Meyer. New Yorker, 8 April 1972, pp. 126-

30.

(N) Format of the Research Paper: Model Research Paper (with endnotes)

Diana Lynn Ikenberry

English 302

January 7, 1977

A Study of the Various Interpretations of

"Young Goodman Brown"

Nathaniel Hawthorne's "Young Goodman Brown" has been sub-
jected to various interpretations. A prime reason for so many
different interpretations is the story's extremely ambiguous
nature. One critic seldom agrees with another as to why various parts of the story are ambiguous. One question that has
engaged many critics is whether Goodman Brown actually went
into the forest and met the devil or whether he only dreamed
that he did. Richard Fogle is one critic who believes that
Hawthorne failed to answer this question definitively, because "the ambiguities of meaning are intentional, an integral
part of his purpose."[1] Fogle feels that the ambiguity results
from unanswered questions like the one above. And it is just
this ambiguity or "device of multiple choice,"[2] as Fogle calls
it, that is the very essence of "Young Goodman Brown."

Critic Thomas F. Walsh, Jr. went a step further in analyzing the ambiguity of Brown's journey into the forest.[3] He
agreed with Fogle that the reader can never be certain whether
the journey was real or imaginary; however, the reader can be
certain "not only of the nature and stages of Goodman Brown's
despair, but also of its probable cause."[4] Walsh also points

2

out that the effect upon Brown, once he emerges from the forest, is quite clear: "Goodman Brown lived and died an unhappy, despairing man."[5] It is Walsh's view that the only solution to the problem of ambiguity in relation to what happened in the forest can be found in the story's complex symbolic pattern.

D. M. McKeithan's view of Brown's journey is unlike any of the previously mentioned views. He feels that, in reality, Goodman Brown neither journeyed into the forest that night nor dreamed that he did. What Brown did do, according to McKeithan, was "to indulge in sin (represented by the journey into the forest that night . . .)," thinking that he could break away from his sinfulness whenever he chose to.[6] However, Brown indulged in sin longer than he expected and "suffered the consequences, which were the loss of religious faith and faith in all other human beings."[7]

All of these critics have something to add to readers' notions about the ambiguous nature of "Young Goodman Brown." It is the purpose of this paper to study some of these critics' interpretations, as well as the interpretations of some critics not yet mentioned, to see just exactly what they have to add to the interpretation of Hawthorne's masterpiece. I will focus primarily on two areas of interpretations: the realizations of Goodman Brown's faith and the over-all implications

of the story itself. These two areas proved to be quite controversial.

Despite all the ambiguities of meaning mentioned above,
I must conclude that young Goodman Brown did come to some realizations about his own personal faith. When Brown starts out
on his journey into the forest, he is confident that his faith
will carry him to heaven. As Thomas E. Connolly points out,
"it is in this concept that his disillusionment will come."[8]
I must agree with Connolly's statement, for Brown thinks that
his wife delayed his journey, but when he arrives at the meeting place with the devil, his Faith is already there. Brown's
confidence in his virtuous wife has been shattered, and from
this point on, he cannot be at peace with himself nor with
any of those around him.

Not only does Connolly suggest Brown's disillusionment,
but he argues that Brown's Calvinistic religion is a major
cause of his disillusionment.[9] Connolly presents this doctrine of Calvinism to his readers:

> Calvinism teaches that man is innately de-
> praved and that he can do nothing to merit
> salvation. He is saved only by the whim
> of God who selects some, through no deserts
> of their own, for heaven while the great
> mass of mankind is destined for hell.[10]

4

I think Goodman Brown was a Calvinist, in the sense that he believed himself to be one of God's Elect. I do not think, however, that Brown found nothing to merit salvation, for even though he believed himself to be one of the Elect, he knew he must cling to his faith in order to get to heaven. One particular group of Calvinists, known as Antinomians,[11] were quite active during the time Hawthorne was writing "Young Goodman Brown." It seems quite possible that this Calvinistic group could have influenced Hawthorne's characterizations. The Antinomians insisted that salvation was a function of faith, for even a man's good works were secondary to his faith. This "mysterious divine grace,"[12] as James W. Mathews calls it, "was contingent on the degree of the individual's faith,"[13] while a strong faith was a good indication of predestined salvation. Extreme Antinomians believed that a man who was of God's Elect could be confident of salvation, no matter how the man conducted himself in his daily living. It seems quite possible, then, that Brown could be classified as an Antinomian, since he was depending on his faith to carry him to heaven.

Mathews makes a strong case for Hawthorne's development of Antinomianism within young Goodman Brown. Brown himself does stress the theoretical rather than the practical side of his religion, as does the Antinomian doctrine. Brown states at one point in the story that "we are a people of prayer,

and good works to boot, and abide no such wickedness."[14]
Later in the story, Brown further adds, "With heaven above
and Faith below, I will yet stand firm against the devil!"
(p. 15). He is quite confident that his being one of God's
Elect, along with his having Faith at home, will prevent any
of the night's evil doings from becoming obstacles in his path
to salvation.

It seems important at this point to look at Faith's relationship with her husband. Brown knows that his journey is
of a sinful nature: "Poor little Faith! . . . What a wretch
am I to leave her on such an errand!" (p. 10). Brown clearly
manifests a sense of guilt for leaving his wife, because he
seems to think it would "kill her" if she knew why he was
going on his journey. However, I think Faith does know his
purpose, because she says to her husband,

> "Dearest heart," whispered she, softly
> and rather sadly . . . "prithee put off
> your journey until sunrise and sleep in
> your own bed tonight. . . . Pray tarry
> with me this night, dear husband, of all
> nights in the year" (p. 10).

Why would Faith be sad to see her husband leave for just one
night, and why would she beg him to stay home on this partic-

6

ular evening? Faith not only realizes her husband's plans but even gives her consent and asks for God's blessing to be with Brown when he insists that he must go: "'Then God bless you!' said Faith, . . . 'and may you find all well when you come back'" (p. 10). I think Faith is particularly concerned with her husband's state of mind <u>after</u> the night's experience. Faith does not appear extremely worried about his leaving, but I think she doubts whether he can accept the consequences. Faith's ability to see that her husband may suffer from the results of his journey is Hawthorne's way of subtly informing his readers that Faith is the wiser and the more realistic of the two. She knows that her husband will soon find out the hard way that Faith--both his wife <u>and</u> his religion--cannot be used at his convenience whenever he is troubled.

Connolly sheds an even brighter light upon young Goodman Brown's faith. He points out that Brown did not lose his faith at all. What Brown did do was not only retain his faith but actually discover "the full and frightening signif- icance of his faith."[15] Connolly illustrates his point with this line from the story: "And when he had lived long, and was borne to his grave a hoary corpse, followed by Faith, an aged woman, and children and grandchildren, . . . they carved no hopeful verse upon his tombstone, for his dying hour was gloom" (p. 21). I must agree with Connolly that Brown's faith--both his wife and his religion--did survive him.

Brown did not lose his wife, even though he did lose the love and trust that had once linked them together happily. And Brown did not lose his religion, for I feel that when Hawthorne wrote this story, he knew that the Calvinistic faith would out-live Goodman Brown. I think Hawthorne realizes that many more "young Goodman Browns" would perish as an indirect result of such a dehumanizing religion.

Besides the subject of faith in "Young Goodman Brown," I would also like to touch upon the over-all implications of the story. Without a doubt, ambiguity is quite prevalent throughout the story. For example, one critic asked, "Does the story have universal significance, or is it merely an in-dividual tragedy?"[16] Another critic questioned whether young Goodman Brown represents the majority of the human race or only a small segment of the human population.[17] Various critics have asked similar questions and have arrived at a variety of answers.

Paul W. Miller is one critic who has struggled with the question of whether Brown should be viewed as an individual or a type, representing either all of mankind or only a seg-ment of it. Miller seems to think that no conclusion can be drawn concerning Brown's representation because the answer depends on "one's understanding of Hawthorne's view of man when he wrote the story, as well as one's interpretation of this enigmatic but nonetheless fascinating tale."[18] Miller

contends that if young Goodman Brown is intended to represent
all mankind, then Hawthorne must be regarded as a totally cyn-
ical man; whereas if Brown represents only a segment of mankind,
then Hawthorne could be viewed less pessimistically. Miller
brings up an interesting point here. If Brown does not represent all mankind, are men like Brown doomed by their nature to
be separated from God, or does the society in which they live
play a major role in separating them from God?[19] I think that,
in Brown's case, the society in which he lives has developed a
religion that refuses to acknowledge sin as an inevitable human weakness. Man is responsible for his separation from God,
but the Calvinistic religion seems to suggest that a man's re-
unification with God is unobtainable if he is not one of the
Elect. Human society ultimately strives to develop a religion
to fill man's need for spiritual comfort, but it appears that
the Calvinists developed a religion that tortured man's spirit.
What portion of mankind, then, does Brown represent? Miller
contends that

> he represents those weaker members of a
> puritanical society who are traumatized,
> arrested in their spiritual development,
> and finally destroyed by the discovery
> that their society is full of "whited
> sepulchres."[20]

I find Miller's interpretation more acceptable than other critics' views. Young Goodman Brown's spiritual development has been not only retarded but warped at the same time, but I do not think Brown himself can be fully blamed.

I can agree only in part with D. M. McKeithan's opinion about the over-all implication of the story.[21] He contends that

> this is not a story of the disillusionment
> that comes to a person when he discovers
> that many supposedly religious and virtuous
> people are really sinful; it is, rather, a
> story of a man whose sin led him to consider
> all other people sinful.[22]

I think Brown is extremely disillusioned when he realizes the sinful nature of Goody Cloyse, Deacon Gookin, and his own wife, Faith. As I view the story, this disillusionment, which denies all that Brown had previously believed, is a major factor in the over-all meaning of the story. Those persons who had always seemed virtuous, pure, and representative of Brown's religion were suddenly seen in a different light--a definite disillusionment for young Goodman Brown. Contrary to McKeithan's view, the story does seem to imply that Brown is disillusioned when he discovers that certain virtuous people

10

are sinful and that Brown becomes painfully aware of his own sinfulness and of the sinfulness of his fellowmen. However, even with the disillusionment that Brown faces and the realization of his own sinful nature, he still fails to perceive two very important characteristics of sin: its universal and inevitable nature.

I also agree, in part, with Herbert Schneider, who places particular importance on Hawthorne's concern with the sinful side of human nature. He writes of Hawthorne,

> For him sin is an obvious and conspicuous
> fact, to deny which is foolish. Its con-
> sequences are inevitable and to seek escape
> from them is childish. The only relief
> from sin comes from public confession. Any-
> thing private or concealed works internally
> until it destroys the sinner's soul.[23]

I strongly agree with Schneider that Hawthorne's denial of sin is foolish and that its consequences are inevitable. However, I question whether Hawthorne feels that a <u>public</u> confession is the sole relief from sin. I think Hawthorne would feel that a private confession could adequately render a sense of relief from one's sinfulness. Young Goodman Brown was unable to bring himself to make either a public or a private confession. He

could not accept the sin he saw in others nor the sin present
within himself, primarily because Calvinistic teachings failed
to inform him that sin in man is inevitable. Paul Miller sums
up my feelings quite well when he says,

> In "Young Goodman Brown," then, Hawthorne
> . . . is pleading that what survives of
> Puritan rigorism in society be sloughed off
> and replaced by a striving for virtue start-
> ing from the confession of common human
> weakness. Such a society would be based
> upon the firm foundation of humility and
> honesty rather than the sinking sands of
> human pride and the hypocrisy that accom-
> panies it.[24]

I do agree with Miller that even a type like Brown could survive in a society like the one described above. Society can
truly have an adverse effect upon man, as did Goodman Brown's
society. But, at the same time, man must face the realities
of society, as Faith seemed to do, even though the pressures
of society oftentimes seem unbearable.

  Doesn't it seem slightly odd that the mere actions of one
character could elicit so many interpretations from critics?
That there should be so many different interpretations seems

12

quite out of the ordinary to me. Yet when one considers the questions that Nathaniel Hawthorne was dealing with in "Young Goodman Brown," the ambiguity present in the story seems as inevitable as the sin that is present in man. In "Young Goodman Brown," Hawthorne found himself dealing with the mysteries that naturally stimulate man to question. And this questioning will go on forever, hopefully, because unless man finds answers to questions concerning his spiritual being or to questions concerning all the intricacies of the human mind, life will hardly be worth living.

I think Hawthorne truly valued this questioning when he wrote this masterpiece. By his dealing with man's faith and man's society, Hawthorne was able to stimulate man to question his beliefs and his own personal role in society. Hawthorne wanted to point out to the Calvinists in a subtle way that their religious teachings were having an adverse effect upon certain people. And I think he wanted the Calvinists to see that the society--not the individual--needed the reform. Through his characterization of Faith, Hawthorne was able to show that man could be considered virtuous, even though he is guilty of some degree of sin. And, finally, I think Hawthorne wanted his readers to see that man's doubtfulness concerning his salvation was <u>natural</u> and <u>necessary</u>, for if man definitely knew that he was one of God's Elect, he would take love and

13

peace of mind for granted.   Young Goodman Brown lost all doubt
concerning his salvation for only one night, but his experience
on that one night caused Brown to live the rest of his life as
an extremely unhappy man.

Notes

[1] Richard H. Fogle, "Ambiguity and Clarity in Hawthorne's 'Young Goodman Brown,'" <u>New England Quarterly</u>,18 (1945), 448.

[2] Fogle, p. 449.

[3] Thomas F. Walsh, Jr., "The Bedeviling of Young Goodman Brown," <u>Modern Language Quarterly</u>, 19 (1958), 331-6.

[4] Walsh, p. 332.

[5] Walsh, p. 336.

[6] D. M. McKeithan, "Hawthorne's 'Young Goodman Brown': An Interpretation," <u>Modern Language Notes</u>, 67 (Feb.1952), 96.

[7] McKeithan, p. 96.

[8] Thomas E. Connolly, "Hawthorne's 'Young Goodman Brown': An Attack on Puritanic Calvinism," <u>American Literature</u>, 28 (1956), 372.

[9] Connolly, p. 375.

15

[10] Connolly, p. 374.

[11] James W. Mathews, "Antinomianism in 'Young Goodman Brown,'" <u>Studies in Short Fiction</u>, 3 (Fall 1965), 73-5.

[12] Mathews, p. 73.

[13] Mathews, p. 73.

[14] This and subsequent quotations from the story "Young Goodman Brown" are taken from the text of the story as reprinted in <u>Nathaniel Hawthorne: Young Goodman Brown</u>, ed. Thomas E. Connolly (Columbus, Ohio: Merrill, 1968), pp. 10-21. Hereafter, quotations from this version of the story will be documented with page numbers in parentheses at the end of the quotation.

[15] Connolly, p. 371.

[16] Paul W. Miller, "Hawthorne's 'Young Goodman Brown': Cynicism or Meliorism?" <u>Nineteenth-Century Fiction</u>, 14 (1959), 255.

[17] Miller, p. 255.

16

[18] Miller, p. 255.

[19] Miller, p. 256.

[20] Miller, p. 262.

[21] McKeithan, pp. 93-6.

[22] McKeithan, pp. 95-6.

[23] Herbert W. Schneider, <u>The Puritan Mind</u> (New York: Holt, 1930), p. 260.

[24] Miller, p. 264.

Writing Research Papers, Letters, and Résumés

Bibliography

Connolly, Thomas E. "Hawthorne's 'Young Goodman Brown': An
    Attack on Puritanic Calvinism." <u>American Literature</u>,
    28 (1956), 370-5.

Fogle, Richard H. "Ambiguity and Clarity in Hawthorne's 'Young
    Goodman Brown.'" <u>New England Quarterly</u>, 18 (1945), 448-65.

Hawthorne, Nathaniel. "Young Goodman Brown." In <u>Nathaniel
    Hawthorne: Young Goodman Brown</u>. Ed. Thomas E. Connolly.
    Columbus, Ohio: Merrill, 1968, pp. 10-21.

McKeithan, D. M. "Hawthorne's 'Young Goodman Brown': An
    Interpretation." <u>Modern Language Notes</u>, 67 (Feb. 1952),
    93-6.

Mathews, James W. "Antinomianism in 'Young Goodman Brown.'"
    <u>Studies in Short Fiction</u>, 3 (Fall 1965), 73-5.

Miller, Paul W. "Hawthorne's 'Young Goodman Brown': Cynicism
    or Meliorism?" <u>Nineteenth-Century Fiction</u>, 14 (1959),
    255-64.

● Format of the Research Paper

18

Schneider, Herbert W.   The Puritan Mind.   New York: Holt, 1930.

Walsh, Thomas F., Jr.   "The Bedeviling of Young Goodman Brown."
   Modern Language Quarterly, 19 (1958), 331-6.

Writing Research Papers, Letters, and Résumés

(O) Format of the Research Paper: The APA System of Documentation

If the MLA system of documentation, illustrated in the previous section, is predominant in the humanities, the American Psychological Association (APA) system is predominant in such fields as psychology, education, psycholinguistics, and many of the social sciences. Over a hundred scholarly journals in the United States now prescribe the APA style of documentation. The highlights of this system will be presented here; for a fuller treatment, consult the readily available paperback edition of *Publication Manual of the American Psychological Association*, 2nd ed. (Washington, D. C.: American Psychological Association, 1974).

The two principal differences between the MLA and the APA systems are as follows:

(1)   Whereas the MLA system documents quotations and other kinds of references in endnotes at the end of the paper or footnotes at the bottom of the page of the citation, the APA system documents all citations *within parentheses in the text.*

(2)   Whereas the MLA system supplies complete bibliographic information about a work the first time that work is cited in an endnote or a footnote, the APA system supplies only the *last name of the author,* the *publication date of the work,* and sometimes the *page number.*

Here is how the first reference to a book would be documented, first in the MLA (footnote) style and then in the APA style:

```
    3Mina P. Shaughnessy, Errors and Expecta-
tions: A Guide for the Teacher of Basic Writing
(New York: Oxford University Press, 1977),
p. 57.

    (Shaughnessy, 1977, p. 57).
```

Readers who wanted fuller information about the work cited in the parenthetical reference could turn to the list of references at the end of the paper. There, in an alphabetical listing, the Shaughnessy work would be entered in double-spaced type-script as follows:

```
Shaughnessy, M. P.  Errors and expectations: A

    guide for the teacher of basic writing.  New

    York: Oxford University Press, 1977.
```

VARIATIONS ON THE BASIC APA STYLE OF DOCUMENTATION

(a) If a whole work is being referred to, only the author's last name and the date of the work are given in parentheses.

```
A recent study has confirmed that twelve-year-

olds grow at an amazingly rapid rate (Swanson,

1969).
```

Writing Research Papers, Letters, and Résumés

(b) A page number or a chapter number is supplied only if part of a work is being referred to. Quotations always demand the addition of a page number.

> The committee boldly declared that "morality
> could not be enforced, but it could be bought"
> (Dawson, 1975, p. 105).

(c) Any information supplied in the text itself need not be repeated in the parentheses.

> Anderson (1948) found that only middle-class
> Europeans disdained our cultural values.
>
> In 1965, Miller professed his fervent admira-
> tion of our admissions policy.

(d) If a work has two authors, both authors should be cited each time a reference is made to that text. If a work has three or more authors, all the authors should be cited the first time, but subsequently only the name of the first author followed by **et al.** needs to be given.

> The circulation of false rumors poisoned the
> environment of that conference (Getty & Howard,
> 1979).

The overall effect of the smear tactics was a
marked decline in voter registrations (Abraham,
Davis & Keppler, 1952).

In three successive national elections, voters
from Slavic neighborhooks showed a 72% turnout
(Abraham et al., 1952, pp. 324-327).

(e)   If several works are cited at the same point in the text, the works should be arranged alphabetically according to the last name of the author and should be separated with semi-colons.

All the studies of the problem agree that the
proposed remedy is worse than the malady (Brown
& Turkell, 1964; Firkins, 1960; Howells, 1949;
Jackson, Miller, & Naylor, undated; Kameron,
in press).

(f)   If several works by the same author are cited in the same reference, the works are distinguished by the publication dates, arranged in chronological order and separated with commas. Two or more works published by the same author in the same year are distinguished by the letters **a, b, c,** etc., added to the repeated date. In such chronological listings, works "in press" are always listed last.

> A consistent view on this point has been re-
> peatedly expressed by the Canadian member of
> the Commission (Holden, 1959, 1965, 1970, 1971a,
> 1971b, 1976).

(g) If no author is given for a work, two or three words from another part of the entry (usually from the title) should be used to refer to the work.

> The voters' apathy was decried in the final
> spring meeting of the city council ("The
> Gradual Decline," 1976).

LIST OF REFERENCES

The *References* page appended to a paper that observes the APA style is comparable to, and yet different from, the *Bibliography* page in a paper that observes the MLA style. Both systems give full bibliographic information about the works cited in the body of the writing, and both systems arrange the entries alphabetically according to the last name of the author. In both systems, the names of the authors are inverted (surname first), but in the APA system, only the initials of first and middle names are given, and when there are two or more authors for a work, the names of *all* the authors are inverted.

The conventions of sequence, punctuation, and capitalization in the APA style for the *References* section can most easily be illustrated with examples.

(1) A book by a single author:

```
Luria, A. R.  The working brain: An introduct-
     ion to neuro-psychology. London: Penguin,
     1973.
```

Note that the title of the book is underlined but that only the first word of the title and the first word following the colon in the title are capitalized. (Any proper nouns in a title would also be capitalized; see the following example.) The three main parts of an entry—author, title, and publication data—are separated with periods.

(2) A book by several authors:

```
Koslin, S., Koslin, B.L., Pargament, R., &
     Pendelton, S.  An evaluation of fifth grade
     reading programs in ten New York City Com-
     munity School Districts, 1973-1974.  New
     York: Riverside Research Institute, 1975.
```

Note that the names of all the authors are inverted, that the names are separated with commas, and that an ampersand (**&**) is put before the last name in the series (even when there are only two names; see the following example.)

Writing Research Papers, Letters, and Résumés

(3) An article in an edited collection:

```
Bobrow, D. G., & Norman, D. A. Some principles

    of memory schemata.  In D. G. Bobrow & A. M.

    Collins (Eds.), Representation and under-

    standing: Studies in cognitive science.  New

    York: Academic Press, 1975.
```

Note that the title of the article (**Some principles** etc.) is not enclosed in quotation marks and that only the first word of this title is capitalized. (Any proper nouns in the title of the article would, of course, be capitalized.) Note also that the subsequent names of the two editors (**Eds.**) of the collection are not inverted and that there is no comma between the names.

(4) An article in a journal:

```
Stahl, A.  The structure of children's composi-

    tions: Developmental and ethnic differences.

    Research in the Teaching of English, 1977,

    11, 156-163.
```

Note that all substantive words in the title of the journal are capitalized and that the title of the journal is underlined. Note also that the year comes before the volume number and that the volume number (*11*) is underlined. For a journal that begins the numbering of its pages with page 1 in each issue, the number of the issue should be indicated with an Arabic number following the volume number—*11(3).*

(5) A book by a corporate author:

American Psychological Association. <u>Standards</u>
<u>for</u> <u>educational</u> and <u>psychological</u> <u>tests</u> <u>and</u>
<u>manuals</u>. Washington, DC: Author, 1966.

Books and articles with corporate authors are listed alphabetically according to the first significant word of the entry (here **American**). The word **Author** listed with the publication data indicates that the publisher of the work is the same as the group named in the author slot. If, however, the publisher is different from the corporate author, the name of that publisher would be given right after the place of publication.

These five models cover most of the kinds of published material likely to be used in a research paper. For additional models, consult the *Publication Manual of the American Psychological Association* (2nd ed.).

For an illustration of the physical appearance, in typescript, of a research paper and of a *References* page done according to the APA system of documentation, see the following pages, taken from a twenty-one-page article by Carl Bereiter of the Ontario Institute for Studies in Education: "Development in Writing," in *Testing, Teaching and Learning* (Washington, D. C.: National Institute of Education, 1979), pp. 146–166. This article was later reprinted in its entirety in L. W. Gregg and E. R. Steinberg, eds., *Cognitive Processes in Writing* (Hillsdale, N. J.: Erlbaum, 1979).

DEVELOPMENT IN WRITING

Carl Bereiter

Although there is a substantial body of data on the development of writing skills, it has not seemed to have much implication for instruction. Reviews of writing research from an educational perspective have given scant attention to it (Blount, 1973; Braddock, Lloyd-Jones, & Schoer, 1963; Lyman, 1929; West, 1967). Generally speaking, developmental research has educational significance only when there is a conceptual apparatus linking it with questions of practical significance.

Almost all of the data on writing development consist of frequency counts--words per communication unit, incidence of different kinds of dependent clauses, frequency of different types of writing at different ages, and so on. The conceptual frameworks used for interpreting these data have come largely from linguistics (e.g., Hunt, 1965; Loban, 1976; O'Donnell, Griffin, & Norris, 1967). However informative these analyses might be to the student of language development, they are disappointing from an educational point of view. The variables they look at seem unrelated to commonly held purposes of writing instruction (Nystrand, 1977).

The purpose of this paper is to synthesize findings on the growth of writing skills within what may be called an "applied cognitive-developmental" framework. Key issues within an applied cognitive-developmental framework are the cognitive strategies children use and how these are adapted to their limited information processing capacities (Case, 1975, 1978; Klahr & Wallace, 1976; Scardamalia, in press). Although this paper will not deal with instructional implications, it will become evident that the issues considered within an applied cognitive-developmental framework are relevant to such concerns of writing instruction as fluency, coherence, correctness, sense of audience, style, and thought content.

What Is Development in Writing?

Students' writing will undoubtedly reflect their overall language development (Loban, 1976; O'Donnell et al., 1967) and also their level of cognitive development (Collis & Biggs, undated; Scardamalia, in press). It is to be expected that it will also at times reflect their level of moral development, social cognition, etc. Given the small role that writing plays in most children's lives, it is therefore reasonable to suppose that there is no such thing as writing development as such—that it is merely the resultant of other, more basic kinds of development. This view is implicit in the speech-primacy position of researchers like Loban (1963, 1966, 1976), who treat children's writing simply as another source of data on their language development.

While it may be reasonable to treat writing development as a reflection of other kinds of development, it is not very useful to do so. An educationally relevant account of writing development would have to give prominence to whatever is distinctive about writing and potentially susceptible to direct influence. The following have been recognized as distinctive characteristics of writing.

1. Written English may be recognized as a subsystem of English, along with spoken English, and distinguishable from the latter in a number of ways. It is usually more compact, contains more elaborately specified subjects, and shows less local variation than spoken English, and generally shows a different distribution of linguistic devices and usages (Allen, 1972; Gleason, 1965; Long, 1961).

2. Written English and spoken English are predominately, but not

Writing

17

References

Allen, R. L. <u>English grammars and English grammar</u>. New York: Scribner's, 1972.

Blount, N. S. Research on teaching literature, language, and composition. In R. M. W. Travers (Ed.), <u>Second handbook of research on teaching</u>. Chicago: Rand-McNally, 1973.

Braddock, R., Lloyd-Jones, R., & Schoer, L. <u>Research in written composition</u>. Champaign, IL: National Council of Teachers of English, 1963.

Case, R. Gearing the demands of instruction to the developmental capacities of the learner. <u>Review of Educational Research</u>, 1975, <u>45</u>(1), 59-87.

Case, R. Implications of developmental psychology for the design of effective instruction. In A. M. Lesgold, J. W. Pellegrino, S. D. Fokemma, & R. Glaser (Eds.), <u>Cognitive psychology and instruction</u>. Plenum, NY: Division of Plenum Publishing Corporation, 1978.

Collis, K. F., & Biggs, J. B. Classroom examples of cognitive development phenomena. ERDC Funded Project 7/41, University of Newcastle, undated.

Gleason, H. A., Jr. <u>Linguistics and English grammar</u>. New York: Holt, Rinehart & Winston, 1965.

Hunt, K. W. <u>Grammatical structures written at three grade levels</u>. Champaign, IL: National Council of Teachers of English, 1965. (Research Report No. 3.)

Klahr, D., & Wallace, J. G. <u>Cognitive development: An information-processing view</u>. Hillsdale, NJ: Erlbaum, 1976.

Writing

18

Loban, W. *The language of elementary school children*. Urbana, IL:
National Council of Teachers of English, 1963. (Research Report No. 1.)

Loban, W. *Problems in oral English*. Urbana, IL: National Council
of Teachers of English, 1966. (Research Report No. 5.)

Loban, W. *Language development: Kindergarten through grade twelve*.
Urbana, IL: National Council of Teachers of English, 1976. (Research
Report No. 18.)

Long, R. B. *The sentence and its parts: A grammar of contemporary
English*. Chicago: University of Chicago Press, 1961.

Lyman, R. Summary of investigations relating to grammar, language, and
composition. Chicago: University of Chicago, 1929. (Supplementary
educational Monographs, No. 36, published in conjunction with
The School Review and *The Elementary School Journal*.)

Nystrand, M. *Assessing written communication competence: A textual
cognition model*. Toronto, Canada: The Ontario Institute for
Studies in Education, 1977. (ERIC Document Reproduction Service
No. ED 133 732.)

O'Donnell, R. C., Griffin, W. J., & Norris, R. C. *Syntax of kinder-
garten and elementary school children: A transformational analysis*.
Champaign, IL: National Council of Teachers of English, 1967.
(Research Report No. 8.)

Scardamalia, M. How children cope with the cognitive demands of
writing. In C. H. Frederiksen, M. S. Whiteman, & J. F. Dominic (Eds.),
*Writing: The nature, development, and teaching of written communi-
cation*, in press.

West, W. W. Written composition. *Review of Educational Research*, 1967,
37(2), 159-167.

Writing Research Papers, Letters, and Résumés

● Forms for letters

General Instructions

The one type of writing that most people engage in after they leave school is letter-writing. They will almost certainly write letters to parents, friends, and acquaintances, and they may have to write letters in connection with their jobs. Occasionally, they may feel compelled to write a letter to the editor of a newspaper or magazine, and sometimes, they may write more formal letters to institutions or officials for such purposes as applying for a job, requesting information or service, or seeking redress of some grievance. Although they do not have to be much concerned about the niceties of form when they are writing to intimate friends, they would be well advised to observe the conventions of form and etiquette in letters addressed to people that they do not know well enough to call by their first names.

FORMAT OF FAMILIAR LETTER

Letters written to acquaintances are commonly referred to as *familiar letters*. Although usually "anything goes" in letters to acquaintances, one should keep in mind that even the most intimate acquaintance is flattered if the author of the letter observes certain amenities of form. Here is a list of the conventions for the familiar letter:

(a)   Familiar letters may be written on lined or unlined paper of any size, but usually they are written on note-size stationery of some pastel color.

(b)   Familiar letters may be handwritten and may be written on both sides of the sheet of paper.

(c)   The author of the letter usually puts his or her address and the date at the right-hand side of the heading but does not, as in a business letter, put at the left-hand side of the heading the name and address of the person to whom the letter is addressed.

(d)   Depending on the degree of intimacy with the addressee, the writer may use salutations like these: **Dear Mom, Dear Jim, Dear Julie, Dear Ms. Worth.** The salutation is often followed by a comma rather than the more formal colon.

(e)   The body of the letter may be written in indented paragraphs, single- or double-spaced.

(f)   Depending on the degree of intimacy with the addressee, the writer may use complimentary closes like these: **Sincerely, Cordially, Affectionately, Yours, Much love, Fondly, As ever**.

(g)   Depending on the degree of intimacy with the addressee, the writer may sign his or her full name or just a first name or a nickname.

FORMAT OF BUSINESS LETTER

Formal letters addressed to organizations or strangers or superiors are commonly called *business letters.* The form of business letters is more strictly prescribed than the form of familiar letters. Models for a business letter appear on pp. 382 and 383. Here is a list of the conventions for the business letter:

(a)   Business letters are written on 8½ x 11 unlined paper or on 8½ x 11 with a printed letterhead.

(b)   Business letters must be typewritten, single-spaced, on one side of the paper only.

Writing Research Papers, Letters, and Résumés

(c)   In the sample business letter that is typed on the printed letterhead stationery (p. 383), the so-called *full block* format of formal business letters is illustrated. Note that in this format, everything—date, address, greeting, text, salutation, etc.— begins at the left-hand margin. Compare this format with the *semi-block* format of the sample business letter that is typed on plain white paper (p. 382). All the other directions about format (d, e, f, g, h, i, j) apply to both kinds of formal business letters.

(d)   Flush with the left-hand margin and in single-spaced block form, the writer should type the name and address of the person or the organization to whom the letter is written. (The same form will be used in addressing the envelope.)

(e)   Two spaces below this inside address and flush with the left-hand margin, the writer should type the salutation, followed by a colon. In addressing an organization rather than a specific person in that organization, the writer can use salutations like **Dear Sir** or **Gentlemen** or **Dear Madam** or **Ladies**. If the writer knows the name of the person, he or she should use the last name, prefaced with **Mr.** or **Miss** or **Mrs.** or, if uncertain about the marital status of a woman, **Ms.**—e.g. **Dear Mr. Toler, Dear Miss Cameron, Dear Mrs. Nakamura, Dear Ms. Ingrao**. Women who feel that marital status should be no more specified in their own case than in that of a man (for whom **Mr.** serves, irrespective of whether he is married) prefer **Ms.** to **Mrs.** and **Miss.** The plural of **Mr.** is **Messrs.**; the plural of **Mrs.** or **Ms.** is **Mmes.**; the plural of **Miss** is **Misses.** Professional titles may also be used in the salutation: **Dear Professor Newman, Dear Dr. Marton**. (*Webster's New Collegiate Dictionary* carries an extensive list of the forms of address for various dignitaries [judges, clergy, legislators, etc.].)

(f)   The body of the letter should be single-spaced, except for double-spacing between paragraphs. Paragraphs are not indented but start flush with the left-hand margin.

(g) The usual complimentary closes for business letters are these: **Sincerely yours, Yours truly, Very truly yours**. The complimentary close is followed by a comma.

(h) The writer should type his or her name about three or four spaces below the complimentary close. The typed name should not be prefaced with a professional title (e.g. **Dr., Rev.**) nor followed with a designation of academic degrees (e.g. **M.A., Ph.D.**), but below the typed name, the writer may indicate his or her official capacity (e.g. **President, Director of Personnel, Managing Editor**). The writer should sign his or her name in the space between the complimentary close and the typed name.

(i) If one or more copies of the letter are being sent to others, that fact should be indicated with a notation like the following in the lower left-hand side of the page (**cc.** is the abbreviation of **carbon copy**):

cc: Mary Hunter
Robert Allison

(j) If the letter was dictated to, and typed by, a secretary, that fact should be indicated by a notation like the following, which is typed flush with the left-hand margin and below the writer's signature (the writer's initials are given in capital letters, the secretary's in lowercase: **WLT/cs** or **WLT:cs.**

See the following models for the text and envelope of the two styles of business letters.

239 Riverside Road
Columbus, OH 43210
January 5, 1981

Mr. Thomas J. Weiss
Manager, Survey Division
Acme Engineering Company, Inc.
5868 Fanshawe Drive
Omaha, NB 68131

Dear Mr. Weiss:

Mr. Robert Miller, sales representative of the Rushmore Caterpillar
Company of Columbus and a long-time friend of my father, told me that
when he saw you at a convention in Chicago recently, you indicated
you would have two or three temporary positions open this summer in
your division. Mr. Miller kindly offered to write you about me, but
he urged me to write also.

By June, I will have completed my junior year in the Department of
Civil Engineering at Ohio State University. Not only do I need to
work this summer to finance my final year of college, but I also need
to get some practical experience in surveying tracts on a large road-
building project such as your company is now engaged in. After check-
ing with several of the highway contractors in this area, I have
learned that all of them have already hired their quota of engineering
students for next summer.

For the last three summers, I have worked for the Worley Building
Contractors of Columbus as a carpenter's helper and as a cement-
finisher. Mr. Albert Michaels, my foreman for the last three summers,
has indicated that he would write a letter of reference for me, if
you want one. He understands why I want to get some experience in
surveying this summer, but he told me that I would have priority for
a summertime job with Worley if I wanted it.

Among my instructors in civil engineering, the two men who know me best
are Dr. Theodore Sloan, who says that he knows you, and Mr. A. M.
Slater. Currently, I have a 3.2 quality-point average in all my subjects,
but I have straight A's in all my engineering courses. For the last two
quarters, I have worked as a laboratory assistant for Professor Sloan.

I am anxious to get experience in my future profession, and I am quite
willing to establish temporary residence in Omaha during the summer.
I own a four-cylinder sub-compact car that I could use to travel to
the job site each day. I am in good health, and I would be available
to work for long hours and at odd hours during the summer months. If
you want any letters of recommendation from any of the men named in
my letter, please let me know.

Sincerely yours,

Oscar Jerman

cc. Robert Miller

Scott, Foresman and Company   1900 East Lake Avenue   Glenview, Illinois 60025   312/729-3000
College Division

January 26, 1982

Professor Don M. Murray
Department of English
Northern Illinois University
De Kalb, IL 60115

Dear Professor Murray:

Thank you for your recent letter. I am looking forward to being a
part of your careers program on April 7th.

I will be calling on Northern during the day and will stop by your
office if that is convenient for you. It is all right to put me last
on the program; I hope my presentation will warrant that position of
emphasis. I will plan on speaking for ten minutes. My remarks will
concentrate on publishing careers, but I also hope to include some
personal experiences as an English major in the job market.

Again, thank you for your invitation. I will see you on the 7th if
we do not get a chance to talk before then.

Sincerely yours,

Michael Anderson

Michael Anderson
Acquisitions Editor
English Skills/ESL

MA/dc
cc: Harriett Prentiss

ADDRESSED BUSINESS-SIZE ENVELOPE

Oscar Jerman
239 Riverside Road
Columbus, OH 43210

Mr. Thomas J. Weiss
Manager, Survey Division
Acme Engineering Company, Inc.
5868 Fanshawe Drive
Omaha, NB 68131

LETTERHEAD BUSINESS ENVELOPE

Michael Anderson

Scott, Foresman and Company   Glenview, Illinois 60025
1900 East Lake Avenue

Professor Don M. Murray
Department of English
Northern Illinois University
De Kalb, IL 60115

●

The two-letter postal abbreviations

Here is the U.S. Postal Service list of two-letter abbreviations of the fifty states, the District of Columbia, and outlying areas. These abbreviations should be set down in capital letters without a period and should be followed by the appropriate five-digit ZIP code—for example, Tempe, AZ 85281.

● Forms for Letters

Alabama	**AL**	Montana	**MT**
Alaska	**AK**	Nebraska	**NB**
Arizona	**AZ**	Nevada	**NV**
Arkansas	**AR**	New Hampshire	**NH**
California	**CA**	New Jersey	**NJ**
Colorado	**CO**	New Mexico	**NM**
Connecticut	**CT**	New York	**NY**
Delaware	**DE**	North Carolina	**NC**
District of Columbia	**DC**	North Dakota	**ND**
Florida	**FL**	Ohio	**OH**
Georgia	**GA**	Oklahoma	**OK**
Guam	**GU**	Oregon	**OR**
Hawaii	**HI**	Pennsylvania	**PA**
Idaho	**ID**	Puerto Rico	**PR**
Illinois	**IL**	Rhode Island	**RI**
Indiana	**IN**	South Carolina	**SC**
Iowa	**IA**	South Dakota	**SD**
Kansas	**KS**	Tennessee	**TN**
Kentucky	**KY**	Texas	**TX**
Louisiana	**LA**	Utah	**UT**
Maine	**ME**	Vermont	**VT**
Maryland	**MD**	Virgin Islands	**VI**
Massachusetts	**MA**	Virginia	**VA**
Michigan	**MI**	Washington	**WA**
Minnesota	**MN**	West Virginia	**WV**
Mississippi	**MS**	Wisconsin	**WI**
Missouri	**MO**	Wyoming	**WY**

Writing Research Papers, Letters, and Résumés

●

The memorandum

The memorandum or, as it is referred to colloquially, the memo is a common form of writing for communications within a company, especially for interoffice communications. If executives need to communicate with a large group of people—for instance, fifty or more—they usually resort to a fairly formal let-

---

MEMORANDUM

Date: April 10, 1981

TO: Sales Managers in the Midwest Region

FROM: Thomas K. Martin *JKM*
       Vice President in Charge of Sales

SUBJECT: Launching of Sales Campaign for Musk Cologne

On May 1, 1981, we are going to launch our sales campaign for our long-awaited new product, Musk Cologne. According to the plans formulated last fall, we are going to test-market Musk in our Midwest market exclusively for a period of four months. If we can get all the bugs out of our advertising and merchandising procedures during this four-month period, we can put Musk on the market nationally by September 1, 1981.

I want all of you to put your most conscientious effort into the inauguration of this new product, which has the potential of being our bestselling item since we launched Tiger Cologne six years ago. I want you all to be as accommodating as you reasonably can in arranging for special deals with local wholesalers or with purchasing agents for individual stores. Two months ago, you were provided with the price schedule worked out on the computer for orders of various sizes. Suggestions were made there about "special incentive discounts" for unusually large orders. Initially, I suppose that we cannot expect orders larger than a gross by any one store, but if the product catches on through aggressive sales and promotions, we will be able to induce at least our chain-store customers to start ordering Musk in truckload lots. That challenge will call for the most imaginative kind of salesmanship.

I know that some of you are apprehensive about launching a new product in the summer months. But our company has proven before that the notion of the summer months being a poor time to introduce a new product is pure myth. It is true, of course, that during the summer months, people are very much preoccupied with their forthcoming vacations. But to offset that preoccupation, people do not have to be worried about fuel bills and school bills during the summer months. Besides, we are advertising Musk as an especially refreshing cologne for the warm days. All of you know, from personal tests that you made last fall, of the cooling effect of this extraordinary cologne.

I need not remind you of the all-expenses trips to Hawaii that will be awarded to the top six sales managers and top six sales persons during this camapign. The chance to get this potential money-maker off to a good start and the prospect of a ten-day vacation in lovely Honolulu should make this MUSK campaign a MUST campaign for all of you.

---

ter. If they need to communicate with a particular person, they pick up the telephone or arrange for a private conference with that person in their office. If they have to communicate some information or directive to a relatively small group of people within the company, they often resort to the memorandum. The memorandum has the advantage over telephone conversations with all the parties involved in that the message has to be stated only once and there is a permanent record of the communiqué.

The memorandum is such a common form in the business world that many companies provide their office staff with printed memo forms. Some of these might be half-sheets for very short communiqués. This form might have the word MEMORANDUM printed at the top of the page. Along the lefthand margin would be printed the words TO, FROM, and SUBJECT, each followed with a colon, and on the righthand side of the page might be printed the word *Date*. Following the FROM, put the name of the author of the memo (usually one person) and the author's title, if it is not familiar to all the addressees. Following the TO, put the names of those to whom the memo is addressed (if there are only a few of them) or the name of the group if there are more people than can be conveniently listed (for example, All Supervisors in the Production Department). Following SUBJECT, put a phrase indicating the matter dealt with in the memo.

The tone of the memorandum is usually relaxed and casual, often with a liberal use of the pronouns *I* and *you*. Because "time is money" in the business world, the author will try to make the memo brief enough to be fitted on one sheet of paper. A memo can usually be made brief because the author does not have to provide the audience with much background information about the subject being dealt with. The memo is not signed at the end, as a letter is, but often the author will scribble his or her initials opposite the name that follows FROM at the head of the memo.

Writing Research Papers, Letters, and Résumés

●
The résumé

A résumé (pronounced *rez-oo-may*) is a one- or two-page summary, presented in the form of a list, of a job-applicant's life, relevant personal experiences, education, work experience, extracurricular activities, honors, goals, etc. It is usually submitted, along with such documents as academic transcripts, letters of reference, and specimens of one's writing, as part of a formal application for a job. The résumé is also referred to, and sometimes even labeled with, the Latin phrases *curriculum vitae* (the course of one's life) or *vita brevis* (a short life) or simply *vita*.

Under the headings of Education, Work Experience, and Extracurricular Activities, items are usually listed in a reverse chronological order, starting with the most recent and ending with the earliest. (See the sample résumé).

A dossier (mentioned in the sample résumé) is a collection of one's documents (transcripts, letters of reference, etc.), which is kept on file in a school's placement office and which will be mailed out, upon request, to prospective employers. The letters of reference in a dossier, written by teachers, employers, and acquaintances, are usually confidential—that is, they are never seen by the applicant. (According to a federal law passed in 1975, however, applicants must be allowed to see any letters of reference about themselves if the letters were written after the law was passed and if the applicants have not signed a waiver to see the letters.) The names and addresses of other people who have agreed to write letters of reference upon request are often listed in the résumé as Additional References.

Résumé

Mary Watson Evans
239 E. Torrence Rd.
Columbus, OH 43214
Tel: (614) 267-4819 (home)
    (614) 422-6866 (office)

PERSONAL: Born, Milwaukee, Wisconsin, August 5, 1958

MARITAL STATUS: Married, James Evans, 1981; no children

EDUCATION: 1980-82, MBA (expected in June, 1982), Ohio State University, Columbus, OH
            Major--Accounting
          1976-80, BA, Marquette University, Milwaukee, WI, graduated <u>magna cum laude</u>, 1980
            Major--Economics
            Minor--History
          1972-76, Westside High School, Milwaukee, WI, graduated <u>summa cum laude</u>, 1976

WORK EXPERIENCE: Research assistant for Robert Moberly, Professor of Finance,
                  Ohio State University, 1980-82
                Check-out clerk, weekends and summers, A&P grocery store,
                  Milwaukee, WI, 1979-80
                Clerk-typist, summer of 1976, Allis Chalmers of Milwaukee
                Clerk, Saturdays and summers, Gimbel's Department Store,
                  Milwaukee, WI, 1974-75

EXTRA-CURRICULAR ACTIVITIES: Yearbook assistant editor, Marquette University, 1980
                            Freshman representative on Student Council, Marquette
                              University, 1976-77
                            Reporter, Westside High School newspaper, 1974;
                              editorial writer, 1975; editor, 1976

HONORS: $500 Scholarship from Rush Foundation, 1976-77
        Full-tuition Scholarship from Omicron Society, 1979-80
        Quill and Scroll award for Best Reporting, 1974

CAREER GOALS: Position as accountant or editor of in-house journal in a large
              accounting firm or bank in the Chicago area, where my husband,
              who will take his law degree in June, 1982, has accepted a position.
              I plan to take night courses in commercial law.

REFERENCES: My dossier is on file at the Placement Office, Ohio State University,
            164 W. 17th Avenue, Columbus, OH 43210

            Additional letters of reference (besides those in my dossier):

                        Mr. John Anderson
                        Personnel Manager
                        Allis Chalmers Corporation
                        West Allis, WI 53214

                        Mr. Hans Schmitz
                        Manager, A&P Stores (retired)
                        2841 N. 70th Street
                        Milwaukee, WI 53210

The Readings

Chapter 10
Narration

○ Salvation

Langston Hughes

Langston Hughes (1902–1967) has won a secure place in the history of American literature mainly as a poet, but he was versatile enough to have also made his mark with novels, plays, essays, short stories, and at least two volumes of autobiography The Big Sea *(1940) and* I Wonder as I Wander *(1956). In the following autobiographical piece, Hughes recounts a traumatic event that he experienced when he was about to become a teenager—his faked testimony of "salvation" in front of a church congregation. In the invention process, Hughes must have relied primarily on his memory to recall the particulars of the event. Once he had recovered the details of this boyhood event, he used chronology as the organizing principle of his narrative. Here is a good example of a narrative that is presented mainly by telling rather than by showing. We get a sense of the drama of the event primarily through the revelation of the boy's thoughts on this occasion. Because of our exposure to this internal drama, we understand the ironic thesis of this narrative: he who was ostensibly "saved" does not now even believe in Jesus. Langston Hughes's piece is the most intensely personal of the "personal narratives" presented in this section.*

Narration

1   I was saved from sin when I was going on thirteen. But not really saved. It happened like this. There was a big revival at my Auntie Reed's church. Every night for weeks there had been much preaching, singing, praying, and shouting, and some very hardened sinners had been brought to Christ, and the membership of the church had grown by leaps and bounds. Then just before the revival ended, they held a special meeting for children, "to bring the young lambs to the fold." My aunt spoke of it for days ahead. That night I was escorted to the front row and placed on the mourners' bench with all the other young sinners, who had not yet been brought to Jesus.

2   My aunt told me that when you were saved you saw a light, and something happened to you inside! And Jesus came into your life! And God was with you from then on! She said you could see and hear and feel Jesus in your soul. I believed her. I had heard a great many old people say the same thing and it seemed to me they ought to know. So I sat there calmly in the hot, crowded church, waiting for Jesus to come to me.

3   The preacher preached a wonderful rhythmical sermon, all moans and shouts and lonely cries and dire pictures of hell, and then he sang a song about the ninety and nine safe in the fold, but one little lamb was left out in the cold. Then he said: "Won't you come? Won't you come to Jesus? Young lambs, won't you come?" And he held out his arms to all us young sinners there on the mourners' bench. And the little girls cried. And some of them jumped up and went to Jesus right away. But most of us just sat there.

4   A great many old people came and knelt around us and prayed, old women with jet-black faces and braided hair, old men with work-gnarled hands. And the church sang a song about

the lower lights are burning, some poor sinners to be saved. And the whole building rocked with prayer and song.

Still I kept waiting to *see* Jesus. 5

Finally all the young people had gone to the altar and were 6 saved, but one boy and me. He was a rounder's son named Westley. Westley and I were surrounded by sisters and deacons praying. It was very hot in the church, and getting late now. Finally Westley said to me in a whisper: "God damn! I'm tired o' sitting here. Let's get up and be saved." So he got up and was saved.

Then I was left all alone on the mourners' bench. My aunt 7 came and knelt at my knees and cried, while prayers and songs swirled all around me in the little church. The whole congregation prayed for me alone, in a mighty wail of moans and voices. And I kept waiting serenely for Jesus, waiting, waiting—but he didn't come. I wanted to see him, but nothing happened to me. Nothing! I wanted something to happen to me, but nothing happened.

I heard the songs and the minister saying: "Why don't you 8 come? My dear child, why don't you come to Jesus? Jesus is waiting for you. He wants you. Why don't you come? Sister Reed, what is this child's name?"

"Langston," my aunt sobbed. 9

"Langston, why don't you come? Why don't you come and be 10 saved? Oh, Lamb of God! Why don't you come?"

Now it was really getting late. I began to be ashamed of my- 11 self, holding everything up so long. I began to wonder what God thought about Westley, who certainly hadn't seen Jesus either, but who was now sitting proudly on the platform, swinging his knickerbockered legs and grinning down at me, surrounded by deacons and old women on their knees praying. God had not struck Westley dead for taking his name in vain or for lying in the temple. So I decided that maybe to save further trouble, I'd better lie, too, and say that Jesus had come, and get up and be saved.

12   So I got up.

13   Suddenly the whole room broke into a sea of shouting, as they saw me rise. Waves of rejoicing swept the place. Women leaped in the air. My aunt threw her arms around me. The minister took me by the hand and led me to the platform.

14   When things quieted down, in a hushed silence, punctuated by a few ecstatic "Amens," all the new young lambs were blessed in the name of God. Then joyous singing filled the room.

15   That night, for the last time in my life but one—for I was a big boy twelve years old—I cried. I cried, in bed alone, and couldn't stop. I buried my head under the quilts, but my aunt heard me. She woke up and told my uncle I was crying because the Holy Ghost had come into my life, and because I had seen Jesus. But I was really crying because I couldn't bear to tell her that I had lied, that I had deceived everybody in the church, that I hadn't seen Jesus, and that now I didn't believe there was a Jesus any more, since he didn't come to help me.

○ The Geese

E. B. White

Many of those who read this account of the conflict between an old gander and a young gander have read, or had read to them, Elwyn Brooks White's classic children's books Stuart Little *(1945) and* Charlotte's Web *(1952). E. B. White (b. 1899) joined the staff of* The New Yorker *in 1926, a year after it was founded, and together with James Thurber, helped set the tone and the standard of excellence of that magazine. Although he still writes for* The New Yorker, *he has for many years been retired on his farm near Brooklin, Maine, the setting of the episode that he narrates here. The story is mainly told to us by White, but occasionally, he gives us direct glimpses of the action and the scene. He functions like the chorus in a Greek tragedy, commenting on the larger dimensions of the drama that is taking place before our eyes. White almost "humanizes" the story, depicting it in terms of a domestic drama, and at times, he is quite explicit in his expression of empathy and sympathy. The parts of the narrative are arranged chronologically, of course, but even within that overall chronological pattern, there is a cause-and-effect relationship between the incidents.*

During the last week in May, Apathy, having produced only 1 three eggs of her own but having acquired ten through the kind offices of her sister and me, became broody and began to sit. Liz, with a tally of twenty-five eggs, ten of them stolen, showed not the slightest desire to sit. Laying was her thing. She laid and laid, while the other goose sat and sat. The old gander, marveling at what he had wrought, showed a great deal of interest in both nests. The young gander was impressed but subdued. I continued to remove the early eggs from Liz's nest, holding her to a clutch of fifteen and discarding the extras. In late June, having produced forty-one eggs, ten of which were under Apathy, she at last sat down.

I had marked Apathy's hatching date on my desk calendar. 2 On the night before the goslings were due to arrive, when I made my rounds before going to bed, I looked in on her. She hissed, as usual, and ran her neck out. When I shone my light at her, two tiny green heads were visible, thrusting their way through her feathers. The goslings were here—a few hours ahead of schedule. My heart leapt up. Outside, in the barnyard, both ganders stood vigil. They knew very well what was up: ganders

Narration

take an enormous interest in family affairs and are deeply impressed by the miracle of the egg-that-becomes-goose. I shut the door against them and went to bed.

3   Next morning, Sunday, I rose early and went straight to the barn to see what the night had brought. Apathy was sitting quietly while five goslings teetered about on the slopes of the nest. One of them, as I watched, strayed from the others, and, not being able to find his way back, began sending out cries for help. They were the kind of distress signal any anxious father would instantly respond to. Suddenly, I heard sounds of a rumble outside in the barnyard where the ganders were—loud sounds of scuffling. I ran out. A fierce fight was in progress—it was no mere skirmish, it was the real thing. The young gander had grabbed the old one by the stern, his white head buried in feathers right where it would hurt the most, and was running him around the yard, punishing him at every turn—thrusting him on ahead and beating him unmercifully with his wings. It was an awesome sight, these two great male birds locked in combat, slugging it out—not for the favors of a female but for the dubious privilege of assuming the responsibilities of parenthood. The young male had suffered all spring the indignities of a restricted life at the pond; now he had turned, at last, against the old one, as though to get even. Round and round, over rocks and through weeds, they raced, struggling and tripping, the old one in full retreat and in apparent pain. It was a beautiful late-June morning, with fair-weather clouds and a light wind going, the grasses long in the orchard—the kind of morning that always carries for me overtones of summer sadness, I don't know why. Overhead, three swallows circled at low altitude, pursuing one white feather, the coveted trophy of nesting time. They were like three tiny fighter planes giving air support to the battle that raged below. For a moment, I thought of climbing the fence and trying to separate the combatants, but instead I just watched.

The engagement was soon over. Plunging desperately down the lane, the old gander sank to the ground. The young one let go, turned, and walked back, screaming in triumph, to the door behind which his newly won family were waiting: a strange family indeed—the sister who was not even the mother of the babies, and the babies who were not even his own get.

When I was sure the fight was over, I climbed the fence and closed the barnyard gate, effectively separating victor from vanquished. The old gander had risen to his feet. He was in almost the same spot in the lane where his first wife had died mysteriously more than a year ago. I watched as he threaded his way slowly down the narrow path between clumps of thistles and daisies. His head was barely visible above the grasses, but his broken spirit was plain to any eye. When he reached the pasture bars, he hesitated, then painfully squatted and eased himself under the bottom bar and into the pasture, where he sat down on the cropped sward in the bright sun. I felt very deeply his sorrow and his defeat. As things go in the animal kingdom, he is about my age, and when he lowered himself to creep under the bar, I could feel in my own bones his pain at bending down so far. Two hours later, he was still sitting there, the sun by this time quite hot. I had seen his likes often enough on the benches of the treeless main street of a Florida city—spent old males, motionless in the glare of the day. 4

Toward the end of the morning, he walked back up the lane as far as the gate, and there he stood all afternoon, his head and orange bill looking like the head of a great snake. The goose and her goslings had emerged into the barnyard. Through the space between the boards of the gate, the old fellow watched the enchanting scene: the goslings taking their frequent drinks of water, climbing in and out of the shallow pan for their first swim, closely guarded by the handsome young gander, shepherded by the pretty young goose. 5

6   After supper, I went into the tie-ups and pulled the five remaining, unhatched eggs from the nest and thought about the
five lifeless chicks inside the eggs—the unlucky ones, the ones
that lacked what it takes to break out of an egg into the light of
a fine June morning. I put the eggs in a basket and set the
basket with some other miscellany consigned to the dump. I
don't know anything sadder than a summer's day.

○ # Some Who Died Trying
Newsweek Magazine

*The following selection is the purest example in this sec-
tion of what is called in Chapter 7 "public narrative," an
account of something that really happened but one in
which we are not made aware of the one who is relaying
the account to us. This piece represents a segment of a
long article that was published in a special issue of
Newsweek magazine on the veterans of the Vietnam War.
Like the whole article, this piece was written by some of
the editors of Newsweek from dozens of news stories
filed by reporters. Our emotions are touched but one in this
straightforward account of how three American soldiers
were killed in the war, but our emotions are touched in
much subtler ways than they are in other pieces in this
section on Narration where the reporter of the event makes
explicit comments on what is happening. One of these
subtle ways is the low-keyed but unflinching account of
how each of these three men met his death. Except for
the families of these men, these casualties existed in the
newspapers and in the Pentagon records primarily as
statistics. Thanks to the artistry of the authors of this story,
Fritz Suchomel, Rick Garcia, and Bobby Eugene Jones
are fleetingly brought to life so that we can see how they
died in the service of their country.*

○ *Newsweek*/Some Who Died Trying

Some never made it back to The World. In April Fritz Suchomel   1
bought it at 19, his lungs screaming for air at the bottom of an
abandoned well. Suchomel had got a Dear John letter from a
girlfriend back in Wisconsin, and some of his buddies had sat
up most of the night with him in a bunker at Fire Base Jim,
sharing some joints and trying to cheer him up. In the morning
he went out with a squad on recon and they stumbled on the
well—the kind the VC routinely used as ammo caches. Somebody tossed in a couple of concussion grenades, just in case.
Somebody else had to go down for a look, and Suchomel was
a natural tunnel rat at roughly 5 feet 4.

So Suchomel started down on a rope, and nobody figured   2
until he got there that a concussion grenade will blow the oxygen out of an enclosed space along with everything else. They
heard him call out after ten minutes or so that he was feeling
dizzy and faint, and they hauled him up for a breath of air. Then
he dropped back down, and in ten more minutes they heard
him again: "Hey guys, pull me out. I think I'm gonna faint." He
went limp at the end of the tope. They pulled at it. He was stuck
and maybe dying, and his pal Smitty went in after him.

They were improbable buddies: Fritz and Smitty, white and   3
black, a skinny towhead straight off Main Street and a pave-
ment-tough ghetto brother with a mostly undiscriminating dislike
for whites. The proximity of death forged friendships like that;
when they carried you off the battlefield, Omega Harris used to
think, it didn't matter what color your were—*the boots hang over
the side of that poncho the same way.* So Smitty went down the
well after Fritz, and he was overcome, too. An armored person-

---

Narration

nel carrier finally backed up to the hole and helped drag both men out. Suchomel was dead, and Smitty was the next thing to it, his brain starved of oxygen.

4   In May they lost Rick Garcia, the kid with the Burton smile and the wife back home saving quarters in a piggy bank so they could meet in Honolulu for his R&R. He and some buddies were riding shotgun on a U.S. tank column on a stretch of Highway 13 north of Saigon called Thunder Road when the VC popped a 'bush, raking the column with grenades, rifles and machine-gun fire. The citation that came home with Garcia's Silver Star said he was cut down by enemy shrapnel trying to help a stunned comrade out of the path of one of the tanks. The troopers who were with him didn't see that part; they remember only that Garcia jumped or fell off the tank he was riding when the shooting started and was himself crushed to death—under its treads.

5   In January 1970 the freedom birds were flying the boys home from Vietnam, but Bobby Eugene Jones, a black kid from North Carolina, seemed to know he wasn't going to make it to the plane. He sat up one night with his Carolina pals James Green and Leroy Pringle, talking about his premonitions. He said he was writing home to Princeville, N.C., to have his bank account changed from his own name to his mother's—he was that sure something was going to happen to him.

6   He was out on patrol the next day when he stepped on a tripwire and set off a booby trap; it blew away both his legs, one above the knee, the other below. Nobody had told Jones that when Green went to see him at the field hospital in Lai Khe. He was conscious, even laughing; all he remembered was seeing the wire too late, and he wanted to know what had happened. Green ducked his questions. But ten days later he heard that Jones had died in Okinawa. *He must have found out,* Green thought: he found out his legs were gone, and it killed him.

○ The Fight

Maya Angelou

In this excerpt from her autobiographical I Know Why the Caged Bird Sings *(1970), Maya Angelou (b. 1928), a playwright, actress, singer, and poet, gives us an account of what it was like when she was a girl to listen to a Joe Louis fight broadcast over the radio in the black community. The Joe Louis fight was, of course, a public event, but because Angelou herself was part of the scene that she narrates, we can classify her account of the event as a "personal narrative." In her story, she sometimes uses the pronoun* I *when she speaks of herself, but because she is an integral part of the community that is clustered around the radio, she more often uses the pronoun* we. *Instead of just telling us about the event, she dramatizes it. The main events of the fight taking place many hundreds of miles away are conveyed to us through snatches of the radio announcer's commentary. As the narrator of the scene in the Store, Angelou gives us anonymous snatches of what people around the radio are saying and fleeting glimpses of their behavior as they listen to the fight. Because we are allowed to relive the scene with the narrator, we get a vivid sense not only of the dramatic suspense of the fight but also of the symbolic value, for the black community, of Joe Louis's victory that night.*

The last inch of space was filled, yet people continued to wedge themselves along the walls of the Store. Uncle Willie had turned the radio up to its last notch so that youngsters on the porch wouldn't miss a word. Women sat on kitchen chairs, dining-room chairs, stools and upturned wooden boxes. Small children and

1

Narration

babies perched on every lap available and men leaned on the shelves or on each other.

2   The apprehensive mood was shot through with shafts of gaiety, as a black sky is streaked with lightning.

3   "I ain't worried 'bout this fight. Joe's gonna whip that cracker like it's open season."

4   "He gone whip him till that white boy call him Momma."

5   At last the talking was finished and the string-along songs about razor blades were over and the fight began.

6   "A quick jab to the head." In the Store the crowd grunted. "A left to the head and a right and another left." One of the listeners cackled like a hen and was quieted.

7   "They're in a clench, Louis is trying to fight his way out."

8   Some bitter comedian on the porch said, "That white man don't mind hugging that niggah now, I betcha."

9   "The referee is moving in to break them up, but Louis finally pushed the contender away and it's an uppercut to the chin. The contender is hanging on, now he's backing away. Louis catches him with a short left to the jaw."

10   A tide of murmuring assent poured out the doors and into the yard.

11   "Another left and another left. Louis is saving that mighty right . . ." The mutter in the Store had grown into a baby roar and it was pierced by the clang of a bell and the announcer's "That's the bell for round three, ladies and gentlemen."

12   As I pushed my way into the Store I wondered if the announcer gave any thought to the fact that he was addressing as "ladies and gentlemen" all the Negroes around the world who sat sweating and praying, glued to their "master's voice."

13   There were only a few calls for R.C. Colas, Dr. Peppers, and Hire's root beer. The real festivities would begin after the fight. Then even the old Christian ladies who taught their children and tried themselves to practice turning the other cheek would buy

soft drinks, and if the Brown Bomber's victory was a particularly bloody one they would order peanut patties and Baby Ruths also.

Bailey and I lay the coins on top of the cash register. Uncle Willie didn't allow us to ring up sales during a fight. It was too noisy and might shake up the atmosphere. When the gong rang for the next round we pushed through the near-sacred quiet to the herd of children outside. 14

"He's got Louis against the ropes and now it's a left to the body and a right to the ribs. Another right to the body, it looks like it was low . . . Yes, ladies and gentlemen, the referee is signaling but the contender keeps raining the blows on Louis. It's another to the body, and it looks like Louis is going down." 15

My race groaned. It was our people falling. It was another lynching, yet another Black man hanging on a tree. One more woman ambushed and raped. A Black boy whipped and maimed. It was hounds on the trail of a man running through slimy swamps. It was a white woman slapping her maid for being forgetful. 16

The men in the Store stood away from the walls and at attention. Women greedily clutched the babes on their laps while on the porch the shufflings and smiles, flirtings and pinching of a few minutes before were gone. This might be the end of the world. If Joe lost we were back in slavery and beyond help. It would all be true, the accusations that we were lower types of human beings. Only a little higher than the apes. True that we were stupid and ugly and lazy and dirty and unlucky and worst of all, that God Himself hated us and ordained us to be hewers of wood and drawers of water, forever and ever, world without end. 17

We didn't breathe. We didn't hope. We waited. 18

"He's off the ropes, ladies and gentlemen. He's moving towards the center of the ring." There was no time to be relieved. The worst might still happen. 19

"And now it looks like Joe is mad. He's caught Carnera with a left hook to the head and a right to the head. It's a left jab to 20 the body and another left to the head. There's a left cross and a right to the head. The contender's right eye is bleeding and he can't seem to keep his block up. Louis is penetrating every block. The referee is moving in, but Louis sends a left to the body and it's the uppercut to the chin and the contender is dropping. He's on the canvas, ladies and gentlemen."

21   Babies slid to the floor as women stood up and men leaned toward the radio.

22   "Here's the referee. He's counting. One, two, three, four, five, six, seven . . . Is the contender trying to get up again?"

23   All the men in the store shouted, "NO."

24   "—eight, nine, ten." There were a few sounds from the audience, but they seemed to be holding themselves in against tremendous pressure.

25   "The fight is all over, ladies and gentlemen. Let's get the microphone over to the referee . . . Here he is. He's got the Brown Bomber's hand, he's holding it up . . . Here he is . . ."

26   Then the voice, husky and familiar, came to wash over us— "The winnah, and still heavyweight champeen of the world . . . Joe Louis."

27   Champion of the world. A Black boy. Some Black mother's son. He was the strongest man in the world. People drank Coca-Colas like ambrosia and ate candy bars like Christmas. Some of the men went behind the Store and poured white lightning in their soft-drink bottles, and a few of the bigger boys followed them. Those who were not chased away came back blowing their breath in front of themselves like proud smokers.

28   It would take an hour or more before the people would leave the Store and head for home. Those who lived too far had made arrangements to stay in town. It wouldn't do for a Black man and his family to be caught on a lonely country road on a night when Joe Louis had proved that we were the strongest people in the world.

○ Four Generations

Joyce Maynard

Joyce Maynard (b. 1953) became a professional writer when she was only twenty years old. While still an undergraduate at Yale University, she published her first book Looking Backward: A Chronicle of Growing Up Old in the Sixties *(1973). By the time "Four Generations" appeared in 1979 in the* New York Times Magazine, *she was married and had given birth to Audrey, the daughter mentioned in the story. The four generations are represented, respectively, by her grandmother, by her mother, by Maynard herself, and by Audrey; and although the focal character is the dying grandmother, every one of those links in the familial chain plays a part in the narrative. Maynard is the filter through which we get all the details of the story. The event in the foreground is her visit, with her daughter, to the grandmother in Winnipeg, Canada, but Maynard provides a background for that event by relating some pertinent vignettes from the past. Some readers may complain that not much "happens" here. But Maynard is not as much interested in what "happens" as she is in the "meaning" of what happens. Very often in personal narratives, the real "action" of the story takes place in the mind of the narrator.*

My mother called last week to tell me that my grandmother is 1 dying. She has refused an operation that would postpone, but not prevent, her death from pancreatic cancer. She can't eat, she has been hemorrhaging, and she has severe jaundice. "I always prided myself on being different," she told my mother. "Now I *am* different. I'm yellow."

Narration

2   My mother, telling me this news, began to cry. So I became the mother for a moment, reminding her, reasonably, that my grandmother is eighty-seven, she's had a full life, she has all her faculties, and no one who knows her could wish that she live long enough to lose them. Lately my mother has been finding notes in my grandmother's drawers at the nursing home, reminding her, "Joyce's husband's name is Steve. Their daughter is Audrey." In the last few years she hadn't had the strength to cook or garden, and she's begun to say she's had enough of living.

3   My grandmother was born in Russia, in 1892—the oldest daughter in a large and prosperous Jewish family. But the prosperity didn't last. She tells stories of the pogroms and the cossacks who raped her when she was twelve. Soon after that, her family emigrated to Canada, where she met my grandfather.

4   Their children were the center of their life. The story I loved best, as a child, was of my grandfather opening every box of Cracker Jack in the general store he ran, in search of the particular tin toy my mother coveted. Though they never had much money, my grandmother saw to it that her daughter had elocution lessons and piano lessons, and assured her that she would go to college.

5   But while she was at college, my mother met my father, who was blue-eyed and blond-haired and not Jewish. When my father sent love letters to my mother, my grandmother would open and hide them, and when my mother told her parents she was going to marry this man, my grandmother said if that happened, it would kill her.

6   Not likely, of course. My grandmother is a woman who used to crack Brazil nuts open with her teeth, a woman who once lifted a car off the ground, when there was an accident and it had to be moved. She has been representing her death as imminent ever since I've known her—twenty-five years—and has

discussed, at length, the distribution of her possessions and her lamb coat. Every time we said goodbye, after our annual visit to Winnipeg, she'd weep and say she'd never see us again. But in the meantime, while every other relative of her generation, and a good many of the younger ones, has died (nursed usually by her), she has kept making knishes, shopping for bargains, tending the healthiest plants I've ever seen.

After my grandfather died, my grandmother lived, more than 7 ever, through her children. When she came to visit, I would hide my diary. She couldn't understand any desire for privacy. She couldn't bear it if my mother left the house without her.

This possessiveness is what made my mother furious (and 8 then guilt-ridden that she felt that way, when of course she owed so much to her mother). So I harbored the resentment that my mother—the dutiful daughter—would not allow herself. I—who had always performed specially well for my grandmother, danced and sung for her, presented her with kisses and good report cards—stopped writing to her, ceased to visit.

But when I heard that she was dying I realized I wanted to go 9 to Winnipeg to see her one more time. Mostly to make my mother happy, I told myself (certain patterns being hard to break). But also, I was offering up one more particularly fine accomplishment: my own dark-eyed, dark-skinned, dark-haired daughter, whom my grandmother had never met.

I put on my daughter's best dress for our visit to Winnipeg, 10 the way the best dresses were always put on me, and I filled my pockets with animal crackers, in case Audrey started to cry. I scrubbed her face mercilessly. On the elevator going up to her room, I realized how much I was sweating.

Grandma was lying flat with an IV tube in her arm and her 11 eyes shut, but she opened them when I leaned over to kiss her. "It's Fredelle's daughter, Joyce," I yelled, because she doesn't hear well anymore, but I could see that no explanation was necessary. "You came," she said. "You brought the baby."

12 Audrey is just one, but she has seen enough of the world to know that people in beds are not meant to be so still and yellow, and she looked frightened. I had never wanted, more, for her to smile.

13 Then Grandma waved at her—the same kind of slow, finger-flexing wave a baby makes—and Audrey waved back. I spread her toys out on my grandmother's bed and sat her down. There she stayed, most of the afternoon, playing and humming and sipping on her bottle, taking a nap at one point, leaning against my grandmother's leg. When I cranked her Snoopy guitar, Audrey stood up on the bed and danced. Grandma wouldn't talk much anymore, though every once in a while she would say how sorry she was that she wasn't having a better day. "I'm not always like this," she said.

14 Mostly she just watched Audrey. Sometimes Audrey would get off the bed, inspect the get-well cards, totter down the hall. "Where is she?" Grandma kept asking. "Who's looking after her?" I had the feeling, even then, that if I'd said "Audrey's lighting matches," Grandma would have shot up to rescue her.

15 We were flying home that night, and I had dreaded telling her, remembering all those other tearful partings. But in the end, I was the one who cried. She had said she was ready to die. But as I leaned over to stroke her forehead, what she said was, "I wish I had your hair" and "I wish I was well."

16 On the plane flying home, with Audrey in my arms, I thought about mothers and daughters, and the four generations of the family that I know most intimately. Every one of those mothers loves and needs her daughter more than her daughter will love or need her some day, and we are, each of us, the only person on earth who is quite so consumingly interested in our child.

17 Sometimes I kiss and hug Audrey so much she starts crying—which is, in effect, what my grandmother was doing to my mother,

all her life. And what makes my mother grieve right now, I think, is not simply that her mother will die in a day or two, but that, once her mother dies, there will never again be someone to love her in quite such an unreserved, unquestioning way. No one else who believes that, fifty years ago, she could have put Shirley Temple out of a job, no one else who remembers the moment of her birth. She will only be a mother, then, not a daughter anymore.

Audrey and I have stopped over for a night in Toronto, where   18
my mother lives. Tomorrow she will go to a safe-deposit box at the bank and take out the receipt for my grandmother's burial plot. Then she will fly back to Winnipeg, where, for the first time in anybody's memory, there was waist-high snow on April Fool's Day. But tonight she is feeding me, as she always does when I come, and I am eating more than I do anywhere else. I admire the wedding china (once my grandmother's) that my mother has set on the table. She says (the way Grandma used to say to her, of the lamb coat), "Some day it will be yours."

○ The Easter Ham and the Bumpus Hounds

Jean Shepherd

Jean Shepherd (b. 1929) was born in Chicago, Illinois, but was raised in the steel-mill town of Hammond, Indiana, the scene of many of the humorous tales about his boyhood years. During the 1960s, Jean Shepherd became something of a cult figure with people in the northeastern part of the United States as a result of his late-night radio show emanating out of WOR in New York City. Although most of his humorous tales originally appeared in Playboy, *probably his largest group of readers is the legion of fans who faithfully read his column in* Car and

Narration

Driver *magazine. It has always been difficult to discriminate fact from fiction in Shepherd's tales. Undoubtedly, the episodes he narrates are based in general on something that happened to him or to somebody that he knows, but just as certainly, Shepherd enhances his "factual" narratives with incidents and details that he has invented. The humor of the "tragedy" related here is heightened when this episode is read as the climax of a series of misadventures between the narrator's family and the passel of hillbillies that moved next door. Pay special attention to the way in which Shepherd uses exact, minute details to conjure up the scene and to stir memories in his readers—details like "the greasy twisted twine" that binds the hams in the grocery store, "the big dark-blue oval pot," the maraschino cherry in the center of each slice of Del Monte pineapple.*

1   These feast days are always associated with major holidays: turkey for Thanksgiving and Christmas, roast chicken for birthdays and, in our house, Easter always meant ham. My father was totally ape over ham. The week before Easter, usually on Friday night, he'd say, "I'll tell you what let's do. What do you say we all pile in the car, drive down to the A. & P. and pick out a great big ham for Easter?"

2   He said it almost nonchalantly, but his eyes would be lit with a wild and ravenous light. It was no small thing he was suggesting, since "a great big ham" meant about half his pay check in those days.

3   My mother almost always would come back with, "Well, gee, I don't know. Can we afford it this year? We can always get a nice little pot roast."

4   "Ah, come on! What the hell. You only live once. What do you say?" And she would always relent.

5   Quivering slightly, he would throw on his coat and rush to the

door. He could already see the ham half eaten, rich and red, weeks of magnificent pickings. Nothing goes with Atlas Praeger like cold ham after a session at the bowling alley.

We'd race to the A. & P. All the hams would be laid out, 6 wrapped in white paper, some marked Armour Star, others Swift; not to mention Hormel. There were always great arguments as to which was really best. These were not dinky little canned hams but weighty monsters smoked darkly and tied with greasy, twisted twine.

The old man would go up and down the case, poking, peer- 7 ing, hefting, sniffing, occasionally punching, until, eventually, *the* ham was isolated from the common herd. Somehow, it looked a little different from the rest. It was *our* ham.

We would leave the market with at least four giant bags of 8 groceries, our fare for the week: loaves of Wonder Bread, Campbell's tomato soup, Ann Page pork and beans, eggs, a two-pound jar of grape jelly, fig bars, oatmeal, Cream of Wheat— real *people* food—and the ham. *The* ham.

When we got the ham home, my mother immediately stripped 9 off the white paper and the string in the middle of our chipped white-enamel kitchen table. There it lay, exuding heavenly per- fumes—proud, arrogant, regal. It had a dark, smoked, leathery skin, which my mother carefully peeled off with her sharpened bread knife. Then the old man, the only one who could lift the ham without straining a gut, placed it in the big dark-blue oval pot that was used only for hams. My mother then covered the ham with water, pushed it onto the big burner and turned up the gas until it boiled. It just sat there on the stove and bubbled away for maybe two hours, filling the house with a smell that was so luscious, so powerful as to have erotic overtones. The old man paced back and forth, occasionally lifting the lid and prodding the ham with a fork, inhaling deeply. The ham frenzy was upon him.

Narration

10   After about an hour, the whole neighborhood knew what we were having for Easter. Finally, the next phase began. Grunting and straining, my mother poured off the water into another pot. It would later form the base of a magnificent pea soup so pungent as to bring tears to the eyes. She then sprinkled a thick layer of brown sugar, dotted with butter, over the ham. She stuck cloves in it in a crisscross design, then added several slices of Del Monte pineapple, thick and juicy, and topped it off with a maraschino cherry in the center of each slice. She then sprinkled more brown sugar over the lot, a few teaspoons of molasses, the juice from the pineapple can, a little salt, a little pepper, and it was shoved into the oven. Almost instantly, the brown sugar melted over the mighty ham and mingled with the ham juice in the pan.

11   By this time, the old man, humming nervously to himself, had checked his carving set several times, to make sure the knife was honed, the fork tines sharp—while in the oven, the ham baked on and on, until late Saturday night, when my mother finally turned off the gas, leaving the oven unopened and the ham inside. She said, as she always did, "Never eat a baked ham right after it's baked. Let it sit in the oven for twelve hours at least."

12   All night long, I would lie in my bed and smell the ham. The next day was Easter: Easter eggs and chocolate bunnies and all that. But the ham and only the ham was what really counted—not only for itself but because it always put my father in a great mood. We would play catch tomorrow; he would drink beer and tell stories. For once, the Bumpuses would be forgotten. Who the hell cares about a bunch of hillbillies, when there's baked ham on the table? I lay in my bed, awake, the dark, indescribable aroma of ham coiling sinuously into my bedroom from the kitchen. In the next room, my father snored lustily, resting up for the great feast.

○ **Shepherd/The Easter Ham**

Immediately after breakfast the next morning, while my brother 13
and I crawled around the house, looking for Easter eggs, my
mother turned on the oven to heat the ham ever so slowly. This
is important, she told us. The flame must be very low.

By 1:30 that afternoon, the tension had risen almost to the 14
breaking point. The smell of ham saturated the drapes. And on
my trip down to Pulaski's for the Sunday paper, I found that it
could be smelled at least four blocks away. Finally, at about two
o'clock, we all gathered around while my mother opened the
blue pot—releasing a blast of fragrance so overwhelming that
my knees wobbled—and surrounded the ham with sliced sweet
potatoes to bake in the brown sugar and pineapple juice.

We usually had our Easter meal around three. Everything was 15
timed carefully around the ham and the Parker House rolls. About
30 minutes before H hour, my mother took the ham out of the
oven and laid it out on a big sheet of wax paper, right in the
middle of the kitchen table, to let it cool a bit and set—the thick,
sweet, brown molasses and sugar oozing down over the sides,
the pineapple slices baked brown, the cloves like tiny black insects soaking in the hot ham gravy.

Easter that year was the way all Easters should be but rarely 16
are. Spring had come early, for a change. There were years
when winter's hard rock ice was still visible along the curbs,
blackened and filthy, coated with steel-mill grime, until late in
May. But this Easter was different; gentle breezes blew through
the kitchen screen door. Already the stickers in our yard gave
promise of a bumper crop. The air was balmy and heavy with
spring passion about to burst.

The spring sunlight slanted in through the kitchen window and 17
bathed the ham in a golden, suffused light, just like any good
religious experience should be lit. The old man was in an exalted state of anticipation. Whenever he really got excited, he
would crack his knuckles loudly. On this fateful day, he was

417

popping them like a set of Brazilian castanets. He had on the new white shirt that he had gotten the week before at J. C. Penney.

18   While the ham sat basking in our gaze, my mother busily spread the lace tablecloth on the dining-room table and set out our best china, which was used only three or four times a year at the maximum. My father picked up his carving knife again, for one last stroke on the whetstone. He held the blade up to the light. Everything was ready. He went into the living room and sat down.

19   "Ah."

20   His eyes glowed with the primal lust of a cave man about to dig into the kill, which would last us at least four months. We would have ham sandwiches, ham salad, ham gravy, ham hash—and, finally, about ten gallons of pea soup made with the gigantic ham bone.

21   When it happened, he was sitting knee-deep in the *Chicago Tribune* sports section. I had been called in to wash up. My mother was in the bedroom, removing the curlers from her hair. My Aunt Glenn and Uncle Tom were on their way over to have Easter dinner with us. Uncle Tom always gave me a dollar. It was going to be a day to remember. Little did I suspect why.

22   I had just left the bathroom and my kid brother had just gone in for his fumigation, when suddenly and without warning:

23   BLAM!

24   The kitchen door flew open. It had been left ajar just a crack to let the air come in to cool the ham.

25   I rushed to the kitchen just in time to see 4,293 blue-ticked Bumpus hounds roar through the screen door in a great, roiling mob. The leader of the pack—the one that almost got the old man every day—leaped high onto the table and grabbed the butt end of the ham in his enormous slavering jaws.

○ Shepherd/The Easter Ham

The rest of the hounds—squealing, yapping, panting, rolling over one another in a frenzy of madness—pounded out the kitchen door after Big Red, trailing brown sugar and pineapple slices behind him. They were in and out in less than five seconds. The screen door hung on one hinge, its screen ripped and torn and dripping with gravy. Out they went. Pow, just like that.

26

"HOLY CHRIST!" The old man leaped out of his chair.

27

"THE HAM! THE HAM! THOSE GODDAMN DOGS! THE HAM!!"

28

He fell heavily over the footrest as he struggled to get into the kitchen, his voice a high-pitched scream of disbelief and rage. My mother just stood in the dining room, her face blank and staring, two aluminum hair curlers still in place. I ran through the kitchen, following my old man out to the back porch.

29

The snarling mob had rolled across the back yard and was now battling it out next to the garage, yipping and squealing with excitement. Occasionally, one of them would be hurled out of the pack, flipping over backward in the air, to land heavily amid the barrel staves and sardine cans. Instantly, he would be back in the fray, biting and tearing at whatever moved.

30

The ham didn't last eight seconds. Old Grandpa Bumpus and a dozen other Bumpuses stuck their heads out of various windows, to see what all the yowling was about. Without pausing to aim, he reared back and spit a great big gob of tobacco juice—a new long-distance record—right into the middle of the pack. It was a direct hit on our ham—or what was left of it.

31

Chapter 11
Description

○ **On the Ball**

Roger Angell

The following description of a baseball was the first paragraph of a rather long article on the art of pitching in the game of baseball. The author of many articles in the New Yorker *about major-league baseball, Roger Angell (b. 1920) here forces the reader to view the familiar object from a startlingly new perspective. First, he gives you precise information about its weight and dimensions; then he unwraps the baseball and shows you the materials from which it is made and displays its structure; then he forces you to imagine that you have a finished baseball in your hand and invites you to turn it over so that you can tactually experience its heft and its symmetry. The thesis of this eye-opening description is expressed in the sentence, "No other small package comes as close to the ideal in design and utility."*

It weighs just over five ounces and measures between 2.86 and 2.94 inches in diameter. It is made of a composition-cork nucleus encased in two thin layers of rubber, one black and one red, surrounded by 121 yards of tightly wrapped blue-gray wool yarn, 45 yards of white wool yarn, 53 more yards of blue-gray wool yarn, 150 yards of fine cotton yarn, a coat of rubber cement, and a cowhide (formerly horsehide) exterior, which is held together with 216 slightly raised red cotton stitches. Printed certifications, endorsements, and outdoor advertising spherically attest to its authenticity. Like most institutions, it is considered inferior in its present form to its ancient archetypes, and in this case the complaint is probably justified; on occasion in recent years it has actually been known to come apart under the demands of its brief but rigorous active career. Baseballs are assembled and hand-stitched in Taiwan (before this year the work was done in Haiti, and before 1973 in Chicopee, Massachusetts), and contemporary pitchers claim that there is a tangible variation in the size and feel of the balls that now come into play in a single game; a true peewee is treasured by hurlers, and its departure from the premises, by fair means or foul, is secretly mourned. But never mind: any baseball is beautiful. No other small package comes as close to the ideal in design and utility. It is a perfect object for a man's hand. Pick it up and it instantly suggests its purpose; it is meant to be thrown a considerable distance—thrown hard and with precision. Its feel and heft are the beginning of the sport's critical dimensions; if it were a fraction of an inch larger or smaller, a few centigrams heavier or lighter, the game of baseball would be utterly different. Hold a baseball in your hand. As it happens, this one is not brand-new. Here, just to one side of the curved surgical welt of stitches, there is a pale-green grass smudge, darkening on one edge almost to black—the mark of an old infield play, a tough grounder now lost in memory. Feel the ball, turn it over in your hand; hold it across the seam or the other way, with the seam just to the side of your middle finger. Speculation stirs. You want to get outdoors and throw this spare and sensual object to somebody or, at the very least, watch somebody else throw it. The game has begun.

Description

○ A Winter Day on Paine Mountain

Floyd C. Stuart

*Floyd Stuart, a poet and essayist, is an associate pro-
fessor at Norwich University. The following passage is
the beginning of a longer article describing his climb up
Paine Mountain in Vermont. In this exemplary description
of a scene, he conveys to his readers a sense of the
almost arrested frigidity of a clear, sunny, wintry morning. Probably from his long experience of writing poetry,
he knows that the best way to convey a verbal picture of
a scene is to use precise, concrete, sensory words,
and fortunately he has the vocabulary resources to be
able to paint the picture. We know his point of view: the
vantage point from just outside the door of his house one
sunshiny morning in the dead of winter. He gives us one
or two appeals to the sense of smell ("the cold smells
clean") and the sense of touch ("glues the moist sides of
your nostrils together at each intake"), but, as is appropriate on such a frozen morning, most of his images appeal to the sense of sight ("brilliant," "white," "smoke,"
"shafts," "shining," "swirls") and the sense of hearing
("squeaks," "yap," "crunching"). And he reinforces these
sensory words with vivid similes and metaphors ("like line-
dried sheets," "packages of cornflakes," ghosts slipping out of the mouth, "icicles lengthening from the land").*

1   I walk out of my house, snowshoes over my shoulder, into brilliant morning, into the kind of cold that, if you've lived here a
while, you've learned to respect. This cold smells clean, like line-
dried sheets, and glues the moist sides of your nostrils together
at each intake. Snow squeaks in such cold. Walking down the
plowed lane (white, for salt the past five days hasn't melted snow,
which compresses toward ice), I hear my boots crunching

From "Paine Mountain" by Floyd C. Stuart from *Blair & Ketchum's Country Journal,*
Vol. IX, No. 1, January 1982. Copyright © 1982 by Floyd C. Stuart. Reprinted by
permission.

packages of cornflakes. This cold hones each sound like a knife. The sharp dog yap up-valley seems at my heels. The ghost slipping out of my mouth looms up before my face. I trudge on through it. Smoke from our village chimneys stands straight up, dozens of white, unwavering shafts, icicles lengthening from the land. Wind itself is frozen solid. A lens of haze hovers over the village this shining day, the steam of the town's warm living that can't break through the lid of cold. But the rest of the sky is eye-aching blue. Those who have asthma or heart trouble don't walk out.

Ten minutes from my door, I strap on the snowshoes and begin a day's trek in the mountains. The snow, so cold, is dry, and even with the modified bear paws, I sink in a foot at each step. Diamond dust swirls up before me in the sun. I wallow across the tilted snowfield, an old freighter churning out toward the horizon.

2

○ **Of Hog Wallow and the New Jersey Wilderness**

John McPhee

There is nothing special about the atmosphere of a so-phisticated college town like Princeton, New Jersey, the birthplace of John McPhee (b. 1931), that would condition a person to become a writer about the rugged out-doors; but almost all of the pieces that McPhee has written for The New Yorker *or for his books, like* Coming into the Country *(1977, about Alaska) and* Basin and Range *(1981, about geological explorations in the mountain ranges of Utah and Nevada), have dealt with the out-door scene—as does the article from which the following description was taken. Descriptions of setting and of*

Description

1   One resident of Hog Wallow is Frederick Chambers Brown. I met him one summer morning when I stopped at his house to ask for water. Fred Brown's house is on an unpaved road that curves along the edge of a wide cranberry bog. What attracted me to it was the pump that stands in his yard. It was something of a wonder that I noticed the pump, because there were, among other things, eight automobiles in the yard, two of them on their sides and one of them upside down, all ten years old or older. Around the cars were old refrigerators, vacuum cleaners, partly dismantled radios, cathode-ray tubes, a short wooden ski, a large wooden mallet, dozens of cranberry picker's boxes, many tires,

an orange crate dated 1946, a cord or so of firewood, mandolines, engine heads, and maybe a thousand other things. The house itself, two stories high, was covered with tarpaper that was peeling away in some places, revealing its original shingles, made of Atlantic white cedar from the stream courses of the surrounding forest. I called out to ask if anyone was home, and a voice inside called back, "Come in. Come in. Come on the hell in."

I walked through a vestibule that had a dirt floor, stepped up 2 into a kitchen, and went on into another room that had several overstuffed chairs in it and a porcelain-topped table, where Fred Brown was seated, eating a pork chop. He was dressed in a white sleeveless shirt, ankle-top shoes, and undershorts. He gave me a cheerful greeting and, without asking why I had come or what I wanted, picked up a pair of khaki trousers that had been tossed onto one of the overstuffed chairs and asked me to sit down. He set the trousers on another chair, and he apologized for being in the middle of his breakfast, explaining that he seldom drank much but the night before he had had a few drinks and this had caused his day to start slowly. "I don't know what's the matter with me, but there's got to be something the matter with me, because drink don't agree with me anymore," he said. He had a raw onion in one hand, and while he talked he shaved slices from the onion and ate them between bites of the chop. He was a muscular and well-built man, with short, bristly white hair, and he had bright, fast-moving eyes in a wide-open face. His legs were trim and strong, with large muscles in the calves. I guessed that he was about sixty and for a man of sixty he seemed to be in remarkably good shape. He was actually seventy-nine. "My rule is: Never eat except when you're hungry," he said, and he ate another slice of the onion.

In a straight-backed chair near the doorway to the kitchen sat 3 a young man with long black hair, who wore a visored red leather

Description

cap that had darkened with age. His shirt was coarse-woven and had eyelets down a V neck that was laced with a thong. His trousers were made of canvas, and he was wearing gum boots. His arms were folded, his legs were stretched out, he had one ankle over the other, and as he sat there he appeared to be sighting carefully past his feet, as if his toes were the outerframe of a gunsight and he could see some sort of target in the floor. When I had entered, I had said hello to him, and he had nodded without looking up. He had a long, straight nose and high cheekbones, in a deeply tanned face that was, somehow, gaunt. I had no idea whether he was shy or hostile. Eventually, when I came to know him, I found him to be as shy a person as I have ever had a chance to know. His name is Bill Wasovwich, and he lives alone in a cabin about half a mile from Fred.

○ # Yellowstone and the Kiowas

N. Scott Momaday

In 1969, N. Scott Momaday (b. 1934) won the Pulitzer Prize for his novel House Made of Dawn. *In that same year, Momaday published* The Way to Rainy Mountain, *a collection of legends about the Kiowa Indians, his native tribe. Born in Oklahoma, the site of Rainy Mountain, he was raised on several Indian reservations. Eventually, he earned his Ph.D. at Stanford University, where he now teaches. In this excerpt, Momaday gives us an account of a pilgrimage he once made to the lands in the northern part of the United States that his ancestors had inhabited many centuries ago before settling in Oklahoma. In this description of the Yellowstone Park area and the great plains that slope eastward from there, the author*

○ Momaday/Yellowstone and the Kiowas

*does not give us the kind of minute detail that we have
encountered in other descriptions in this section. Instead, he gives us the kind of panoramic view of the
scene that we might get in the opening scene of a movie
about the big-sky areas of the American West. With his
Olympian perspective on the scene and with his lyrical,
highly metaphorical language, Momaday gives his readers an overview of the awesome, majestic beauty of the
land of his ancestral roots. We might call this a "holistic
description," a picture that gives us a sense, an impression, of the scene as a whole.*

Although my grandmother lived out her long life in the shadow   1
of Rainy Mountain, the immense landscape of the continental
interior lay like memory in her blood. She could tell of the Crows,
whom she had never seen, and of the Black Hills, where she
had never been. I wanted to see in reality what she had seen
more perfectly in the mind's eye, and traveled fifteen hundred
miles to begin my pilgrimage.

Yellowstone, it seemed to me, was the top of the world, a   2
region of deep lakes and dark timber, canyons and waterfalls.
But, beautiful as it is, one might have the sense of confinement
there. The skyline in all directions is close at hand, the high wall
of the woods and deep cleavages of shade. There is a perfect
freedom in the mountains, but it belongs to the eagle and the
elk, the badger and the bear. The Kiowas reckoned their stature
by the distance they could see, and they were bent and blind
in the wilderness.

Descending eastward, the highland meadows are a stairway   3
to the plain. In July the inland slope of the Rockies is luxuriant
with flax and buckwheat, stonecrop and larkspur. The earth un-
folds and the limit of the land recedes. Clusters of trees, and

Description

animals grazing far in the distance, cause the vision to reach
away and wonder to build upon the mind. The sun follows a
longer course in the day, and the sky is immense beyond all
comparison. The great billowing clouds that sail upon it are
shadows that move upon the grain like water, dividing light. Far-
ther down, in the land of the Crows and Blackfeet, the plain is
yellow. Sweet clover takes hold of the hills and bends upon itself
to cover and seal the soil. There the Kiowas paused on their
way; they had come to the place where they must change their
lives. The sun is at home on the plains. Precisely there does it
have the certain character of a god. When the Kiowas came to
the land of the Crows, they could see the dark lees of the hills
at dawn across the Bighorn River, the profusion of light on the
grain shelves, the oldest diety ranging after the solstices. Not
yet would they veer southward to the caldron of the land that
lay below; they must wean their blood from the northern winter
and hold the mountains a while longer in their view. They bore
Tai-me in procession to the east.

○ # The Destructive Power of a Nuclear Bomb

Jonathan Schell

*The description below was taken from the first of three
installments of an article that appeared in* The New Yorker
*during February 1982 and that was published later that
year as a book entitled* The Fate of the Earth. *The ultimate purpose of this description—and of the article from
which it is excerpted—is to alert people everywhere to
the horrendous consequences of a nuclear explosion and
thereby to dissuade nations from even contemplating a*

○ Schell/Destructive Power of a Nuclear Bomb

nuclear war. What Jonathan Schell (b. 1943) is describing here is something that has not happened but that could happen. So incredible is the destructive power of modern nuclear bombs that Schell has a very real problem in finding words and images that can adequately convey the horrors of a nuclear explosion. He tries to help us imagine the destructive powers of the bomb by picturing what would happen if a bomb were dropped over a specific spot in the heart of Manhattan. In the first paragraph, he tries by various means to give us an idea of the extent of the devastation, and in the second paragraph, he tries to make us experience, by appeals to several of our senses, the succession of fiery horrors that would follow the explosion of the bomb. Ironically, in the event of the "real thing," no eye-witness to the event would live to give us a description like the one Jonathan Schell conjures up here.

One way to begin to grasp the destructive power of present-day nuclear weapons is to describe the consequences of the detonation of a one-megaton bomb, which possesses eighty times the explosive power of the Hiroshima bomb, on a large city, such as New York. Burst some eighty-five hundred feet above the Empire State Building, a one-megaton bomb would gut or flatten almost every building between Battery Park and 125th Street, or within a radius of four and four-tenths miles, or in an area of sixty-one square miles, and would heavily damage buildings between the northern tip of Staten Island and the George Washington Bridge, or within a radius of about eight miles, or in an area of about two hundred square miles. A conventional explosive delivers a swift shock, like a slap, to whatever it hits, but the blast wave of a sizable nuclear weapon en-

Description

dures for several seconds and "can surround and destroy whole buildings" (Glasstone). People, of course, would be picked up and hurled away from the blast along with the rest of the debris. Within the sixty-one square miles, the walls, roofs, and floors of any buildings that had not been flattened would be collapsed, and the people and furniture inside would be swept down onto the street. (Technically, this zone would be hit by various over-pressures of at least five pounds per square inch. Overpressure is defined as the pressure in excess of normal atmospheric pressure.) As far away as ten miles from ground zero, pieces of glass and other sharp objects would be hurled about by the blast wave at lethal velocities. In Hiroshima, where buildings were low and, outside the center of the city, were often constructed of light materials, injuries from falling buildings were often minor. But in New York, where the buildings are tall and are con-structed of heavy materials, the physical collapse of the city would certainly kill millions of people. The streets of New York are nar-row ravines running between the high walls of the city's build-ings. In a nuclear attack, the walls would fall and the ravines would fill up. The people in the buildings would fall to the street with the debris of the buildings, and the people in the street would be crushed by this avalanche of people and buildings. At a distance of two miles or so from ground zero, winds would reach four hundred miles an hour, and another two miles away they would reach a hundred and eighty miles an hour. Mean-while, the fireball would be growing, until it was more than a mile wide, and rocketing upward, to a height of over six miles. For ten seconds, it would broil the city below. Anyone caught in the open within nine miles of ground zero would receive third-degree burns and would probably be killed; closer to the ex-plosion, people would be charred and killed instantly. From Greenwich Village up to Central Park, the heat would be great enough to melt metal and glass. Readily inflammable materials, such as newspapers and dry leaves, would ignite in all five boroughs (though in only a small part of Staten Island) and west to the Passaic River, in New Jersey, within a radius of about nine and a half miles from ground zero, thereby creating an area of more than two hundred and eighty square miles in which mass fires were likely to break out.

If it were possible (as it would not be) for someone to stand at Fifth Avenue and Seventy-second Street (about two miles from ground zero) without being instantly killed, he would see the following sequence of events. A dazzling white light from the fireball would illumine the scene, continuing for perhaps thirty seconds. Simultaneously, searing heat would ignite everything flammable and start to melt windows, cars, buses, lampposts, and everything else made of metal or glass. People in the street would immediately catch fire, and would shortly be reduced to heavily charred corpses. About five seconds after the light appeared, the blast wave would strike, laden with the debris of a now nonexistent midtown. Some buildings might be crushed, as though a giant fist had squeezed them on all sides, and others might be picked up off their foundations and whirled uptown with the other debris. On the far side of Central Park, the West Side skyline would fall from south to north. The four-hundred-mile-an-hour wind would blow from south to north, die down after a few seconds, and then blow in the reverse direction with diminished intensity. While these things were happening, the fireball would be burning in the sky for the ten seconds of the thermal pulse. Soon huge, thick clouds of dust and smoke would envelop the scene, and as the mushroom cloud rushed overhead (it would have a diameter of about twelve miles) the light from the sun would be blotted out, and day would turn to night. Within minutes, fires, ignited both by the thermal pulse and by broken gas mains, tanks of gas and oil, and the like, would begin to spread in the darkness, and a strong, steady wind

2

Description

would begin to blow in the direction of the blast. As at Hiroshima, a whirlwind might be produced, which would sweep through the ruins, and radioactive rain, generated under the meteorological conditions created by the blast, might fall. Before long, the individual fires would coalesce into a mass fire, which, depending largely on the winds, would become either a conflagration or a firestorm. In a conflagration, prevailing winds spread a wall of fire as far as there is any combustible material to sustain it; in a firestorm, a vertical updraft caused by the fire itself sucks the surrounding air in toward a central point, and the fires therefore converge in a single fire of extreme heat. A mass fire of either kind renders shelters useless by burning up all the oxygen in the air and creating toxic gases, so that anyone inside the shelters is asphyxiated, and also by heating the ground to such high temperatures that the shelters turn, in effect, into ovens, cremating the people inside them. In Dresden, several days after the firestorm raised there by Allied conventional bombing, the interiors of some bomb shelters were still so hot that when they were opened the inrushing air caused the contents to burst into flame. Only those who had fled their shelters when the bombing started had any chance of surviving. (It is difficult to predict in a particular situation which form the fires will take. In actual experience, Hiroshima suffered a firestorm and Nagasaki suffered a conflagration.)

Chapter 12
Exposition

○ Nature's Odds

Robert Ardrey

Robert Ardrey (b. 1908) was a fairly successful play-wright, screenwriter, and novelist before he turned, rather late in life, to the writing of books and articles on anthro-pology. Perhaps his best-known books of anthropology are African Genesis: A Personal Investigation into the An-imal Origins and Nature of Man *(1961) and* The Territorial Imperative: A Personal Inquiry into the Animal Origins of Property and Nations *(1966). Writers sometimes use Analogy as part of a description, an argument, or, an exposition (and occasionally, but less frequently, as part of a narrative). In the following excerpt from an exposi-tory piece on genetic mutation, Ardrey resorts to an analogy to illustrate the thesis that he articulates at the end of the second paragraph: "The change of one [gene] changes the system and modifies the value of all other genes." If his analogy is to serve its purpose, what he compares the mutation of genes to must be something that his audience is familiar with and that bears a number of pertinent similarities to what the audience is less fa-miliar with. It would be a rare person in his audience who was not familiar with the game of draw poker. Most peo-ple would know how the card or cards drawn in this game can make all the difference in whether one's hand is a complete "bust"—a "disaster," to use Ardrey's term—or a "winner"—a "benevolent mutation," in Ardrey's terms. In his final paragraph, Ardrey makes some rather ex-plicit applications of his analogy. But whereas in the ear-lier paragraphs he spends most of his time pointing out the similarities between the mutation of genes and the mutation of a poker hand, at the end he emphasizes some important differences.*

Exposition

1   The theory of mutation . . . is a concept as exalted as that of time or death.

2   The gene is a chemical unit of atomic proportions buried in every living cell. It determines the structure of an organism, and frequently its ways. It is capable of self-reproduction, and is inheritable. The gene developed as the determinant of life, in all probability, in the long beginnings of Pre-Cambrian simplicity; but genes by the thousands are required to handle the complexities of higher animals. And mutation is the abrupt change in the character of a gene in a reproductive cell, resulting in an abrupt and usually diastrous change in the character of the descendant organism. And while one might think that the change of a single gene among, say, a thousand would have small consequence, still it is not so, for genes operate as a system. The change of one changes the system and modifies the value of all other genes.

3   We may best compare the play of genes to a hand of draw poker. You hold the ten, jack, queen, and king of hearts, along with the nine of spades. The nine gives the other cards a considerable value, and you are in business with a high straight. But discard the nine of spades and draw. If you draw a lesser card, then you are out of the game. Your ten, jack, queen, and king of hearts are suddenly of no value; you have suffered a normal mutation, and you are dead. Or you may draw a higher card, any but an ace. Your high straight is gone, and you are reduced to a pair. You are not dead, but suffer many such hands and you will be out of the game. Draw the ace of hearts, however. Every other card will leap in value. You will have a royal flush, the pot on the table, and in all probability a heart attack.

In only this last qualification does such a draw differ from a benevolent mutation.

Nature's odds are poorer than poker's. One mutation in a hundred may be regarded as benevolent, and generally we may say that the other ninety-nine mutations will kill the organism immediately, or so damage its genetic system that natural selection will accomplish its discard. But when a change however rare opens a new evolutionary road better suited to an environment, then natural selection will protect and multiply the lucky heirs and seek further mutations among them.

4

○ The Skull as Architecture

Ashley Montagu

Ashley Montagu (b. 1906) was born in London, England, but became a naturalized citizen of the United States in 1940, shortly after he took his Ph.D. degree at Columbia University in New York City. Although Montagu has been a professor of anatomy at schools like New York University and Rutgers University, he is best known today as an anthropologist. This article from the regular column "Human Nature" in Science Digest *is a good example of the use of Analogy to explain something to someone. The basic strategy is to compare the something to something else that your audience is likely to be familiar with and to point out the ways in which the two things are similar. Montagu wants to give his readers some idea of the structure of the human skull. He knows that most of the regular readers of* Science Digest *are interested in science and probably have an expert knowledge of one or two of the sciences. So he can presume that his readers will not be thrown as much by a technical vocabulary as the general lay audience might be. Here most of the technical vocabulary comes from the*

Exposition

field of anatomy—occipital bone, sagittal arch, zygomatic bone (see the illustrative sketch of a skull in your
desk dictionary). His language is least technical when he
talks about architecture, but he obviously presumes that
his readers are familiar enough with architecture that they
won't be thrown by a technical term like Gothic arch, the
key term that he uses to give his readers an idea of the
basic structure of the human skull. Even if you do not
have as much general knowledge of science as most of
Montagu's primary audience has, you probably get from
his exposition a fairly clear image of the structure of the
human skull, and you are probably persuaded that, as
Montagu claims, the "human skull is one of the most
structurally efficient pieces of architecture ever developed."

1   Your head and the Cathedral of Notre Dame have more in
common than you might think.

2   The human skull is one of the most structurally efficient pieces
of architecture ever developed. The brain and the sensory organs located in the head require a housing able to resist strains
of all sorts and able to distribute stress so that it is rendered
harmless. The skull fulfills these requirements perfectly.

3   One might think that the skull is subject to assault only during
such events as a football game or a mugging. Not so. Serious
stress is constant, produced almost entirely through the action
of the lower jaw—the only movable portion of the adult skull—
upon the upper. Every movement of the lower jaw, or mandible,
that brings its teeth in contact with those of the upper jaw produces a series of shocks that affect the whole skull.

4   The freely hinged mandible also creates stress through the
muscles that move and support it, pulling on the skull when the
mouth is open and pressing against it when the mouth is closed.

"The Skull As Architecture" by Ashley Montagu originally appeared in Science Digest, February 1982. Reprinted by permission of the author.

○ **Montagu/The Skull as Architecture**

Wiggle your jaw; you'll see how freely it moves and how great, in consequence, must be the variety of forces that act upon the skull.

The arrangement for distributing force through the teeth represents a marvel of design. Architecturally, the skull more closely approaches the Gothic style than any other. It can be considered an arch or series of arches, the pillars of which are supported and reinforced by a number of buttresses. The three main arches are formed by large curved plates running from side to side: the frontal bone, the occipital bone and the parietal bones. The great sagittal arch runs from the root of the nose to the back of the head. Instead of passing directly to the base of the skull, shocks are distributed throughout the skull's pillars and buttresses, as they would be by any architectural arch. The key buttress of the skull is the quadrangular zygomatic bone, which lies perpendicular to the first molar. All the stresses of teeth clashing pass into this buttress without any injury to the skull or discomfort to the organism.

The whole architectural system of the skull suffers when one of its interdependent components is lost. The jaw can become considerably deformed, for example, by the uneven distribution of stresses produced by the lower jaw after the loss of certain teeth.

The structure of the bones serving as pillars and buttresses makes them highly efficient shock absorbers. They are composed of a spongy, zigzagging latticework sandwiched between two layers of dense bone. Forces traveling along the long axis of a bone will be reduced by the thick layers and dissipated as they are sidetracked into the innumerable struts forming the spongy layer. The spongy layer also absorbs the forces set up by the push and pull of the muscles.

Blows to the top of the head are cushioned partly by the arches of the skull. In addition, the skull contains 22 independent but

Exposition

dovetailing bones. It is at their joints, which maintain a certain amount of give until we reach middle age, that the bones absorb the spread that may be caused by a sudden powerful blow, just as the joints of a building absorb the shocks it receives.

9   Architects and historians have long debated whether the ornate flying buttresses of Gothic cathedrals serve a purpose or exist merely as decoration. Recently, using plastic models and a process called optical stress analysis, Princeton structural engineers have shown that the buttresses indeed play a vital supporting role: apparently they were designed to absorb stresses caused by high winds.

10   Since medieval architects were field-trained and apparently built no models of their great cathedrals, how could they have known intuitively that their buttresses and pillars would work? Could it be that they literally used their heads? The main parts of the skull had certainly been known since Galen (A.D. 130–200) wrote his provocatively titled *Bones for Beginners.* Could architects of the Middle Ages have modeled their cathedrals after the vaulted, buttressed, pillared, beautifully designed human skull?

○ What Do They Mean, SF?

Gene Wolfe

Of all the sub-categories of Exposition, Definition is the one that you might think demands of the author the least concern for the audience: just lay out the definition and let the audience come to terms with it. And indeed some writers are more concerned with the accuracy of their definition than they are with their readers' ability to grasp the definition. In the following selection from a magazine

*for writers, however, the author has assessed his ex-
pected audience and accommodated his definition to their
capacities. Gene Wolfe (b. 1931), a well-known writer
himself of short stories for science fiction magazines,
knows that his title is going to attract knowledgeable authors and readers of science fiction. Accordingly, he can
presume that his audience has some prior knowledge of
the subject he is writing about. He can take lots of short-
cuts in his definitions and can drop names and make
allusions without having to explain them or elaborate on
them. In order to clarify the "overlapping genres" of science fiction, speculative fiction, and science fantasy (all
SF's, as you will note), Wolfe spends most of his time
differentiating the three types. The fact that he refers to
the genres as "overlapping" indicates his awareness that
all three have something in common: probably that element of the out-of-the-ordinary which demands a "willing
suspension of disbelief" on the reader's part. Since he
knows that his primary audience is familiar with all three
types of story, he does not have to dwell on what the
stories have in common; he can best help these dedicated readers by showing them the subtle differences
between the three types of preternatural fiction. A test of
how well Gene Wolfe succeeds in defining his terms for
you would be how well you, in turn, could explain to a
friend the differences between the three genres.*

T o a geographer, I suppose it might be San Francisco, and to   1
a dean, senior fellow. To a writer, SF means **science fiction;**
but to a science fiction writer, SF (or s.f., or sf) can mean any of
three overlapping genres—science fiction, speculative fiction, and
science fantasy.

Needless to say, the name is not the thing named. You might   2
write and sell all three without having any clear idea of the no-

---

From "What Do They Mean, SF?" by Gene Wolfe from *The Writer*, Vol. 93, No. 8,
August 1980. Copyright © 1980 by The Writer, Inc. Reprinted by permission.

Exposition

menclature involved, and even without having heard the terms. When Mary Wollstonecraft Shelley wrote *Frankenstein* back in the early years of the 19th century, she could not possibly have had any idea she was originating "science fiction," which is a 20th century coinage. But if you understand how the three differ and know the basis of each, you will have a considerable advantage.

3   **Science fiction** has the oldest name (although it is not really the oldest form), so we'll deal with it first. It may well be the hardest of the three to write; it is certainly the easiest to sell, when it is written competently.

4   Science fiction is fiction that turns upon the assumption of at least one breakthrough in one of the "hard" sciences. (A hard science is one in which theories are subject to *rigorous* test, usually by experiment. Physics, chemistry, biology, and mathematics are the principal hard sciences.) Mary Shelley, for example, extrapolated from experiments in galvanism and assumed, for the purposes of her book, that the time would soon come when life could be restored to dead flesh. In other words, she assumed a certain breakthrough in biology and biochemistry. When H. G. Wells assumed [in *The Time Machine*] that a machine capable of traveling through time could be built, he was assuming a breakthrough in physics.

5   In both of those books, "we"—members of western civilization—were supposed to have made the breakthrough; but it doesn't actually matter who makes it. Wells's *War of the Worlds* assumes that Martians develop interplanetary flight and come to Earth; it is just as much science fiction as Stanley Weinbaum's "A Martian Odyssey," in which Americans go to Mars.

6   Too often, would-be science-fiction writers suppose that any story that has a rocket ship, a ray gun, or a robot in it is science fiction, and that any story that lacks all three is not. It just isn't so. L. Frank Baum's *Tik-Tok of Oz* is fantasy (very good fantasy,

I might add), although the title character is a robot. It is fantasy because Tik-Tok is fundamentally a large, magical, mechanical toy, and not a triumph of physics and engineering. If you want to examine some contemporary science fiction that does not make use of rockets, ray guns, or robots, you could hardly do better than to read *Who?* and *Michaelmas,* both by the redoubtable Algis Budrys.

Speculative fiction is unquestionably the oldest genre of the three SF's, although as a term, it is the newest. To the best of my knowledge, the phrase originated with Damon Knight, a fine writer who usually produces science fiction. Knight seems to have meant it as a general broadening of science fiction; but it has rapidly come to designate stories in which one or more changes are assumed in the "soft" sciences. (Soft sciences are, obviously, sciences that are not "hard"; psychology, history, economics, and sociology are soft sciences.) The granddad of all speculative fiction is probably *Utopia,* by Thomas More, written almost 500 years ago. Sir Thomas (who has since become Saint Thomas, the undoubtable patron of all SF writers) imagined a way of life radically different from life in the England of his day and wrote a book to answer the question "What if people lived like this?" A superb modern example of the same type of novel is Ursula K. Le Guin's *The Dispossessed,* which compares future capitalism and future communism.

Stories that speculate about the effects of a nuclear war next week or a stock market crash next month are speculative fiction; so are those that wonder what would have happened if the South had won the Civil War, or if England had crushed the revolution in her colonies. In the language of the counterculture, speculative fiction is well described by the title of Thomas M. Disch's story collection *Fun With Your New Head.* Another good collection is the recently published *Interfaces: An Anthology of Speculative Fiction,* edited by Le Guin and Virginia Kidd.

Exposition

9   If this article were to stick strictly to plan, the next genre to be discussed would be science fantasy. But nothing is more typical of the old, unmodified fantasy than that it turns up in unexpected places and in unexpected guises. Some feeling for fantasy—I won't say an understanding, because nobody can really understand it—is necessary to explain science fantasy.

10   Fantasy is mankind's oldest literature. *Gilgamesh,* written on clay tablets 1500 years before the birth of Moses, is fantasy. The first book you ever read was probably some dreary text about Dick, Jane, and Spot. But the first book ever read to you, your real first book, was very possibly fantasy—*Puss in Boots* or *Alice in Wonderland.* It might be said that any story laid in Wonderland is fantasy, but it is by no means true that all fantasy must be laid there. James Thurber's "The Unicorn in the Garden" is fantasy, although the only fantasy element is the unicorn.

11   For twenty years now, modern fantasy has been almost overwhelmed by J. R. R. Tolkien's *The Lord of the Rings,* the book that proved that fantasy in the 20th century A.D. was no more limited to children's stories than it had been in the 20th century B.C. When our 20th century is over and the 21st rolls around, *The Lord of the Rings* will probably remain what it is today—the one book every modern fantasy writer must read, and the one book that no modern fantasy writer should try to imitate.

12   **Science fantasy** is the newest term. A science fantasy story uses the means of science to achieve the spirit of fantasy. Like fantasy, science fantasy rests upon, and often abounds with, "impossible" creatures and objects—girls asleep for centuries, one-eyed giants, weapons that can speak and may rebel. But it uses the methodology of science fiction to show that these things are not only possible but probable.

13   Let's take one of those girls for example. As I write these words, hundreds of medical researchers are seeking a way to achieve suspended animation in human beings. We know it can be done, and indeed among the lower animals it isn't even particularly

uncommon. Those goldfish you saw the last time you went to the dime store probably arrived in a cake of ice. That's the usual method of shipping goldfish, and though some fish in each shipment are dead when the ice is thawed, the fish suffer fewer losses that way than they would if they spent the trip sloshing around in a portable tank. If a goldfish, why not a golden-haired princess?

Alas, there is a reason—we don't know how to do it. But if we did know how, we could vastly reduce the difficulty of—say—an expedition to Mars by princesses. Furthermore, if a golden-haired princess (or anybody else) fell ill of a disease science has not yet learned to cure, she could sleep until a cure was ready. 14

But now suppose that, for whatever reason, no one came to wake her. Perhaps a war was fought—not a war of hydrogen bombs, but a war of deadly viruses. With her biological functions suspended, the princess would not die, though the hospital staff would. When they were gone, she would slumber on, unknowing, while the forests cut by the first settlers grew back around the crumbling walls of International Medical Center. Until one day . . . 15

You get the idea now. . . . That's science fantasy. Or at least, it could be. It would be if the treatment spoke of the mystery of things, even while the words talked among themselves of disease vectors and cryogenics. 16

○ **In Bed**

Joan Didion

In addition to her three novels Run River *(1963),* Play It as It Lays *(1971), and* A Book of Common Prayer *(1977), Joan Didion (b. 1934) has published two collections of essays,* Slouching Towards Bethlehem *(1969) and* The White Album *(1979). In the following excerpt, Didion does not give us the kind of formal, even technical definition*

Exposition

of a migraine headache that we might encounter in an encyclopedia or in a medical textbook. Instead, she gives us an intensely personal account of her long-time experience with migraine headaches. But this highly subjective definition conveys to us—even if we have never experienced a migraine headache ourselves—a keen sense of the stunningly painful and thoroughly incapacitating effects of this dreaded "visitor." A close analysis of how Joan Didion makes her readers "feel" the headache will let you in on the secret of how fiction writers recreate an experience so vividly that readers can "relive" the experience with the narrator. In other words, you will see how a writer uses techniques from the art of fiction to give an exposition of something. You may find that sometimes you can best convey an explanation of something to someone else by resorting to what we might call an "experiential definition."

Three, four, sometimes five times a month, I spend the day in bed with a migraine headache, insensible to the world around me. Almost every day of every month, between these attacks, I feel the sudden irrational irritation and the flush of blood into the cerebral arteries which tell me that migraine is on its way, and I take certain drugs to avert its arrival. If I did not take the drugs, I would be able to function perhaps one day in four. The physiological error called migraine is, in brief, central to the given of my life. When I was 15, 16, even 25, I used to think that I could rid myself of this error by simply denying it, character over chemistry. "Do you have headaches *sometimes? frequently? never?*" the application forms would demand. "Check one." Wary of the trap, wanting whatever it was that the successful circumnavigation of that particular form could bring (a job, a scholarship, the respect of mankind and the grace of God), I would check one. *"Sometimes,"* I would lie. That in fact I spent one or two days a week almost unconscious with pain seemed a shameful secret, evidence not merely of some chemical inferiority but of all my bad attitudes, unpleasant tempers, wrong-think.

For I had no brain tumor, no eyestrain, no high blood pressure, nothing wrong with me at all: I simply had migraine headaches, and migraine headaches were, as everyone who did not have them knew, imaginary. I fought migraine then, ignored the warnings it sent, went to school and later to work in spite of it, sat through lectures in Middle English and presentations to advertisers with involuntary tears running down the right side of my face, threw up in washrooms, stumbled home by instinct, emptied ice trays onto my bed and tried to freeze the pain in my right temple, wished only for a neurosurgeon who would do a lobotomy on house call, and cursed my imagination.

It was a long time before I began thinking mechanistically enough to accept migraine for what it was: something with which I would be living, the way some people live with diabetes. Migraine is something more than the fancy of a neurotic imagination. It is an essentially hereditary complex of symptoms, the most frequently noted but by no means the most unpleasant of which is a vascular headache of blinding severity, suffered by a surprising number of women, a fair number of men (Thomas Jefferson had migraine, and so did Ulysses S. Grant, the day he accepted Lee's surrender), and by some unfortunate children as young as two years old. (I had my first when I was eight. It came on during a fire drill at the Columbia School in Colorado Springs, Colorado. I was taken first home and then to the infirmary at Peterson Field, where my father was stationed. The Air Corps doctor prescribed an enema.) Almost anything can trigger a specific attack of migraine: stress, allergy, fatigue, an abrupt change in barometric pressure, a contretemps over a parking ticket. A flashing light. A fire drill. One inherits, of course, only the predisposition. In other words, I spent yesterday in bed with a headache not merely because of my bad attitudes, un-

2

3

Exposition

pleasant tempers and wrongthink, but because both my grand-
mothers had migraine, my father has migraine and my mother
has migraine.

4   No one knows precisely what it is that is inherited. The chemistry of migraine, however, seems to have some connection with
the nerve hormone named serotonin, which is naturally present
in the brain. The amount of serotonin in the blood falls sharply
at the onset of migraine, and one migraine drug, methysergide,
or Sansert, seems to have some effect on serotonin. Methysergide is a derivative of lysergic acid (in fact Sandoz Pharma-
ceuticals first synthesized LSD-25 while looking for a migraine
cure), and its use is hemmed about with so many contraindica-
tions and side effects that most doctors prescribe it only in the
most incapacitating cases. Methysergide, when it is prescribed,
is taken daily, as a preventive; another preventive which works
for some people is old-fashioned ergotamine tartrate, which helps
to constrict the swelling blood vessels during the "aura," the
period which in most cases precedes the actual headache.

5   Once an attack is under way, however, no drug touches it.
Migraine gives some people mild hallucinations, temporarily blinds
others, shows up not only as a headache but as a gastrointes-
tinal disturbance, a painful sensitivity to all sensory stimuli, an
abrupt overpowering fatigue, a strokelike aphasia, and a crip-
pling inability to make even the most routine connections. When
I am in a migraine aura (for some people the aura lasts fifteen
minutes, for others several hours), I will drive through red lights,
lose the house keys, spill whatever I am holding, lose the ability
to focus my eyes or frame coherent sentences, and generally
give the appearance of being on drugs, or drunk. The actual
headache, when it comes, brings with it chills, sweating, nau-
sea, a debility that seems to stretch the very limits of endurance.
That no one dies of migraine seems, to someone deep into an
attack, an ambiguous blessing.

My husband also has migraine, which is unfortunate for him but fortunate for me: perhaps nothing so tends to prolong an attack as the accusing eye of someone who has never had a headache. "Why not take a couple of aspirin," the unafflicted will say from the doorway, or "I'd have a headache, too, spending a beautiful day like this inside with all the shades drawn." All of us who have migraine suffer not only from the attacks themselves but from this common conviction that we are perversely refusing to cure ourselves by taking a couple of aspirin, that we are making ourselves sick, that we "bring it on ourselves." And in the most immediate sense, the sense of why we have a headache this Tuesday and not last Thursday, of course we often do. There certainly is what doctors call a "migraine personality," and that personality tends to be ambitious, inward, intolerant of error, rather rigidly organized, perfectionist. "You don't look like a migraine personality," a doctor once said to me. "Your hair's messy. But I suppose you're a compulsive housekeeper." Actually my house is kept even more negligently than my hair, but the doctor was right nonetheless: perfectionism can also take the form of spending most of a week writing and rewriting and not writing a single paragraph.

But not all perfectionists have migraine, and not all migrainous 7 people have migraine personalities. We do not escape heredity. I have tried in most of the available ways to escape my own migrainous heredity (at one point I learned to give myself two daily injections of histamine with a hypodermic needle, even though the needle so frightened me that I had to close my eyes when I did it), but I still have migraine. And I have learned now to live with it, learned when to expect it, how to outwit it, even how to regard it, when it does come, as more friend than lodger. We have reached a certain understanding, my migraine and I. It never comes when I am in real trouble. Tell me that my house is burned down, my husband has left me, that there is gunfighting in the streets and panic in the banks, and I will not respond by getting a headache. It comes instead when I am fighting not an open but a guerrilla war with my own life, during weeks of small household confusions, lost laundry, unhappy help, canceled appointments, on days when the telephone rings too much and I get no work done and the wind is coming up. On days like that my friend comes uninvited.

8   And once it comes, now that I am wise in its ways, I no longer fight it. I lie down and let it happen. At first every small apprehension is magnified, every anxiety a pounding terror. Then the pain comes, and I concentrate only on that. Right there is the usefulness of migraine, there in that imposed yoga, the concentration on the pain. For when the pain recedes, ten or twelve hours later, everything goes with it, all the hidden resentments, all the vain anxieties. The migraine has acted as a circuit breaker, and the fuses have emerged intact. There is a pleasant convalescent euphoria. I open the windows and feel the air, eat gratefully, sleep well. I notice the particular nature of a flower in a glass on the stair landing. I count my blessings.

○ **Ducks vs. Hard Rocks**

Deairich Hunter

By the time this piece appeared in Newsweek, *fifteen-year-old Deairich Hunter had returned to his high school in Wilmington, Delaware, where he was a junior and a regular columnist for the school's news magazine. Here, in recalling his experience as a black youth living in a Brooklyn ghetto, Hunter presents his classification of the young people growing up there. The basis for his division of young people into distinct categories is the way in which they attempt to cope with the difficult conditions of their lives in the ghetto. In labeling his two catego-*

○ **Hunter/Ducks vs. Hard Rocks**

*ries—the "ducks" and the "hard rocks"—Hunter resorts
to the metaphors used in the Brooklyn ghetto. Puzzling
out the aptness of these metaphors can lead us to a
deeper understanding of the nature of these two groups
and maybe to an understanding of how these groups
differ—if they do—from comparable groups of young
people growing up in middle-class communities.*

Although the chaos and viciousness of the Miami riot hap-   1
pened months ago, the chaos and viciousness of daily life for
many inner-city black people goes on and on. It doesn't seem
to matter where you are, though some places are worse than
others. A few months ago I left my school in Wilmington, Del.,
moved to Brooklyn, N.Y., and really began to understand.

After you stay in certain parts of New York for awhile, that   2
chaos and viciousness gets inside of you. You get used to seeing
the younger guys flashing pistols and the older ones shooting
them. It's not unusual to be walking down the street or through
the park and see somebody being beaten or held up. It's no
big deal if someone you know is arrested and beat up by the
cops.

In my four months in Brooklyn, I was mugged three times.   3

Although such events may seem extraordinary to you, they   4
are just a part of life in almost any minority neighborhood. It
seems like everybody knows how to use some kind of weapon,
whether it's a pair of nun-chucks (two round sticks attached by
a chain) or an ice pick. As long as it will do the job, you can
use it.

In Brooklyn you fall into one of two categories when you start   5
growing up. The names for the categories may be different in
other cities, but the categories are the same. First, there's the

Exposition

minority of the minority, the "ducks," or suckers. These are the kids who go to school every day. They even want to go to college. Imagine that! School after high school! They don't smoke cheeb (marijuana) and they get zooted (intoxicated) after only one can of beer. They're wasting their lives waiting for a dream that won't come true.

6   The ducks are usually the ones getting beat up on by the majority group—the "hard rocks." If you're a real hard rock you have no worries, no cares. Getting high is as easy as breathing. You just rip off some duck. You don't bother going to school; it's not necessary. You just live with your mom until you get a job—that should be any time a job comes looking for you. Why should you bother to go look for it? Even your parents can't find work.

7   I guess the barrier between the ducks and the hard rocks is the barrier of despair. The ducks still have hope, while the hard rocks are frustrated. They're caught in the deadly, dead-end environment and can't see a way out. Life becomes the fast life—or incredibly boring—and death becomes the death that you see and get used to every day. They don't want to hear any more promises. They believe that's just the white man's way of keeping them under control.

8   Hard rocks do what they want to do when they want to do it. When a hard rock goes to prison it builds up his reputation. He develops a bravado that's like a long, sad joke. But it's all lies and excuses. It's a hustle to keep ahead of the fact that he's going nowhere.

9   Actually, there is one more category, but this group is not really looked upon as human. They're the junkies. They all hang together, but they don't actually have any friends. Everybody in the neighborhood knows that a drug addict would cut his own throat if he could get a fix for it. So everybody knows junkies will stab you in the back for a dollar.

10   A guy often becomes a junkie when he tries to get through

the despair barrier and reach the other side alone. Let's say a hard rock wants to change, to better himself, so he goes back to school. His friends feel he's deserting them, so they desert him first. The ducks are scared of him and won't accept him. Now this hard rock is alone. If he keeps going to school, somebody who is after him out of spite or revenge will probably catch him and work him over. The hard rock has no way to get back. His way of life is over; he loses his friends' respect, becoming more and more of an outcast. Then he may turn to drugs.

I guess the best way to help the hard rocks is to help the ducks. If the hard rocks see the good guy making it, maybe they will change. If they see the ducks, the ones who try, succeed, it might bring them around. The ducks are really the only ones who might be able to change the situation. 11

The problem with most ducks is that after years of effort they develop a negative attitude, too. If they succeed, they know they've got it made. Each one can say he did it by himself and for himself. No one helped him and he owes nobody anything, so he says, "Let the hard rocks and the junkies stay where they are"—the old every-man-for-himself routine. 12

What the ducks must be made to realize is that it was this same attitude that made the hard rocks so hard. They developed a sense of kill or be killed, abuse or be abused, take it or get taken. 13

The hard rocks want revenge. They want revenge because they don't have any hope of changing their situation. Their teachers don't offer it, their parents have lost theirs, and their grandparents died with a heartful of hope but nothing to show for it. 14

Maybe the only people left with hope are the only people who can make a difference—teens like me. We, the ducks, must learn to care. As a 15-year-old, I'm not sure I can handle all that. Just growing up seems hard enough. 15

○ Kinds of Humor

C. S. Lewis

Clive Staples Lewis (1898–1963), during the last ten years of his life, served as Professor of Medieval and Renaissance English literature at Cambridge University in England. The author of many books and articles, he is perhaps best known for his two scholarly books, The Allegory of Love *(1936) and* English Literature in the Sixteenth Century *(1954), his science-fiction novel* Out of the Silent Planet *(1938), and his children's classic* The Lion, the Witch, and the Wardrobe *(1950). To understand what is going on in the following selection, you need to know that this excerpt was taken from Lewis's* The Screwtape Letters *(1942), a series of letters from a devil named Screwtape to his nephew Wormwood on dealing with human "patients." Although Screwtape here uses all the conventional strategies for composing a piece of exposition by means of classifying or dividing a subject into its species, his values are exactly upside-down (note, for instance, what he says at the end of paragraph 2: "it promotes charity, courage, contentment, and many other evils"). He uses the* causes *of humor as the principle for dividing humor into its kinds, and those causes give their names to the types: Joy, Fun, the Joke Proper, and Flippancy. Although Analogy works by looking for the similarities among different things, Classification works by pointing out the differences between kindred things. So when Screwtape talks about each of the four types of humor, he stresses those features that differentiate that type from the other three. He arranges the kinds in a climactic order—from Joy, the lowest form of humor, to Flippancy, the highest form of humor. But notice that his upside-down hierarchy here is the opposite of the order in which normal human beings would rank the types. As we read this example of classificatory exposition, we can enjoy the satirical humor of the piece and also Screwtape's (or Lewis's) skill in executing this classification.*

○ Lewis/Kinds of Humor

I divide the causes of human laughter into Joy, Fun, the Joke 1
Proper, and Flippancy. You will see the first among friends and
lovers reunited on the eve of a holiday. Among adults some
pretext in the way of Jokes is usually provided, but the facility
with which the smallest witticisms produce laughter at such a
time shows that they are not the real cause. What that real cause
is we do not know. Something like it is expressed in much of
that detestable art which the humans call Music, and something
like it occurs in Heaven—a meaningless acceleration in the rhythm
of celestial experience, quite opaque to us. Laughter of this kind
does us no good and should always be discouraged. Besides,
the phenomenon is of itself disgusting and a direct insult to the
realism, dignity, and austerity of Hell.

Fun is closely related to Joy—a sort of emotional froth arising 2
from the play instinct. It is very little use to us. It can sometimes
be used, of course, to divert humans from something else which
the Enemy would like them to be feeling or doing: but in itself it
has wholly undesirable tendencies; it promotes charity, courage, contentment, and many other evils.

The Joke Proper, which turns on sudden perception of incon- 3
gruity, is a much more promising field. I am not thinking primarily of indecent or bawdy humour, which, though much relied
upon by second-rate tempters, is often disappointing in its results. The truth is that humans are pretty clearly divided on this
matter into two classes. There are some to whom "no passion
is as serious as lust" and for whom an indecent story ceases to
produce lasciviousness precisely in so far as it becomes funny:
there are others in whom laughter and lust are excited at the
same moment and by the same things. The first sort joke about
sex because it gives rise to many incongruities; the second cultivate incongruities because they afford a pretext for talking about

Exposition

sex. If your man is of the first type, bawdy humour will not help you—I shall never forget the hours which I wasted (hours to me of unbearable tedium) with one of my early patients in bars and smoking rooms before I learned this rule. Find out which group the patient belongs to—and see that he does *not* find out.

4   The real use of Jokes or Humour is in quite a different direction, and it is specially promising among the English, who take their "sense of humour" so seriously that a deficiency in this sense is almost the only deficiency at which they feel shame. Humour is for them the all-consoling and (mark this) the all-excusing, grace of life. Hence it is invaluable as a means of destroying shame. If a man simply lets others pay for him, he is "mean"; if he boasts of it in a jocular manner and twits his fellows with having been scored off, he is no longer "mean" but a comical fellow. Mere cowardice is shameful; cowardice boasted of with humorous exaggerations and grotesque gestures can be passed off as funny. Cruelty is shameful—unless the cruel man can represent it as a practical joke. A thousand bawdy, or even blasphemous, jokes do not help towards a man's damnation so much as his discovery that almost anything he wants to do can be done, not only without the disapproval but with the admiration of his fellows, if only it can get itself treated as a Joke. And this temptation can be almost entirely hidden from your patient by that English seriousness about Humour. Any suggestion that there might be too much of it can be represented to him as "Puritanical" or as betraying a "lack of humour."

5   But flippancy is the best of all. In the first place it is very economical. Only a clever human can make a real Joke about virtue, or indeed about anything else; any of them can be trained to talk *as if* virtue were funny. Among flippant people the Joke is always assumed to have been made. No one actually makes it; but every serious subject is discussed in a manner which implies that they have already found a ridiculous side to it. If

454

prolonged, the habit of Flippancy builds up around a man the finest armour plating against the Enemy that I know, and it is quite free from the dangers inherent in the other sources of laughter. It is a thousand miles away from joy; it deadens, instead of sharpening, the intellect; and it excites no affection between those who practise it.

○ Friends, Good Friends— and Such Good Friends

Judith Viorst

Judith Viorst, who was born in Newark, New Jersey, and attended Rutgers University, is a poet, journalist, and author of children's books. She has published several volumes of poetry, among them People and Other Aggravations *(1971), and a collection of her prose pieces* Yes, Married: A Saga of Love and Complaint *(1972). The following is an unusual example of exposition by classification. In analyzing a subject into its categories, one usually has a choice of several principles of division. After deciding on one's principle of division, however, one usually sticks to it. But in the following essay, Viorst seems to have used more than one principle for arriving at her categories of friends. As a reaction to her former practice of classifying her acquaintances as either all-out friends or no friends at all, she sets up in the third paragraph four different criteria for classifying friends: (1) levels of intensity, (2) the functions they serve, (3) the needs they meet, and (4) the levels of intimacy. She arrives at eight numbered "varieties of friendships." It is impossible to detect a single principle of division under which all eight varieties could be listed, but when you look at what Viorst says about each of the varieties of friendships, you see that she is discriminating the various types according to one or other of the four criteria that she outlines in the third paragraph.*

Exposition

1 Women are friends, I once would have said, when they totally love and support and trust each other, and bare to each other the secrets of their souls, and run—no questions asked—to help each other, and tell harsh truths to each other (no, you can't wear that dress unless you lose ten pounds first) when harsh truths must be told.

2 Women are friends, I once would have said, when they share the same affection for Ingmar Bergman, plus train rides, cats, warm rain, charades, Camus, and hate with equal ardor Newark and Brussels sprouts and Lawrence Welk and camping.

3 In other words, I once would have said that a friend is a friend all the way, but now I believe that's a narrow point of view. For the friendships I have and the friendships I see are conducted at many levels of intensity, serve many different functions, meet different needs and range from those as all-the-way as the friendship of the soul sisters mentioned above to that of the most nonchalant and casual playmates.

4 Consider these varieties of friendship:

5 1. Convenience friends. These are the women with whom, if our paths weren't crossing all the time, we'd have no particular reason to be friends: a next-door neighbor, a woman in our car pool, the mother of one of our children's closest friends or maybe some mommy with whom we serve juice and cookies each week at the Glenwood Co-op Nursery.

6 Convenience friends are convenient indeed. They'll lend us their cups and silverware for a party. They'll drive our kids to soccer when we're sick. They'll take us to pick up our car when we need a lift to the garage. They'll even take our cats when we go on vacation. As we will for them.

But we don't, with convenience friends, ever come too close 7
or tell too much; we maintain our public face and emotional distance. "Which means," says Elaine, "that I'll talk about being
overweight but not about being depressed. Which means I'll admit being mad but not blind with rage. Which means I might say
that we're pinched this month but never that I'm worried sick
over money."

But which doesn't mean that there isn't sufficient value to be 8
found in these friendships of mutual aid, in convenience friends.

2. Special-interest friends. These friendships aren't intimate, 9
and they needn't involve kids or silverware or cats. Their value
lies in some interest jointly shared. And so we may have an
office friend or a yoga friend or a tennis friend or a friend from
the Women's Democratic Club.

"I've got one woman friend," says Joyce, "who likes, as I do, 10
to take psychology courses. Which makes it nice for me—and
nice for her. It's fun to go with someone you know and it's fun
to discuss what you've learned, driving back from the classes."
And for the most part, she says, that's all they discuss.

"I'd say that what we're doing is *doing* together, not being 11
together," Suzanne says of her Tuesday-doubles friends. "It's
mainly a tennis relationship, but we play together well. And I
guess we all need to have a couple of playmates."

I agree. 12

My playmate is a shopping friend, a woman of marvelous taste, 13
a woman who knows exactly *where* to buy *what,* and furthermore is a woman who always knows beyond a doubt what one
ought to be buying. I don't have the time to keep up with what's
new in eyeshadow, hemlines and shoes and whether the smock
look is in or finished already. But since (oh, shame!) I care a lot
about eyeshadow, hemlines and shoes, and since I don't *want*
to wear smocks if the smock look is finished, I'm very glad to
have a shopping friend.

Exposition

14   3. Historical friends. We all have a friend who knew us when
. . . maybe way back in Miss Meltzer's second grade, when our
family lived in that three-room flat in Brooklyn, when our dad
was out of work for seven months, when our brother Allie got in
that fight where they had to call the police, when our sister married the endodontist from Yonkers and when, the morning after
we lost our virginity, she was the first, the only, friend we told.

15   The years have gone by and we've gone separate ways and
we've little in common now, but we're still an intimate part of
each other's past. And so whenever we go to Detroit we always
go to visit this friend of our girlhood. Who knows how we looked
before our teeth were straightened. Who knows how we talked
before our voice got unBrooklyned. Who knows what we ate
before we learned about artichokes. And who, by her presence,
puts us in touch with an earlier part of ourself, a part of ourself
it's important never to lose.

16   "What this friend means to me and what I mean to her," says
Grace, "is having a sister without sibling rivalry. We know the
texture of each other's lives. She remembers my grandmother's
cabbage soup. I remember the way her uncle played the piano.
There's simply no other friend who remembers those things."

17   4. Crossroads friends. Like historical friends, our crossroads
friends are important for *what was*—for the friendship we shared
at a crucial, now past, time of life. A time, perhaps, when we
roomed in college together; or worked as eager young singles
in the Big City together; or went together, as my friend Elizabeth
and I did through pregnancy, birth and that scary first year of
new motherhood.

18   Crossroads friends forge powerful links, links strong enough
to endure with not much more contact than once-a-year letters
at Christmas. And out of respect for those crossroads years, for
those dramas and dreams we once shared, we will always be
friends.

5. Cross-generational friends. Historical friends and cross- 19
roads friends seem to maintain a special kind of intimacy—dor-
mant but always ready to be revived—and though we may rarely
meet, whenever we do connect, it's personal and intense. Another kind of intimacy exists in the friendships that form across
generations in what one woman calls her daughter-mother and
her mother-daughter relationships.

Evelyn's friend is her mother's age—"but I share so much 20
more than I ever could with my mother"—a woman she talks to
of music, of books and of life. "What I get from her is the benefit
of her experience. What she gets—and enjoys—from me is a
youthful perspective. It's a pleasure for both of us."

I have in my own life a precious friend, a woman of 65 who 21
has lived very hard, who is wise, who listens well; who has been
where I am and can help me understand it; and who represents
not only an ultimate ideal mother to me but also the person I'd
like to be when I grow up.

In our daughter role we tend to do more than our share of 22
self-revelation; in our mother role we tend to receive what's revealed. It's another kind of pleasure—playing wise mother to a
questing younger person. It's another very lovely kind of friendship.

6. Part-of-a-couple friends. Some of the women we call our 23
friends we never see alone—we see them as part of a couple
at couples' parties. And though we share interests in many things
and respect each other's views, we aren't moved to deepen the
relationship. Whatever the reason, a lack of time or—and this is
more likely—a lack of chemistry, our friendship remains in the
context of a group. But the fact that our feeling on seeing each
other is always, "I'm so glad she's here" and the fact that we
spend half the evening talking together says that this too, in its
own way, counts as a friendship.

(Other part-of-a-couple friends are the friends that came with 24

459

Exposition

the marriage, and some of these are friends we could live without. But sometimes, alas, she married our husband's best friend; and sometimes, alas, she *is* our husband's best friend. And so we find ourself dealing with her, somewhat against our will, in a spirit of what I'll call *reluctant* friendship.)

25   7. Men who are friends. I wanted to write just of women friends, but the women I've talked to won't let me—they say I must mention man-woman friendships too. For these friendships can be just as close and as dear as those that we form with women. Listen to Lucy's description of one such friendship:

26   "We've found we have things to talk about that are different from what he talks about with my husband and different from what I talk about with his wife. So sometimes we call on the phone or meet for lunch. There are similar intellectual interests— we always pass on to each other the books that we love—but there's also something tender and caring too."

27   In a couple of crises, Lucy says, "he offered himself, for talking and for helping. And when someone died in his family he wanted me there. The sexual, flirty part of our friendship is very small, but *some*—just enough to make it fun and different." She thinks—and I agree—that the sexual part, though small is always *some,* is always there when a man and a woman are friends.

28   It's only in the past few years that I've made friends with men, in the sense of a friendship that's *mine,* not just part of two couples. And achieving with them the ease and the trust I've found with women friends has value indeed. Under the dryer at home last week, putting on mascara and rouge, I comfortably sat and talked with a fellow named Peter. Peter, I finally decided, could handle the shock of me minus mascara under the dryer. Because we care for each other. Because we're friends.

29   8. There are medium friends, and pretty good friends, and very good friends indeed, and these friendships are defined by

their level of intimacy. And what we'll reveal at each of these levels of intimacy is calibrated with care. We might tell a medium friend, for example, that yesterday we had a fight with our husband. And we might tell a pretty good friend that this fight with our husband made us so mad that we slept on the couch. And we might tell a very good friend that the reason we got so mad in that fight that we slept on the couch had something to do with that girl who works in his office. But it's only to our very best friends that we're willing to tell all, to tell what's going on with that girl in his office.

The best of friends, I still believe, totally love and support and trust each other, and bare to each other the secrets of their souls, and run—no questions asked—to help each other, and tell harsh truths to each other when they must be told. 30

But we needn't agree about everything (only 12-year-old girl friends agree about *everything*) to tolerate each other's point of view. To accept without judgment. To give and to take without ever keeping score. And to *be* there, as I am for them and as they are for me, to comfort our sorrows, to celebrate our joys. 31

○ **How to Mark a Book**

Mortimer J. Adler

Mortimer J. Adler (b. 1902) is now the Chairman of the Board of Editors of the Encyclopaedia Britannica Corporation, but he first came to national prominence in the 1930s when as a young professor of philosophy, he helped launch the Great Books Program in the Midwest. One of the fruits of that program was the 54-volume set of the Great Books of the Western World, *for which Adler served as the general editor. The following article appeared in the* Saturday Review of Literature *in 1940, the same year in which his best-selling and influential book*

Exposition

How To Read a Book *was published. In the first paragraph of the article, he announces the main intent of his
essay: to persuade his readers to write in the pages of
their books. He then devotes paragraphs 2–14 to the task
of persuading his readers that writing in their books is a
good thing. Next, in paragraphs 15–23, he describes
the various ways of "marking a book intelligently and
fruitfully," and in the remaining paragraphs (24–27), he
answers three possible objections to the process. One
significant way in which Adler's exposition of a process
differs from most expositions of a process is that it is not
arranged chronologically—first you do this, then you do
this, etc. In one sense, there is no reason why his seven
(really nine) devices for marking a book should be discussed in the order that they are in the article. But in another sense, the order is not wholly arbitrary either. If you
look closely, you will see that he has arranged his "devices" in an order of increasing complexity or emphasis. Test
out Adler's advice by using several of his "devices" to mark
his essay. Does writing in the text help you to get more out
of this essay and other essays in this book?*

1   You know you have to read "between the lines" to get the most
out of anything. I want to persuade you to do something equally
important in the course of your reading. I want to persuade you
to "write between the lines." Unless you do, you are not likely to
do the most efficient kind of reading.

2   I contend, quite bluntly, that marking up a book is not an act
of mutilation but of love.

3   You shouldn't mark up a book which isn't yours. Librarians (or
your friends) who lend you books expect you to keep them clean,
and you should. If you decide that I am right about the usefulness of marking books, you will have to buy them. Most of the

world's great books are available today, in reprint editions, at less than a dollar.

There are two ways in which one can own a book. The first is the property right you establish by paying for it, just as you pay for clothes and furniture. But this act of purchase is only the prelude to possession. Full ownership comes only when you have made it a part of yourself, and the best way to make yourself a part of it is by writing in it. An illustration may make the point clear. You buy a beefsteak and transfer it from the butcher's icebox to your own. But you do not own the beefsteak in the most important sense until you consume it and get it into your bloodstream to do you any good.

Confusion about what it means to own a book leads people to a false reverence for paper, binding, and type—a respect for the physical thing—the craft of the printer rather than the genius of the author. They forget that it is possible for a man to acquire the idea, to possess the beauty, which a great book contains, without staking his claim by pasting his bookplate inside the cover. Having a fine library doesn't prove that its owner has a mind enriched by books; it proves nothing more than that he, his father, or his wife, was rich enough to buy them.

There are three kinds of book owners. The first has all the standard sets and best-sellers—unread, untouched. (This deluded individual owns woodpulp and ink, not books.) The second has a great many books—a few of them read through, most of them dipped into, but all of them as clean and shiny as the day they were bought. This person would probably like to make books his own, but is restrained by a false respect for their physical appearance.) The third has a few books or many—every one of them dog-eared and dilapidated, shaken and loosened by continual use, marked and scribbled in from front to back. (This man owns books.)

Exposition

7   Is it false respect, you may ask, to preserve intact and un-blemished a beautifully printed book, an elegantly bound edition? Of course not. I'd no more scribble all over the first edition of *Paradise Lost* than I'd give my baby a set of crayons and an original Rembrandt. I wouldn't mark up a painting or a statue. Its soul, so to speak, is inseparable from its body. And the beauty of a rare edition or of a richly manufactured volume is like that of a painting or a statue.

8   But the soul of a book *can* be separated from its body. A book is more like the score of a piece of music than it is like a painting. No great musician confuses a symphony with the printed sheets of music. Arturo Toscanini reveres Brahms, but Toscani-ni's score of the C-minor Symphony is so thoroughly marked up that no one but the maestro himself can read it. The reason why a great conductor makes notations on his musical scores—marks them up again and again each time he returns to study them— is the reason why you should mark up your books. If your respect for magnificent binding or typography gets in the way, buy yourself a cheap edition and pay your respects to the author.

9   Why is marking up a book indispensable to reading it? First, it keeps you awake. (And I don't mean merely conscious; I mean wide awake.) In the second place, reading, if it is active, is thinking, and thinking tends to express itself in words, spoken or written. The marked book is usually the thought-through book. Finally, writing helps you remember the thoughts you had, or the thoughts the author expressed. Let me develop these three points.

10   If reading is to accomplish anything more than passing time, it must be active. You can't let your eyes glide across the lines of a book and come up with an understanding of what you have read. Now an ordinary piece of light fiction, like say, *Gone with the Wind,* doesn't require the most active kind of reading. The

books you read for pleasure can be read in a state of relaxation, and nothing is lost. But a great book, rich in ideas and beauty, a book that raises and tries to answer great fundamental questions, demands the most active reading of which you are capable. You don't absorb the ideas of John Dewey the way you absorb the crooning of Mr. Vallee. You have to reach for them. That you cannot do while you're asleep.

If, when you've finished reading a book, the pages are filled 11 with your notes, you know that you read actively. The most famous *active* reader of great books I know is President Hutchins, of the University of Chicago. He also has the hardest schedule of business activities of any man I know. He invariably reads with a pencil, and sometimes, when he picks up a book and pencil in the evening, he finds himself, instead of making intelligent notes, drawing what he calls "caviar factories" on the margins. When that happens, he puts the book down. He knows he's too tired to read, and he's just wasting time.

But, you may ask, why is writing necessary? Well, the physical 12 act of writing, with your own hand, brings words and sentences more sharply before your mind and preserves them better in your memory. To set down your reaction to important words and sentences you have read, and the questions they have raised in your mind, is to preserve those reactions and sharpen those questions.

Even if you wrote on a scratch pad, and threw the paper away 13 when you had finished writing, your grasp of the book would be surer. But you don't have to throw the paper away. The margins (top and bottom, as well as side), the end-papers, the very space between the lines, are all available. They aren't sacred. And, best of all, your marks and notes become an integral part of the book and stay there forever. You can pick up the book the following week or year, and there are all your points of agreement,

Exposition

disagreement, doubt, and inquiry. It's like resuming an interrupted conversation with the advantage of being able to pick up where you left off.

14   And that is exactly what reading a book should be: a conversation between you and the author. Presumably he knows more about the subject than you do; naturally, you'll have the proper humility as you approach him. But don't let anybody tell you that a reader is supposed to be solely on the receiving end. Understanding is a two-way operation; learning doesn't consist in being an empty receptacle. The learner has to question himself and question the teacher. He even has to argue with the teacher, once he understands what the teacher is saying. And marking a book is literally an expression of your differences, or agreements of opinion, with the author.

15   There are all kinds of devices for marking a book intelligently and fruitfully. Here's the way I do it:

16   1. Underlining: Of major points, of important or forceful statements.

17   2. Vertical lines at the margin: To emphasize a statement already underlined.

18   3. Star, asterisk, or other doo-dad at the margin: To be used sparingly, to emphasize the ten or twenty most important statements in the book. (You may want to fold the bottom corner of each page on which you use such marks. It won't hurt the sturdy paper on which most modern books are printed, and you will be able to take the book off the shelf at any time and, by opening it at the folded-corner page, refresh your recollection of the book.)

19   4. Numbers in the margin: To indicate the sequence of points the author makes in developing a single argument.

20   5. Numbers of other pages in the margin: To indicate where else in the book the author made points relevant to the

point marked; to tie up the ideas in a book, which, though they may be separated by many pages, belong together.

6. Circling of key words or phrases.   21

7. Writing in the margin, or at the top or bottom of the page, 22 for the sake of: Recording questions (and perhaps answers) which a passage raised in your mind; reducing a complicated discussion to a simple statement; recording the sequence of major points right through the book. I use the end-papers at the back of the book to make a personal index of the author's points in the order of their appearance.

The front end-papers are, to me, the most important. Some 23 people reserve them for a fancy bookplate. I reserve them for fancy thinking. After I have finished reading the book and making my personal index on the back end-papers, I turn to the front and try to outline the book, not page by page, or point by point (I've already done that at the back), but as an integrated structure, with a basic unity and an order of parts. This outline is, to me, the measure of my understanding of the work.

If you're a die-hard and anti-book-marker, you may object that 24 the margins, the space between the lines, and the end-papers don't give you room enough. All right. How about using a scratch pad slightly smaller than the page-size of the book—so that the edges of the sheets won't protrude? Make your index, outlines, and even your notes on the pad, and then insert these sheets permanently inside the front and back covers of the book.

Or, you may say that this business of marking books is going 25 to slow up your reading. It probably will. That's one of the reasons for doing it. Most of us have been taken in by the notion that speed of reading is a measure of our intelligence. There is no such thing as the right speed for intelligent reading. Some things should be read quickly and effortlessly, and some should be read slowly and even laboriously. The sign of intelligence in reading is the ability to read different things differently according to their worth. In the case of good books, the point is not to see how many of them you can get through, but rather how many can get through you—how many you can make your own. A few friends are better than a thousand acquaintances. If this be your aim, as it should be, you will not be impatient if it takes more time and effort to read a great book than it does a newspaper.

26   You may have one final objection to marking books. You can't lend them to your friends because nobody else can read them without being distracted by your notes. Furthermore, you won't want to lend them because a marked copy is a kind of intellectual diary, and lending it is almost like giving your mind away.

27   If your friend wishes to read your *Plutarch's Lives,* "Shakespeare," or *The Federalist Papers,* tell him gently but firmly, to buy a copy. You will lend him your car or your coat—but your books are as much a part of you as your head or your heart.

○ The Spider and the Wasp

Alexander Petrunkevitch

Alexander Petrunkevitch (1875–1964) was born in Russia but came to the United States as a young man. He eventually became a world-renowned zoologist and taught at universities like Harvard, Indiana, and Yale. His specialty was spiders. The essay from which the following excerpt was taken first appeared in the magazine Scientific American *over thirty years ago and has become one of the half dozen or so most frequently reprinted modern essays. What has fascinated countless readers is the microscopic particularity and the breathtaking drama of the author's description of an organic process. In the paragraphs reprinted here, Pe-*

○ Petrunkevitch/The Spider and the Wasp

trunkevitch first presents a meticulous description of the tarantula or spider (the two words are used interchangeably in the essay) and of its three senses of touch. Next, he gives a brief description of the Pepsis wasp, and then turns the spotlight on the drama of the wasp's stalking and paralyzing the spider. Like most expositions of a process, this one observes a chronological order—once the actors are put on stage. The writer can learn two valuable lessons from this expertly written piece of exposition: the importance of specific, precise, sensory diction in conjuring up a picture of the thing or the action for the reader; the importance of knowing how to use narration to serve the primary purpose of exposition. Although we seem to be getting an account of a particular conflict between a particular spider and wasp at a particular time, we are left with the dominant impression that this one example is representative of an age-old process.

Most tarantulas live in the Tropics, but several species occur in the temperate zone and a few are common in the southern U.S. Some varieties are large and have powerful fangs with which they can inflict a deep wound. These formidable looking spiders do not, however, attack man; you can hold one in your hand, if you are gentle, without being bitten. Their bite is dangerous only to insects and small mammals such as mice; for a man it is no worse than a hornet's sting.

Tarantulas customarily live in deep cylindrical burrows, from which they emerge at dusk and into which they retire at dawn. Mature males wander about after dark in search of females and occasionally stray into houses. After mating, the male dies in a few weeks, but a female lives much longer and can mate sev-

Exposition

eral years in succession. In a Paris museum is a tropical specimen which is said to have been living in captivity for 25 years.

3   A fertilized female tarantula lays from 200 to 400 eggs at a time; thus it is possible for a single tarantula to produce several thousand young. She takes no care of them beyond weaving a cocoon of silk to enclose the eggs. After they hatch, the young walk away, find convenient places in which to dig their burrows and spend the rest of their lives in solitude. Tarantulas feed mostly on insects and millepedes. Once their appetite is appeased, they digest the food for several days before eating again. Their sight is poor, being limited to sensing a change in the intensity of light and to the perception of moving objects. They apparently have little or no sense of hearing, for a hungry tarantula will pay no attention to a loudly chirping cricket placed in its cage unless the insect happens to touch one of its legs.

4   But all spiders, and especially hairy ones, have an extremely delicate sense of touch. Laboratory experiments prove that tarantulas can distinguish three types of touch: pressure against the body wall, stroking of the body hair and riffling of certain very fine hairs on the legs called trichobothria. Pressure against the body, by a finger or the end of a pencil, causes the tarantula to move off slowly for a short distance. The touch excites no defensive response unless the approach is from above where the spider can see the motion, in which case it rises on its hind legs, lifts its front legs, opens its fangs and holds this threatening posture as long as the object continues to move. When the motion stops, the spider drops back to the ground, remains quiet for a few seconds and then moves slowly away.

5   The entire body of a tarantula, especially its legs, is thickly clothed with hair. Some of it is short and woolly, some long and stiff. Touching this body hair produces one of two distinct reactions. When the spider is hungry, it responds with an immediate and swift attack. At the touch of a cricket's antennae the taran-

tula seizes the insect so swiftly that a motion picture taken at the rate of 64 frames per second shows only the result and not the process of capture. But when the spider is not hungry, the stimulation of its hairs merely causes it to shake the touched limb. An insect can walk under its hairy belly unharmed.

The trichobothria, very fine hairs growing from disklike membranes on the legs, were once thought to be the spider's hearing organs, but we now know that they have nothing to do with sound. They are sensitive only to air movement. A light breeze makes them vibrate slowly without disturbing the common hair. When one blows gently on the trichobothria, the tarantula reacts with a quick jerk of its four front legs. If the front and hind legs are stimulated at the same time, the spider makes a sudden jump. This reaction is quite independent of the state of its appetite.

These three tactile responses—to pressure on the body wall, to moving of the common hair and to flexing of the trichobothria—are so different from one another that there is no possibility of confusing them. They serve the tarantula adequately for most of its needs and enable it to avoid most annoyances and dangers. But they fail the spider completely when it meets its deadly enemy, the digger wasp Pepsis.

These solitary wasps are beautiful and formidable creatures. Most species are either a deep shiny blue all over, or deep blue with rusty wings. The largest have a wing span of about four inches. They live on nectar. When excited, they give off a pungent odor—a warning that they are ready to attack. The sting is much worse than that of a bee or common wasp, and the pain and swelling last longer. In the adult stage the wasp lives only a few months. The female produces but a few eggs, one at a time at intervals of two or three days. For each egg the mother must provide one adult tarantula, alive but paralyzed. The tarantula must be of the correct species to nourish the larva. The

6

7

8

Exposition

mother wasp attaches the egg to the paralyzed spider's abdomen. Upon hatching from the egg, the larva is many hundreds of times smaller than its living but helpless victim. It eats no other food and drinks no water. By the time it has finished its single gargantuan meal and become ready for wasphood, nothing remains of the tarantula but its indigestible chitinous skeleton.

9   The mother wasp goes tarantula-hunting when the egg in her ovary is almost ready to be laid. Flying low over the ground late on a sunny afternoon, the wasp looks for its victim or for the mouth of a tarantula burrow, a round hole edged by a bit of silk. The sex of the spider makes no difference, but the mother is highly discriminating as to species. Each species of Pepsis requires a certain species of tarantula, and the wasp will not attack the wrong species. In a cage with a tarantula which is not its normal prey the wasp avoids the spider, and is usually killed by it in the night.

10   Yet when a wasp finds the correct species, it is the other way about. To identify the species the wasp apparently must explore the spider with her antennae. The tarantula shows an amazing tolerance to this exploration. The wasp crawls under it and walks over it without evoking any hostile response. The molestation is so great and so persistent that the tarantula often rises on all eight legs, as if it were on stilts. It may stand this way for several minutes. Meanwhile the wasp, having satisfied itself that the victim is of the right species, moves off a few inches to dig the spider's grave. Working vigorously with legs and jaws, it excavates a hole 8 to 10 inches deep with a diameter slightly larger than the spider's girth. Now and again the wasp pops out of the hole to make sure that the spider is still there.

11   When the grave is finished, the wasp returns to the tarantula to complete her ghastly enterprise. First she feels it all over once more with her antennae. Then her behavior becomes more ag-

gressive. She bends her abdomen, protruding her sting, and searches for the soft membrane at the point where the spider's leg joins its body—the only spot where she can penetrate the horny skeleton. From time to time, as the exasperated spider slowly shifts ground, the wasp turns on her back and slides along with the aid of her wings, trying to get under the tarantula for a shot at the vital spot. During all this maneuvering, which can last for several minutes, the tarantula makes no move to save itself. Finally the wasp corners it against some obstruction and grasps one of its legs in her powerful jaws. Now at last the harassed spider tries a desperate but vain defense. The two contestants roll over and over on the ground. It is a terrifying sight and the outcome is always the same. The wasp finally manages to thrust her sting into the soft spot and holds it there for a few seconds while she pumps in the poison. Almost immediately the tarantula falls paralyzed on its back. Its legs stop twitching; its heart stops beating. Yet it is not dead, as is shown by the fact that if taken from the wasp it can be restored to some sensitivity by being kept in a moist chamber for several months.

After paralyzing the tarantula, the wasp cleans herself by 12 dragging her body along the ground and rubbing her feet, sucks the drop of blood oozing from the wound in the spider's abdomen, then grabs a leg of the flabby, helpless animal in her jaws and drags it down to the bottom of the grave. She stays there for many minutes, sometimes for several hours, and what she does all that time in the dark we do not know. Eventually she lays her egg and attaches it to the side of the spider's abdomen with a sticky secretion. Then she emerges, fills the grave with soil carried bit by bit in her jaws, and finally tramples the ground all around to hide any trace of the grave from prowlers. Then she flies away, leaving her descendant safely started in life.

In all this the behavior of the wasp evidently is qualitatively 13 different from that of the spider. The wasp acts like an intelligent

Exposition

animal. This is not to say that instinct plays no part or that she reasons as man does. But her actions are to the point; they are not automatic and can be modified to fit the situation. We do not know for certain how she identifies the tarantula—probably it is by some olfactory of chemo-tactile sense—but she does it purposefully and does not blindly tackle a wrong species.

14   On the other hand, the tarantula's behavior shows only confusion. Evidently the wasp's pawing gives it no pleasure, for it tries to move away. That the wasp is not simulating sexual stimulation is certain, because male and female tarantulas react in the same way to its advances. That the spider is not anesthetized by some odorless secretion is easily shown by blowing lightly at the tarantula and making it jump suddenly. What, then, makes the tarantula behave as stupidly as it does?

15   No clear, simple answer is available. Possibly the stimulation by the wasp's antennae is masked by a heavier pressure on the spider's body, so that it reacts as when prodded by a pencil. But the explanation may be much more complex. Initiative in attack is not in the nature of tarantulas; most species fight only when cornered so that escape is impossible. Their inherited patterns of behavior apparently prompt them to avoid problems rather than attack them. For example, spiders always weave their webs in three dimensions, and when a spider finds that there is insufficient space to attach certain threads in the third dimension, it leaves the place and seeks another, instead of finishing the web in a single plane. This urge to escape seems to arise under all circumstances, in all phases of life and to take the place of reasoning. For a spider to change the pattern of its web is as impossible as for an inexperienced man to build a bridge across a chasm obstructing his way.

16   In a way the instinctive urge to escape is not only easier but more efficient than reasoning. The tarantula does exactly what

is most efficient in all cases except in an encounter with a ruth-less and determined attacker dependent for the existence of her own species on killing as many tarantulas as she can lay eggs. Perhaps in this case the spider follows its usual pattern of trying to escape, instead of seizing and killing the wasp, because it is not aware of its danger. In any case, the survival of the tarantula species as a whole is protected by the fact that the spider is much more fertile than the wasp.

○ Better Read Than Dead: A Revised Opinion

Fran Lebowitz

Fran Lebowitz, born in Morristown, New Jersey, is a writer of humorous essays, operating in the mildly satir-ical tradition of Dorothy Parker, Jean Kerr, and Erma Bombeck. Metropolitan Life *(1978), the first collection of her essays, made her an instant celebrity, much in de-mand on talk shows. Although the following example of a comparison-and-contrast essay has a lighthearted tone about it, its underlying theme is a serious one: the gen-eralizations we make about people or nations are often a curious blend of facts and myths. In comparing the eco-nomic systems of Communist Russia and of the United States, Lebowitz finds only differences—exaggerated differences—and when we look at her annotations, we see that the differences she considers concern rather trivial aspects of life—e.g., Americans have peanut butter, but the Russians don't. Nevertheless, Lebowitz's essay shows how a writer might seriously use the differences (and/or the similarities) between two things in order to give us a clear picture of the main thing being explained. Here she accentuates the differences by the typographical device of displaying the contrasts in side-by-side columns.*

Exposition

1   **M**y attendance at grammar school coincided rather unappeal-
ingly with the height of the cold war. This resulted in my spending a portion of each day sitting cross-legged, head in lap, either alone under my desk or, more sociably, against the wall in
the corridor. When not so occupied, I could be found sitting in
class reading avidly about the horrors of life under Communism.
I was not a slow child, but I believed passionately that Communists were a race of horned men who divided their time equally
between the burning of Nancy Drew books and the devising of
a plan of nuclear attack that would land the largest and most
lethal bomb squarely upon the third-grade class of Thomas Jefferson School in Morristown, New Jersey. This was a belief widely
held among my classmates, and it was reinforced daily by
teachers and those parents who were of the Republican persuasion.

2   Among the many devices used to keep this belief alive was a
detailed chart that appeared yearly in our social studies book.
This chart pointed out the severe economic hardships of Communist life. The reading aloud of the chart was accompanied by
a running commentary from the teacher and went something
like this:

3   "This chart shows how long a man must work in Russia in
order to purchase the following goods. We then compare this to
the length of time it takes a man in the United States to earn
enough money to purchase the same goods."

RUSSIA	U.S.A.

A PAIR OF SHOES—38 HOURS

"And they only have brown ox-fords in Russia, so that nobody ever gets to wear shoes without straps even for dress-up. Also they have never even heard of Capezios, and if they did, no one would be allowed to wear them because they all have to work on farms whenever they are not busy making atom bombs."

A PAIR OF SHOES—2 HOURS

"And we have all kinds of shoes, even Pappagallos."

A LOAF OF BREAD—2½ HOURS

"They do not have peanut butter in Russia, or Marshmallow Fluff, and their bread has a lot of crust on it, which they force all the children to eat."

A LOAF OF BREAD—5 MINUTES

"We have cinnamon raisin bread and english muffins and we can put whatever we like on it be-cause we have democracy."

A POUND OF NAILS—6 HOURS

"And they need a lot of nails in Russia because everyone has to work very hard all the time building things—even mothers."

A POUND OF NAILS—8 MINUTES

"Even though we don't need that many nails because we have Scotch tape and staples.

A STATION WAGON—9 YEARS

"If they were even permitted to own them, which they are not, so everyone has to walk every-where even though they are very tired from building so many things like atom bombs."

A STATION WAGON—4 MONTHS

"And we have so many varieties to choose from—some painted to look like wood on the sides and some that are two different colors. We also have lots of other cars, such as convertible sports cars."

Exposition

RUSSIA	U.S.A.

A PAIR OF OVERALLS—11 HOURS

"And everyone has to wear overalls all the time and they're all the same color so nobody gets to wear straight skirts even if they're in high school."

A PAIR OF OVERALLS—1 HOUR

"But since we can choose what we want to wear in a democracy, mostly farmers wear overalls and they like to wear them."

A DOZEN EGGS—7 HOURS

"But they hardly ever get to eat them because eggs are a luxury in Russia and there are no luxuries under Communism."

A DOZEN EGGS—9 MINUTES

"We have lots of eggs here and that is why we can have eggnog, egg salad, even Easter eggs, except for the Jewish children in the class, who I'm sure have something just as nice on their holiday which is called Hanukkah."

A TELEVISION SET—2 YEARS

"But they don't have them. That's right, they do not have TV in Russia because they know that if the people in Russia were allowed to watch *Leave It to Beaver* they would all want to move to the United States, and probably most of them would want to come to Morristown."

A TELEVISION SET—2 WEEKS

"And many people have two television sets and some people like Dougie Bershey have color TV so that he can tell everyone in class what color everything was on *Walt Disney*."

4   All of this was duly noted by both myself and my classmates, and the vast majority of us were rather right-wing all through grammar school. Upon reaching adolescence, however, a num-

ber of us rebelled, and I must admit to distinctly leftist leanings during my teen years. Little by little, though, I have been coming around to my former way of thinking, and while I am not all that enamored of our local form of government, I have reacquired a marked distaste for Theirs.

My political position is based largely on my aversion to large groups, and if there's one thing I know about Communism it's that large groups are definitely in the picture. I do not work well with others, and I do not wish to learn to do so. I do not even dance well with others if there are too many of them, and I have no doubt but that Communist discothèques are hideously over-crowded. "From each according to his ability, to each according to his needs" is not a decision I care to leave to politicians, for I do not believe that an ability to remark humorously on the passing scene would carry much weight with one's comrades or that one could convince them of the need for a really reliable answering service. The common good is not my cup of tea—it is the uncommon good in which I am interested, and I do not deceive myself that such statements are much admired by the members of farming collectives. Communists all seem to wear small caps, a look I consider better suited to tubes of toothpaste than to people. We number, of course, among us our own cap wearers, but I assure you they are easily avoided. It is my un-derstanding that Communism requires of its adherents that they arise early and participate in a strenuous round of calisthenics. To someone who wishes that cigarettes came already lit, the thought of such exertion at any hour when decent people are just nodding off is thoroughly abhorrent. I have been further ad-vised that in the Communist world an aptitude for speaking or writing in an amusing fashion doesn't count for spit. I therefore have every intention of doing my best to keep the Iron Curtain from being drawn across Fifty-seventh Street. It is to this end that I have prepared a little chart of my own for the edification of my fellow New Yorkers.

Exposition

The following chart compares the amount of time it takes a Communist to earn enough to purchase the following goods against the amount of time it takes a New Yorker to do the same.

COMMUNIST	NEW YORKER
A CO-OP APARTMENT IN THE EAST SEVENTIES ON THE PARK—4,000 YEARS. And even then you have to share it with the rest of the collective. There is not a co-op in the city with that many bathrooms.	A CO-OP APARTMENT IN THE EAST SEVENTIES ON THE PARK—No time at all if you were lucky in the parent department. If you have not been so blessed it could take as long as twenty years, but at least you'd have your own bathroom.
A SUBSCRIPTION TO *The New Yorker*—3 WEEKS. And even then it is doubtful that you'd understand the cartoons.	A SUBSCRIPTION TO *The New Yorker*—1 HOUR, maybe less, because in a democracy one frequently receives such things as gifts.
A FIRST-CLASS AIRPLANE TICKET TO PARIS—6 MONTHS—Paris, Comrade? Not so fast.	A FIRST-CLASS AIRPLANE TICKET TO PARIS—Varies widely, but any smart girl can acquire such a ticket with ease if she plays her cards right.
A FERNANDO SANCHEZ NIGHTGOWN—3 MONTHS. With the cap? Very attractive.	A FERNANDO SANCHEZ NIGHTGOWN—1 WEEK, less if you know someone in the business, and need I point out that your chances of being so connected are far greater in a democracy such as ours than they are in Peking.
DINNER AT A FINE RESTAURANT—2 YEARS to earn the money; 27 years for the collective to decide on a restaurant.	DINNER AT A FINE RESTAURANT—No problem if one has chosen one's friends wisely.

○ Grant and Lee: A Study in Contrasts

Bruce Catton

Born in Michigan, Bruce Catton (1899–1978) worked for a number of years as a newspaper reporter in Cleveland, Boston, and Washington, and after a stint as Director of Information for the U.S. Department of Commerce during World War II, he devoted himself full-time to writing Civil War history. Among his many books on the Civil War are Mr. Lincoln's Army *(1951),* Glory Road *(1952), and* A Stillness at Appomattox *(1953), which won a Pulitzer Prize. The following piece is a classic example of an exposition that is developed primarily by comparison and contrast. He emphatically announces the theme of similarities and differences in the one-sentence third paragraph: "They were two strong men, these oddly different generals, and they represented the strengths of two conflicting currents that, through them, had come into final collision." We see exhibited here one of the common patterns of organization of a comparison-and-contrast essay. Paragraphs 4, 5, and 6 are devoted to a characterization of General Lee; paragraphs 7, 8, and 9 are devoted to a characterization of General Grant. Then in paragraphs 10, 11, and 12, Catton points out explicitly the differences between the two men that are implicit in the paragraphs describing the two men. In the final four paragraphs of the essay, Catton delineates the similarities between the two men.*

When Ulysses S. Grant and Robert E. Lee met in the parlor of a modest house at Appomattox Court House, Virginia, on April 9, 1865, to work out the terms for the surrender of Lee's Army of Northern Virginia, a great chapter in American life came to a close, and a great new chapter began.

1

Exposition

2   These men were bringing the Civil War to its virtual finish. To be sure, other armies had yet to surrender, and for a few days the fugitive Confederate government would struggle desperately and vainly, trying to find some way to go on living now that its chief support was gone. But in effect it was all over when Grant and Lee signed the papers. And the little room where they wrote out the terms was the scene of one of the poignant, dramatic contrasts in American History.

3   They were two strong men these oddly different generals, and they represented the strengths of two conflicting currents that, through them, had come into final collision.

4   Back of Robert E. Lee was the notion that the old aristocratic concept might somehow survive and be dominant in American life.

5   Lee was tidewater Virginia, and in his background were family, culture, and tradition . . . the age of chivalry transplanted to a New World which was making its own legends and its own myths. He embodied a way of life that had come down through the age of knighthood and the English country squire. America was a land that was beginning all over again, dedicated to nothing much more complicated than the rather hazy belief that all men had equal rights and should have an equal chance in the world. In such a land Lee stood for the feeling that it was somehow of advantage to human society to have a pronounced inequality in the social structure. There should be a leisure class, backed by ownership of land; in turn, society itself should be keyed to the land as the chief source of wealth and influence. It would bring forth (according to this ideal) a class of men with a strong sense of obligation to the community; men who lived not to gain advantage for themselves, but to meet the solemn obligations which had been laid on them by the very fact that they were privileged. From them the country would get its leadership; to them it could look for the higher values—of thought, of

conduct, or personal deportment—to give it strength and virtue.

Lee embodied the noblest elements of this aristocratic ideal. 6
Through him, the landed nobility justified itself. For four years, the Southern states had fought a desperate war to uphold the ideals for which Lee stood. In the end, it almost seemed as if the Confederacy fought for Lee; as if he himself was the Confederacy . . . the best thing that the way of life for which the Confederacy stood could ever have to offer. He had passed into legend before Appomattox. Thousands of tired, underfed, poorly clothed Confederate soldiers, long since past the simple enthusiasm of the early days of the struggle, somehow considered Lee the symbol of everything for which they had been willing to die. But they could not quite put this feeling into words. If the Lost Cause, sanctified by so much heroism and so many deaths, had a living justification, its justification was General Lee.

Grant, the son of a tanner on the Western frontier, was every- 7
thing Lee was not. He had come up the hard way and embodied nothing in particular except the eternal toughness and sinewy fiber of the men who grew up beyond the mountains. He was one of a body of men who owed reverence and obeisance to no one, who were self-reliant to a fault, who cared hardly anything for the past but who had a sharp eye for the future.

These frontier men were the precise opposites of the tidewa- 8
ter aristocrats. Back of them, in the great surge that had taken people over the Alleghenies and into the opening Western country, there was a deep, implicit dissatisfaction with a past that had settled into grooves. They stood for democracy, not from any reasoned conclusion about the proper ordering of human society, but simply because they had grown up in the middle of democracy and knew how it worked. Their society might have privileges, but they would be privileges each man had won for himself. Forms and patterns meant nothing. No man was

Exposition

born to anything, except perhaps to a chance to show how far he could rise. Life was competition.

9   Yet along with this feeling had come a deep sense of belonging to a national community. The Westerner who developed a farm, opened a shop, or set up in business as a trader could hope to prosper only as his own community prospered—and his community ran from the Atlantic to the Pacific and from Canada down to Mexico. If the land was settled, with towns and highways and accessible markets, he could better himself. He saw his fate in terms of the nation's own destiny. As its horizons expanded, so did his. He had, in other words, an acute dollars-and-cents stake in the continued growth and development of his country.

10   And that, perhaps, is where the contrast between Grant and Lee becomes most striking. The Virginia aristocrat, inevitably, saw himself in relation to his own region. He lived in a static society which could endure almost anything except change. Instinctively, his first loyalty would go to the locality in which that society existed. He would fight to the limit of endurance to defend it, because in defending it he was defending everything that gave his own life its deepest meaning.

11   The Westerner, on the other hand, would fight with an equal tenacity for the broader concept of society. He fought so because everything he lived by was tied to growth, expansion, and a constantly widening horizon. What he lived by would survive or fall with the nation itself. He could not possibly stand by unmoved in the face of an attempt to destroy the Union. He would combat it with everything he had, because he could only see it as an effort to cut the ground out from under his feet.

12   So Grant and Lee were in complete contrast, representing two diametrically opposed elements in American life. Grant was the modern man emerging; beyond him, ready to come on the stage, was the great age of steel and machinery, of crowded cities and a restless burgeoning vitality. Lee might have ridden

down from the old age of chivalry, lance in hand, silken banner fluttering over his head. Each man was the perfect champion of his cause, drawing both his strengths and his weaknesses from the people he led.

Yet it was not all contrast, after all. Different as they were—in background, in personality, in underlying aspiration—these two great soldiers had much in common. Under everything else, they were marvelous fighters. Furthermore, their fighting qualities were really very much alike.   13

Each man had, to begin with, the great virtue of utter tenacity and fidelity. Grant fought his way down the Mississippi Valley in spite of acute personal discouragement and profound military handicaps. Lee hung on in the trenches at Petersburg after hope itself had died. In each man there was an indomitable quality . . . the born fighter's refusal to give up as long as he can still remain on his feet and lift his two fists.   14

Daring and resourcefulness they had, too: the ability to think faster and move faster than the enemy. These were the qualities which gave Lee the dazzling campaigns of Second Manassas and Chancellorsville and won Vicksburg for Grant.   15

Lastly, and perhaps greatest of all, there was the ability, at the end, to turn quickly from war to peace once the fighting was over. Out of the way these two men behaved at Appomattox came the possibility of a peace of reconciliation. It was a possibility not wholly realized, in the years to come, but which did, in the end, help the two sections to become one nation again . . . after a war whose bitterness might have seemed to make such a reunion wholly impossible. No part of either man's life became him more than the part he played in their brief meeting in the McLean house at Appomattox. Their behavior there put all succeeding generations of Americans in their debt. Two great Americans, Grant and Lee—very different, yet under everything very much alike. Their encounter at Appomattox was one of the great moments of American history.   16

Chapter 13
Argumentation

○ **Capital Punishment**

William F. Buckley, Jr.

William F. Buckley, Jr. (b.1925) was one of ten children born into a wealthy family in New York City. He achieved national attention a year after he graduated from Yale University when he published his attack on the kind of education he had received there, God and Man at Yale *(1951). He alienated liberal intellectuals with his book* Up from Liberalism, *published in 1959, and his defense of the public activities of Senator Joseph McCarthy. During that same period, he became the founder and editor of the conservative weekly magazine* National Review. *In the mid-'60s, he started his TV talk show called* Firing Line, *and in the mid-'70s, he began writing popular novels of espionage, such as* Saving the Queen *(1976) and* Stained Glass *(1978). The following argument in favor of retaining capital punishment is more interesting for the cleverness of Buckley's rhetorical strategies than for the soundness of his arguments. For one thing, he tells us at the beginning of the piece (paragraph 2) that he is presenting not his own arguments but the substance of the arguments that the philosopher Ernest van den Haag presented in testimony before the House Committee of the Judiciary. Realizing, however, that some of the arguments will not*

○ **Buckley/Capital Punishment**

*be palatable to some people, he states that he does not
wholeheartedly endorse the case that van den Haag made
for the retention of capital punishment but shrewdly avoids
specifying his points of disagreement. In other words,
he leaves himself an escape hatch in case any of the
arguments are challenged. For another thing, most of
the essay is devoted to refuting five of the arguments
used by those who espouse the abolition of capital punishment. Apparently, Buckley trusts that the mere refutation of the opposition's case will induce his readers to
favor the retention of capital punishment. Readers may
want to discuss the validity and the effectiveness of the
arguments that Buckley uses to refute the five arguments
presented by the abolitionists.*

There is national suspense over whether capital punishment is   1
about to be abolished, and the assumption is that when it comes
it will come from the Supreme Court. Meanwhile, (a) the presti-
gious State Supreme Court of California has interrupted executions, giving constitutional reasons for doing so; (b) the death
wings are overflowing with convicted prisoners; (c) executions
are a remote memory; and—for the first time in years—(d) the
opinion polls show that there is sentiment for what amounts to
the restoration of capital punishment.

The case for abolition is popularly known. The other case less   2
so, and (without wholeheartedly endorsing it) I give it as it was
given recently to the Committee of the Judiciary of the House of
Representatives by Professor Ernest van den Haag, under whose
thinking cap groweth no moss. Mr. van den Haag, a professor
of social philosophy at New York University, ambushed the most

Argumentation

popular arguments of the abolitionists, taking no prisoners.

3   (1) The business about the poor and the black suffering excessively from capital punishment is no argument against capital punishment. It is an argument against the *administration* of justice, not against the penalty. Any punishment can be unfairly or unjustly applied. Go ahead and reform the processes by which capital punishment is inflicted, if you wish; but don't confuse maladministration with the merits of capital punishment.

4   (2) The argument that the death penalty is "unusual" is circular. Capital punishment continues on the books of a majority of states, the people continue to sanction the concept of capital punishment, and indeed capital sentences are routinely handed down. What has made capital punishment "unusual" is that the courts and, primarily, governors have intervened in the process so as to collaborate in the frustration of the execution of the law. To argue that capital punishment is unusual, when in fact it has been made unusual by extra-legislative authority, is an argument to expedite, not eliminate, executions.

5   (3) Capital punishment is cruel. That is a historical judgment. But the Constitution suggests that what must be proscribed as cruel is (a) a particularly painful way of inflicting death, or (b) a particularly undeserved death; and the death penalty, as such, offends neither of these criteria and cannot therefore be regarded as objectively "cruel."

6   Viewed the other way, the question is whether capital punishment can be regarded as useful, and the question of deterrence arises.

7   (4) Those who believe that the death penalty does not intensify the disinclination to commit certain crimes need to wrestle with statistics that, in fact, it can't be proved that *any* punish-

ment does that to any particular crime. One would rationally suppose that two years in jail would cut the commission of a crime if not exactly by 100 percent more than a penalty of one year in jail, at least that it would further discourage crime to a certain extent. The proof is unavailing. On the other hand, the statistics, although ambiguous, do not show either (a) that capital punishment net discourages; or (b) that capital punishment fails net to discourage. "The absence of proof for the additional deterrent effect of the death penalty must not be confused with the presence of proof for the absence of this effect."

The argument that most capital crimes are crimes of passion committed by irrational persons is no argument against the death penalty, because it does not reveal how many crimes might, but for the death penalty, have been committed by rational persons who are now deterred.   8

And the clincher. (5) Since we do not know for certain whether or not the death penalty adds deterrence, we have in effect the choice of two risks.   9

Risk One: If we execute convicted murderers without thereby deterring prospective murderers beyond the deterrence that could have been achieved by life imprisonment, we may have vainly sacrificed the life of the convicted murderer.   10

Risk Two: If we fail to execute a convicted murderer whose execution might have deterred an indefinite number of prospective murderers, our failure sacrifices an indefinite number of victims of future murderers.   11

"If we had certainty, we would not have risks. We do not have certainty. If we have risks—and we do—better to risk the life of the convicted man than risk the life of an indefinite number of innocent victims who might survive if he were executed."   12

○ # Drafting Daughters

Ellen Goodman

*Ellen Goodman (b. 1941), a graduate of Radcliffe Col-
lege, has for some time been a columnist for the* Boston
Globe. *Her column—of which "Drafting Daughters" is an
example—proved to be so popular that it is now syndi-
cated in over 200 newspapers, and in 1980, her column won her a Pulitzer Prize for Commentary. The subject of the following piece is suggested by its title, and
the issue at stake gradually emerges in the first seven
paragraphs of the essay: should young women be drafted
into the armed forces? In paragraph 8, the author for-
mulates the thesis that she will argue for, but the sharp-
est statement of this thesis is found in the first sentence
of the next-to-last paragraph: "So, if we must have a draft
registration, I would include young women as well as
young men." She realizes, however, that this position
will not be readily accepted by most of her readers, because it flouts the traditional values of our culture. So she
has to sell her idea to her audience. How does she persuade that audience? She resorts to a combination of
ethical, emotional, and rational appeals (see Chapter 7
for a discussion of these three appeals). The ethical and
emotional appeals are exerted primarily in the first seven
paragraphs. Ellen Goodman has already established her
credentials, of course, with most of her faithful readers,
but she reinforces and extends those credentials in these
early paragraphs by speaking of herself as a parent concerned about the welfare of her young daughter and as
a citizen of the world concerned about the insanity and
brutality of war. Although in these early paragraphs she
does not stress the fact that she is a woman, she is well
aware that her credibility is enhanced by the fact that
she is a woman advocating a policy that is not, on the
face of it, advantageous to women. As for the rational
appeal, she spends more time giving "good reasons"
for her position than presenting carefully developed arguments. The many two- and three-sentence paragraphs
in this piece indicate that none of her reasons are developed. We will be persuaded in proportion to our perception of her reasons as being "good reasons." (Recall that*

○ **Goodman/Drafting Daughters**

My daughter is eleven, and as we watch the evening news, she turns to me seriously and says, "I don't like the way the world is doing things." Neither do I.   1

My daughter is eleven years and eight months old, to be precise, and I do not want her to grow up and be drafted. Neither does she.   2

My daughter is almost twelve, and thinks about unkindness and evil, about endangered species and war. I don't want her to grow up and be brutalized by war—as soldier or civilian.   3

As I read those sentences over, they seem too mild. What I want to say is that I am horrified by the very idea that she could be sent to fight for fossil fuel or fossilized ideas. What I want to say is that I can imagine no justification for war other than self-defense, and I am scared stiff about who has the power to decide what is "defense."   4

But now, in the last days before President Carter decides whether we will register young people and whether half of those young people will be female, I wonder about something else. Would I feel differently if my daughter were my son? Would I be more accepting, less anguished, at the notion of a son drafted, a son at war?   5

Would I beat the drums and pin the bars and stars on his uniform with pride? Would I look forward to him being tough-   6

---

ened up, be proud of his heroism, and accept his risk as a simple fact of life?

7   I cannot believe it.

8   So, when I am asked now about registering women for the draft along with men, I have to nod yes reluctantly. I don't want anyone registered, anyone drafted, unless it is a genuine crisis. But if there is a draft, this time it can't just touch our sons, like some civilized plague that leaves daughters alone to produce another generation of warriors.

9   We may have to register women along with men anyway. Women may not have won equal rights yet, but they have "won" equal responsibilities. A male-only draft may be ruled unconstitutional.

10   But at a deeper level, we have to register women along with men because our society requires it. For generations, war has been part of the rage so many men have held against women.

11   War is in the hard-hat yelling at an equal rights rally, "Where were you at Iwo Jima?" War is in the man infuriated at the notion of a woman challenging veterans' preference. War is in the mind of the man who challenges his wife for having had a soft life.

12   War has often split couples and sexes apart, into lives built on separate realities. It has been part of the grudge of self-sacrifice, the painful gap of understanding and experience between men's and women's lives. It is the stuff of which alienation and novels are written.

13   But more awesomely, as a male activity, a rite of passage, a test of manhood, war has been gruesomely acceptable. Old men who were warriors have sent younger men to war as if it were their birthright. The women's role until recently was to wave banners and sing slogans, and be in need of protection from the enemy.

14   We all pretended that war was civilized. War had rules and

battlegrounds. War did not touch the finer and nobler things, like women.

This was, of course, never true. The losers, the enemies, the 15 victims, the widows of war were as brutalized as the soldiers. Under duress and in defense, women always fought.

But, perhaps, stripped of its maleness and mystery, its audi- 16 ence and cheerleaders, war can be finally disillusioned. Without the last trappings of chivalry, it can be seen for what it is: the last deadly resort.

So, if we must have a draft registration, I would include young 17 women as well as young men. I would include them because they can do the job. I would include them because all women must gain the status to stop as well as to start wars. I would include them because it has been too easy to send men alone.

I would include them because I simply cannot believe that I 18 would feel differently if my daughter were my son.

○ **The New Immorality**

Joseph Wood Krutch

Born in Tennessee, Joseph Wood Krutch (1893–1970) became a prominent journalist, a literary critic, and, in the final years of his life, a self-taught naturalist. He is best known, however, for his essays, which were col- lected under such titles as The Modern Temper *(1929) and* The Measure of Man *(1954), and for the two works of natural history that he wrote after he retired to a desert area in Arizona,* The Desert Year *(1952) and* The Best of Two Worlds *(1953). The argument presented in the following essay is a blend of induction and deduction (see Chapter 7 for an explanation of these terms). Krutch starts out inductively by offering two examples, supplied*

Argumentation

by testimony, of the moral attitude displayed by two groups of people toward cheating, and from those two examples, he makes the generalization that personal or private morality seems to be declining at a time when social morality seems to be growing. The proposition, the thesis, that he is mainly interested in arguing is the one he articulates in paragraph 9, where he says that "for the individual himself nothing is more important than this personal, interior sense of right and wrong and his determination to follow that rather than to be guided by what everybody does or merely the criterion of 'social usefulness.'" He then devotes all of paragraph 10 to arguing in support of that contention. You should examine that paragraph for the implicit and explicit premises upon which his deductive argument is based. Once you have detected those latent and overt premises, you can ask yourself whether you too subscribe to those premises. If you were persuaded by Krutch, you probably do subscribe to them.

1 The provost of one of our largest and most honored institutions told me not long ago that a questionnaire was distributed to his undergraduates and that 40 percent refused to acknowledge that they believed cheating on examinations to be reprehensible.

2 Recently a reporter for a New York newspaper stopped six people on the street and asked them if they would consent to take part in a rigged television quiz for money. He reported that five of the six said yes. Yet most of these five, like most of the college cheaters, would probably profess a strong social consciousness. They may cheat, but they vote for foreign aid and for enlightened social measures.

3 These two examples exhibit a paradox of our age. It is often said, and my observation leads me to believe it true, that our

Adaptation of "A Commencement Address—1960" from *A Krutch Omnibus* by Joseph Wood Krutch. Copyright © 1960 by Joseph Wood Krutch. Adapted by permission of William Morrow & Company.

seemingly great growth in social morality has oddly enough taken place in a world where private morality—a sense of the supreme importance of purely personal honor, honesty, and integrity—seems to be declining. Beneficent and benevolent social institutions are administered by men who all too frequently turn out to be accepting "gifts." The world of popular entertainment is rocked by scandals. College students put on their honor, cheat on examinations. Candidates for the Ph.D. hire ghost writers to prepare their theses.

But, one may object, haven't all these things always been true? Is there really any evidence that personal dishonesty is more prevalent than it always was? 4

I have no way of making a historical measurement. Perhaps these things are not actually more prevalent. What I do know is that there is an increasing tendency to accept and take for granted such personal dishonesty. The bureaucrat and disk jockey say, "Well, yes, I took presents, but I assure you that I made just decisions anyway." The college student caught cheating does not even blush. He shrugs his shoulders and comments: "Everybody does it, and besides, I can't see that it really hurts anybody." 5

Jonathan Swift once said: "I have never been surprised to find men wicked, but I have often been surprised to find them not ashamed." It is my conviction that though men may be no more wicked than they always have been, they seem less likely to be ashamed. If anybody does it, it must be right. Honest, moral, decent mean only what is usual. This is not really a wicked world, because morality means mores or manners and usual conduct is the only standard. 6

The second part of the defense, "it really doesn't hurt anybody," is equally revealing. "It doesn't hurt anybody" means it doesn't do that abstraction called society any harm. The harm it did the bribe-taker and the cheater isn't important; it is purely 7

Argumentation

personal. And personal as opposed to social decency doesn't count for much. Sometimes I am inclined to blame sociology for part of this paradox. Sociology has tended to lay exclusive stress upon social morality, and tended too often to define good and evil as merely the "socially useful" or its reverse.

8   What social morality and social conscience leave out is the narrower but very significant concept of honor—as opposed to what is sometimes called merely "socially desirable conduct." The man of honor is not content to ask merely whether this or that will hurt society, or whether it is what most people would permit themselves to do. He asks, and he asks first of all, would it hurt him and his self-respect? Would it dishonor him personally?

9   It was a favorite and no doubt sound argument among early twentieth-century reformers that "playing the game" as the gentleman was supposed to play it was not enough to make a decent society. They were right: it is not enough. But the time has come to add that it is indeed inevitable that the so-called social conscience unsupported by the concept of personal honor will create a corrupt society. But suppose that it doesn't? Suppose that no one except the individual suffers from the fact that he sees nothing wrong in doing what everybody else does? Even so, I still insist that for the individual himself nothing is more important than this personal, interior sense of right and wrong and his determination to follow that rather than to be guided by what everybody does or merely the criterion of "social usefulness." It is impossible for me to imagine a good society composed of men without honor.

10   We hear it said frequently that what present-day men most desire is security. If that is so, then they have a wrong notion of what the real, the ultimate, security is. No one who is dependent on anything outside himself, upon money, power, fame, or whatnot, is or ever can be secure. Only he who possesses himself

and is content with himself is actually secure. Too much is being said about the importance of adjustment and "participation in the group." Even cooperation, to give this thing its most favorable designation, is no more important than the ability to stand alone when the choice must be made between the sacrifice of one's own integrity and adjustment to or participation in group activity.

No matter how bad the world may become, no matter how   11
much the mass man of the future may lose such of the virtues as he still has, one fact remains. If one person alone refuses to go along with him, if one person alone asserts his individual and inner right to believe in and be loyal to what his fellow men seem to have given up, then at least he will still retain what is perhaps the most important part of humanity.

○ What If Shakespeare Had Had a Sister?

Virginia Woolf

Virginia Woolf (1882–1941) was born in London, England, and began her own literary career as a reviewer for the London Times Literary Supplement. *She made her mark chiefly as a novelist, however, with such experimental fiction as* Mrs. Dalloway *(1922),* To the Lighthouse *(1927),* The Waves *(1931). Many of her essays too are likely to endure, in such collections as* The Common Reader: First Series *(1925),* The Common Reader: Second Series *(1932), and* A Room of One's Own *(1929), from which the following excerpt was taken. At the age of fifty-nine, despondent over her poor health and the war in Europe, she drowned herself in the River Ouse, near her country home in Rodmell, England. The following selec-*

Argumentation

tion from a longer essay is an extraordinary example of argumentation, because it attempts to make its point with invented data. Although Woolf may not have consciously used the problem-solving device for finding "proofs" for her essay (see Problem-Solving in Chapter 3), we can regard her essay as an example of that technique. She starts out with a problem or a question: why is it that no Elizabethan woman wrote any of the remarkable literature of that period? To answer that question, she sets up a hypothesis: what if William Shakespeare had had a sister? Is it conceivable that this sibling, raised in the same environment, could have written any of the great poetry of that age? It is in testing out her hypothesis that Woolf resorts to imaginary data, because, as she said, the "facts" about the women of that time are hard to come by. But two things can be said about her resort to fiction here: (1) she uses her invented data in the same way that someone would who wanted to support a case with hard facts; (2) the details she presents about the social conditions of women in Shakespeare's time are remarkably close to the actual conditions that scholars have been able to discover from the historical and literary documents of the time. The conclusion she seems to come to from her unusual inductive approach is that it would have been impossible for any woman, even Shakespeare's sister, to have written any of the great literature of the Elizabethan period. But is there not just a touch of irony in the concessions she makes in the final paragraph to the deceased bishop? Does she really believe that no woman of the times was intellectually capable of writing great poetry?

1   It is a perennial puzzle why no woman wrote a word of that extraordinary literature [of the Elizabethan period] when every other man, it seemed, was capable of song or sonnet. What were the conditions in which women lived, I asked myself; for

---

fiction, imaginative work that is, is not dropped like a pebble upon the ground, as science may be; fiction is like a spider's web, attached ever so lightly perhaps, but still attached to life at all four corners. Often the attachment is scarcely perceptible; Shakespeare's plays, for instance, seem to hang there complete by themselves. But when the web is pulled askew, hooked up at the edge, torn in the middle, one remembers that these webs are not spun in midair by incorporeal creatures, but are the work of suffering human beings, and are attached to grossly material things, like health and money and the house we live in. . . .

Here am I asking why women did not write poetry in the Elizabethan age, and I am not sure how they were educated; whether they were taught to write; whether they had sitting-rooms to themselves; how many women had children before they were twenty-one; what, in short, they did from eight in the morning till eight at night. They had no money evidently; according to Professor Trevelyan [in his *History of England*] they were married whether they liked it or not before they were out of the nursery, at fifteen or sixteen very likely. It would have been extremely odd, even upon this showing, had one of them suddenly written the plays of Shakespeare, I concluded, and I thought of that old gentleman, who is dead now, but was a bishop, I think, who declared that it was impossible for any woman, past, present, or to come, to have the genius of Shakespeare. He wrote to the papers about it. He also told a lady who applied to him for information that cats do not as a matter of fact go to heaven, though they have, he added, souls of a sort. How much thinking those old gentlemen used to save one! How the borders of ignorance shrank back at their approach! Cats do not go to heaven. Women cannot write the plays of Shakespeare.

Be that as it may, I could not help thinking, as I looked at the works of Shakespeare on the shelf, that the bishop was right at least in this; it would have been impossible, completely and en-

2

3

499

Argumentation

tirely, for any woman to have written the plays of Shakespeare in the age of Shakespeare. Let me imagine, since facts are so hard to come by, what would have happened had Shakespeare had a wonderfully gifted sister, called Judith, let us say. Shakespeare himself went, very probably—his mother was an heiress—to the grammar school, where he may have learnt Latin—Ovid, Virgil and Horace—and the elements of grammar and logic. He was, it is well known, a wild boy who poached rabbits, perhaps shot a deer, and had, rather sooner than he should have done, to marry a woman in the neighbourhood, who bore him a child rather quicker than was right. That escapade sent him to seek his fortune in London. He had, it seemed, a taste for the theatre; he began by holding horses at the stage door. Very soon he got work in the theatre, became a successful actor, and lived at the hub of the universe, meeting everybody, knowing everybody, practising his art on the boards, exercising his wits in the streets, and even getting access to the palace of the queen. Meanwhile his extraordinarily gifted sister, let us suppose, remained at home. She was as adventurous, as imaginative, as agog to see the world as he was. But she was not sent to school. She had no chance of learning grammar and logic, let alone of reading Horace and Virgil. She picked up a book now and then, one of her brother's perhaps, and read a few pages. But then her parents came in and told her to mend the stockings or mind the stew and not moon about with books and papers. They would have spoken sharply but kindly, for they were substantial people who knew the conditions of life for a woman and loved their daughter—indeed, more likely than not she was the apple of her father's eye. Perhaps she scribbled some pages up in an apple loft on the sly, but was careful to hide them or set fire to them. Soon, however, before she was out of her teens, she was to be betrothed to the son of a neighbouring wool-stapler. She cried out that marriage was hateful to her, and for that she was severely beaten by her father. Then he ceased to scold her. He begged her instead not to hurt him, not to shame him in this matter of her marriage. He would give her a chain of beads or a fine petticoat, he said; and there were tears in his eyes. How could she disobey him? How could she break his heart? The force of her own gift alone drove her to it. She made up a small parcel of her belongings, let herself down by a rope one summer's night and took the road to London. She was not seventeen. The birds that sang in the hedge were not more musical than she was. She had the quickest fancy, a gift like her brother's, for the tune of words. Like him, she had a taste for the theatre. She stood at the stage door; she wanted to act, she said. Men laughed in her face. The manager—a fat, loose-lipped man—guffawed. He bellowed something about poodles dancing and women acting—no woman, he said, could possibly be an actress. He hinted—you can imagine what. She could get no training in her craft. Could she even seek her dinner in a tavern or roam the streets at midnight? Yet her genius was for fiction and lusted to feed abundantly upon the lives of men and women and the study of their ways. At last—for she was very young, oddly like Shakespeare the poet in her face, with the same grey eyes and rounded brows—at last Nick Greene the actor-manager took pity on her; she found herself with child by that gentleman and so—who shall measure the heat and violence of the poet's heart when caught and tangled in a woman's body?—killed herself one winter's night and lies buried at some crossroads where the omnibuses now stop outside the Elephant and Castle.

That, more or less, is how the story would run, I think, if a woman in Shakespeare's day had had Shakespeare's genius. But for my part, I agree with the deceased bishop, if such he was—it is unthinkable that any woman in Shakespeare's day should have had Shakespeare's genius. For genius like Shake-

4

speare's is not born among labouring, uneducated, servile people. It was not born in England among the Saxons and the Britons. It is not born today among the working classes. How, then, could it have been born among women whose work began, according to Professor Trevelyan, almost before they were out of the nursery, who were forced to it by their parents and held to it by all the power of law and custom?

○ **I Have a Dream**
Martin Luther King, Jr.

Born in Atlanta, Georgia, the son of a Baptist minister, Martin Luther King, Jr. (1929–1968) was himself ordained as a Baptist minister. He first became prominent in the civil-rights movement in 1955, when he led a boycott in protest against the segregated city buses in Montgomery, Alabama. He became the first president of the Southern Christian Leadership Conference, and in 1964, he was awarded the Nobel Peace Prize. He was assassinated in Memphis, Tennessee in April of 1968. Today, in many states, his birthday on January 15 is an official holiday. "I Have a Dream" is the only argumentative piece in this section that was first delivered to an audience as a speech. On August 28, 1963, at a mass rally in Washington, D.C., to commemorate the centennial of Abraham Lincoln's Emancipation Proclamation, Martin Luther King, Jr. led a march of over 200,000 people from the Washington Monument to the Lincoln Memorial, where he delivered this speech to the assembled crowd and to millions of other people via television. This memorable speech is a classic example of the ceremonial or epideictic oration, which comprises such common forms of speech as Fourth of July orations, graduation speeches, most inaugural addresses, and funeral sermons. A good deal of the impact of this speech on the audiences that heard it when it was first delivered was exerted by the eloquent style of the piece and by the manner of its de-

*livery. Much of the emotional effect of the speech, for
instance, was achieved by the skillful use of figures of
speech and special artistic sentence patterns (see Chapter
5 under these headings). Many of the metaphors are familiar, even trite, figures—like "beacon of hope," "doors
of opportunity,"—but King deliberately chose these oft-
repeated metaphors because he knew they would stir
his audience just by their familiarity. He achieves the same
effect with the series of echoes in the speech, such as
the Biblical echoes in paragraph 18 and, fittingly for this
speech, the echo from the Gettysburg Address in the
opening phrase of the speech ("Five score years ago").
But King shows himself capable of fresh, creative uses
of metaphor too: the cluster of banking metaphors in paragraphs 3–4 (like "promissory note," "a blank check,");
the contrasting pairs of metaphor ("quicksands of racial
injustice"/"solid rock of brotherhood"); the new-minted
metaphor in "the tranquillizing drugs of gradualism." The
rhythms of the speech come straight out of the incanta-
tory style of delivery of the Southern black preachers. The
most notable of these sound effects are the repetitive initial patterns (the Greeks called them* anaphora*): "One
hundred years later . . . ." "I have a dream . . . ." "Let
freedom ring . . . ." One has to develop a sense for
knowing when such consciously artistic style and delivery will be appropriate and effective.*

Five score years ago, a great American, in whose symbolic   1
shadow we stand, signed the Emancipation Proclamation. This
momentous decree came as a great beacon light of hope to
millions of Negro slaves who had been seared in the flames of
withering injustice. It came as a joyous daybreak to end the long
night of captivity.

But one hundred years later, we must face the tragic fact that   2
the Negro is still not free. One hundred years later, the life of the
Negro is still sadly crippled by the manacles of segregation and

Argumentation

the chains of discrimination. One hundred years later, the Negro lives on a lonely island of poverty in the midst of a vast ocean of material prosperity. One hundred years later, the Negro is still languishing in the corners of American society and finds himself an exile in his own land. So we have come here today to dramatize an appalling condition.

3   In a sense we have come to our nation's capital to cash a check. When the architects of our republic wrote the magnificent words of the Constitution and the Declaration of Independence, they were signing a promissory note to which every American was to fall heir. This note was a promise that all men would be guaranteed the unalienable rights of life, liberty, and the pursuit of happiness.

4   It is obvious today that America has defaulted on this promissory note insofar as her citizens of color are concerned. Instead of honoring this sacred obligation, America has given the Negro people a bad check; a check which has come back marked "insufficient funds." But we refuse to believe that the bank of justice is bankrupt. We refuse to believe that there are insufficient funds in the great vaults of opportunity of this nation. So we have come to cash this check—a check that will give us upon demand the riches of freedom and the security of justice. We have also come to this hallowed spot to remind America of the fierce urgency of *now*. This is no time to engage in the luxury of cooling off or to take the tranquilizing drugs of gradualism. *Now* is the time to make real the promises of Democracy. *Now* is the time to rise from the dark and desolate valley of segregation to the sunlit path of racial justice. *Now* is the time to open the doors of opportunity to all of God's children. *Now* is the time to lift our nation from the quicksands of racial injustice to the solid rock of brotherhood.

5   It would be fatal for the nation to overlook the urgency of the moment and to underestimate the determination of the Negro.

This sweltering summer of the Negro's legitimate discontent will not pass until there is an invigorating autumn of freedom and equality. 1963 is not an end, but a beginning. Those who hope that the Negro needed to blow off steam and will now be content will have a rude awakening if the nation returns to business as usual. There will be neither rest nor tranquillity in America until the Negro is granted his citizenship rights. The whirlwinds of revolt will continue to shake the foundations of our nation until the bright day of justice emerges.

But there is something that I must say to my people who stand   6
on the warm threshold which leads into the palace of justice. In the process of gaining our rightful place we must not be guilty of wrongful deeds. Let us not seek to satisfy our thirst for freedom by drinking from the cup of bitterness and hatred. We must forever conduct our struggle on the high plane of dignity and discipline. We must not allow our creative protest to degenerate into physical violence. Again and again we must rise to the majestic heights of meeting physical force with soul force. The marvelous new militancy which has engulfed the Negro community must not lead us to a distrust of all white people, for many of our white brothers, as evidenced by their presence here today, have come to realize that their destiny is tied up with our destiny and their freedom is inextricably bound to our freedom. We cannot walk alone.

And as we walk, we must make the pledge that we shall march   7
ahead. We cannot turn back. There are those who are asking the devotees of civil rights, "When will you be satisfied?" We can never be satisfied as long as the Negro is the victim of the unspeakable horrors of police brutality. We can never be satisfied as long as our bodies, heavy with the fatigue of travel, cannot gain lodging in the motels of the highways and the hotels of the cities. We cannot be satisfied as long as the Negro's basic mobility is from a smaller ghetto to a larger one. We can never

Argumentation

be satisfied as long as a Negro in Mississippi cannot vote and a Negro in New York believes he has nothing for which to vote. No, no, we are not satisfied, and we will not be satisfied until justice rolls down like waters and righteousness like a mighty stream.

8   I am not unmindful that some of you have come here out of great trials and tribulations. Some of you have come fresh from narrow jail cells. Some of you have come from areas where your quest for freedom left you battered by the storms of persecution and staggered by the winds of police brutality. You have been the veterans of creative suffering. Continue to work with the faith that unearned suffering is redemptive.

9   Go back to Mississippi, go back to Alabama, go back to South Carolina, go back to Georgia, go back to Louisiana, go back to the slums and ghettos of our northern cities, knowing that somehow this situation can and will be changed. Let us not wallow in the valley of despair.

10   I say to you today, my friends, that in spite of the difficulties and frustrations of the moment I still have a dream. It is a dream deeply rooted in the American dream.

11   I have a dream that one day this nation will rise up and live out the true meaning of its creed: "We hold these truths to be self-evident; that all men are created equal."

12   I have a dream that one day on the red hills of Georgia the sons of former slaves and the sons of former slaveowners will be able to sit down together at the table of brotherhood.

13   I have a dream that one day even the state of Mississippi, a desert state sweltering with the heat of injustice and oppression, will be transformed into an oasis of freedom and justice.

14   I have a dream that my four little children will one day live in a nation where they will not be judged by the color of their skin but by the content of their character.

15   I have a dream today.

I have a dream that one day the state of Alabama, whose   16
governor's lips are presently dripping with the words of interpo-
sition and nullification, will be transformed into a situation where
little black boys and black girls will be able to join hands with
little white boys and white girls and walk together as sisters and
brothers.

I have a dream today.   17

I have a dream that one day every valley shall be exalted,   18
every hill and mountain shall be made low, the rough places will
be made plain, and the crooked places will be made straight,
and the glory of the Lord shall be revealed, and all flesh shall
see it together.

This is our hope. This is the faith with which I return to the   19
South. With this faith we will be able to hew out of the mountain
of despair a stone of hope. With this faith we will be able to
transform the jangling discords of our nation into a beautiful
symphony of brotherhood. With this faith we will be able to work
together, to pray together, to struggle together, to go to jail together, to stand up for freedom together, knowing that we will
be free one day.

This will be the day when all of God's children will be able to   20
sing with new meaning

> My country, 'tis of thee,
> Sweet land of liberty,
>   Of thee I sing:
> Land where my fathers died,
> Land of the pilgrims' pride,
> From every mountain-side
>   Let freedom ring.

And if America is to be a great nation this must become true.   21
So let freedom ring from the prodigious hilltops of New Hampshire. Let freedom ring from the mighty mountains of New York.

Argumentation

Let freedom ring from the heightening Alleghenies of Pennsylvania!

22   Let freedom ring from the snowcapped Rockies of Colorado!

23   Let freedom ring from the curvaceous peaks of California!

24   But not only that; let freedom ring from Stone Mountain of Georgia!

25   Let freedom ring from Lookout Mountain of Tennessee!

26   Let freedom ring from every hill and molehill of Mississippi. From every mountainside, let freedom ring.

27   When we let freedom ring, when we let it ring from every village and every hamlet, from every state and every city, we will be able to speed up that day when all of God's children, black men and white men, Jews and Gentiles, Protestants and Catholics, will be able to join hands and sing in the words of the old Negro spiritual, "Free at last! free at last! thank God almighty, we are free at last!"

○ Declaration of Independence

Thomas Jefferson

Every American schoolchild is familiar with the name of Thomas Jefferson, and some of them can recite, on command, some specific biographical details about him—that he was born in Virginia in 1743 and died in 1826, that he attended William and Mary College and later founded what is now the University of Virginia, that he served two terms, from 1801 to 1809, as the third President of the United States, and that as a member of the Continental Congress in 1775–1776, he was the one mainly responsible for the spirit and the phrasing of our "Declaration of Independence," which was formally adopted on July 4, 1776. The opening paragraph of this classic manifesto explains why the document was written and points out who the audience for the document is ("a decent respect to the opinion of mankind"). The basic syllogistic structure of the argument in this document can be paraphrased in these terms:

If a monarch violates the inalienable rights of his subjects, his subjects have the right and the duty to sever the bonds of allegiance to that monarch.

King George III, the monarch of Great Britain and of the Colonies, has violated the inalienable rights of the Colonists.

Therefore, the Colonists have the right and the duty to sever the bonds of allegiance to that monarch.

The second paragraph of the document lays out the principles upon which the major premise (the first proposition in the scheme above) is based. The reason the "we" do not present any arguments to establish the truth of that major premise is that they regard this proposition as one of the "self-evident" truths. Paragraphs 3–30 present the bill of particulars, which serves to "prove" the minor premise (the second proposition above). The charges listed there against George III are not documented in the "Declaration," but we are left with the impression that these well-known "facts" could be amply documented if they were challenged. The final paragraph, after defining the "we" that has been speaking throughout the document ("We . . . the Representatives of the United States of America"), makes the formal declaration of independence. Is the argument vulnerable in any sections of the "Declaration"? Some people, for instance, have questioned whether the truths enunciated in the second paragraph are indeed self-evident. The question about the soft spots in the argument lends itself to a lively discussion.

When in the course of human events, it becomes necessary   1
for one people to dissolve the political bands which have connected them with another, and to assume among the Powers of

Argumentation

the earth, the separate and equal station to which the Laws of Nature and of Nature's God entitle them, a decent respect to the opinions of mankind requires that they should declare the causes which impel them to the separation.

2   We hold these truths to be self-evident, that all men are created equal, that they are endowed by their Creator with certain unalienable Rights, that among these are Life, Liberty and the pursuit of Happiness. That to secure these rights, Governments are instituted among Men, deriving their just powers from the consent of the governed. That whenever any Form of Government becomes destructive of these ends, it is the Right of the People to alter or to abolish it, and to institute a new Government, laying its foundation on such principles and organizing its powers in such form, as to them shall seem most likely to effect their Safety and Happiness. Prudence, indeed, will dictate that Governments long established should not be changed for light and transient causes; and accordingly all experience hath shown that mankind are more disposed to suffer, while evils are sufferable, than to right themselves by abolishing the forms to which they are accustomed. But when a long train of abuses and usurpations pursuing invariably the same Object evinces a design to reduce them under absolute Despotism, it is their right, it is their duty, to throw off such government, and to provide new Guards for their future security. Such has been the patient sufferance of these Colonies; and such is now the necessity which constrains them to alter their former Systems of Government. The history of the present King of Great Britain is a history of repeated injuries and usurpations, all having in direct object the establishment of an absolute Tyranny over these States. To prove this, let Facts be submitted to a candid world.

3   He has refused his Assent to Laws, the most wholesome and necessary for the public good.

○ **Jefferson/Declaration of Independence**

He has forbidden his Governors to pass Laws of immediate 4
and pressing importance, unless suspended in their operation
till his Assent should be obtained; and when so suspended, he
has utterly neglected to attend to them.

He has refused to pass other Laws for the accommodation of 5
large districts of people, unless those people would relinquish
the right of Representation in the Legislature, a right inestimable
to them and formidable to tyrants only.

He has called together legislative bodies at places unusual, 6
uncomfortable, and distant from the depository of their Public
Records, for the sole purpose of fatiguing them into compliance
with his measures.

He has dissolved Representative Houses repeatedly, for 7
oposing with manly firmness his invasions on the rights of the
people.

He has refused for a long time, after such dissolutions, to cause 8
others to be elected; whereby the Legislative Powers, incapable
of Annihilation, have returned to the People at large for their
exercise; the State remaining in the mean time exposed to all
the dangers of invasion from without, and convulsions within.

He has endeavored to prevent the population of these States; 9
for that purpose obstructing the Laws of Naturalization of Foreigners; refusing to pass others to encourage their migration
hither, and raising the conditions of new Appropriations of Lands.

He has obstructed the Administration of Justice, by refusing 10
his Assent to Laws for establishing Judiciary Powers.

He has made Judges dependent on his Will alone, for the 11
tenure of their offices, and the amount and payment of their salaries.

He has erected a multitude of New Offices, and sent hither 12
swarms of Officers to harass our People, and eat out their substance.

Argumentation

13   He has kept among us, in time of peace, Standing Armies without the consent of our Legislature.

14   He has affected to render the Military independent of and superior to the Civil Power.

15   He has combined with others to subject us to jurisdictions foreign to our constitution, and unacknowledged by our laws; giving his Assent to their acts of pretended Legislation:

16   For quartering large bodies of armed troops among us:

17   For protecting them, by a mock Trial, from Punishment for any Murders which they should commit on the Inhabitants of these States:

18   For cutting off our Trade with all parts of the world:

19   For imposing Taxes on us without our Consent:

20   For depriving us in many cases, of the benefits of Trial by Jury:

21   For transporting us beyond Seas to be tried for pretended offenses:

22   For abolishing the free System of English Laws in a Neighbouring Province, establishing therein an Arbitrary government, and enlarging its boundaries so as to render it at once an example and fit instruments for introducing the same absolute rule into these Colonies:

23   For taking away our Charters, abolishing our most valuable Laws, and altering fundamentally the Forms of our Governments:

24   For suspending our own Legislatures, and declaring themselves invested with Power to legislate for us in all cases whatsoever.

25   He has abdicated Government here, by declaring us out of his Protection and waging War against us.

26   He has plundered our seas, ravaged our Coasts, burnt our towns and destroyed the Lives of our people.

27   He is at this time transporting large Armies of foreign Mercenaries to compleat the works of death, desolation and tyranny,

already begun with circumstances of Cruelty & Perfidy scarcely paralleled in the most barbarous ages, and totally unworthy the Head of a civilized nation.

He has constrained our fellow Citizens taken Captive on the high Seas to bear Arms against their Country, to become the executioners of their friends and Brethren, or to fall themselves by their Hands. 28

He has excited domestic insurrections amongst us, and has endeavored to bring on the inhabitants of our frontiers, the merciless Indian Savages, whose known rule of warfare, is an undistinguished destruction of all ages, sexes and conditions. 29

In every stage of these Oppressions We Have Petitioned for Redress in the most humble terms: Our repeated petitions have been answered only by repeated injury. A Prince, whose character is thus marked by every act which may define a Tyrant, is unfit to be the ruler of a free People. 30

Nor have We been wanting in attention to our British brethren. We have warned them from time to time of attempts by their legislature to extend an unwarrantable jurisdiction over us. We have reminded them of the circumstances of our emigration and settlement here. We have appealed to their native justice and magnanimity, and we have conjured them by the ties of our common kindred to disavow these usurpations, which would inevitably interrupt our connections and correspondence. They too have been deaf to the voice of justice and of consanguinity. We must, therefore, acquiesce in the necessity, which denounces our Separation, and hold them, as we hold the rest of mankind, Enemies in War, in Peace Friends. 31

We, therefore, the Representatives of the United States of America, in General Congress, Assembled, appealing to the Supreme Judge of the world for the rectitude of our intentions, do, in the Name, and by Authority of the good People of these Colonies, solemnly publish and declare, That these United Colonies are, and of Right ought to be, Free and Independent States; that 32 they are Absolved from all Allegiance to the British Crown, and that all political connection between them and the State of Great Britain, is and ought to be totally dissolved; and that as Free and Independent States, they have full power to levy War, conclude Peace, contract Alliances, establish Commerce, and to do all other Acts and Things which Independent States may of right do. And for the support of this Declaration, with a firm reliance on the protection of Divine Providence, we mutually pledge to each other our lives, our Fortunes and our sacred Honor.

○ The Art of Teaching Science

Lewis Thomas

Lewis Thomas (b. 1913), who was born in Flushing, New York, took his B.S. degree from Princeton University and his M.D. degree from Harvard University. For a number of years, he taught at the Yale University Medical School, but since 1973, he has been the chief executive officer of the Memorial Sloan-Kettering Cancer Center in New York City. In 1971, he began contributing a column, entitled "Notes of a Biology Watcher," to the New England Journal of Medicine. *A collection of these columns under the title of* The Lives of a Cell *won a National Book Award in 1975. The latest collection of his columns bears the title* The Medusa and the Snail: More Notes of a Biology Watcher *(1979). What he is arguing for in this piece is a change in the way that the sciences are taught in the schools. His procedure is, first of all, to point out the two major weaknesses in the way that the scientific community has presented the sciences in the schools (paragraphs 3–4). In paragraphs 5, 6, and 7 then, he presents arguments against that way of presenting the sciences. In paragraph 9, he suggests, in a general way, how the teaching of the sciences might be fruitfully*

○ Thomas/The Art of Teaching Science

changed: put the mystery, the wonder, back into science so that we can entice students to take up the study of the sciences. Then in paragraphs 12–19, he spells out in more detail what the new curriculum would be like. Lewis Thomas is not addressing this argument primarily to scientists and teachers of science but is addressing it to the general audience that reads the articles in the New York Times Magazine *every Sunday. His assessment of the current situation and his prescriptions for remedying it will carry considerable weight with that audience, partly because he is a scientist himself, who is exposing the weaknesses of his own professional province, and partly because he has established his credentials with that audience through his previous writings. Does his characterization of the scientific community accord with your experiences of that community during your schooling?*

Everyone seems to agree that there is something wrong with the way science is being taught these days. But no one is at all clear about when it went wrong or what is to be done about it. The term "scientific illiteracy" has become almost a cliché in educational circles. Graduate schools blame the colleges; colleges blame the secondary schools; the high schools blame the elementary schools, which in turn, blame the family. 1

I suggest that the scientific community itself is partly, perhaps largely, to blame. Moreover, if there are disagreements between the world of the humanities and the scientific enterprise as to the place and importance of science in a liberal-arts education and the role of science in 20th-century culture, I believe that the scientists are themselves responsible for a general misunderstanding of what they are really up to. 2

During the last half-century, we have been teaching the sciences as though they were the same collection of academic 3 subjects as always, and—here is what has really gone wrong—as though they would always be the same. Students learn today's biology, for example, the same way we learned Latin when I was in high school long ago: first, the fundamentals; then, the underlying laws; next, the essential grammar and, finally, the reading of texts. Once mastered, that was that: Latin was Latin and forever after would always be Latin. History, once learned, was history. And biology was precisely biology, a vast array of hard facts to be learned as fundamentals, followed by a reading of the texts.

4   Furthermore, we have been teaching science as if its facts were somehow superior to the facts in all other scholarly disciplines—more fundamental, more solid, less subject to subjectivism, immutable. English literature is not just one way of thinking; it is all sorts of ways; poetry is a moving target; the facts that underlie art, architecture and music are not really hard facts, and you can change them any way you like by arguing about them. But science, it appears, is an altogether different kind of learning: an unambiguous, unalterable and endlessly useful display of data that only needs to be packaged and installed somewhere in one's temporal lobe in order to achieve a full understanding of the natural world.

5   And, of course, it is not like this at all. In real life, every field of science is incomplete, and most of them—whatever the record of accomplishment during the last 200 years—are still in their very earliest stages. In the fields I know best, among the life sciences, it is required that the most expert and sophisticated minds be capable of changing course—often with a great lurch—every few years. In some branches of biology the mind-changing is occurring with accelerating velocity. Next week's issue of any scientific journal can turn a whole field upside down, shaking out any number of immutable ideas and installing new bodies of dogma. This is an almost everyday event in physics,

in chemistry, in materials research, in neurobiology, in genetics, in immunology.

On any Tuesday morning, if asked, a good working scientist will tell you with some self-satisfaction that the affairs of his field are nicely in order, that things are finally looking clear and making sense, and all is well. But come back again on another Tuesday, and the roof may have just fallen in on his life's work. All the old ideas—last week's ideas in some cases—are no longer good ideas. The hard facts have softened, melted away and vanished under the pressure of new hard facts. Something strange has happened. And it is this very strangeness of nature that makes science engrossing, that keeps bright people at it, and that ought to be at the center of science teaching.

The conclusions reached in science are always, when looked at closely, far more provisional and tentative than are most of the assumptions arrived at by our colleagues in the humanities. But we do not talk much in public about this, nor do we teach this side of science. We tend to say instead: These are the facts of the matter, and this is what the facts signify. Go and learn them, for they will be the same forever.

By doing this, we miss opportunity after opportunity to recruit young people into science, and we turn off a good many others who would never dream of scientific careers but who emerge from their education with the impression that science is fundamentally boring.

Sooner or later, we will have to change this way of presenting science. We might begin by looking more closely at the common ground that science shares with all disciplines, particularly with the humanities and with social and behavioral science. For there is indeed such a common ground. It is called bewilderment. There are more than seven times seven types of ambiguity in science, all awaiting analysis. The poetry of Wallace Stevens is crystal clear alongside the genetic code.

Argumentation

10   One of the complaints about science is that it tends to flatten everything. In its deeply reductionist way, it is said, science removes one mystery after another, leaving nothing in the place of mystery but data. I have even heard this claim as explanation for the drift of things in modern art and modern music: Nothing is left to contemplate except randomness and senselessness; God is nothing but a pair of dice, loaded at that. Science is linked somehow to the despair of the 20th-century mind. There is almost nothing unknown and surely nothing unknowable. Blame science.

11   I prefer to turn things around in order to make precisely the opposite case. Science, especially 20th-century science, has provided us with a glimpse of something we never really knew before, the revelation of human ignorance. We have been accustomed to the belief, from one century to another, that except for one or two mysteries we more or less comprehend everything on earth. Every age, not just the 18th century, regarded itself as the Age of Reason, and we have never lacked for explanations of the world and its ways. Now, we are being brought up short. We do not understand much of anything, from the episode we rather dismissively (and, I think, defensively) choose to call the "big bang," all the way down to the particles in the atoms of a bacterial cell. We have a wilderness of mystery to make our way through in the centuries ahead. We will need science for this but not science alone. In its own time, science will produce the data and some of the meaning in the data, but never the full meaning. For perceiving real significance when significance is at hand, we will need all sorts of brains outside the fields of science.

12   It is primarily because of this need that I would press for changes in the way science is taught. Although there is a perennial need to teach the young people who will be doing the science themselves, this will always be a small minority. Even

more important, we must teach science to those who will be needed for thinking about it, and that means pretty nearly everyone else—most of all, the poets, but also artists, musicians, philosophers, historians and writers. A few of these people, at least, will be able to imagine new levels of meaning which may be lost on the rest of us.

In addition, it is time to develop a new group of professional 13 thinkers, perhaps a somewhat larger group than the working scientists and the working poets, who can create a discipline of scientific criticism. We have had good luck so far in the emergence of a few people ranking as philosophers of science and historians and journalists of science, and I hope more of these will be coming along. But we have not yet seen specialists in the fields of scientific criticism who are of the caliber of the English literary and social critics F. R. Leavis and John Ruskin or the American literary critic Edmund Wilson. Science needs critics of this sort, but the public at large needs them more urgently.

I suggest that the introductory courses in science, at all levels 14 from grade school through college, be radically revised. Leave the fundamentals, the so-called basics, aside for a while, and concentrate the attention of all students on the things that are not known. You cannot possibly teach quantum mechanics without mathematics, to be sure, but you can describe the strangeness of the world opened up by quantum theory. Let it be known, early on, that there are deep mysteries and profound paradoxes revealed in distant outline by modern physics. Explain that these can be approached more closely and puzzled over, once the language of mathematics has been sufficiently mastered.

At the outset, before any of the fundamentals, teach the still 15 imponderable puzzles of cosmology. Describe as clearly as possible, for the youngest minds, that there are some things going on in the universe that lie still beyond comprehension, and make it plain how little is known.

16   Do not teach that biology is a useful and perhaps profitable science; that can come later. Teach instead that there are structures squirming inside each of our cells that provide all the energy for living. Essentially foreign creatures, these lineal descendants of bacteria were brought in for symbiotic living a billion or so years ago. Teach that we do not have the ghost of an idea how they got there, where they came from, or how they evolved to their present structure and function. The details of oxidative phosphorylation and photosynthesis can come later.

17   Teach ecology early on. Let it be understood that the earth's life is a system of interdependent creatures, and that we do not understand at all how it works. The earth's environment, from the range of atmospheric gases to the chemical constituents of the sea, has been held in an almost unbelievably improbable state of regulated balance since life began, and the regulation of stability and balance is somehow accomplished by the life itself, like the autonomic nervous system of an immense organism. We do not know how such a system works, much less what it means, but there are some nice reductionist details at hand, such as the bizarre proportions of atmospheric constituents, ideal for our sort of planetary life, and the surprising stability of the ocean's salinity, and the fact that the average temperature of the earth has remained quite steady in the face of at least a 25 percent increase in heat coming in from the sun since the earth began. That kind of thing: something to think about.

18   Go easy, I suggest, on the promises sometimes freely offered by science. Technology relies and depends on science these days, more than ever before, but technology is far from the first justification for doing research, nor is it necessarily an essential product to be expected from science. Public decisions about the future of technology are totally different from decisions about

science, and the two enterprises should not be tangled together. The central task of science is to arrive, stage by stage, at a clearer comprehension of nature, but this does not at all mean, as it is sometimes claimed to mean, a search for mastery over nature.

Science may someday provide us with a better understanding of ourselves, but never, I hope, with a set of technologies for doing something or other to improve ourselves. I am made nervous by assertions that human consciousness will someday be unraveled by research, laid out for close scrutiny like the workings of a computer, and then—and *then . . .!* I hope with some fervor that we can learn a lot more than we now know about the human mind, and I see no reason why this strange puzzle should remain forever and entirely beyond us. But I would be deeply disturbed by any prospect that we might use the new knowledge in order to begin doing something about it—to improve it, say. This is a different matter from searching for information to use against schizophrenia or dementia, where we are badly in need of technologies, indeed likely one day to be sunk without them. But the ordinary, everyday, more or less normal human mind is too marvelous an instrument ever to be tampered with by anyone, science or no science.

The education of humanists cannot be regarded as complete, or even adequate, without exposure in some depth to where things stand in the various branches of science, particularly, as I have said, in the areas of our ignorance. Physics professors, most of them, look with revulsion on assignments to teach their subject to poets. Biologists, caught up by the enchantment of their new power, armed with flawless instruments to tell the nucleotide sequences of the entire human genome, nearly matching the physicists in the precision of their measurements of living processes, will resist the prospect of broad survey courses;

Argumentation

each biology professor will demand that any student in his path master every fine detail within that professor's research program.

21   The liberal-arts faculties for their part, will continue to view the scientists with suspicion and apprehension. "What do the scientists want?" asked a Cambridge professor in Francis Cornford's wonderful "Microcosmographia Academica." "Everything that's going," was the quick answer. That was back in 1912, and scientists haven't much changed.

22   But maybe, just maybe, a new set of courses dealing systematically with ignorance in science will take hold. The scientists might discover in it a new and subversive technique for catching the attention of students driven by curiosity, delighted and surprised to learn that science is exactly as the American scientist and educator Vannevar Bush described it: an "endless frontier." The humanists, for their part, might take considerable satisfaction in watching their scientific colleagues confess openly to not knowing everything about everything. And the poets, on whose shoulders the future rests, might, late nights, thinking things over, begin to see some meanings that elude the rest of us. It is worth a try.

23   I believe that the worst thing that has happened to science education is that the fun has gone out of it. A great many good students look at it as slogging work to be got through on the way to medical school. Others are turned off by the premedical students themselves, embattled and bleeding for grades and class standing. Very few recognize science as the high adventure it really is, the wildest of all explorations ever taken by human beings, the chance to glimpse things never seen before, the shrewdest maneuver for discovering how the world works. Instead, baffled early on, they are misled into thinking that baf-

flement is simply the result of not having learned all the facts. They should be told that everyone else is baffled as well—from the professor in his endowed chair down to the platoons of post-doctoral students in the laboratories all night. Every important scientific advance that has come in looking like an answer has turned, sooner or later—usually sooner—into a question. And the game is just beginning.

If more students were aware of this, I think many of them would 24 decide to look more closely and to try and learn more about what *is* known. That is the time when mathematics will become clearly and unavoidably recognizable as an essential, indispensable instrument for engaging in the game, and that is the time for teaching it. The calamitous loss of applied mathematics from what we might otherwise be calling higher education is a loss caused, at least in part, by insufficient incentives for learning the subject. Left by itself, standing there among curriculum offerings, it is not at all clear to the student what it is to be applied to. And there is all of science, next door, looking like an almost-finished field reserved only for chaps who want to invent or apply new technologies. We have had it wrong, and presented it wrong to class after class for several generations.

An appreciation of what is happening in science today, and 25 how great a distance lies ahead for exploring, ought to be one of the rewards of a liberal-arts education. It ought to be good in itself, not something to be acquired on the way to a professional career but part of the cast of thought needed for getting into the kind of century that is now just down the road. Part of the intellectual equipment of an educated person, however his or her time is to be spent, ought to be a feel for the queernesses of nature, the inexplicable thing, the side of life for which informed bewilderment will be the best way of getting through the day.

○ **A Modest Proposal**

For Preventing the Children of Poor People in Ireland
from Being a Burden to Their Parents or Country,
and for Making Them Beneficial to the Public

Jonathan Swift

*Jonathan Swift (1667–1745) was the son of English par-
ents who had settled in Ireland. He spent a good part of
his early adult life in London, enmeshed in the fierce
political struggles that went on between the Whigs and
the Tories. In 1713, Queene Anne appointed him as the
Dean of St. Patrick's Cathedral in Dublin, where he spent
most of his remaining years. A famous writer of satire, in
both verse and prose, Swift is probably best remembered for his novel* Gulliver's Travels *(1726). "A Modest
Proposal" (1729), however, is his most famous short
piece and is one of the three or four most-anthologized
essays in English. It is a classic example of a piece of
argumentation about a very serious social problem. Three
consecutive years of drought and sparse crops had reduced many thousands of Irish people (35,000 by one
estimate) to a condition of beggary in the streets. The
absentee English landlords seemed to be indifferent to
the plight of the Irish poor. Many writers and speakers
had tried to rouse the landlords or the government to do
something about the pitiful situation, but to no avail. Swift
decided to use the shock treatment. His "modest" proposal urges that the Irish poor sell their year-old children
to be eaten by the rich. Swift's essay, which was published as a pamphlet, did not immediately effect a
change, but it certainly aroused the conscience of a nation. His main rhetorical device in the essay is irony: saying one thing but meaning just the opposite. In order to
be able to analyze Swift's argumentative strategies,
readers have to be able to discriminate the two voices
or personas operating in the essay. First of all, there is
the voice of the proposer, the "I" of the essay. Then there
is the implied voice of the author, of Jonathan Swift himself. What Swift is arguing for is something quite different
from what the proposer is arguing for. To get the full im-*

pact of the essay, you have to believe that the proposer is perfectly serious about his proposal and about the arguments he presents to support his proposal. A more reasonable solution for the Irish problem and the one that Swift and other writers would endorse is suggested by the list of "other expedients" in paragraph 29. One of the great ironies about this famous ironic essay is that despite the outrageousness of the proposal, the arguments that the proposer offers in support of his proposal make perfect sense—if you can accept cannibalism as a legitimate resort for survival.

I t is a melancholy object to those who walk through this great   1
town or travel in the country, when they see the streets, the roads, and cabin doors, crowded with beggars of the female sex, followed by three, four, or six children all in rags and importuning every passenger for an alms. These mothers, instead of being able to work for their honest livelihood, are forced to employ all their time in strolling to beg sustenance for their helpless infants, who, as they grow up, either turn thieves for want of work, or leave their dear native country to fight for the Pretender in Spain, or sell themselves to the Barbados.

I think it is agreed by all parties that this prodigious number   2
of children in the arms, or on the backs, or at the heels of their mothers, and frequently of their fathers, is in the present deplorable state of the kingdom a very great additional grievance; and therefore whoever could find out a fair, cheap, and easy method of making these children sound, useful members of the commonwealth would deserve so well of the public as to have his statue set up for a preserver of the nation.

But my intention is very far from being confined to provide   3
only for the children of professed beggars; it is of a much greater extent, and shall take in the whole number of infants at a certain age who are born of parents in effect as little able to support them as those who demand our charity in the streets.

As to my own part, having turned my thoughts for many years   4

Argumentation

upon this important subject, and maturely weighed the several schemes of other projectors, I have always found them grossly mistaken in their computation. It is true, a child just dropped from its dam may be supported by her milk for a solar year, with little other nourishment; at most not above the value of two shillings, which the mother may certainly get, or the value in scraps, by her lawful occupation of begging; and it is exactly at one year that I propose to provide for them in such a manner as instead of being a charge upon their parents or the parish, or wanting food and raiment for the rest of their lives, they shall on the contrary contribute to the feeding, and partly to the clothing, of many thousands.

5   There is likewise another great advantage in my scheme, that it will prevent those voluntary abortions, and that horrid practice of women murdering their bastard children, alas, too frequent among us, sacrificing the poor innocent babes, I doubt, more to avoid the expense than the shame, which would move tears and pity in the most savage and inhuman breast.

6   The number of souls in this kingdom being usually reckoned one million and a half, of these I calculate there may be about two hundred thousand couples whose wives are breeders; from which number I subtract thirty thousand couples who are able to maintain their own children, although I apprehend there cannot be so many under the present distress of the kingdom; but this being granted, there will remain an hundred and seventy thousand breeders. I again subtract fifty thousand for those women who miscarry, or whose children die by accident or disease within the year. There only remain an hundred and twenty thousand children of poor parents annually born. The question therefore is, how this number shall be reared and provided for, which, as I have already said, under the present situation of affairs, is utterly impossible by all the methods hitherto proposed. For we can neither employ them in handicraft or agri-

culture; we neither build houses (I mean in the country) nor cultivate land. They can very seldom pick up a livelihood by stealing till they arrive at six years old, except where they are of towardly parts; although I confess they learn the rudiments much earlier, during which time they can however be looked upon only as probationers, as I have been informed by a principal gentleman in the country of Cavan, who protested to me that he never knew above one or two instances under the age of six, even in a part of the kingdom so renowned for the quickest proficiency in that art.

I am assured by our merchants that a boy or a girl before   7
twelve years old is no salable commodity; and even when they come to this age they will not yield above three pounds, or three pounds and half a crown at most on the Exchange; which cannot turn to account either to the parents or the kingdom, the charge of nutriment and rags having been at least four times that value.

I shall now therefore humbly propose my own thoughts, which   8
I hope will not be liable to the least objection.

I have been assured by a very knowing American of my ac-   9
quaintance in London, that a young healthy child well nursed is at a year old a most delicious, nourishing, and wholesome food, whether stewed, roasted, baked, or boiled; and I make no doubt that it will equally serve in a fricassee or a ragout.

I do therefore humbly offer it to public consideration that of   10
the hundred and twenty thousand children, already computed, twenty thousand may be reserved for breed, whereof only one fourth part to be males, which is more than we allow to sheep, black cattle, or swine; and my reason is that these children are seldom the fruits of marriage, a circumstance not much regarded by our savages, therefore one male will be sufficient to serve four females. That the remaining hundred thousand may at a year old be offered in sale to the persons of quality and

fortune through the kingdom, always advising the mother to let them suck plentifully in the last month, so as to render them plump and fat for a good table. A child will make two dishes at an entertainment for friends; and when the family dines alone, the fore or hind quarter will make a reasonable dish, and seasoned with a little pepper or salt will be very good boiled on the fourth day, especially in winter.

11   I have reckoned upon a medium that a child just born will weigh twelve pounds, and in a solar year if tolerably nursed increaseth to twenty-eight pounds.

12   I grant this food will be somewhat dear, and therefore very proper for landlords, who, as they have already devoured most of the parents, seem to have the best title to the children.

13   Infant's flesh will be in season throughout the year, but more plentiful in March, and a little before and after. For we are told by a grave author, an eminent French physician, that fish being a prolific diet, there are more children born in Roman Catholic countries about nine months after Lent than at any other season; therefore, reckoning a year after Lent, the markets will be more glutted than usual, because the number of popish infants is at least three to one in this kingdom; and therefore it will have one other collateral advantage, by lessening the number of Papists among us.

14   I have already computed the charge of nursing a beggar's child (in which list I reckon all cottagers, laborers, and four-fifths of the farmers) to be about two shillings per annum, rags included; and I believe no gentleman would repine to give ten shillings for the carcass of a good fat child, which, as I have said, will make four dishes of excellent nutritive meat, when he hath only some particular friend or his own family to dine with him. Thus the squire will learn to be a good landlord, and grow popular among the tenants; the mother will have eight shillings net profit, and be fit for work till she produces another child.

Those who are more thrifty (as I must confess the times re-   15
quire) may flay the carcass; the skin of which artificially dressed
will make admirable gloves for ladies, and summer boots for
fine gentlemen.

As to our city of Dublin, shambles may be appointed for this   16
purpose in the most convenient parts of it, and butchers we may
be assured will not be wanting; although I rather recommend
buying the children alive, and dressing them hot from the knife
as we do roasting pigs.

A very worthy person, a true lover of his country, and whose   17
virtues I highly esteem, was lately pleased in discoursing on this
matter to offer a refinement upon my scheme. He said that many
gentlemen of his kingdom, having of late destroyed their deer,
he conceived that the want of venison might be well supplied
by the bodies of young lads and maidens, not exceeding fourteen years of age nor under twelve, so great a number of both
sexes in every county being now ready to starve for want of
work and service; and these to be disposed of by their parents,
if alive, or otherwise by their nearest relations. But with due de-
ference to so excellent a friend and so deserving a patriot, I
cannot be altogether in his sentiments; for as to the males, my
American acquaintance assured me from frequent experience
that their flesh was generally tough and lean, like that of our
schoolboys, by continual exercise, and their taste disagreeable;
and to fatten them would not answer the charge. Then as to the
females, it would, I think with humble submission, be a loss to
the public, because they soon would become breeders themselves; and besides, it is not improbable that some scrupulous
people might be apt to censure such a practice (although indeed very unjustly) as a little bordering upon cruelty; which, I
confess, hath always been with me the strongest objection against
any project, how well soever intended.

But in order to justify my friend, he confessed that this expe-   18

529

Argumentation

dient was put into his head by the famous Psalmanazar, a native
of the island Formosa, who came from thence to London above
twenty years ago, and in conversation told my friend that in his
country when any young person happened to be put to death,
the executioner sold the carcass to persons of quality as a prime
dainty; and that in his time the body of a plump girl of fifteen,
who was crucified for an attempt to poison the emperor, was
sold to his Imperial Majesty's prime minister of state, and other
great mandarins of the court, in joints from the gibbet, at four
hundred crowns. Neither indeed can I deny that if the same use
were made of several plump young girls in this town, who without one single groat to their fortunes cannot stir abroad without
a chair, and appear at the playhouse and assemblies in foreign
fineries which they never will pay for, the kingdom would not be
the worse.

19   Some persons of a desponding spirit are in great concern
about that vast number of poor people who are aged, diseased,
or maimed, and I have been desired to employ my thoughts
what course may be taken to ease the nation of so grievous an
encumbrance. But I am not in the least pain upon that matter,
because it is very well known that they are every day dying and
rotting by cold and famine, and filth and vermin, as fast as can
be reasonably expected. And as to the younger laborers, they
are now in almost as hopeful a condition. They cannot get work,
and consequently pine away for want of nourishment to a degree that if any time they are accidentally hired to common labor, they have not strength to perform it; and thus the country
and themselves are happily delivered from the evils to come.

20   I have too long digressed, and therefore shall return to my
subject. I think the advantages by the proposal which I have
made are obvious and many, as well as of the highest importance.

21   For first, as I have already observed, it would greatly lessen

the number of Papists, with whom we are yearly overrun, being the principal breeders of the nation as well as our most dangerous enemies; and who stay at home on purpose to deliver the kingdom to the Pretender, hoping to take their advantage by the absence of so many good Protestants, who have chosen rather to leave their country than to stay at home and pay tithes against their conscience to an Episcopal curate.

Secondly, the poorer tenants will have something valuable of   22
their own, which by law may be made liable to distress, and help to pay their landlord's rent, their corn and cattle being already seized and money a thing unknown.

Thirdly, whereas the maintenance of an hundred thousand   23
children, from two years old and upwards, cannot be computed at less than ten shillings a piece per annum, the nation's stock will be thereby increased fifty thousand pounds per annum, besides the profit of a new dish introduced to the tables of all gentlemen of fortune in the kingdom who have any refinement in taste. And the money will circulate among ourselves, the goods being entirely of our own growth and manufacture.

Fourthly, the constant breeders, besides the gain of eight   24
shillings sterling per annum by the sale of their children, will be rid of the charge of maintaining them after the first year.

Fifthly, this food would likewise bring great custom to taverns,   25
where the vintners will certainly be so prudent as to procure the best receipts for dressing it to perfection, and consequently have their houses frequented by all the fine gentlemen, who justly value themselves upon their knowledge in good eating; and a skillful cook, who understands how to oblige his guests, will contrive to make it as expensive as they please.

Sixthly, this would be a great inducement to marriage, which   26
all wise nations have either encouraged by rewards or enforced by laws and penalties. It would increase the care and tenderness of mothers toward their children, when they were sure of a

Argumentation

settlement for life to the poor babes, provided in some sort by the public, to their annual profit instead of expense. We should see an honest emulation among the married women, which of them could bring the fattest child to the market. Men would become as fond of their wives during the time of their pregnancy as they are now of their mares in foal, their cows in calf, or sows when they are ready to farrow; nor offer to beat or kick them (as is too frequent a practice) for fear of a miscarriage.

27   Many other advantages might be enumerated. For instance, the addition of some thousand carcasses in our exportation of barreled beef, the propagation of swine's flesh, and improvements in the art of making good bacon, so much wanted among us by the great destruction of pigs, too frequent at our tables, which are no way comparable in taste or magnificence to a well-grown, fat, yearling child, which roasted whole will make a considerable figure at a lord mayor's feast or any other public entertainment. But this and many others I omit, being studious of brevity.

28   Supposing that one thousand families in this city would be constant customers for infants' flesh, besides others who might have it at merry meetings, particularly weddings and christenings, I compute that Dublin would take off annually about twenty thousand carcasses, and the rest of the kingdom (where probably they will be sold somewhat cheaper) the remaining eighty thousand.

29   I can think of no one objection that will possibly be raised against this proposal, unless it should be urged that the number of people will be thereby much lessened in the kingdom. This I freely own, and it was indeed one principal design in offering it to the world. I desire the reader will observe, that I calculate my remedy for this one individual kingdom of Ireland and for no other that ever was, is, or I think ever can be upon earth. Therefore let no man talk to me of other expedients: of taxing our

absentees at five shillings a pound: of using neither clothes nor household furniture except what is of our own growth and manufacture: of utterly rejecting the materials and instruments that promote foreign luxury: of curing the expensiveness of pride, vanity, idleness, and gaming in our women: of introducing a vein of parsimony, prudence, and temperance: of learning to love our country, in the want of which we differ even from Laplanders and the inhabitants of Topinamboo: of quitting our animosities and factions, nor acting any longer like the Jews, who were murdering one another at the very moment their city was taken: of being a little cautious not to sell our country and conscience for nothing: of teaching landlords to have at least one degree of mercy toward their tenants: lastly, of putting a spirit of honesty, industry, and skill into our shopkeepers; who, if a resolution could now be taken to buy only our native goods, would immediately unite to cheat and exact upon us in the price, the measure, and the goodness, nor could ever yet be brought to make one fair proposal of just dealing, though often and earnestly invited to it.

Therefore I repeat, let no man talk to me of these and the like   30
expedients, till he hath at least some glimpse of hope that there will ever be some hearty and sincere attempt to put them in practice.

But as to myself, having been wearied out for many years with   31
offering vain, idle, visionary thoughts, and at length utterly despairing of success, I fortunately fell upon this proposal, which, as it is wholly new, so it hath something solid and real, of no expense and little trouble, full in our own power, and whereby we can incur no danger in disobliging England. For this kind of commodity will not bear exportation, the flesh being of too tender a consistence to admit a long continuance in salt, although perhaps I could name a country which would be glad to eat up our whole nation without it.

Argumentation

32   After all, I am not so violently bent upon my own opinion as to reject any offer proposed by wise men, which shall be found equally innocent, cheap, easy, and effectual. But before something of that kind shall be advanced in contradiction to my scheme, and offering a better, I desire the author or authors will be pleased maturely to consider two points. First, as things now stand, how they will be able to find food and raiment for an hundred thousand useless mouths and backs. And secondly, there being a round million of creatures in human figure throughout this kingdom, whose sole subsistence put into a common stock would leave them in debt two millions of pounds sterling, adding those who are beggars by profession to the bulk of farmers, cottagers, and laborers, with their wives and children who are beggars in effect; I desire those politicians who dislike my overture, and may perhaps be so bold to attempt an answer, that they will first ask the parents of these mortals whether they would not at this day think it a great happiness to have been sold for food at a year old in this manner I prescribe, and thereby have avoided such a perpetual scene of misfortunes as they have since gone through by the oppression of landlords, the impossibility of paying rent without money or trade, the want of common sustenance, with neither house nor clothes to cover them from the inclemencies of the weather, and the most inevitable prospect of entailing the like or greater miseries upon their breed forever.

33   I profess, in the sincerity of my heart, that I have not the least personal interest in endeavoring to promote this necessary work, having no other motive than the public good of my country, by advancing our trade, providing for infants, relieving the poor, and giving some pleasure to the rich. I have no children by which I can propose to get a single penny; the youngest being nine years old, and my wife past childbearing.

○ The Achievement of Desire

Richard Rodriguez

Richard Rodriguez (b. 1944) the son of Mexican-Americans, was born in San Francisco and attended Catholic elementary and secondary schools in Sacramento, California. After graduating from Stanford University, he did graduate work at Columbia University and the Warburg Institute in London. He became a professor at the University of California at Berkeley after earning his Ph.D. there. In 1981, he published Hunger of Memory: The Education of Richard Rodriguez. *In the segment reprinted here, Rodriguez argues that there was a cause-and-effect relationship between the education that he received as a young man and the subsequent course of his life. He conducts his argument within a narrative mode, and his "proofs" consist primarily of incidents (examples) from his life as a schoolboy, incidents which point up his growing awareness of the sharp contrasts between his home life and his school life, between his role as a "good student" and his role as a 'troubled son." He keeps relating his own experiences to what Richard Hoggart had said, in an abstract way, about the life of a typical "scholarship boy."*

What I am about to describe to you has taken me twenty years   1
to admit: *The primary reason for my success in the classroom
was that I couldn't forget that schooling was changing me and
separating me from the life I had enjoyed before becoming a
student.* (That simple realization!) For years I never spoke to

From "The Achievement of Desire: Personal Reflections on Learning 'Basics' " by Richard Rodriguez from *College English*, Vol. 40, No. 3, November 1978. Copyright © 1978 by The National Council of Teachers of English. Reprinted by permission of the publisher and the author.

Argumentation

anyone about this boyhood fear, my guilt and remorse. I never mentioned these feelings to my parents or my brothers. Nor to my teachers or classmates. From a very early age, I understood enough, just enough, about my experiences to keep what I knew vague, repressed, private, beneath layers of embarrassment. Not until the last months that I was a graduate student, nearly thirty years old, was it possible for me to think about the reasons for my success. Only then. At the end of my schooling, I needed to determine how far I had moved from my past. The adult finally confronted—and now must publicly say—what the child shuddered from knowing and could never admit to the faces which smiled at his every success.

2   At the end, in the British Museum (too distracted to finish my dissertation), for weeks I read, speed-read, books by sociologists and educationists only to find infrequent and brief mention of scholarship students, "successful working-class students." Then one day I came across Richard Hoggart's *The Uses of Literacy* and saw, in his description of the scholarship boy,[1] myself. For the first time I realized that there were others much like me, and I was able to frame the meaning of my academic failure and success.

3   What Hoggard understands is that the scholarship boy moves between environments, his home and the classroom, which are at cultural extremes, opposed. With his family, the boy has the pleasure of an exuberant intimacy—the family's consolation in feeling public alienation. Lavish emotions texture home life. *Then* at school the instruction is to use reason primarily. Immediate needs govern the pace of his parents' lives; from his mother and

---

[1] For reasons of tone and verbal economy only, I employ the expression, scholarship *boy*, throughout this essay. I do not intend to imply by its usage that the experiences I describe belong to or are the concern solely of male students.

father he learns to trust spontaneity and non-rational ways of knowing. *Then* at school there is mental calm; teachers emphasize the value of a reflectiveness which opens a space between thinking and immediate action.

It will require years of schooling for the boy to sketch the cultural differences as abstractly as this. But he senses those differences early. Perhaps as early as the night he brings home some assignment from school and finds the house too noisy for study.

> He has to be more and more alone, if he is going to "get on." He will have, probably unconsciously, to oppose the ethos of the hearth, the intense gregariousness of the working-class family group. Since everything centres upon the living room, there is unlikely to be a room of his own; the bedrooms are cold and inhospitable, and to warm them or the front room, if there is one, would not only be expensive, but would require an imaginative leap—out of the tradition—which most families are not capable of making. There is a corner of the living-room table. On the other side Mother is ironing, the wireless is on, someone is singing a snatch of song or Father says intermittently whatever comes into his head. The boy has to cut himself off mentally so as to do his homework as well as he can.[2]

The next day, the lesson is as apparent at school. There are even rows of desks. The boy must raise his hand (and rehearse his thoughts) before speaking in a loud voice to an audience of

---

[2]Richard Hoggart, *The Uses of Literacy* (London: Chatto and Windus, 1957), p. 241.

Argumentation

students he barely knows. And there is time enough and silence to think about ideas ("big ideas") never mentioned at home.

5   Not for the working-class child alone is adjustment to the classroom difficult. Schooling requires of any student alteration of childhood habits. But the working-class child is usually least prepared for the change. Unlike most middle-class children, moreover, he goes home and sees in his parents a way of life that is not only different, but starkly opposed to that of the classroom. They talk and act in precisely the ways his teachers discourage. Without his extraordinary determination and the great assistance of others—at home and at school—there is little chance for success. Typically, most working-class children are barely changed by the classroom. The exception succeeds. Only a few become scholarship students. Of these, Richard Hoggart estimates, most manage a fairly graceful transition. They somehow learn to live in the two very different worlds of their day. There are some others, however, those Hoggart terms scholarship boys, for whom success comes with awkwardness and guilt.

6   Scholarship boy: good student, troubled son. The child is "moderately endowed," intellectually mediocre, Hoggart suggests—though it may be more pertinent to note the special qualities of temperament in the boy. Here is a child haunted by the knowledge that one chooses to become a student. (It is not an inevitable or natural step in growing up.) And that, with the decision, he will separate himself from a life that he loves and even from his own memory of himself.

7   For a time, he wavers, balances allegiance. "The boy is himself (until he reaches, say, the upper forms) very much of *both* the worlds of home and school. He is enormously obedient to the dictates of the world of school, but emotionally still strongly wants to continue as part of the family circle" (p. 241). Gradually, because he needs to spend more time studying, his balance is lost. He must enclose himself in the "silence" permitted

and required by intense concentration. Thus, he takes the first step toward academic success. But a guilt sparks, flickers, then flares up within him. He cannot help feeling that he is rejecting the attractions of family life. (There is no logic here, only the great logic of the heart.)

From the very first days, through the years following, it will be with his parents—the figures of lost authority, the persons toward whom he still feels intense emotion—that the change will most powerfully be measured. A separation will unravel between him and them. Not the separation, "the generation gap," caused by a difference of age, but one that results from cultural factors. The former is capable of being shortened with time, when the child, grown older, comes to repeat the refrain of the newly adult: "I realize now what my parents knew. . . ." Age figures in the separation of the scholarship boy from his parents, but in an odder way. Advancing in his studies, the boy notices that his father and mother have not changed as much as he. Rather, as he sees them, they often remind him of the person he was once, and the life he earlier shared with them. In a way he realizes what Romantics also know when they praise the working-class for the capacity for human closeness, qualities of passion and spontaneity, that the rest of us share in like measure only in the earliest part of our youth. For Romantics, this doesn't make working-class life childish. Rather, it becomes challenging just because it is an *adult* way of life.

The scholarship boy reaches a different conclusion. He cannot afford to admire his parents. (How could he and still pursue such a contrary life?) He permits himself embarrassment at their lack of education. And to evade nostalgia for the life he has lost, he concentrates on the benefits education will give him. He becomes an especially ambitious student. "[The scholarship boy] tends to make a father-figure of his form master" (p. 243), Hoggart writes with the calm prose of the social scientist. His remark

8

9

only makes me remember with what urgency I *idolized* my teachers.

10   I began imitating their accents, using their diction, trusting their every direction. Any books they told me to read, I read—and then waited for them to tell me which books I enjoyed. I was awed by how much they knew. I copied their most casual opinions; I memorized all that they taught. I stayed after school and showed up on Saturdays in order "to help"—to get their attention. It was always their encouragement that mattered to me. *They* understood exactly what my achievements entailed. My memory clutched and caressed each word of praise they bestowed so that, still today, their compliments come quickly to mind.

11   I cannot forget either, though it is tempting to want to forget, some of the scenes at home which followed my resolution to seek academic success. During the crucial first months, the shy, docile, obedient student came home a shrill and precocious son—as though he needed to prove (to himself? to his parents?) that he had made the right choice. After a while, I developed quiet tact. I grew more calm. I became a conventionally dutiful son; politely affectionate; cheerful enough; even—for reasons beyond choosing—my father's favorite. And in many ways, much about my home life was easy, calm, comfortable, happy in the rhythm of the family's routine: the noises of radios and alarm clocks, the errands, the rituals of dinner and going to bed in flannel pyjamas.

12   But withheld from my parents was most of what deeply mattered to me; the extraordinary experience of my education. My father or mother would wonder: "What did you learn today?" Or say: "Tell us about your new courses." I would barely respond. "Just the usual things. . . ." (Silence. Silence!) In place of the sounds of intimacy which once flowed easily between us there was the silence. (The toll of my guilt and my loss.) After dinner, I would rush away to a bedroom with papers and books. As

often as possible I resisted parental pleas to "save lights" by coming to the kitchen to work. I kept so much, so often to myself. Sad. Guilty for the excitement of coming upon new ideas, new possibilities. Eager. Fascinated. I hoarded the pleasures of learning. Alone for hours. Enthralled. Afraid. Quiet (the house noisy), I rarely looked away from my books—or back on my memories. Times when relatives visited and the front rooms were warmed by Spanish sounds, I slipped out of the house.

It mattered that education was changing me. It never ceased   13
to matter. I would not have become a scholarship boy had it not mattered so much.

Walking to school with classmates sometimes, I would hear   14
them tell me that their parents read to them at night. Strange-sounding books like *Winnie the Pooh*. Immediately, I asked them: "What is it like?" But the question only confused my companions. So I learned to keep it to myself and silently imagined the scene of parent and child reading together.

One day—I must have been nine or ten years old at the time—   15
my mother asked for a "nice" book to read. ("Something not too hard that you think I might like.") Carefully, I chose one. I think it was Willa Cather's *My Antonia*. But when, several weeks later, I happened to see it next to her bed, unread except for the first few pages, I was furious with impatience. And then suddenly I wanted to cry, I grabbed up the book and took it back to my room.

"Why didn't you tell us about the award?" my mother scolded—   16
though her face was softened with pride. At the grammar school ceremony, some days later, I felt such contrary feelings. (There is no simple roadmap through the heart of the scholarship boy.) Nervously, I heard my father speak to my teacher and felt my familiar shame of his accent. Then guilty for the shame. My instructor was so soft-spoken and her words were edged clear. I

Argumentation

admired her until it seemed to me that she spoke too carefully. Sensing that she was condescending to them, I was suddenly resentful. Protective. I tried to move my parents away. "You must both be so proud of him," she said. They quickly answered in the affirmative. They were proud. "We are proud of all our children." Then, this afterthought: "They sure didn't get their brains from us." I smiled. The three of them laughed.

17   But tightening the irony into a knot was the knowledge that my parents were always behind me. In many ways, they made academic success possible. They evened the path. They sent their children to parochial schools because "the nuns teach better." They paid a tuition they couldn't afford. They spoke English at home. ("¡Hablanos en English!")Their voices united to urge me past my initial resistance to the classroom. They always wanted for my brothers and me the chances they never had.

18   It saddened my mother to learn about Mexican-American parents who wanted their children to start working after finishing high school. In schooling she recognized the key to job advancement. And she remembered her past. As a girl, new to America, she had been awarded a diploma by high school teachers too busy or careless to notice that she hardly spoke English. On her own she determined to learn to type. That skill got her clean office jobs and encouraged an optimism about the possibility of advancement. (Each morning when her sisters put on uniforms for work, she chose a bright-colored dress.) She became an excellent speller—of words she mispronounced. ("And I've never been to college," she would say smiling when her children asked about a word they didn't want to look up in a dictionary.)

19   When her youngest child started going to high school, my mother found full-time employment. She worked for the (California) state government, in civil service positions, positions carefully numbered and acquired by examinations. The old ambition

of her youth was still bright then. She consulted bulletin boards for news of new jobs, possible advancement. Then one day saw mention of something called an "anti-poverty agency." A typing job. A glamorous job—part of the governor's staff. ("A knowledge of Spanish desired.") She applied without hesitation and grew nervous only when the job was suddenly hers.

"Everyone comes to work all dressed up," she reported at 20 night. And didn't need to say more than that her co-workers wouldn't let her answer the phone. She was only a typist. Though a fast typist. And an excellent speller. There was a letter one day to be sent to a Washington cabinet officer. On the dictating tape my mother heard mention of "urban guerillas." She typed (the wrong word, correctly): "gorillas." Everyone was shocked. The mistake horrified the anti-poverty bureaucrats who, several days later, returned her to her previous position. She would go no further. She willed her ambition to her children.

After one of her daughters got a job ironing for some rich 21 people we knew, my mother was nervous with fear. ("I don't want you wearing a uniform.") Another summer, when I came home from college, she refused to let me work as a gardener. "You can do much better than that," she insisted. "You've got too much education now." I complied with her wish, though I really didn't think of schooling as job-training. It's true that I planned by that time to become a teacher, but it wasn't an occupation I aimed for as much as something more elusive and indefinite: I wanted to know as much as my teachers; to possess their confidence and authority; even to assume a professor's persona.

For my father, education had a value different from that it had 22 for my mother. He chuckled when I claimed to be tired by reading and writing. It wasn't real work I did, he would say. "You'll never know what real work is." His comment would recall in my mind his youth. Orphaned when he was eight, he began working after two years in school. He came to America in his twenties, dreaming of returning to school and becoming an engineer. ("Work for my hands and my head.") But there was no money and too little energy at the end of a day for more than occasional night-school courses in English and arithmetic. Days were spent in factories. He no longer expected ever to become an engineer. And he grew pessimistic about the ultimate meaning of work or the possibility of ever escaping its claims. ("But look at all you've accomplished," his best friend once said to him. My father said nothing, and only smiled weakly.)

23   But I would see him looking at me with opened-mouth curiosity sometimes when I glanced up from my books. Other times, I would come upon him in my bedroom, standing at my desk or bookshelves, fingering the covers of books, opening them to read a few lines. He seemed aware at such moments of some remarkable possibility implied by academic activity. (Its leisure? Its splendid uselessness?) At the moment our eyes met, we each looked quickly away and never spoke.

24   Such memories as these slammed together in the instant of hearing that familiar refrain (all scholarship boys hear) from strangers and friends: 'Your parents must be so proud." Yes, my parents were happy at my success. They also were proud. The night of the awards ceremony my mother's eyes were brighter than the trophy I won. Pushing back the hair from my forehead, she whispered that I had "shown" the *gringos*. Years later, my father would wonder why I never displayed my awards and diplomas. He said that he liked to go to doctors' offices and notice the schools they had attended. My awards got left in closets. The golden figure atop a trophy was broken, wingless, after hitting the ground. Medals were put into a jar. My father found my high school diploma when it was about to be thrown out with the trash. He kept it afterwards with his own things.

25   "We are proud of all of our children."

The Handbook

Note to the Writer

You are fortunate if you have an instructor or an editor or a knowledgeable friend who will read what you have written and call attention to the strengths and weaknesses of your prose by writing comments in the margin or at the end of your paper. Comments of that sort, especially when they are judicious and constructive, can be of great help to you in improving your writing. You should value those personal notes, and whenever the correction, question, suggestion, praise, or blame in them strikes you as being well grounded, you would do well to heed it.

To call attention, however, to routine matters of grammar, style, paragraphing, punctuation, or mechanics, your accommodating critic may resort to some kind of shorthand notations. If he knows that you have a copy of this handbook, he may underline or encircle something in your manuscript and write a number in the margin. If, for instance, he scribbles the number 83 in the margin, he is suggesting that you look at item **83** in the section on mechanics. Turning to this item in the handbook, you will find that it has to do with italicizing certain kinds of titles. Perhaps you failed to italicize the title of a book you mentioned, or perhaps instead of italicizing the title of the book, you enclosed it in quotation

Note to the Writer

marks. The principle stated opposite the number **83** may be all that you need to read. But if you need further enlightenment about what you have done wrong, you can look at the graphic diagram of the structure involved (if one is presented for that principle) or at the examples printed below the principle, or you can go on to read the explanation of the principle.

For more complicated matters, the explanation in the handbook may not be sufficient to point out what you have done wrong or to prevent you from making the mistake again. If so, you should arrange to have a conference with the critic of your prose. Although the correction symbols in the margin may strike you as being heartlessly impersonal, it would be a mistake for you to regard them as petulant slaps on the wrist. They are intended to help you discover how to put your written prose in the "proper" form.

This handbook is also intended to serve as a guide to the writer who does not have an instructor or a friend to read and criticize what he has written. Usually, once a writer has completed a Freshman English course or an advanced composition course of some kind, he no longer enjoys the advantage of frequent, expert criticism of his prose. (If he does, he probably has to pay for the service.) If kept at hand, along with such other reference books as a dictionary and a thesaurus, this handbook can be a useful guide for the writer when he sits down to write something that he wants others to read. The reference charts on the endpages will direct him to the section that deals with his particular problem of the moment. For example, "Should the modifying clause in this sentence be enclosed with commas?" Somewhere in its pages, the handbook probably provides a straightforward answer to that query.

Legend

Some of the conventions presented in this handbook, especially those having to do with punctuation, are illustrated with graphic models using these symbols:

1

☐ = word

A word inside the box designates a particular part of speech, e.g. noun

2

_____ = phrase

The following abbreviations on the horizontal line designate a particular kind of phrase, e.g. _prep._.

prep. = prepositional phrase (**on the bus**)
part. = participial phrase (**having ridden on the bus**)
ger. = gerund phrase (**riding on the bus** pleased him)
inf. = infinitive phrase (he wanted to **ride on the bus**)

Legend

3

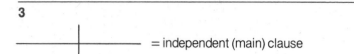 = independent (main) clause

An independent clause, sometimes referred to as a main clause, can stand by itself as a grammatically complete sentence, e.g. **He rode on the bus.**
The vertical line indicates the separation of subject from predicate.

4

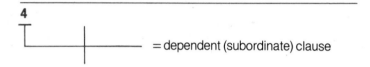 = dependent (subordinate) clause

A dependent clause, sometimes referred to as a subordinate clause, cannot stand by itself as a grammatically complete sentence. The following abbreviations printed above the first vertical line designate a particular kind of dependent clause, e.g.

noun

 = dependent (subordinate) noun clause

   noun = noun clause (He claimed **that he rode on the bus.**)
   adj. = adjective clause (The man **who rode on the bus** was pleased.)
   adv. = adverb clause (He was late **because he rode on the bus.**)

If the examples provided above do not give you a clear enough idea of the difference between a *clause* and a *phrase* or between an *independent clause* and a *dependent clause*, perhaps the following fuller explanation will be helpful.

What a clause and a phrase have in common is that they are made up of two or more words. Not every group of two or more words, however, constitutes a phrase or a clause. The group of words must make some sense to native speakers of the language. For instance, the group of words **the big red balloon** qualifies as a phrase because it is a string of two or more words that presents an intelligible thought unit in the English language. The group of words **red the balloon big** does not qualify as a phrase, however, because it does not make sense, does not present a recognizable thought unit in English. Note that all the examples of phrases and clauses are made up of two or more words that make sense—e.g. **on the bus, to ride on the bus, he rode on the bus, because he rode on the bus**.

The difference between a clause and a phrase is that whereas a clause has both a *subject* (usually a noun or pronoun) and a *predicate* (a finite verb—that is, a verb that is fixed, by its form, in regard to person, number, and tense), a phrase lacks a subject and a predicate. In the examples above, the two groups of words **he rode on the bus** and **because he rode on the bus** both qualify as clauses because they have a subject (the pronoun **he**) and a predicate (the finite verb **rode**). The group of words **on the bus**, however, does not qualify as a clause because it lacks both a subject and a predicate. Note that none of the above groups of boldfaced words marked with the abbreviations *prep., part., ger.,* and *inf.* has a subject or a predicate.

In order to consistently write complete sentences and to punctuate them properly, a writer must have a firm understanding of the difference not only between a phrase and a clause but also between an independent clause and a dependent

Legend

clause. Having noted the difference between a clause and a phrase, let us now look at the difference between an independent clause and a dependent clause.

What an independent clause and a dependent clause have in common is that somewhere in the group of words, there is a subject and a predicate (a finite verb). We call the two groups of words **he rode on the bus** and **that he rode on the bus** clauses because in the string of words we can find a word that serves as a subject (**he**) and a word that serves as a predicate (**rode**). We can change the subject or the predicate, but as long as we retain both a subject and a predicate, we still have a clause. The following groups of words all qualify as clauses because they have a subject and a predicate:

He rides on the bus.

The **man rode** on the bus.

My **aunt was riding** on the bus.

Amy Pearson has ridden on the bus.

Have you ever **ridden** on a bus?

John Morris said that **he had ridden** on a bus.

Now let us consider the crucial difference between an independent clause and a dependent clause. As its name implies, an independent clause can stand by itself. A dependent clause cannot stand by itself. We can put an independent clause down on paper with an initial capital letter and a period at the end—e.g. **His mother rode on the bus.**—and have a sentence. But simply by adding some subordinating word to the front end of that group of words, we change it from an independent clause to a dependent one—**when his mother rode on the bus.** By adding the subordinating conjunction *when*, we make this group of words *depend* on an independent clause for its completion—e.g. **When his mother rode on the bus, the axle broke.** Adding any subordinating conjunction, (*because, if, although, etc.*) to the front end of a clause or substituting a relative pronoun (*who, which, that*) for the subject word will "cripple" the clause and make it dependent for "support" on an independent (main) clause:

> if his mother rode the bus
> because his mother rode the bus
> after his mother rode the bus
> that his mother rode the bus
> who rode the bus
> which rode the bus

If you read those strings of words aloud, you sense that they are not completed or finished. (You would not drop your voice at the end of the string, as you would in reading this string aloud: **His daring, adventuresome mother intrepidly rode the bus on the narrow mountain roads.**) In writing those strings of words, you would not begin them with a capital letter or terminate them with a period.

Format of Manuscript

In preparing the final draft of a manuscript, follow the specific directions about format given by your instructor or editor. However, if no specific directions are given, you can be confident that the format of your manuscript will be acceptable if you observe the following conventions:

10

Write on one side of the paper only.

11

Double-space the lines of prose, whether you handwrite or typewrite.

A manuscript submitted to an editor for consideration must be typewritten and double-spaced.

12

Preserve a left-hand and a right-hand margin.

On the left-hand side, leave at least a 1½-inch margin. On the right-hand side, try to preserve about a 1-inch margin. If you are handwriting your manuscript on theme paper, the vertical red line will set your left-hand margin. Try to leave an inch of space between the last line and the bottom edge of the page.

13

Put the title of your paper at the top of the first page of your manuscript—even though you may have put the title on a cover sheet.

See **84** for instructions about how to set down the title of your paper.

14

Number all pages, except the first one (which is never numbered), at the top of the page—either in the middle or at the right-hand margin.

Be sure to assemble the pages of your manuscript in the right sequence.

15

Secure your manuscript with a paper clip—*never* with a staple or pin.

Many editors will not even read a manuscript that is stapled together.

16

Use the proper kind of paper.

If you typewrite your manuscript, use white, unlined, opaque paper. If you handwrite your manuscript, use white, lined theme paper. Never submit a formal written assignment on pages torn from a spiral notebook.

Grammar

Grammar may be defined as the study of how a language "works"—a study of how the structural system of a language combines with a vocabulary to convey meaning. When we study a foreign language in school, we must study both **vocabulary** and **grammar,** and until we can put the two together, we cannot translate the language. Sometimes we know the meaning of every word in a foreign-language sentence, and yet we cannot translate the sentence because we cannot figure out its grammar. On the other hand, we sometimes can figure out the grammar of the foreign-language sentence, but because we do not know the meaning of one or more words in the sentence, we still cannot translate the sentence.

If native speakers of English heard or read this sequence of words

> The porturbs in the brigger torms have tanted the makrets' rotment brokly.

they would perceive that the sequence bears a marked resemblance to an English sentence. Although many words in that sequence would be unfamiliar to them, they would detect that the sequence had the structure of the kind of English sentence that

Grammar

makes a statement, and they might further surmise that this kind of statement pattern was one that said that *porturbs* (whoever they are) had done something to *rotment* (whatever that is), or, to put it another way, that *porturbs* was the subject of the sentence, that *have tanted* was the predicate verb, and that *rotment* was the object of that verb, the receiver of the action performed by the doer, *porturbs*. How were they able to make that much "sense" out of that sequence of strange words? They were able to detect that much sense by noting the following structural signals:

☐ **Function words:**

The three occurrences of the article **the,** the preposition **in,** and the auxiliary verb **have.**

☐ **Inflections and affixes:**

The **-s** added to nouns to form the plural, the **-er** added to adjectives to form the comparative degree, the **-ed** added to verbs to form the past tense or the past participle, the **-s'** added to nouns to form the plural possessive case, the affix **-ment** added to certain words to form an abstract noun, and the **-ly** added to adjectives to form adverbs.

☐ **Word order:**

The basic pattern of a statement or declarative sentence in English is S (subject) + V (verb) + C (complement) or NP (noun phrase) + VP (verb phrase). In the sequence, **The porturbs in the brigger torms** appears to be the S or NP part of the sentence and **have tanted the makrets' rotment brokly** the VP part of the sentence (**have tanted** being the V and **the makrets' rotment brokly** being the C).

☐ **Intonation (stress, pitch, and juncture):**

If the sequence were spoken aloud, native speakers would detect that the sequence had the intonational pattern of a declarative sentence in spoken English.

Punctuation and mechanics:

If the sequence were written out (as it is here), native speakers would observe that it began with a capital letter and ended with a period, two typographical devices that signal a statement in written English.

Native speakers of English would be able to read a relational sense or structural meaning into the string of nonsense words simply by observing the grammatical devices of **inflections, function words, word order,** and **intonation** (if spoken) or **punctuation** (if written). Now, if they had a dictionary that defined such words as **porturb, brig, torm, tant, makret, rotment,** and **brok,** they would be able to translate the full meaning of the sentence. But by observing the structural or grammatical devices alone, native speakers of English could perceive that the sequence of words

The porturbs in the brigger forms have tanted the makrets' rotment brokly.

exactly matches the structure of an English sentence like this one:

The citizens in the larger towns have accepted the legislators' commitment enthusiastically.

What they have been concentrating on is the *grammar* of the sentence, and it is in this structural sense that we use the term *grammar* in the section that follows.

Most children master the fundamentals of this grammatical system of English by the time they begin school. They "master" grammar in the sense that they can form original and meaningful English sentences of their own and can understand English sentences uttered by others. They may not "know" grammar in the sense that they can analyze the structure of sentences and label the parts, but they know grammar in the sense that they

Grammar

can *perform appropriately* in the language—that is, that they can utter, and respond to, properly formed sentences.

The grammar of a language is, for the most part, a convention. We form sentences in a certain way because communities of native speakers of the language, over a long period of time, have developed, and tacitly agreed on, certain ways of saying something. The grammar of a language allows some choices but proscribes others. For instance, if you wanted to tell someone that a certain lawyer scolded a certain defendant in a certain manner, English grammar would allow you to choose from these patterns:

The lawyer scolded the defendant vehemently.

The lawyer vehemently scolded the defendant.

Vehemently the lawyer scolded the defendant.

The defendant was vehemently scolded by the lawyer.

English grammar would not allow you to use one of these patterns:

The vehemently lawyer the defendant scolded.

Scolded lawyer the vehemently defendant the.

The defendant scolded the lawyer vehemently.

(*This last sentence is grammatical, but because of the altered word order, it does not say what you wanted it to say. Here the defendant is the doer of the action, and the lawyer is the receiver of the action—the exact opposite of your meaning.*)

The choice of which grammatically acceptable pattern a writer will use is a concern of style, which will be dealt with in the next section.

In this section on grammar, we are dealing with those devices of *inflection, function words,* and *word order* that make it possible for written sentences to convey to readers, clearly and unmistakably, a writer's intended meaning. We are not concerned here with *intonation*, because this handbook deals only with the written language. In a later section, we shall consider the fourth grammatical device of written English, *punctuation*.

20

Use an apostrophe for the possessive case of the noun.

Here are some guidelines on forming the possessive case of the English noun:

(a) As the diagrams above indicate, most English nouns form the possessive case with **'s** (singular) or **s'** (plural). An alternative form of the possessive case consists of an **of** phrase: **the commands of the general** (instead of **the general's commands**).

(b) Nouns that form their plural in ways other than by adding an **s** form their possessive in the plural by adding **'s** to the plural of the noun: **woman's/women's, man's/men's, child's/children's, ox's/oxen's, deer's/deer's, mouse's/mice's**.

(c) Some writers simply add an apostrophe to form the possessive case of nouns ending in **s**:

the goddess' fame

the alumnus' contribution

Grammar

Keats' odes

Dickens' novels

However, other writers add the usual **'s** to form the possessive case of such nouns: **goddess's, alumnus's** (plural **alumni's**), **Keats's, Dickens's.** Take your choice, but be consistent.

(d) The rules for forming the possessive case of pairs of nouns are as follows: (1) in the case of *joint* possession, add **'s** only to the second member of the pair: **John and Mary's mother, the brother and sister's car,** and (2) in the case of *individual* possession, add **'s** to each member of the pair: **the boy's and girl's bedrooms, John's and Mary's tennis rackets, the men's and women's locker rooms**.

(e) Form the possessive case of group nouns or compound nouns by adding **'s** to the end of the unit: **commander in chief's, someone else's, president-elect's, editor in chief's, son-in-law's**. In the case of those compounds that form their plural by adding **s** to the first word, form the plural possessive case by adding **'s** to the end of the unit: **editors in chief's, sons-in-law's**.

(f) Normally the **'s** or **s'** is reserved for the possessive case of nouns naming animate creatures (human beings and animals). The **of** phrase is commonly used for the possessive case of inanimate nouns: not **the house's roof** but **the roof of the house**. Usage, however, now sanctions the use of **'s** with some inanimate nouns: **a day's wages, a week's work, the year's death toll, the school's policies, the car's performance, the radio's tone**.

21

Its is the possessive case of the pronoun it; it's is the contraction of it is or it has.

More mistakes have been made with the pronoun **it** than with any other single word in the English language. The mistakes result from confusion about the two **s** forms of this pronoun. **It's** is often used where **its** is the correct form (**The dog broke it's leg** instead of the correct form, **The dog broke its leg**), and **its** is often used where **it's** is the correct form (**Its a shame that the girl broke her leg** instead of the correct form, **It's a shame that the girl broke her leg**).

Those who use **it's** for the possessive case of **it** are probably influenced by the **'s** that is used to form the possessive case of the singular noun (**man's hat**). They might be helped to avoid this mistake if they were reminded that *none of the personal pronouns uses 's to form its possessive case*: **I/my, you/your, he/his, she/her, it/its, we/our, they/their**. So they should write, **The company lost its lease**.

Writers might also be helped to avoid this mistake if they would remember that the apostrophe has another function in written English: to indicate the omission of one or more letters in an English word, as in contractions (**I'll, don't, she'd**). The apostrophe in the word **it's** signals the contraction of the expression **it is** or **it has**. So they should write, **It's the first loss that the company has suffered** or **It's come to my attention that you are frequently late**.

Don't let this little word defeat you. Get **it** right, once and for all.

Grammar

22

The predicate verb should agree in number with its subject.

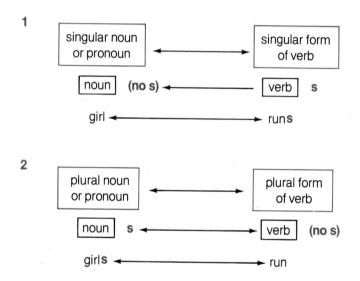

Some typical examples of faulty agreement:

1 He **don't care** about anything.

2 The lawyer and his/her client **agrees** on a fee.

3 If any one of the substations **are knocked** out, we can resort to reserve stations.

4 The jury **has made** up their minds.

5 He finds it impossible to live with the ignorance, injustice, poverty, and prejudice that **surrounds** him.

6 Neither the gambler nor Jake **are** really bitter about his bad luck or **blame** anyone for his misfortunes.

22 Subject/Verb Agreement

In addition to such differentiated forms of the verb in the third person, present tense as **run** and **runs,** we have to be concerned about the few differentiated forms of the verb **to be (am/is/are; was/were)** and of auxiliary verbs **(has/have; does/do).**

The English verb has been evolving toward a single form for the singular and plural of all three persons (first, second, third)—as witness the **-ed** ending added to the verb in all three persons, singular and plural, of the past tense—and we may yet live to see the day when a totally simplified form of the English verb is achieved. Meanwhile, the few remaining differentiated forms of the verb will probably continue to give writers some trouble.

Expressions like **He don't care about anything** are not so much "mistakes" in agreement as carry-overs from the dialect that people speak, quite acceptably, in their own communities. Such people should be made aware of the standard form of the verb in written prose: **He doesn't care about anything** (a singular verb with a singular subject).

Most errors of agreement in written prose are the result of carelessness, inadvertence, or uncertainty. The writer often knows better but merely slips up. Errors in agreement often occur when several words intervene between the simple subject of the sentence and the predicate verb, as in sentence : **If any one of the substations are knocked out**. . . . The simple subject of the **if** clause here is **one,** but because the plural noun **substations** (the object of the preposition **of**) intervened between that singular subject and the verb, the writer was influenced to use the plural form of the verb **(are knocked out)** instead of the correct singular form **(is knocked out).** Careful proofreading will often catch such inadvertent errors of agreement.

Errors due to uncertainty are another matter. Uncertainty

Grammar

about whether the verb should be singular or plural arises in cases where (1) the subject is compound, (2) the subject is a collective noun, (3) the subject of the sentence follows the structure **there is/there are**, and (4) the subject takes the form of structures like **one of those who** and **this man as well as.** Here are some guidelines for these puzzling cases:

(a) Compound subject

(1) Singular subjects joined by **and** usually take a plural verb.

John and his sister **were questioned** by the police.

(2) Singular subjects joined by **or** or by the correlative conjunctions **either** . . . **or, neither** . . . **nor** take a singular verb.

John or his sister **runs** the store during the week.

Neither the gambler nor Jake **is** really bitter about his bad luck or **blames** anyone for his misfortunes.

(3) When both subjects are plural, the verb is plural.

The detectives and the insurance agents **have expressed** their belief in the innocence of the brother and sister.

Neither the detectives nor the insurance agents **have expressed** any doubts about the innocence of the brother and sister.

(4) When one subject is singular and the other subject is plural and the subjects are joined by **or** or by the correlative conjunctions **either . . . or, neither . . . nor,** the verb agrees in number with the closest subject.

Either John or his parents **have agreed** to cooperate with the police.

Neither the brothers nor the sister **appears** to be cooperative.

However, plural or singular subjects joined by the correlative conjunctions **both** . . . **and** or **not only** . . . **but (also)** take a plural verb.

> Both John and his sister **have agreed** to cooperate with the police.
>
> Not only the brother but also the sister **appear** to be cooperative.

(b) Collective noun as subject

(1) If the collective noun is considered as a **group,** the verb is singular.

> The jury **has made up** its mind.
>
> The committee **was elected** unanimously.
>
> The number of students who failed **has increased** by 50 percent.

(2) If the collective noun is considered as **individuals,** each acting on his or her own, the verb is plural.

> The jury **have made up** their minds.
>
> The committee **wish** to offer their congratulations to the new chairperson.
>
> A number of students **have asked** the dean for an extension.

(c) The structure **there is/are, there was/were**

(1) If the delayed or real subject following **there** is singular, the verb is singular.

> There **is** a remarkable consensus among the committee members.

(2) If the delayed or real subject following **there** is plural, the verb is plural.

> There **were** ten dissenting votes from the stockholders.

(d) Special structures

(1) In the structure **one of the** [plural noun] **who,** the predicate verb of the **who** clause is plural, because the antecedent of the subject **who** is the plural noun rather than the singular **one.**

> Matilda is one of the women who **refuse** to accept the ruling.
>
> (*here the antecedent of* **who** *is the plural noun* **women**)

(2) Exception: if **the only** precedes **one of the** [plural noun] **who,** the predicate verb of the **who** clause is singular, because the subject **who** in that case refers to the singular **one** rather than to the plural object of the preposition **of.**

> Matilda is the only one of the women who **refuses** to accept the ruling.

(3) A singular subject followed by structures like **as well as, in addition to, together with** takes a singular verb.

(A plural subject, of course, followed by any of these structures, would take a plural verb. See the third example below.)

> The sergeant as well as his superior officers **praises** his platoon.
>
> Linda Myers along with her roommate **has denied** the charges.
>
> The students together with their counselor **deny** that there has been any distribution of drugs in the dorms.

(4) Nouns that do not end in *s* but that are plural in meaning take a plural verb.

> The bacteria **require** constant attention.
>
> These data **are** consistent with the judge's findings.
>
> The deer **are running** loose in the state park.

(5) Nouns that end in *s* but that are singular in meaning take a singular verb.

> My grandmother's scissors **was** very dull.

Ten dollars **is** a fair price for the coat.

Two weeks **seems** a long time when you are waiting for someone you love.

(6) Noun clauses serving as the subject of the sentence always take a singular verb.

That Sara decided to go to college **pleases** me very much.

What caused the accident **was** two stones in the road.

(7) In inverted structures, where the subject follows the verb, a singular subject takes a singular verb, and a plural subject takes a plural verb.

At each checkpoint **stands** a heavily armed soldier.

Happy **were** they to see us arrive.

Among the crew **were** Carson, Barton, and Farmon.

Here are the corrected versions of all the sample sentences:

1 He **doesn't care** about anything.
2 The lawyer and her client **agree** on a fee.
3 If any one of the substations **is knocked** out, we can resort to reserve stations.
4 The jury **have made** up their minds.
5 He finds it impossible to live with the ignorance, injustice, poverty, and prejudice that **surround** him.
6 Neither the gambler nor Jake **is** really bitter about his bad luck or **blames** anyone for his misfortunes.

Grammar

23

A pronoun must agree in person, number, and gender with its antecedent noun.

Examples of faulty agreement between a pronoun and its antecedent:

1 A **family** cannot go camping these days without a truckload of gadgets to make **your** campsite look just like home.

2 The woman threw some floatable **items** overboard for the sailor, even though she knew that **it** would probably not save him.

3 The **university** did not live up to **his** promise to the students.

4 The **student** should bring **his** schedule cards to the bursar's office.

Pronouns, which are substitutes for nouns, share the following features with nouns: **number** (singular or plural) and **gender** (masculine or feminine or neuter). What nouns and pronouns do not share in common is the full range of **person.** All nouns are **third person** exclusively; but some pronouns are **first person (I, we),** some are **second person (you),** and some are **third person (he, she, it, they, one, some, none, all, everybody).**

A firm grammatical principle is that a pronoun must correspond with whatever features of person, number, and gender it has in common with its antecedent noun. A second-person pronoun should not be linked with a third-person noun (see sentence **1**). A singular pronoun should not be linked with a plural noun (see sentence **2**). A masculine pronoun should not be linked with a neuter noun (see sentence **3**).

Sentence **4** is not so much an instance of faulty agreement as it is an instance of *inappropriate* agreement. The problem in that example stems from the fact that the English language has no convenient pronoun for indicating masculine-*or*-feminine gender. It has been a common practice in the past to use the generic he **(him, his)** to refer to nouns of common gender like *student, teacher, writer, candidate, driver.* In recent years, however, the use of generic *he* and its derivative forms **(his, him)** to refer to singular nouns that could be either masculine or feminine has been considered an example of the sexist bias of the English language. Many writers today are making a genuine effort to avoid offending readers with any kind of sexist language.

How does one deal with the agreement problem exhibited in sentence **4**? One way is to resort to the use of an admittedly awkward pronoun form like **his or her, his/her,** or **his (her),** as in the following sentence: "The **student** should bring **his or her** schedule cards to the bursar's office." Another way is to use a plural noun wherever possible: "**Students** should bring **their** schedule cards to the bursar's office." In some cases, it is possible to reword the sentence so that no pronoun has to be used, as in this revision: "The **student** should bring all schedule cards to the bursar's office."

Mismatchings of nouns and pronouns in person and gender are not very common in written prose. Most mismatchings of nouns and pronouns involve number—a singular pronoun referring to a plural noun (**items. . . it,** as in sentence **2**) or a plural pronoun referring to a singular noun (**student . . . their**). Another agreement problem derives from the ambiguity of number of such pronouns as **everyone, everybody, all, none, some, each.** Although there are exceptions, the following guidelines are generally reliable:

(a) **Everyone, everybody, anybody, anyone** invariably takes singular verbs and, in formal usage at least, should be referred to by a singular pronoun.

Grammar

Everyone brings **his or her** schedule cards to the bursar's office.

Anybody who wants to run in the race has to pay **her** entry fee by Friday.

(b) **All** and **some** are singular or plural according to the context. If the **of** phrase following the pronoun specifies a *mass* or a *bulk* of something, the pronoun is singular. If the **of** phrase specifies a *number* of things or persons, the pronoun is plural.

Some of the fabric lost **its** coloring.

All of the sugar was spoiled by **its** own chemical imbalance.

Some of the students complained about **their** dormitory rooms.

All of the women registered **their** protests at City Hall.

(c) **None** is singular or plural according to the context. (The distinction in particular cases is sometimes so subtle that a writer could justify either a singular or a plural pronoun.)

None of the young men **was** willing to turn in **his** driver's license. (*but* **were ... their** *could also be justified in this case*)

None of the young men in the hall **were** as tall as **their** fathers. (*here it would be harder to justify the singular forms* **was. . . his**)

(d) **Each** is almost invariably singular.

Each of them declared **her** allegiance to democracy.

(e) For guidelines about the **number** of collective nouns, see **(b)** in the previous section **(22)**

Here are corrected versions of the sample sentences:

1 A family cannot go camping these days without a truckload of gadgets to make **their** [or **its**] campsite look just like home.

2 The woman threw some floatable items overboard for the sailor, even though she knew that **they** would probably not save him.

3 The university did not live up to **its** promise to the students.

4 Students should bring **their** schedule cards to the bursar's office.

If you match up your pronouns in person, number, and gender with their antecedent nouns, you will make it easier for your reader to figure out what the pronouns refer to.

24

A pronoun should have a clear antecedent.

?.... pronoun

Examples of no antecedent or an unclear antecedent for the pronoun:

1 Mayor Worthington, acting on the advice of her physician, resigned her office, and the city council, responding to a mandate from the voters, was swift to accept **it**

   (what did the council accept?)

2 John told his father that **his** car wouldn't start.

   (whose car? the father's or John's?)

3 I decided to break the engagement with my girlfriend, **which** distressed my parents very much.

   (just what was it that distressed your parents?)

4 The league's first major step was to sponsor a cleanup day, but **it** could not enlist enough volunteers.

   (a pronoun should not refer to a noun functioning as a possessive or as a modifier—here **league's**)

5 I enjoyed the sun and the sand and the surf, and **this** revealed to me that I really prefer a vacation at the beach.

   (what does **this** refer to?)

Careless handling of the pronoun often blocks communication between writer and reader. The writer always knows what he or she meant the pronoun to stand for, but if there is no antecedent (a noun in the previous group of words to which the pronoun

Grammar

can refer) or if it is difficult to find the antecedent (the noun) to which the pronoun refers, the reader will not know—and will have to guess—what the pronoun stands for.

A good piece of advice for apprentice writers is that whenever they use a pronoun, they should check to see whether there is a noun in the previous group of words that they could put in the place of the pronoun. Let's apply this test to sentence 1. There are three neuter, singular nouns to which the final pronoun **it** could refer: **advice, office, mandate.** But when we put each of these nouns, successively, in the place of the **it**, we see that none of them names what the council accepted. If we pondered the sentence long enough, we might eventually figure out that what the council accepted was the mayor's *resignation*. But since the noun *resignation* appears nowhere in the sentence, the writer must use the noun phrase **his resignation** instead of the pronoun **it.**

Sentence **2** is an example of an unclear antecedent. The pronoun reference is unclear because the pronoun **his** is ambiguous—that is, there are two nouns to which the masculine, singular pronoun **his** could refer: **John** and **father**. So we cannot tell whether it was the father's car or John's car that wouldn't start. If the context in which that sentence occurred did not help us determine whose car was being referred to, the writer could avoid the ambiguity by turning the sentence into a direct quotation: either **John told his father, "Your car won't start"** or **John told his father, "My car won't start."**

The use of the pronoun **this** or **that** to refer to a whole idea in a previous clause or sentence has long been a common practice in spoken English, and it is now becoming common in written English as well. Although the practice is gaining the approval of usage, writers should be aware that by using the demonstrative pronoun **this** or **that** to refer to a whole idea in the previous clause or sentence, they run the risk that the reference of the pronoun will be vague or ambiguous for their read-ers. If they do not want to run that risk, they can use **this** or **that** (or the corresponding plural, **these** or **those**) as an adjective in-stead of as a pronoun. The adjective would go before some noun summing up what **this** or **that** stands for. The writer of sentence **5** could avoid the vague pronoun reference by phras-ing the sentence in this fashion: "I enjoyed the sun and the sand and the surf, and **this experience** revealed to me that I really prefer a vacation at the beach."

The use of the relative pronoun **which** or **that** to refer to a whole idea in the main clause rather than to a specific noun in that clause is also becoming more common. But there is a risk in this use similar to the one that attends the use of **this** or **that** to refer to a whole idea. The writer who worries about whether the reader will be even momentarily baffled by the **which** in a sentence like **3** will supply a summary noun to serve as the an-tecedent for that relative pronoun: "I decided to break the en-gagement with my girlfriend, a **decision which** distressed my parents very much."

The problem with the pronoun reference in sentence **4** stems from the linguistic fact that a pronoun does not readily reveal its antecedent if it refers to a noun that is functioning in a subordinate structure such as a possessive (the **school's** prin-cipal), a modifier of a noun (the **school** term), or an object of a preposition (in the **school**). One remedy for the vague pronoun reference in sentence **4** is to use the noun **league** rather than the pronoun **it**: ". . . but the **league** could not enlist enough vol-unteers." Another remedy is to make **league** the subject of the first clause so that the **it** in the second clause would have an antecedent: "The **league** took as its first major step the spon-sorship of a cleanup day, but **it** could not enlist enough volun-teers."

25

An introductory verbal or verbal phrase must find its "doer" in the subject of the main clause.

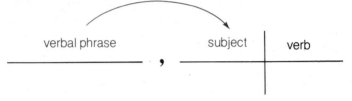

verbal phrase		subject	verb

Examples of "dangling" verbal phrases:

1 Revolving at a rate of 2200 revolutions per minute, the janitor turned off the overheated generator.

2 By stressing positive action, her inferiority complex can be eliminated.

3 Refusing to be inducted into the army, the World Boxing Association stripped Muhammad Ali of his title.

4 To pass the examinations, it is necessary for us to study diligently.

In English, an introductory verbal phrase (dominated by a participle, a gerund, or an infinitive) naturally adheres to the subject of the main clause. When the subject of the main clause is not the "doer" of the action indicated in the verbal, we say that the verbal **dangles**—that it is not attached to the proper agent. In each of the sentences above, the subject of the main clause is not the "doer" of the action specified by the introductory verbal (**revolving, stressing, refusing, to pass**).

To prevent dangling verbals, writers should make sure that the subject of the main clause is the doer of the action specified in the preceding verbal. If the authors of the sample sentences above had observed this caution, they would have revised their sentences to read as follows:

1 Revolving at the rate of 2200 revolutions per minute, the overheated generator was turned off by the janitor. **OR:** The janitor turned off the overheated generator, which was revolving at a rate of 2200 revolutions per minute.

2 By stressing positive action, she can eliminate her inferiority complex.

3 Refusing to be inducted into the army, Muhammad Ali was stripped of his title by the World Boxing Association. **OR:** The World Boxing Association stripped Muhammad Ali of his title for refusing to be inducted into the army.

4 To pass the examinations, we must study diligently.

Sometimes in revising our sentence to make the subject of the main clause the doer of the action specified in our introductory verbal, we have to resort to a rather awkward passive verb, as we did in revisions **1** and **3** above. In such cases, we may decide to recast the sentence so that it doesn't begin with a verbal phrase.

26

Misplaced modifiers lead to a misreading of the sentence.

Examples of misplaced modifiers:

1 Anyone who reads a newspaper **frequently** will notice that many people are now concerned about pollution.

2 He has **only** a face that a mother could love.

3 Matilda **even** smiles when she is sleeping.

4 The judge explained why traffic violations are a menace to society **on Tuesday**.

5 **After you entered the park**, the sponsors of the Summerfest de-

cided that you would not have to spend any more money at the concession stands.

6 She paid $5.00 for a dress at the county fair **that she despised**.

Because English is a language that depends heavily on word order to protect meaning, related words, phrases, and clauses should be placed as close as possible to one another. Adverbial and adjectival modifiers especially must be placed as close as possible to words that they modify. Failure to juxtapose related words, phrases, or clauses may lead to a misreading—that is, to a reading different from what the author intended.

In sentence **1**, we have an example of what is called a **squinting modifier**, a modifier that looks in two directions at once. In that sentence, the adverb **frequently** sits between two verbs that it could modify—**reads** and **will notice**. If the writer intends the adverb to modify the act of *reading* rather than the act of *noticing*, the position of **frequently** should be shifted so that the sentence reads as follows: **Anyone who frequently reads a newspaper will notice that many people are now concerned about pollution**. If, however, the writer intends the adverb to modify the act of *noticing*, **frequently** should be shifted to a position between **will** and **notice** or after **notice**.

Because **only** in sentence **2** is placed in the wrong clause of the sentence, it modifies **a face**. The writer could avoid getting an unwanted laugh from readers by putting **only** in the clause where it belongs: **He has a face that only a mother could love**.

Chances are that the writer of sentence **3** did not intend **even** to modify the act of *smiling*. Shifting **even** will make the sentence say what the writer probably meant it to say: **Matilda smiles even when she is sleeping**.

Because the prepositional phrase **on Tuesday** has been put in the wrong place in sentence **4**, it does not modify the word that it should be modifying (**explained**) and therefore does not say what the writer intended to say. The sentence should be revised to read as follows: **The judge explained on Tuesday why traffic violations are a menace to society**.

Notice how shifting the position of the modifying clauses in sentences **5** and **6** makes the sentences say what they were probably intended to say:

> The sponsors of the Summerfest decided that after you entered the park you would not have to spend any more money at the concession stands.

> At the county fair, she paid $5.00 for a dress that she despised.

Reading sentences aloud will sometimes reveal the misplacement of modifying words, phrases, and clauses.

27

Preserve parallel structure by using units of the same grammatical kind.

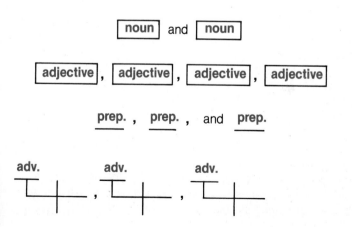

Grammar

Examples of breakdown in parallelism:

1 The old beliefs about theft have been rejected as **superstitions** and **detrimental** to one's prestige.

   (noun and adjective)

2 He was a **miser,** a **bachelor,** and **egotistical.**

   (noun, noun, adjective)

3 John was **healthy, wealthy,** and an **athlete.**

   (adjective, adjective, noun)

4 First of all, Daisy was an **adult, married,** and **had a young daughter.**

   (noun, adjective, verb phrase)

5 Lincoln was a man **of the people, for the people,** and **loved by the people.**

   (prepositional phrase, prepositional phrase, participial phrase)

6 The president commended the steelworkers **for their patriotism** and **because they did not ask for a wage increase.**

   (prepositional phrase, adverb clause)

7 I enjoy reading simply **for personal enlightenment** and **to develop mental sharpness.**

   (prepositional phrase, infinitive phrase)

8 The advertisers **not only** convince the reader that the Continental is a luxury car **but also** that the car confers status on its owner.

   (violation of parallelism with correlative conjunctions)

The principle governing parallel structure is that a pair or a series (three or more) of units serving the same function in a sentence should be composed of similar ·elements—e.g. nouns with nouns, adjectives with adjectives, not a mixture of nouns and adjectives. A breakdown in parallelism wrenches coherence because it disrupts the expectation that is set up for a reader when a series starts out with one kind of element and then shifts to another kind.

27 Parallelism

The obvious way to correct a breakdown in parallelism is to convert all the members of the pair or the series to units of the same grammatical kind. Let us first correct all the violations of parallelism in the sample sentences and then comment on the revisions.

1 The old beliefs about theft have been rejected as **superstitious** and **detrimental** to one's prestige.

   (adjective and adjective)

2 He was a **miser,** a **bachelor,** and an **egotist.**

   (noun, noun, noun)

3 John was **healthy, wealthy,** and **athletic.**

   (adjective, adjective, adjective)

4 First of all, Daisy was an **adult,** a married **woman,** and the **mother** of a young daughter.

   (noun, noun, noun)

5 Lincoln was a man **who was born of the people, who worked for the people,** and **who was loved by the people.**

   (adjective clause, adjective clause, adjective clause)

6 The president commended the steelworkers **for their patriotism** and **for their restraint**

   (prepositional phrase, prepositional phrase)

7 I enjoy reading simply **to gain personal enlightenment** and **to develop mental sharpness**

   (infinitive phrase, infinitive phrase)

8 The advertisers convince the reader not only **that the Continental is a luxury car** but also **that the car confers status on its owner.**

   (noun clause, noun clause)

In converting all the members of a pair or a series to units of the same grammatical kind, a writer sometimes has an either/ or choice available, but usually one of the options will be stylisti-

Grammar

cally preferable to the other. In sentences **2**, **6**, and **7**, the writer could have chosen another option:

2 He was **miserly, single,** and **egotistical**.

6 The president commended the steelworkers **because they were patriotic and because they did not ask for a wage increase**.

7 I enjoy reading simply **for personal enlightenment** and **for mental sharpness**.

Whenever alternative ways of repairing the breakdown in parallelism are available, the writer has to exercise judgment in deciding which is the better stylistic choice in a particular case.

Sentences , , and , however, do not readily lend themselves to alternative revisions. In sentence , for instance, the writer could convert the pair to two nouns (**superstitions** and **detriments**), but that wording is not as stylistically satisfactory as the conversion to two adjectives (**superstitious** and **detrimental**). The predicate terms in sentence cannot be converted to three nouns because there are no single-word noun equivalents of the adjectives **healthy** and **wealthy**; so this sentence can be made parallel only by turning all three units into adjectives. The use of noun phrases was the only option available for the revision of sentence because there is no noun or adjective equivalent of the verb phrase **had a young daughter**.

Correcting the violation of parallelism in sentence was almost impossible because of the unavailability of three equivalent prepositional phrases or three equivalent participial phrases. The best that could be done in that case was to use three **who** clauses, but although that revision makes the sentence grammatically parallel, it is not stylistically satisfactory.

Sentence illustrates a violation of parallelism when correlative conjunctions are used: **either . . . or; neither . . . nor; not (only) . . . but (also).** The principle operating with correlative conjunctions is that the same grammatical structure must be on the right-hand side of both conjunctions. We can more easily see the breakdown in parallelism if we lay out sentence **8** in two layers:

> The advertisers **not only** convince the reader that the Continental is
> a luxury car
> **but also** that the car confers status on its owner.

On the right-hand side of **not only**, the writer has this grammatical sequence: a verb (**convince**), a noun (**the reader**), and a noun clause (**that the Continental is a luxury car**). On the right-hand side of **but also**, however, the writer has *only* the noun clause (**that the car confers status on its owner**). The faulty parallelism can be revised in either of two ways:

> The advertisers **not only** convince the reader that the Continental
> is a luxury car
> **but also** convince the reader that the car confers
> status on its owner.
> The advertisers convince the reader **not only** that the Continental
> is a luxury car
> **but also** that the car confers
> status on its owner.

In both revisions, we now have the same grammatical structures on the right-hand side of both correlative conjunctions. But because the second revision has fewer words and less repetition than the first one, it is probably the better of the two revisions.

Note how parallelism is preserved in the following two sentences using correlative conjunctions:

> **Either** he will love the one and hate the other, **or** he will hate the one
> and love the other.
> He will **either** love the one and hate the other **or** hate the one and
> love the other.

Grammar

The principle governing parallelism: **like must be joined with like**.

28

Use the subordinate conjunction *that* if it will prevent a possible misreading.

Examples where it would be advisable to insert **that**:

1 My father believed∧his doctor, who was a boyhood friend, was wholly trustworthy.

2 A more realistic person would probably assert∧these statements about the ad were frivolous and sentimental.

3 He discovered∧the radio and the tape recorder in his roommate's closet had been stolen.

4 The author reported∧as soon as a Jew became intensely depressed in camp and lost all purpose for living, death came shortly after.

5 Professor Clements maintained ∧communism rejected capitalism and∧democracy rejected collective ownership.

The tendency of any language is toward economy of means. So we omit syllables in such contractions as **he's, she'll, we'd, won't,** and we resort to such common elliptical expressions as **not all [of] the men; she is taller than I [am tall]; when [I was] in the fourth grade, I went to the zoo with my mother.** We also frequently omit the conjunction **that**, which introduces a noun clause serving as the object of a verb, as in "He said [**that**] he was going" and "He announced [**that**] I was a candidate for office."

Whether to use the conjunction **that** in written prose will be a problem only when a noun clause is being used as the direct object of a verb—but not in every instance of such use. If there is no chance that a sentence will be misread, it is all right, even in written prose, to omit **that.** But if there is a chance that a noun phrase following the verb may be read as the object of the verb rather than as the subject of the subsequent clause, then the writer can prevent even a momentary misreading by inserting **that** at the beginning of the noun clause. What follows may make all of this discussion clearer.

In a sentence like "He believed they were going," it is safe to omit **that** after **believed** because **they** cannot possibly be read as the object of **believed**. (If **they** were the object of the verb here, the pronoun would have to be **them—He believed them**.) But in a sentence like **1**, it is not only possible but likely that the noun phrase **his doctor** will initially be read as the object of **believed** (**he believed his doctor**). Of course, as soon as readers come to the predicate **was wholly trustworthy**, they realize that they have misread the sentence, and so they have to back up and reread the sentence as the writer intended it to be read. But the writer could have prevented that initial misreading by inserting **that** after **believed—My father believed that his doctor, who was a boyhood friend, was wholly trustworthy**. Then the sentence can be read in only one way— the way in which the writer intended it to be read.

Read the other sample sentences aloud, the first time omitting **that**, the second time inserting **that** where the (∧) is. By doing this double reading of the sentences aloud, you will notice how the insertion of **that** ensures that the sentences will be read in the way the writer intended them to be read.

Whenever a reader has to reread a sentence in order to make sense of it, the writer is often the one to blame. Inserting **that** where it is necessary or advisable is one way to spare readers from having to reread a sentence.

29

Avoid the careless or indefensible use of sentence fragments.

Examples of questionable sentence fragments:

1 They tried to explain to the police that they intended to drive the brakeless car only two blocks to the repair shop. **Although they soon became aware that neither of the police officers was paying any attention to their explanation.**

2 **The reason for Holden's disappointment being that his sister wasn't there to comfort him.**

3 Both men are alike in that they try to help people if the effort does not result in too much trouble for themselves. **Herenger, in his idea that it is good to help someone with "so little trouble to himself," and the Baron, who believes in giving money to someone as long as there is no further responsibility involved.**

4 The bond between Gretta and Michael was strong enough to make him face death rather than be separated from her. **The tragedy here that such a love could not be consummated and that one so young should be cut off just at the dawn of life.**

5 I know what you're thinking. **The wife trying to maintain her stubborn pride, the husband feeling guilty and remorseful, the children looking desperately for somebody to reconcile their parents.**

A sentence fragment can be defined as a string of words, between an initial capital letter and a period or a question mark, that lacks a subject or a finite-verb predicate (or both) or that has a subject and a finite-verb predicate but is made part of a larger structure by a relative pronoun (**who, which, that**) or by a subordinating conjunction (**although, because, if, when,** etc.). (For a further discussion of the difference between a phrase and a clause and between an independent (main) clause and a dependent (subordinate) clause, see the LEGEND section at the front of the book.)

In example **1**, the string of words beginning with **although** and terminating with a period is a sentence fragment because although it has a subject (**they**) and a finite-verb predicate (**became**), it is turned into a dependent clause by the subordinating conjunction **although** at the beginning of it. If instead of using the subordinating conjunction **although**, the writer had used a coordinating conjunction (**but**) or a conjunctive adverb (**however**), the words that follow would be a complete sentence. But if **although** is used to begin that string of words, then the words must be made a part of the preceding independent clause:

> They tried to explain to the police that they intended to drive the brakeless car only two blocks to the repair shop, although they soon became aware that neither of the police officers was paying any attention to their explanation.

Example **2** is a sentence fragment because there is no finite-verb predicate for the noun **reason**. (There is a finite verb in the string—**wasn't**—but that verb is the predicate of the dependent noun clause **that his sister wasn't there to comfort him**.) There is a verbal here (the participle **being**), but by itself, that participle cannot serve as the predicate for **reason**. The simplest way to make that fragment a complete sentence is to convert the participle **being** into the finite verb **was**:

> The reason for Holden's disappointment was that his sister wasn't there to comfort him.

The boldface string of words in example **3** is a sentence fragment because neither **Herenger** nor **Baron**, both of which appear to be "subjects," has a predicate verb. By supplying the finite verb **believes** for both subjects, we can convert that fragment into an independent clause, which can stand by itself:

Grammar

> Both men are alike in that they try to help people if the effort does not result in too much trouble for themselves. Herenger believes that it is good to help someone with "so little trouble to himself," and the Baron believes in giving money to someone as long as there is no further responsibility involved.

Apparently, the author of example **4** left out the verb in the boldface string of words, owing to mere carelessness. If the author had read the string aloud, he or she would probably have noticed that the predicate verb was missing. Simply putting in a verb like **was** will correct this sentence fragment:

> The bond between Gretta and Michael was strong enough to make him face death rather than be separated from her. The tragedy here was that such a love could not be consummated and that one so young should be cut off just at the dawn of life.

Because example **5** lacks a predicate verb in the boldface string, it is difficult—if not impossible—for us readers to figure out what the relationship between the two groups of words is and therefore what the author was trying to say. Because we cannot figure out what the author was trying to say, we can only suggest possible revisions. The following revision is only one of a number of ways of rewriting the strings in order to eliminate the sentence fragment:

> I know what you're thinking. You're thinking that the wife is trying to maintain her stubborn pride, the husband is feeling guilty and remorseful, and the children are looking desperately for somebody to reconcile their parents.

Whether a string of words constitutes a complete sentence or only a sentence fragment is a grammatical concern; whether the use of a sentence fragment is appropriate in a particular context and is therefore justifiable is a rhetorical or stylistic concern. It is a fact of life that we sometimes communicate with

29 Sentence Fragments

one another in sentence fragments. Take for instance the following exchange:

Where are you going tonight?
The movies.
Who with?
Jack.
Where?
The Palace.
What time?
About 8:30.
By car?
No, by bus.
Can I go?
Sure.

Once the context of that dialogue was established, both speakers communicated in fragments. Notice, though, that the dialogue had to be initiated by a complete sentence (the question **Where are you going tonight?**) and that later the first speaker had to resort again to a complete sentence **(Can I go?)** because there was no way to phrase that question clearly in a fragmentary way.

Native speakers of a language can converse in fragments because each of them is capable of mentally supplying what is missing from an utterance. When in response to the initial question the second speaker answers, **The movies**, that phrase conveys a meaning because the first speaker is able to supply, mentally and perhaps subconsciously, the missing elements in the fragmentary reply: **(I am going to) the movies.**

All of us have encountered sentence fragments in the written prose of some very reputable writers. Predicateless sentences are most likely to be found in mood-setting descriptive and nar-

Grammar

rative prose, as in this first paragraph of Charles Dickens's novel *Bleak House*:

> London. Michaelmas Term lately over, and the Lord Chancellor sitting in Lincoln's Inn Hall. Implacable November weather. As much mud in the streets, as if the waters had but newly retired from the face of the earth, and it would not be wonderful to meet a Megalosaurus, forty feet long or so, waddling like an elephantine lizard up Holborn Hill. Smoke lowering down from chimney-pots, making a soft black drizzle, with flakes of soot in it as big as full-grown snow-flakes—gone into mourning, one might imagine, for the death of the sun. Dogs, undistinguishable in mire. Horses, scarcely better; splashed to their blinkers. Foot passengers, jostling one another's umbrellas, in a general infection of illtemper, and losing their foothold at street-corners, where tens of thousands of other foot passengers have been slipping and sliding since the day broke (if this day ever broke), adding new deposits to the crust upon crust of mud, sticking at those points tenaciously to the pavement and accumulating at compound interest.

In that paragraph, there are a few clauses (that is, groups of words with a subject and a finite-verb predicate), but the paragraph consists primarily of nouns and noun phrases, some of them modified by participial phrases (e.g. **sitting in Lincoln's Inn Hall, splashed to their blinkers, jostling one another's umbrellas**). (It might be a good exercise for you to go through the paragraph and see if you can distinguish the sentence fragments from the complete sentences.) But although the passage is largely lacking in statements made with finite verbs, the sequence of sentence fragments does create effects that Dickens could not have achieved—or achieved as well—with complete sentences.

The points to be made in citing these examples of spoken and written discourse are (1) that sentence fragments are a part of the English language (in that sense, they are "grammatical''), (2) that in certain contexts they do communicate meaning, and (3) that in some circumstances and for some purposes they are appropriate and therefore acceptable, effective, and even stylistically desirable. But writers should be aware of what they are doing. They should be conscious that they are deliberately using a sentence fragment instead of a complete sentence; otherwise, they will be guilty of a *careless* use of a sentence fragment. And they should have some purpose or effect in mind when they use a sentence fragment; otherwise, they will be guilty of an *indefensible* use of a sentence fragment. In every case, they should be aware of the possibility that the sentence fragment may not communicate clearly with readers.

30

Independent clauses cannot be spliced simply with a comma.

Examples of comma splices:

1 We are not allowed to think for ourselves, that privilege is reserved for administrators.

2 The biggest government spender, according to *Time* magazine, is the Department of Agriculture, the next biggest spender is the Department of Defense.

3 Our minds are never challenged by the television set, it is just so much easier to sit there than to read a book.

4 The members of the city council are convinced of the need for wheelchair lifts on public buses, however, they can't figure out how the city or the bus companies could finance such equipment.

Grammar

A comma splice is the result of joining independent clauses with nothing but a comma. *A comma is a separating device, not a joining device.* A comma splice is, therefore, an error in punctuation, but since punctuation is, for the written language, the grammatical equivalent of vocal intonation in the spoken language, this error in punctuation can also be considered an error in grammar.

Independent clauses must be joined either by a coordinating conjunction (**and, but, or, for, nor, yet, so**) or by a semicolon. In addition to these two ways of properly splicing independent clauses, there are two other ways of fixing up a comma splice: by making separate sentences of the two clauses and by subordinating one of the clauses. Using each of these methods in turn, let us correct the comma splice in the first sample sentence above.

(a) Insert the appropriate coordinating conjunction after the comma:

We are not allowed to think for ourselves **,** **for** that privilege is reserved for administrators. ·

(b) Substitute a semicolon for the comma:

We are not allowed to think for ourselves **;** that privilege is reserved for administrators.

(c) Subordinate one of the independent clauses:

We are not allowed to think for ourselves **,** **because** that privilege is reserved for administrators.

(d) Put a period at the end of the first independent clause and begin a new sentence with the first word of the second independent clause:

We are not allowed to think for ourselves **.** That privilege is reserved for administrators.

Although these four ways of repairing a comma splice are always available, one of them will usually be better in a particular instance. In sentence **1**, splicing the two clauses with a semicolon would probably be best: **We are not allowed to think for ourselves; that privilege is reserved for administrators.** The semicolon here effects the closest union of the two related clauses and best points up the irony between the thoughts in the two clauses. We have made our choice of the semicolon on stylistic grounds; grammatically, the other three options are equally correct.

In the following revisions of the remaining sample sentences, we have corrected the comma splice by one of the four available methods, but it must be understood that each of the comma splices could have been corrected by one of the other three methods.

2 The biggest government spender, according to *Time* magazine, is the Department of Agriculture **, but** the next biggest spender is the Department of Defense.

3 Our minds are never challenged by the television set **.** It is just so much easier to sit there than to read a book.

4 **Although** the members of the city council are convinced of the need for wheelchair lifts on public buses, they can't figure out how the city or the bus companies could finance such equipment.

See **66** and **67** in the section on punctuation for the proper use of the semicolon.

31

Do not run independent clauses together without a conjunction or the proper punctuation.

Examples of independent clauses run together:

1 Why am I qualified to speak on this subject I just finished three dreadful years of high school.

2 Those shiny red apples sitting on my desk pleased me very much they were tokens of affection from my pupils.

3 Two suspects were arrested last week one of them was a cripple.

4 Leggatt was blackballed for having killed a man thus he would never be able to work on a ship again.

The term commonly used to label two or more independent clauses that have been run together without any conjunction or punctuation is **fused sentence** or **run-on sentence.** Fused sentences are not as common in writing as comma splices, but when they occur, they are even more of a stumbling block for a reader than comma splices are. If the writers of the sample sentences above had read their strings of words aloud, they would have detected a natural stopping place—a place where the expression of one thought ended and the expression of another began.

Once the writers had detected the fused sentence, they could then consider how best to revise it. Fused sentences can be corrected in the same four ways that comma splices can be corrected:

(a) Join the independent clauses with the appropriate coordinating conjunction:

Those shiny red apples sitting on my desk pleased me very much, **for** they were tokens of affection from my pupils.

(b) Splice the independent clauses with a semicolon:

Two suspects were arrested last week; one of them was a cripple.

(c) Subordinate one of the independent clauses:

Because Leggatt was blackballed for having killed a man, he would never be able to work on a ship again.

(d) Make separate sentences of the independent clauses:

Why am I qualified to speak on this subject? I just finished three dreadful years of high school.

As with comma splices, all four of these ways are usually available for correcting a fused sentence, but in a particular instance, one of them will probably be better than the others. Furthermore, some fused sentences do not readily lend themselves to correction by all four means. For instance, because sentence 1 fuses a question and a statement—**Why am I qualified to speak on this subject** (question) and **I just finished three dreadful years of high school** (statement)—it most readily lends itself to correction by the fourth method, that of making separate sentences of the two clauses. Sentence 3 does not readily lend itself to correction by the use of a coordinating conjunction. The coordinating conjunctions **or, nor, for, yet, so** just do not fit with the sense of the two clauses. Depending on the larger context in which the sentence occurred, joining the two independent clauses with the coordinating conjunctions **and** or **but** might work, but this way of revising the sentence would not be as satisfactory as joining the clauses with a semicolon.

Reading one's prose aloud will usually disclose instances where independent clauses have been run together.

Grammar

32

Choose words and put them together so that they make sense.

Examples of confused or puzzling sentences:

1 Much later in the story, the dinner conversation the function of the "small talk" seems to be about the old times.

2 The youth, rejected by his parents, by the world, by God, and tragically and ultimately he has rejected himself.

3 William Faulkner presents in his short story "Barn Burning" a human character that is as nonhuman as is feasible to a person's mind.

4 Now in the third stanza, the poet starts her descent. She brings about her conclusion of the boy, which can be paralleled to mankind.

5 Of course, this situation of rundown houses is not always the case, but instead the high rent that the tenants have to pay, which leaves little money for anything else.

A confused or puzzling sentence is one that because of some flaw in the *choice* of words or in the *arrangement* of words reveals no meaning or a scrambled meaning or a vague meaning. Unlike the stylistic flaws discussed in **40, 41,** and **42,** which produce vague or imprecise or inept sentences, this flaw of diction or arrangement produces what might be called a "non-English" sentence—a sentence that is semantically or grammatically impossible in the English language. For example, a sentence like "The ice cube froze" is a non-English sentence because of the choice of the semantically incompatible words **ice cube** and **froze.** (We can say, "The water froze," but we are uttering nonsense if we say, "The ice cube froze.") A sentence like "Harshly me teacher scolded the yesterday" is a non-English sentence because English grammar does not allow that arrangement of words. To make sense, those words would have to be arranged in an order like "The teacher scolded me harshly yesterday."

Some of the sample sentences are confused or puzzling mainly because of the choice of words. In sentence **3**, for example, there is some incompatibility between **human character** and **nonhuman,** and the word **feasible** simply does not fit in that context. In sentence **4**, the choice of **conclusion** produced the non-English phrase "her conclusion of the boy." The use of **paralleled** in the final clause of that sentence is an error in idiom, resulting in a non-English clause.

The other sample sentences are examples of confused or puzzling sentences produced by faulty syntax (arrangement of words). The writers of those sentences started out on a certain track but got derailed, or they switched to another track. Sentence **1**, for instance, starts out well enough—**Much later in the story, the dinner conversation. . .**—but then gets derailed. Sentence **2** starts out on one track and then switches to another.

If readers cannot figure out what the writer meant to say, they often cannot analyze what went wrong with the sentence, and they certainly cannot suggest how the bewildering sentence might be fixed up. The best they can do is to point out that the sentence makes no sense and urge the writer to rephrase it.

In the following revisions, (1) a guess has been made about what the author meant to say, (2) as many of the original words as possible have been retained, and (3) none of the needed stylistic changes has been made. We have merely tried to repair the sentences so that they make some kind of sense.

1 Much later in the story—during the dinner conversation—the function of the "small talk" seems to be to recall the old times.

Grammar

2 The youth, rejected by his parents, by the world, by God, has tragically and ultimately rejected himself.

3 William Faulkner presents in his short story "Barn Burning" a character that is as unlike a normal human being as a person could imagine.

4 Now in the third stanza, the poet starts her descent. She draws her conclusion about the boy, which is similar to the generalization that could be made about the rest of mankind.

5 Of course, the houses are not invariably rundown, but the high rent that the tenants have to pay leaves little money for anything else.

If reading sentences aloud to oneself does not help in detecting confused or puzzling sentences, it may be necessary to read them aloud to someone else.

33

Use the proper form of the verb.

Examples of the wrong form of the verb:

1 Before television came along, children **use** to read for hours by the fireplace.

2 Whenever I went shopping with my sister, I had the urge to buy everything I **seen.**

3 In that environment, it seemed that whatever you would **liked** to do was sinful.

4 Many parents never ask their children, "**Have** you **drank** your milk yet?"

5 Yesterday, when customers **lay** their umbrellas on the counter while paying their bills, they usually walked off without them.

6 When the incident at Three Mile Island occurred, many people **are frightened.**

7 On the top of the hill, there is a sturdy log cabin, which **was** three years old.

8 The *Delta Queen* **leaves** Davenport tomorrow. It **will arrive** in St. Louis on Tuesday, and it **stays** there for a day and a half.

Native speakers of English are often not aware of how subtly complicated the English verb system is, especially the system of tenses, which indicate the *time* of an action or a state of being. But foreigners who have to learn English in school are painfully aware of the subtleties of the verb system. English is doubly difficult for those foreigners whose native languages do not have a system of tenses for their verbs. Instead of indicating time by making some change in the *form* of the verb (e.g. **walk—walked; sleep—slept**), these languages indicate time by adding some *word* to the sentence—as English sometimes does to indicate future time even when the verb indicates present time (e.g. **She goes tomorrow**).

Native speakers of English, who learn the language in the natural way, as part of the normal process of growing up, usually handle the complicated verb system quite well. Occasionally, however, they use the wrong form of a verb, as did the writers of the sample sentences above. Let us analyze and correct the sample sentences and then review some of the basic conventions governing the formation of the past tense and the past participle of the English verb.

The omission of the **-d** at the end of **use** in a sentence like **1** above is understandable, because in speaking, we are scarcely conscious of pronouncing that final **-d**. But this expression must always be written as **used to**. The verb in sentence **4** (**drank**) has the past-tense form, but it should have the past-participle form (**drunk**) so that it will fit with its auxiliary verb **have**. The verb in the *when* clause of sentence **5** clearly needs to be put into the past tense, but the proper form of the past tense of the verb *lay* is **laid**.

Grammar

Of the three verbs in sentence **2**, one is in the wrong tense: **seen** should be **saw**. This mistake is the reverse of the situation in **4**. The verb in sentence **3** has a **-d** ending that should not be there: **liked** should be **like** (the reverse of **1**). The writer of that sentence may have been influenced to add the **-d** ending to **like** because of the other past-tense signals in the sentence (**seemed, would,** and **was**) or because of the sound of **t** in **to** (*like to = liket = liked*).

Sentences **6, 7,** and **8** illustrate the error known as **faulty sequence of tenses**—that is, a needless or an unjustifiable shift of tenses in successive clauses or sentences. In sentence **6**, the past tense (**occurred**) in the *when* clause is followed by an incompatible present tense (**are frightened**) in the main clause. Sentence **7** has a present tense (**is**) in the main clause and an unjustifiable past tense (**was**) in the adjective clause. In sentence **8**, there is a sequence of present tense (**leaves**), future tense (**will arrive**), and present tense (**stays**). The context here seems to demand that all three verbs have the future-tense form. But one could also justify putting the three verbs in the present tense (**leaves, arrives, stays**).

Here now are all eight sample sentences with corrected verb forms:

1 Before television came along, children **used** to read for hours by the fireplace.

2 Whenever I went shopping with my sister, I had the urge to buy everything I **saw**

3 In that environment, it seemed that whatever you would **like** to do was sinful.

4 Many parents never ask their children, "**Have** you **drunk** your milk yet?"

5 Yesterday, when customers **laid** their umbrellas on the counter while paying their bills, they usually walked off without them.

6 When the incident at Three Mile Island occurred, many people **were frightened**

7 On the top of the hill, there is a sturdy log cabin, which **is** three years old.

8 The *Delta Queen* **will leave** Davenport tomorrow. It **will arrive** in St. Louis on Tuesday, and it **will stay** there for a day and a half.

Most of the errors that writers make with verbs involve the lack of agreement in person or number between the subject and predicate or the wrong past-tense form or the wrong past-participle form. Subject-predicate agreement is dealt with in section **22.** This section has dealt mainly with improper past-tense and past-participle forms. The majority of English verbs form their past tense and past participle by adding **-ed** or **-d** to the stem form (e.g. **walk—walked; believe—believed**). These verbs are called *regular verbs* or sometimes *weak verbs*.

The so-called *irregular verbs* or *strong verbs* form their past tense and past participle by means of a change in spelling (e.g. **sing—sang—sung; hide—hid—hidden**). Most native speakers of English know the principal parts of most of these irregular verbs. When they do not know, or are not sure of, the principal parts, they consult a good dictionary, which regularly supplies the past tense and past participle of all irregular verbs. But for your convenience, here are the principal parts of some of the most commonly used irregular verbs. (Incidentally, the *stem form* of the verb is the form that combines with *to* to become the infinitive—**to walk, to go**; the stem form is also the form that the verb has when it is used with the first-person pronouns in the present tense—**I walk, we go**.)

Grammar

PRINCIPAL PARTS OF SOME IRREGULAR VERBS

stem form	past tense form	past-participle form
begin	began	begun
bite	bit	bitten
blow	blew	blown
break	broke	broken
choose	chose	chosen
do	did	done
drink	drank	drunk
drive	drove	driven
eat	ate	eaten
fall	fell	fallen
fly	flew	flown
forget	forgot	forgotten
give	gave	given
go	went	gone
know	knew	known
lay	laid	laid
lie	lay	lain
pay	paid	paid
ride	rode	ridden
ring	rang	rung
rise	rose	risen
run	ran	run
see	saw	seen
sit	sat	sat
speak	spoke	spoken
swear	swore	sworn
take	took	taken
throw	threw	thrown
wear	wore	worn

Style

Style is the result of the choices that a writer makes from the available vocabulary and syntactical resources of a language. A writer may not choose—or should not choose

☐ **Words and structures that are not part of the language:**

The defendants have **klinded** the case to the Supreme Court.

(no such word in the English language)

All gas stations **have being closed** for the duration of the emergency.

(no such verb structure in the English language)

☐ **Words and structures that make no sense:**

The mountains lucidly transgressed sentient rocks.

(a grammatical but nonsensical sentence)

☐ **Words and structures that do not convey a clear, unambiguous meaning:**

The teacher gave the papers to the students that were chosen by the committee.

*(was it the **papers** or the **students** that were chosen by the committee?)*

Style

Aside from these unavailable or inadvisable choices, however, the rich vocabulary and the flexible syntax of the English language offer the writer a number of alternative but synonymous ways of saying something. For instance, one may choose to use an active verb or a passive verb:

He reported the accident to the police.

OR

The accident was reported by him to the police.

Or one may shift the position of some modifiers:

He reported the accident to the police when he was ready.

OR

When he was ready, he reported the accident to the police.

Or one may substitute synonymous words and phrases:

He informed the police about the accident at the intersection.

OR

John notified Sergeant James Murphy about the collision at the corner of Fifth and Main.

A number of other stylistic choices may be open to the writer:

(a) whether to write a long sentence or to break up the sentence into a series of short sentences.

(long sentence)

In a sense, we did not have history until the invention of the alphabet, because before that invention, the records of national events could be preserved only if there were bards inspired enough to sing about those events and audiences patient enough to listen to a long, metered recitation.

OR

(a series of short sentences)

In a sense, we did not have history until the invention of the alphabet. Before that invention, the records of national events were passed on by singing bards. But those bards had to have audiences patient enough to listen to a long, metered recitation.

(b) whether to write a compound sentence or to subordinate one of the clauses.

(compound sentence)

None of the elegies that were delivered at funerals in eighteenth-century village churches have been preserved, but the "short and simple annals of the poor" have been preserved on thousands of gravestones from that era.

OR

(subordinate one of the clauses)

Although none of the elegies that were delivered at funerals in eighteenth-century village churches have been preserved, the "short and simple annals of the poor" have been preserved on thousands of gravestones from that era.

(c) whether to modify a noun with an adjective clause or with a participial phrase or merely with an adjective.

(adjective clause)

The house, which was painted a garish red, did not find a buyer for two months.

OR

(participial phrase)

The house, painted a garish red, did not find a buyer for two months.

OR

(adjective)

The garishly red house did not find a buyer for two months.

Style

(d) whether to use literal language or figurative language.

(literal)

The president walked into a room filled with angry reporters.

OR

(figurative)

The president walked into a hornet's nest.

(e) whether to use a "big" word or an ordinary word (*altercation* or *quarrel*), a specific word or a general word (*sauntered* or *walked*), a formal word or a colloquial word (*children* or *kids*).

(big, formal words)

Everyone was astonished by her phenomenal equanimity.

OR

(ordinary, colloquial words)

Everyone was flabbergasted by her unusual cool.

(f) whether to begin a succession of sentences with the same word and the same structure or to vary the diction and the structure.

(same word, same structure)

We wanted to preserve our heritage. We wanted to remind our children of our national heroes. We wanted to inspire subsequent generations to emulate our example.

OR

(different words, different structures)

We wanted to preserve our heritage. Our children, in turn, needed to be reminded of our national heroes. Could we inspire subsequent generations to emulate our example?

The availability of options such as these gives writers the opportunity to achieve variety in their style. *By varying the length, the rhythm, and the structure of their sentences, writers can avoid monotony, an attention-deadening quality in prose.* The previous sentence is a good example of the variety made possible by the availability of options. All the meanings packed into that sentence can be laid out in a series of short sentences. (Transformational grammarians refer to these "meanings" that are laid out in the "kernel sentences" as the *deep structure*. The *surface structure* of a sentence represents the choice of words and syntax that a writer uses to express that deep structure. Here is the deep structure of the sentence:

> Writers vary the length of their sentences.
>
> Writers vary the rhythm of their sentences.
>
> Writers vary the structure of their sentences.
>
> Writers can avoid monotony.
>
> Monotony in prose deadens the attention of readers.

One *could* choose precisely that succession of simple sentences as the surface structure to express the deep structure. Although these elementary sentences would be appropriate in a first-grade Dick-and-Jane reader, a succession of such monotonous sentences would soon turn adult readers away. By a series of transformations that involve **combining** (compounding), **embedding** (subordinating), **shifting** (rearranging), or **deleting** (omitting) the five sentences, one can produce a single neat sentence that emphasizes the main idea and holds the readers' attention. Here is one way that the writer might have chosen to express the deep structure:

> If writers vary the length, the rhythm, and the structure of their sentences, they can avoid monotony, which deadens readers' attention.

Style

The writer of the first sentence (in italics) chose to combine some of the same elements combined by the writer of the sentence immediately above—e.g. compounding the "meanings" of the first three kernel sentences. On the other hand, the first writer chose a different way of embedding some of the elements—e.g. instead of using the adverbial *if* clause, the writer used an *-ing* gerund phrase (**varying**); and instead of using the adjectival *which* clause, the writer reduced the clause, by a series of deletions of words, to a compound adjective (**attention-deadening**). So instead of

> If writers vary the length, the rhythm, and the structure of their sentences, they can avoid monotony, which deadens readers' attention.

we get

> By varying the length, the rhythm, and the structure of their sentences, writers can avoid monotony, an attention-deadening quality in prose.

By using a different combination of combining, embedding, shifting, and deleting, other writers would come up with other ways of expressing all the meanings. The different ways result in different styles.

Choice is the key word in connection with style. Some choices a writer may not, or should not, make. As was pointed out at the beginning of this section, a writer may not choose what the grammar of the language does not allow. Furthermore, a writer cannot choose resources of language he or she does not command. A writer would also be ill-advised to choose words and structures that are inappropriate for the subject matter, the occasion, or the audience.

Aside from those constraints, however, a writer has hundreds of decisions to make about the choice of vocabulary or syntax while writing. Grammar will determine whether a particular stylistic choice is *correct*—that is, whether a particular locution complies with the conventions of the language. Rhetoric will determine whether a particular stylistic choice is *effective* —that is, whether a particular locution conveys the intended meaning with the clarity, economy, emphasis, and tone appropriate to the subject matter, occasion, audience, and desired effect.

The previous section dealt with what the grammar of the language permits—or, more accurately, with what the conventions of Edited American English permit. This section on style will guide writers in making judicious choices from among the available options. Questions about style are not so much questions about *right* and *wrong* as questions about *good, better, best.*

40

Choose the right word or expression for what you intend to say.

Examples of wrong words or expressions:

1 If you do not **here** from me within three weeks, give me a call.

2 The shortstop played very **erotically** in the first game of the double-header.

3 The typical surfer has long **ignominious** hair bleached by the **pid** sun.

4 A thief and a liar **are vices** that we should avoid.

5 Abused children **should not be tolerated** in our society.

6 The source of Hemingway's title **is taken** from a sermon by John Donne.

7 The reason she didn't come to class **is because** she was sick.

Style

8 The beach **is where** I get my worst sunburn.

9 An example of honesty **is when** someone finds a wallet and brings it to the police.

A word is labeled "wrong" when it does not express the author's intended meaning. The most obvious instance of a "wrong word" is the substitution, usually due to carelessness, of a homonym (a like-sounding word) for the intended word— e.g. **through** for **threw, there** for **their, sole** for **soul, son** for **sun, loose** for **lose**. Sentence 1 has one of these homonyms —**here** for **hear**.

Another kind of "wrong word" is called a **malapropism**, after Mrs. Malaprop in Sheridan's play *The Rivals.* Mrs. Malaprop would say things like "as headstrong as an *allegory* on the banks of the Nile," when she should have used the word *alligator*. There is a malapropism in sentence 2. "Played erratically" is a common phrase, but by using the approximate-sounding word **erotically** in that phrase, the writer has produced a howler.

The occurrence of a "wrong word" is commonly the result of a writer's using a word that is new and somewhat unfamiliar to him or her. In sentence 3, the word *ignominious* is wrong for that context. The denotative meaning of the word is "disgraceful," "shameful," but although we can speak of "an ignominious act," the word is "wrong" when applied to **hair**. In the same sentence, if the writer meant to say that the sun was sluggish, **torpid** is the right word; but "torrid sun" comes closer to what the writer probably intended to say.

Wrong words commonly occur as part of the predication of a sentence. This fault is so common that it has acquired its own label—**faulty predication**. A faulty predication occurs when the predicate of a clause (either the verb itself or the whole verb phrase) does not fit semantically or syntactically with the subject of the clause.

40 Wrong Word and Faulty Predication

Sentences **4**, **5**, and **6** illustrate a semantic mismatch between the subject and the predicate. Thieves and liars cannot be called vices; *thievery* and *lies* are vices. Sentence **5** says that we should not tolerate abused children. Probably what the writer meant to say is that the abuse of children should not be tolerated. In sentence **6**, the predicate **is taken** is incompatible with the subject **source**. It was the title, not the source, that was taken from Donne's sermon.

Sentences **7**, **8**, and **9** illustrate common instances of **faulty predication** involving a syntactical mismatch between the subject and the predicate. The adverb clauses in those sentences cannot serve as complements for the verb **to be.** (No more could a simple adverb serve as the complement of the verb **to be:** "he is swiftly.") One way to correct such faulty predications is to put some kind of nominal structure after the **to be** verb—a noun, a noun phrase, or a noun clause. Avoid this kind of predication:

The reason is because . . .

An example is when . . .

A ghetto is where . . .

Here are the revisions of the "wrong word" sentences:

1 If you do not hear from me within three weeks, give me a call.

2 The shortstop played very erratically in the first game of the doubleheader.

3 The typical surfer has long, stringy hair bleached by the torrid sun.

4 A thief and a liar practice vices that we should avoid.

5 The abuse of children should not be tolerated in our society.

6 The source of Hemingway's title is a sermon by John Donne.

7 The reason she didn't come to class is that she was sick.

8 The beach is the place where I get my worst sunburn.

9 Honesty is the virtue exemplified when someone finds a wallet and brings it to the police.

41

Choose the precise word for what you want to say.

Examples of imprecise words:

1 I liked the movie *Breaking Away* because it was **interesting**
2 What most impressed me about the poem was the poet's **descriptive** language.
3 Has-been athletes always have a **sore** look on their face.
4 To prevent her from catching a cold, he insisted that she wear the **gigantic** galoshes.
5 Honesty is a **thing** that we should value highly.
6 Jane sold her car, **as** she was planning to take a trip to Europe.

Whereas a "wrong word" misses the target entirely, an "imprecise word" hits all around the bull's-eye and never on dead center. But the governing principle here is that one should strive only for as much precision in diction as the situation demands.

In the spoken medium, diction is often imprecise. But fortunately, in many conversational situations, our diction does not have to be sharply precise in order to communicate adequately. In a conversation, for instance, if someone asked, "How did you like him?" we might respond, "Oh, I thought he was very nice." The word *nice* does not convey a precise meaning, but for the particular situation, it may be precise enough. The word *nice* here certainly conveys the meaning that we approve of the person, that we are favorably impressed by the person. In speech, we do not have the leisure to search for the words that express our meaning exactly. If the woman who asked the question were not satisfied with our general word of approval, *nice*, she could ask us to be more specific.

In the written medium, however, we do have the leisure to search for a precise word, and we are not available to the reader who may want or need more specific information than our words supply. Generally, the written medium requires that the words we choose be as exact, as specific, as unequivocal as we can make them. Consulting a thesaurus or, better yet, a dictionary that discriminates the meanings of synonyms will frequently yield the word that conveys our intended meaning precisely.

The word **interesting** in sentence 1 is too general to convey a precise meaning. A reader's response to a general word like that would be to ask, "In what way was the movie interesting?" If the writer had said "innovative" or "spellbinding" or "thought-provoking," readers might want some more particulars, but at least they would have a clearer idea of the sense in which the writer considered the movie to be interesting.

The word **descriptive** in sentence 2 is too vague. Expressions like "the poet's simple, concrete words" or "the poet's specific adjectives for indicating colors" would give readers a more exact idea of the kind of descriptive language that impressed the writer of the sentence.

Sore in sentence 3 is ambiguous—that is, it has more than one meaning in its context. The word **sore** could mean either "angry, disgruntled" or "aching, painful." The choice of a more exact word here will clarify the writer's meaning.

Gigantic in sentence 4 above is exaggerated. Unless the word were deliberately chosen to create a special effect of humor or irony, the writer should use a word more proportionate to the circumstances, such as *big* or *heavy* or *ungainly*.

In the oral medium, we can get by with a catchall word like **thing**, as in sentence 5, but writing allows us the leisure to search for a word that will serve as a more accurate predicate complement for *honesty*. We can use words like *policy, virtue, habit, disposition*—whichever fits best with what we want to say about honesty here.

Style

The subordinating conjunction **as** carries a variety of meanings, and it is not always possible to tell from the context which of its several meanings it carries in a particular sentence. In sentence **6**, we cannot tell whether **as** is being used in its sense of "because" or "since" or "when" or "while." We should use the conjunction that exactly expresses our intended meaning: **because** she was planning; **when** she was planning; **while** she was planning. We should reserve the conjunction **as** for those contexts in which there is no possibility of ambiguity, as in sentences like "In that kind of situation, he acts exactly **as** he should" and "Do **as** I say."

Here, for each of the sample sentences, is one possible revision for greater precision:

1 I liked the movie *Breaking Away* because the theme was poignant.

2 What most impressed me about the poem was the poet's vivid, sensory diction.

3 Has-been athletes always have a disgruntled look on their face.

4 To prevent her from catching a cold, he insisted that she wear the big galoshes.

5 Honesty is a virtue that we should value highly.

6 Jane sold her car, because she was planning to take a trip to Europe.

42

Choose words that are appropriate to the context.

Examples of inappropriate words:

1 He didn't want to **exacerbate** his mother's **sangfroid,** so he **indited** an **epistolary message** to inform her of his unavoidable **retardation**

2 Whenever I visit a new city, I browse through a secondhand bookstore and eventually **cheapen** a book.

3 The conclusion that I have come to is that **kids** should not have to suffer for the sins of their fathers.

4 Merchants in areas where the freeway would be built have persistently opposed the project, claiming that it would disturb the residents and **freak out** all the **weirdos** in the area.

A word is inappropriate if it does not fit, if it is out of tune with, the subject matter, the occasion, the audience, or the personality of the writer. It is a word that is conspicuously "out of place" with its environment.

No word in isolation can be labeled inappropriate; it must first be seen in the company of other words. Although one would feel safer in making a judgment if one had a larger context, the boldfaced words in the sample sentences above seem to be inappropriate.

Sentence **1** exhibits the kind of language used by (usually beginning) writers who are passing through a phase in which they seem unable to say even a simple thing in a simple way. Young writers consciously striving to enlarge their vocabulary often produce sentences like this one. Instead of using a thesaurus to find an accurate or precise word, they use it to find an unusual or polysyllabic word that they think will make their prose sound "literary" or learned or both. Fortunately, most of those who are ambitious enough to want to expand their working vocabulary develop eventually enough sophistication to be able to judge when their language is appropriate and when it is not.

Sentence **2** illustrates another kind of inappropriateness. The word **cheapen** was once a perfectly appropriate word as used in this context. During the Elizabethan period in England, it was a common verb meaning "to bid for," "to bargain for." If you look up the word in a modern dictionary, you will discover that

Style

cheapen in this sense is labeled archaic. The label means that the word in that sense can no longer be used in a modern context.

The more common fault of inappropriateness, however, is diction that is too colloquial or too slangy for its context. This fault is illustrated in sentences **3** and **4**. Although there are contexts in which the colloquial word **kids** would be more appropriate than the word *children*, sentence **3** seems not to be one of those contexts. There are contexts where slang and even the jargon of particular social groups would be perfectly appropriate, but the slang in sentence **4** seems to be out of tune with the subject matter and with almost all of the other words in the sentence.

Since dictionaries, thesauruses, and handbooks will not be of much help in telling a writer that a word is inappropriate, the writer will have to rely on the criteria of subject matter, occasion, audience, desired effect, and personality of the author. Another way of putting this precept is to say that the writer's "voice" must remain in harmony with the overall tone that he or she has established in a particular piece of writing.

Here are some revisions of the sample sentences, with more appropriate diction:

1 He didn't want to upset his mother, so he wrote her a note to inform her that he would be late.

2 Whenever I visit a new city, I browse through a secondhand bookstore and eventually bid for a book.

3 The conclusion that I have come to is that children should not have to suffer for the sins of their fathers.

4 Merchants in areas where the freeway would be built have persistently opposed the project, claiming that it would disturb the residents and disconcert the eccentric transients in the area.

43

Use the proper idiom.

Examples of lapse of idiom:

1 Although I agree **to** a few of Socrates' principles, I must disagree **to** many of them.

2 Formerly devoted **on** a theatrical career, she developed a strong passion **in** gourmet cooking.

3 Conformity has been a common tendency throughout **the** American history.

4 Nobody seems immune **from** pressures.

5 It's these special characters and their motives that I intend **on concentrating** in this paper.

6 Abner had no interest or respect **for** the boy.

To label a locution unidiomatic is to indicate that native speakers of the language do not say it that way—in any dialect of the language. Unidiomatic expressions are one of the commonest weaknesses to be found in the prose of unpracticed writers. Why do lapses of idiom occur so frequently? That is a good question to ask, because writers presumably do not hear other native speakers use the curious expressions that they write down on paper. One explanation for the frequency of idiomatic lapses is that in writing, unpracticed writers use words and structures that they seldom or never use in speech; and because they have not paid close enough attention to the way native speakers say something, they make a guess—usually a wrong guess—at how the expression should be phrased.

No word by itself is ever unidiomatic. Only combinations of words can be unidiomatic. The commonest kind of idiomatic lapse is the one that occurs with a preposition. Three of the first

Style

four sample sentences above involve idiomatic lapses in the use of prepositions.

A number of prepositions fit idiomatically with the verbs **agree** and **disagree**, but the preposition that fits idiomatically with the sense of **agree** and **disagree** in sentence **1** is **with**. There will be other contexts when the correct preposition to use with **agree** will be **to** ("They agreed to the conditions we laid down") or **on** ("They can't agree on the wording of the proposal").

There are two unidiomatic prepositions in sentence **2**. Native speakers don't say "devoted **on**" or "a passion **in**"; they say "devoted **to**" and "a passion **for**." In a sentence like **4**, above, native speakers don't say "immune **from**"; they say "immune **to**."

No native speaker of English would use the article **the** in the phrase **throughout the American history** (see sentence **3**). However, an American speaker would say, "He was in the hospital," whereas a British speaker would say, "He was in hospital." Some Asian speakers have trouble with the English article, because their language does not use a part of speech like it.

Sentence **5** above is clearly an instance of a writer's using a structure that he or she has never attempted before and failing to recall how native speakers phrase it. The structure should be phrased in this way: "intend **to concentrate on**."

Unidiomatic expressions often appear in compounded phrases, as in sentence **6**. The preposition **for** fits with **respect** ("respect **for** the boy"), but it does not fit with **interest** (not "interest **for** the boy" but "interest **in** the boy"). In such cases, the idiomatic preposition must be inserted for both members of the compound (see the revision below).

What prevents a handbook from setting reliable guidelines for proper idiom is the fact that logic plays little or no part in establishing the idioms of a language. If logic were involved in establishing idioms, we would say, "He looked *down* the word in the dictionary" instead of what we do say, "He looked *up* the word in the dictionary." Likewise, the logical preposition to use with the verb **center** is **on**—"Her efforts centered on community service." But more and more, usage seems to be establishing the idiom of **around** with **center**—"Her efforts centered around community service." Editors or teachers can call your attention to an unidiomatic expression and can insert the correct idiom, but they cannot give you any rule that will prevent other lapses of idiom. You simply have to learn proper idioms by reading more and by listening more intently.

Here are the revisions of the unidiomatic expressions:

1 Although I agree **with** a few of Socrates' principles, I must disagree **with** many of them.

2 Formerly devoted **to** a theatrical career, she developed a strong passion **for** gourmet cooking.

3 Conformity has been a common tendency throughout American history.

4 Nobody seems immune **to** pressures.

5 It's these special characters and their motives that I intend **to concentrate on** in this paper.

6 Abner had no interest **in,** or respect **for,** the boy.

44

Avoid trite expressions.

Examples of trite expressions:

1 I returned from the picnic **tired but happy,** and that night **I slept like a log**

Style

2 My primary objective in coming to college was to get a **well-rounded education**

3 The construction of two new hotels was a **giant step forward** for the community.

4 In the last few years, the popularity of ice hockey has grown **by leaps and bounds.**

5 Convinced now that drugs are a temptation for young people, the community must **nip the problem in the bud** before it **runs rampant**

There is nothing grammatically or idiomatically wrong with a trite expression. A trite expression is *stylistically* objectionable—mainly because it is a *tired* expression. Whether an expression is "tired" is, of course, a relative matter. What is lackluster for some readers may be bright-penny new for others. But it would be surprising if the expressions in the examples above were not jaded for most readers.

Trite expressions are certain combinations of words or certain figures of speech that have been used so often that they have lost their freshness and even their meaning for most readers. Rhetorically, the price that writers pay for their use of trite language is the alienation of their readers. Readers stop paying attention. Writers may have something new and important to say, but if their message is delivered in threadbare language, they will lose or fail to capture the attention of their readers.

Figures of speech are especially prone to staleness. Metaphors like "nip in the bud," "slept like a log," "giant step" were once fresh and cogent; they are now wilted from overuse. Trite combinations of words like "tired but happy," "by leaps and bounds," "runs rampant" produce glazed-eyed readers. Ironically, one of the ways in which to revise sentences that have trite language is to use the most familiar, ordinary language. Sentence 1, for example, would be improved if the **but happy** part of the combination were dropped and if a simple adverb were substituted for the simile **like a log**:

> I returned from the picnic tired, and that night I slept soundly.

Sometimes, making a daring alteration in a tired expression can rejuvenate the sentence. Look at what happens to the yawn-producing **well-rounded education** in this revision of sentence 2:

> My primary objective in coming to college was to get a well-squared education.

If you make an effort to invent your own figures of speech, you may produce awkward, strained figures, but at least they will be fresh. Instead of borrowing the hackneyed metaphor **nip the problem in the bud**, make up your own metaphor:

> Convinced now that drugs are a temptation for young people, the community should excise the tumor before it becomes a raging cancer.

It takes a great deal of sophistication about language even to recognize trite expressions, and those who don't read very much can hardly be expected to detect tired language, because almost all the expressions that they encounter are relatively new to them. They may have to rely on others to point out the trite language in their prose.

Be wary of weary words.

45

Rephrase awkwardly constructed sentences.

Examples of awkward sentences:

1 You could get a dose of the best exercise a person could undertake,

walking. I believe a person should walk at a leisurely pace, with no set goal on distance.

2 The football player has had many broken noses, with which he ends up looking like a prizefighter.

3 I and probably everybody else who started drinking beer in their sophomore year of high school thought the only thing to do was get drunk and go to school activities where we could meet and have a good time.

The fault dealt with in **32**, in the Grammar section, concerns sentences that are so badly put together that they reveal no meaning or only a vague meaning. Awkward sentences, which are dealt with in this section, are sentences so ineptly put together that they are difficult—but not impossible—for readers to understand. They are sentences that are grammatically passable but stylistically weak.

The problem is that those who write awkwardly constructed sentences are usually not aware that they are doing so; they have to be told that their sentences are awkward. The ear, however, is a reliable resource for detecting awkward sentences. If writers adopt the practice of reading their sentences aloud, they will often detect clumsy, odd-sounding combinations of words. Thus alerted, they can then examine their sentences for the presence of any of the usual causes of awkwardness:

(a) Excessive number of words (see sentence **3**)

(b) Words and phrases out of their normal order (note the position of **walking** in sentence **1**)

(c) Successions of prepositional phrases ("the president of the largest chapter of the national fraternity of students of dentistry")

(d) Pretentious circumlocutions ("the penultimate month of the year" for "November")

(e) Split constructions ("I, chastened by my past experiences, resolved to never consciously and maliciously circulate, even if true, damaging reports about my friends")

(f) Successions of rhyming words ("She tries wisely to revise the evidence supplied by her eyes")

In rephrasing awkward sentences, writers might try expressing the same thoughts in the way they would if they were *speaking* the sentences to others. These spoken versions might need some further touching up, but they probably would no longer be awkward. For example, the phrasing "the president of the largest fraternity chapter of dental students" gets rid of two of the four prepositional phrases that were in the original version **(c)** Shifting the word order gets rid of some of the awkwardness caused by the split constructions **(d)**: "Chastened by my past experiences, I resolved never to circulate damaging reports about my friends consciously and maliciously, even if they were true." Choosing synonymous words eliminates the series of rhyming words **(f)**: "She attempts a judicious alteration of the evidence presented by her eyes." A writer might still want to polish those sentences further, but whatever other faults those revisions still have, at least the awkwardness has been removed.

The sample sentences at the beginning of this section are awkward for a variety of reasons, but what they all have in common is wordiness. Pruning some of the deadwood, rearranging some of the parts, using simpler, more idiomatic phrases, we can improve the articulation of those clumsy sentences:

1 Walking is the best exercise. A person should walk at a leisurely pace and only as far as he feels like going.

2 The football player has broken his nose so often that he looks like a prizefighter.

3 Like everybody else who started drinking beer as a high-school

sophomore, I thought that getting drunk and going to school activities would be the best way to ensure a good time.

Construct your sentences so smoothly that your readers won't have to stumble through them.

46

Cut out unnecessary words.

Examples of wordy sentences:

1 He was justified in trying to straighten out his mother on her backward ideas about her attitude toward blacks.

2 In this modern world of today, we must get an education that will prepare us for a job in our vocation in life.

3 In the "Garden of Love," the poem relates the sad experience of a child being born into a cruel world.

4 The meaning, at least in my own eyes, that he is trying to convey in the poem "Arms and the Boy" is of the evilness of war in that it forces innocent people to take up the instruments of death and destruction and then tries to teach them to love to use them to kill other human beings.

5 These rivers do not contain fish, due to the fact that the flow of water is too rapid.

A "wordy sentence" is one in which a writer has used more words than are needed to say what has to be said. The superfluous words simply clutter up a sentence and impede its movement. Speakers are especially prone to verbosity because words come so easily to their tongues. But writers too are prone to verbosity once they acquire a certain facility with words. Facile writers have to make a conscious effort to control their expenditure of words. Writers would soon learn to cultivate restraint if they were charged for every word used, as they are when they send a telegram. They should not, of course, strive for a "telegraphic" or a "headline" style, but they should learn to value words so much that they spend words sparingly.

Let us see if we can trim the sample sentences without substantially altering their meaning:

1 He was justified in trying to straighten out his mother's attitude toward blacks. (from 19 to 13 words)

2 In the modern world, we must get an education that will prepare us for a job. (from 23 to 13 words)

3 The "Garden of Love" relates the sad experience of a child born into a cruel world. (from 20 to 16 words)

4 As I see it, the poet's thesis in "Arms and the Boy" is that war is evil because it not only forces people to take up arms but makes them use these weapons to kill other human beings. (from 58 to 38 words)

5 These rivers do not contain fish, because they flow too rapidly. (from 18 to 11 words)

Each of the revised sentences uses fewer words than the original. The retrenchment ranges from four words to twenty words. If the writers were being charged a quarter a word, they could probably find other superfluous words to prune. The writer of the fourth sentence, for instance, would lop off **As I see it** and would condense **to kill other human beings** to **to kill others**.

One should not become obsessed with saving words, but one should seize every opportunity, in the revising stage, to clear out obvious deadwood. As Alexander Pope said,

> Words are like leaves, and where they most abound,
> Much fruit of sense beneath is rarely found.

47

Avoid careless or needless repetition of words and ideas.

Examples of careless or needless repetition:

1 Mrs. Bucks, a **fellow colleague**, offered to intercede with the dean.

2 He does not rely on the **surrounding environment** as much as his sister does.

3 The objective point of view accentuates the emotional intensity of the love affair and the **impending** failure that will **eventually happen.**

4 **In Larry's mind** he **thinks**, "I have never met anyone so absorbed in himself."

5 There are some striking similarities between Segal and Hemingway, for **both** have studied life and love and found them **both** to be failures.

6 After **setting** up camp, we **set** off to watch the sun **set.**

A "careless or needless repetition" refers either to the recurrence of a word in the same sentence or in adjoining sentences or to the use of synonymous words that produces what is called a **redundancy** or a **tautology.**

The emphasis in this caution about repetition should be put on the words *careless* and *needless*, for there are cases where repetition serves a purpose. Item **51** in the next section, for instance, shows that the repetition of key words can be an effective means of achieving coherence in a paragraph. Sometimes too it is better to repeat a word, even in the same sentence, than to run the risk of ambiguity or misunderstanding. In the first sentence of this paragraph, for example, the word **repetition** has been repeated because the use of the pronoun *it* in place of **repetition** would be ambiguous ("The emphasis in this caution about repetition should be put on the words *careless* and *needless*, for there are cases where **it** serves a purpose").

The boldfaced words in the first four examples above are instances or redundancy or tautology (needless repetition of the same idea in different words). **Fellow** and **colleague, surrounding** and **environment, impending** and **eventually happen** are examples of needless repetition. In sentence **4**, the phrase **In Larry's mind** is superfluous (where else does one **think** but in the mind?). The repetition of the pronoun **both** in sentence **5** is especially careless because the repeated pronouns have different antecedents (the first one refers to **Segal** and **Hemingway**, the second to **life** and **love.** In sentence **6**, we have an instance of the same basic verb form (**set**) repeated in three different senses.

Here are revisions of the sample sentences to eliminate the repetitions:

1 Mrs. Bucks, a **colleague,** offered to intercede with the dean.

2 He does not rely on the **environment** as much as his sister does.

3 The objective point of view accentuates the emotional intensity of the love affair and its **impending** failure.

4 Larry **thinks**, "I have never met anyone so absorbed in himself."

5 There are some striking similarities between Segal and Hemingway, for both of them have studied life and love and found them to be failures.

6 After preparing camp, we took off to watch the sun set.

48

Avoid mixed metaphors.

Examples of mixed metaphors:

1 Sarty finally comes to the point where his inner turmoil reaches its **zenith** and **stagnates in a pool** of lethargy.

2 In "The Dead," James Joyce uses small talk as an effective **weapon** to **illustrate** his thesis.

3 She tried to **scale the wall** of indifference between them but found that she couldn't **burrow** through it.

4 The experience struck a **spark** that **massaged** the poet's imagination.

5 When we tried to get the mayor's campaign **off the ground,** we found that his campaign **sank in a sea** of indifference.

A mixed metaphor is the result of a writer's failure to keep a consistent image in mind. All metaphors are based on the perceived likenesses between things that exist in different orders of being—as for instance between a *man* and a *greyhound* ("The lean shortstop is a greyhound when he runs the bases"), *fame* and a *spur* ("Fame is the spur to ambition"), *mail* and an *avalanche* ("The mail buried the staff under an avalanche of complaints"). Whenever any detail is incompatible with one or other of the terms of the analogy, the metaphor is said to be mixed.

Zenith, in sentence 1, connotes something rising to its highest point, and therefore that image of ascending motion is incompatible with the detail of **stagnation**. Likewise, a **weapon** is not used to **illustrate** something. If one were climbing (**scaling**) a wall, one could not dig (**burrow**) through it at the same time. A **spark** could start a fire, but it couldn't **massage** anything. The basic metaphor in the first half of the fifth sentence above is that of an airplane taking off, but in the second half of the sentence, the metaphor shifts to that of a ship sinking.

The following revisions unscramble the mixed metaphors:

1 Sarty finally comes to the point where his inner turmoil reaches its **zenith** and **fizzles out** into lethargy.

2 In "The Dead," James Joyce uses small talk as a **mirror** to **reflect** his thesis.

3 She tried to **scale the wall** of indifference between them but found that she couldn't **surmount** it.

4 The experience struck a **spark** that **ignited** the poet's imagination.

5 When we tried to get the mayor's campaign **off the ground**, we found that the campaign didn't **get up enough speed** to become **airborne**

Forming and maintaining a clear picture of the notion one is attempting to express figuratively will ensure a consistent metaphor.

49

Consider whether an active verb would be preferable to a passive verb.

Examples of questionable use of the passive voice:

1 Money **was borrowed** by the couple so that they could pay off all their bills.

2 His love for her **is shown** by his accepting her story and by his remaining at her side when she is in trouble.

3 From these recurrent images of hard, resistant metals, it **can be inferred** by us that she was a mechanical, heartless person.

4 Talking incessantly, he **was overwhelmed** by the girl.

Style

The passive voice of the verb is a legitimate and useful part of the English language. A sentence using a passive verb as its predicate is a different but synonymous way of expressing the thought conveyed by a sentence using an active verb. The basic formula for a sentence using an active-verb construction is as follows:

NOUN PHRASE₁   +   VERB   +   NOUN PHRASE₂

The judge   pronounced   the verdict

The formula for transforming that active-verb construction into a passive-verb construction is as follows:

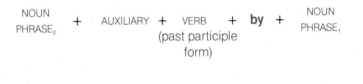

NOUN PHRASE₂   +   AUXILIARY   +   VERB (past participle form)   +   **by**   +   NOUN PHRASE₁

The verdict   was   pronounced   by   the judge

Notice the changes that have taken place in the second sentence: (1) Noun Phrase₁ and Noun Phrase₂ have switched positions, and (2) two words have been added, the auxiliary **was** and the preposition **by.** Although the second sentence expresses the same thought as the first sentence, it is longer, by two words, than the first sentence.

If the use of a passive verb is questionable, it is questionable stylistically, not grammatically. To question the use of a passive verb is to ask the writer to consider whether the sentence would not be more emphatic or more economical or less awkward or somehow "neater" if an active verb were used. Challenged to consider the options available in a particular case, the writer is the final judge of the best choice in that case.

Writers sometimes decide to use the passive verb because they want to give special emphasis to some word in the sentence. In sentence **1**, the word **money** gets special emphasis because it occupies the initial position. If the active verb were used, the word **couple** would get the special emphasis. It would be more difficult to cite emphasis as the justification for the choice of passive verbs in sentences **2** and **3**. Writers can also justify the use of a passive verb when they do not know the agent of an action or prefer not to reveal the agent or consider it unnecessary to indicate the agent, as in the sentence ''The story was reported to all the newspapers.''

Dangling verbals often result from the use of a passive verb in the main clause of the sentence (see **25** on dangling verbals). The context of sentence **4** suggests that the lead-off participial phrase (**talking incessantly**) may be dangling—that is, that it was not the boy (**he**) but **the girl** who was talking incessantly. If that is so, the writer may not choose the passive verb for the main clause but must use the active verb.

The writers of the sample sentences should consider whether their sentences would be improved by the use of an active verb, as in these revisions:

1 The couple **borrowed** money so that they could pay off all their bills.

2 He **shows** his love for her by accepting her story and by remaining at her side when she is in trouble.

3 From these recurrent images of hard, resistant metals, we **can infer** that she was a mechanical, heartless person.

4 Talking incessantly, the girl **overwhelmed** him.

Paragraphing

One way to regard paragraphing is to view it as a system of punctuating stages of thought presented in units larger than the word and the sentence. Paragraphing is a means of alerting readers to a shift of focus in the development of the main idea of the whole discourse. It marks off for the reader's convenience the individually distinct but related parts of the whole discourse. How paragraphing facilitates reading would be made dramatically evident if a whole discourse were written or printed—as ancient manuscripts once were—in a single, unbroken block.

Like punctuation and mechanics, paragraphing is a feature only of the written language. Some linguists claim that speakers of connected discourse signal their "paragraphs" by pauses and by shifts in the tone of their voice. (The next time you hear a speech being delivered from a written text, see if you can detect when the speaker shifts to another paragraph of his or her text.) But speakers are not conscious—especially in extemporaneous stretches of talk—of paragraphing the stream of sound as writers must be when they are writing their manuscripts.

The typographical device most commonly used to mark off paragraphs is *indentation.* The first line of each new paragraph starts several spaces (usually five or six spaces on the typewriter) from the left-hand margin. Another convention for marking paragraphs is the block system: beginning the first line at the left-hand margin but leaving double or triple spacing between paragraphs. One of the forms of writing that regularly uses the block system is the single-spaced, typewritten business letter.

In this section, only three aspects of the paragraph are treated: unity, coherence, and adequate development. The traditional means of developing the central idea of a paragraph are mentioned in the section on adequate development, but they are not discussed at length. The means of developing paragraphs are fundamentally a concern of invention, which is the province of a rhetoric text rather than of a handbook. However, if writers take care of unity, coherence, and adequate development, they will be attending to the three most persistent and common problems that beset the composition of written paragraphs.

50

Preserve the unity of the paragraph.

Examples of paragraphs lacking unity:

1 The eminence of Samuel Johnson inclines modern scholars to study his thoughts and opinions. His multifarious knowledge intrigued his contemporaries. Although he manifested his interest in the drama by editing Shakespeare, he did not enjoy the theater. He was envious too of his former pupil David Garrick, the greatest actor of the eighteenth century.

2 "The Cradle Song" from the *Songs of Innocence* has internal rhyme. In this poem, the child is quiet and happy. It has a heavenly

Paragraphing

image, and throughout the poem, the mother sheds tears of joy. It has a persona—that is, one who speaks for the poet—who is naive and innocent. The poem "Infant Sorrow" contrasts with "The Cradle Song," and this contrast is very distinct. One can see a screaming and devilish child. The piping is a harsh sound, and the child, who's against restrictions, is looking back and realizing that there is no paradise on earth.

3 Dr. Rockwell let his feelings be known on only one subject: the administration. He felt that the administrative system was outdated. Abolishing grades, giving the student a voice in administration, and revamping the curriculum were three steps he felt should be taken to improve the system. Dr. Rockwell taught in this manner. In class, a mysterious aura surrounded him. He was "hip" to what was going on, but he preferred to hear the members of the class rather than himself. He was quiet and somewhat shy. His eyes caught everything that went on in class. His eyes generated a feeling of understanding.

The principle governing paragraph unity is that a paragraph should develop a single topic or thesis, which is often—but not always—announced in a topic sentence. Every sentence in the paragraph should contribute in some way to the development of that single idea. When writers introduce other ideas into the paragraph, they violate the unity of the paragraph and disorient their readers.

In a sense, all three of the sample paragraphs discuss a single idea or topic: **1** talks about Samuel Johnson; **2** talks about William Blake's poetry; **3** talks about a teacher, Dr. Rockwell. But in another sense, all three paragraphs present a confusing mixture of unrelated ideas.

The first sentence of paragraph **1**, which has the air of being a "topic sentence," mentions that modern scholars have turned their attention to a study of Samuel Johnson. Instead of the second sentence going on to develop that idea, it mentions what

Dr. Johnson meant to his contemporaries. The third sentence talks about his attitude toward drama and the theater. The fourth sentence mentions his envy of his former pupil David Garrick. What we have in this paragraph is four topics. A whole paragraph or paper could be devoted to the development of each of these four topics, but here they are packed into a single paragraph.

Paragraph 2, as we have already observed, has a certain unity: each sentence is saying something about a poem by William Blake. Even though this paragraph discusses two different poems by Blake, we can detect some unity in the paragraph if we view it as developing a contrast between two poems by the same author. And, indeed, midway through the paragraph, the writer explicitly announces that the two poems contrast with one another. But even if we were generous enough to concede that much unity to the paragraph, it would be difficult for us to perceive a unifying theme among the many disparate things said about the two poems.

Paragraph 3 also has a certain unity: each sentence in the paragraph is talking about the teacher, Dr. Rockwell. And there is a tight unity in the first three sentences: each of these sentences talks about Dr. Rockwell's attitude toward the administration. But with the fourth sentence of the paragraph, the writer introduces another and unrelated topic: a description of how Dr. Rockwell conducted himself in the classroom. If the writer had broken up this stretch of prose into two paragraphs, each of the two paragraphs would have had its own unity.

Each of the following revisions constitutes one of several ways in which the corresponding sample paragraph might have been unified:

1 The eminence of Samuel Johnson inclines modern scholars to study his thoughts and opinions. A number of recent books and articles

Paragraphing

have dealt with his viewpoints on a variety of his interests. One of those interests was the drama. Curiously, however, although he manifested this interest by writing his own play for the stage and by editing all the plays of Shakespeare, he did not enjoy the theater. Some modern scholars have speculated that he did not enjoy the theater because of his poor eyesight and impaired hearing. Others have speculated that he disliked the theater because he was jealous of his former pupil David Garrick, who very early in his career acquired the reputation of being the greatest actor of his day.

2 William Blake's "The Cradle Song" contrasts distinctly with his poem "Infant Sorrow." Whereas the child in "The Cradle Song" is quiet and happy, the child in "Infant Sorrow" is strident and devilish. Both poems have a persona—that is, one who speaks for the poet—but the persona in "The Cradle Song" is naive and innocent, whereas the persona in the other poem is worldly-wise and guilt-ridden. The rhythms and rhymes in the first poem are smooth and pleasant, but the rhythms and rhymes of the second poem are harsh and discordant. One poem presents an overall mood of contentment; the other presents a mood of disillusionment.

3 Dr. Rockwell let his feelings be known on only one subject: the administration. His estimate of the administrative system of the school was largely negative. He felt, for instance, that the administrative system was outdated. Abolishing grades, giving students a voice in administration, and revamping the curriculum were three steps he felt should be taken to improve the system.

Dr. Rockwell's demeanor in the classroom was remarkable. Although there was a mysterious aura about him, he was always "hip" to what was going on. His eyes caught everything that went on in class, but they generated a feeling of understanding. Even though he was a very learned scholar, this quiet, somewhat shy man preferred to listen to the members of the class rather than himself.

A paragraph will have unity, will have "oneness," if every sentence in it has an obvious bearing on the development of a single topic. When writers sense that they have shifted to the discussion of another topic, they should begin a new paragraph.

51

Compose the paragraph so that it reads coherently.

Examples of incoherent paragraphs:

1 The first stanza of "The Echoing Green" does not correspond with any other poem by Blake. The glory of nature's beauty is presented in vivid details. Emotional intensity is the overall effect of the poem. Blake resents the mechanization which has been brought about by the Industrial Revolution. The rhythm of the verses contributes to the meditative mood.

2 The preceding account illustrates all the frustrations that a beginning golfer experiences. The dominant philosophy is that the golfer who looks the best plays the best. He complicates the game by insisting on perfection the first time he sets foot on the course. More time and money are spent on clothes and equipment than on the most important aspect, skill. Winning is the only goal. Where is the idea of recreation? Try playing without a caddy sometime, and see how much exercise you get.

3 After the program has been written, each line is punched onto a card. The deck of cards is known as the "program source deck." The next step is to load the program compiler into the computer. The compiler is a program written in machine language for a particular computer, which reads the source deck and performs a translation of the program language into machine language. The machine language, in the form of instructions, is punched onto cards. This machine-language deck of cards is known as the "object deck." After the object deck has been punched, the programmer is then able

Paragraphing

to execute his program. The program is run by loading the object deck into the computer. The run of the program marks the end of the second step.

Coherence is that quality which makes it easy for a reader to follow a writer's train of thought from sentence to sentence and from paragraph to paragraph. Coherence facilitates reading because it ensures that the reader will be able to detect the relationship of the parts of a discourse. It also reflects the clear thinking of the writer because it results from the writer's arrangement of ideas in some kind of perceptible order and from the use of those verbal devices that help to stitch thoughts together. In short, as the Latin roots of the word suggest (*co*, "together," + *haerēre*, "to stick"), coherence helps the parts of a discourse "stick together."

Here are some ways in which to achieve coherence in a paragraph (not all of these devices, of course, have to be used in every paragraph):

(a) Repeat key words from sentence to sentence or use recognizable synonyms for key words.

(b) Use pronouns for key nouns. (Because a pronoun gets its meaning from the noun to which it refers, it is by its very nature one of those verbal devices that help to stitch sentences together.)

(c) Use demonstrative adjectives, "pointing words" (**this** statement, **that** plan, **these** developments, **those** disasters).

(d) Use conjunctive adverbs, "thought-connecting words" **(however, moreover, also, nevertheless, therefore, thus, subsequently, indeed, then, accordingly).**

(e) Arrange the sequence of sentences in some kind of perceivable order (for instance, a **time order,** as in a narrative of what happened or in an explanation of how to do something;

a **space order,** as in the description of a physical object or a scene; a **logical order,** such as cause to effect, effect to cause, general to particular, particular to general, whole to part, familiar to unfamiliar).

Paragraph 3 above attempts to describe computer programming, a process that most readers would find difficult to follow because it is unfamiliar and complicated. But the process will be doubly difficult for readers if it is not described coherently. What makes this description of computer programming especially difficult to follow is that the writer is doing two things at once in the paragraph: (1) designating the chronological sequence of steps in the process, and (2) defining the technical terms used in the description of the process. It would have been better if the writer had devoted one paragraph to defining such terms as **program source deck, compiler, object deck.** Then the writer could have devoted another paragraph exclusively to the description of the process of "running a program"—first you do this, then you do that, after that you do this, etc. As the paragraph now stands, readers get lost because they are kept bouncing back and forth between definition of the terms and description of the process.

It is more difficult to suggest ways of revising paragraphs 1 and 2; they are so incoherent that it is almost impossible to discover what the principal points were that the writers wanted to put across in them. If we could confer with the writers and ask them what the main idea of their paragraphs was supposed to be, we could then advise them about which of the sentences contributed to the development of that idea (and which sentences had to be dropped because they threatened the unity of the paragraph), about the order of the sentences in the given paragraph, and about the verbal devices that would help to knit the sequence of sentences together.

Paragraphing

Each of the following revisions constitutes one of a number of ways in which the corresponding sample might have been written to give it coherence:

1 It is interesting to note how William Blake achieves the emotional intensity that he does in "The Echoing Green." He achieves that intensity partly by presenting the glory of nature in vivid details that contrast with the dull, gray mechanization of the urban scene that has been produced by the Industrial Revolution. The slow rhythm of the verses also contributes to the emotional intensity by creating a meditative mood. The extraordinary collection of images in the first stanza of the poem also serves to exert a strong emotional effect on the reader.

2 The beginning golfer is often frustrated by the false sense of values that he has been sold. For one thing, he spends more time and money on buying clothes and equipment than on acquiring the most important aspect, skill. Apparently, he has bought the philosophy that the golfer who looks the best plays the best. Moreover, because he has bought the philosophy that winning is the only goal, he has lost sight of the goal of recreation. He insists on perfection the first time he sets foot on the course instead of being satisfied with the fun and exercise he gets from playing a round of eighteen holes.

3 Before you can understand the process of "running a program," you need some definitions of technical terms. After the program discussed in the previous paragraph has been written, each line of that program is punched onto an IBM card. The collection of these cards is known as the "program source deck." Another set of cards is known as the "compiler." The compiler "reads" the source deck and translates it into machine language. The machine-language deck of cards that results from the operation of the compiler is known as the "object deck."

The first step in the process is to put the program source deck into the computer. Then in order to translate the program language of the source deck into machine language, the compiler set must be inserted. Following that step, the object deck, with its instructions written out in machine language, is put into the computer. Now the program is ready to be "run" through the computer.

Coherence is a difficult writing skill to master, but until writers acquire at least a measure of that skill, they will continue to be frustrated in their efforts to communicate with others on paper. They must learn how to compose paragraphs so that the sequence of thoughts flows smoothly, easily, and logically from sentence to sentence. They must provide those bridges or links that will allow the reader to pass from sentence to sentence without being puzzled about the relationship of what is said in one sentence to what is said in the next sentence.

Note how a skillful writer like Thomas Babington Macaulay stitches sentences together by repeating key words and by using pronouns, conjunctive words, and parallel structures:

It will be seen that we do not consider Bacon's ingenious analysis of the inductive method as a very useful performance. Bacon was not, as we have already said, the inventor of the inductive method. He was not even the person who first analyzed the inductive method correctly, though he undoubtedly analyzed it more minutely than any who preceded him. He was not the person who first showed that by the inductive method alone new truth could be discovered. But he was the person who first turned the minds of speculative men, long occupied in verbal disputes, to the discovery of new and useful truth; and by doing so, he at once gave to the inductive method an importance and dignity which had never belonged to it. He was not the maker of that road; he was not the discoverer of that road; he was not the person who first surveyed and mapped that road. But he was the person who first called the public attention to an inexhaustible mine of wealth, which had been utterly neglected and which was accessible by that road alone. By doing so, he caused that road, which had previously been trodden only by peasants and higglers, to be frequented by a higher class of travellers.

52

Paragraphs should be adequately developed.

Examples of inadequately developed paragraphs:

1 The government has resorted to many methods of preventing tax frauds. Most of these methods have proved ineffective so far.

2 The young people now growing up in this drug-oriented atmosphere should be made aware of the disadvantages of their indulging in drugs, just as the young people of the previous generation were cautioned about the disadvantages of their engaging in premarital sex. In both cases, responsibility for one's actions is the chief lesson to be taught.

3 Before we seek answers to those questions, however, we should settle on a definition of the term *illiteracy*. For most people, *illiteracy* signifies the inability to read and write.

Generally, one- and two-sentence paragraphs are not justifiable, except for purposes of emphasis, transition, or dialogue.

Note that this last sentence is also a paragraph, justifiable as such on the grounds that the writer wanted to give special emphasis to a principle by setting it aside in a paragraph by itself. Separate paragraphing for emphasis is a graphic device comparable to underlining a word or a phrase in a sentence for emphasis. Set aside in a paragraph by itself, an important idea achieves a prominence that would be missed if the idea were merged with other ideas in the same paragraph.

A one- or two-sentence paragraph can also be used to mark or signal a transition from one major division of a discourse to the next major division. These transitional paragraphs facilitate reading because they orient readers, reminding them of what has been discussed and alerting them to what is going to be discussed. Such paragraphs are like signposts marking the major stages of a journey. Note how the following two-sentence transitional paragraph looks backward to what has been discussed and forward to what will be discussed:

> After presenting his introduction to *Songs of Experience*, William Blake apparently feels that his readers have been sufficiently warned about their earthly predicament. Let us see now how he uses the poems in *Songs of Experience* to illustrate what the people might do to solve their problems.

One of the conventions of printing is that in representing dialogue in a story, we should begin a new paragraph every time the speaker changes. A paragraph of dialogue can be one sentence long or ten sentences long (any number of sentences, in fact). A paragraph of dialogue may also consist of only a phrase or a single word. Note the paragraphing of the following stretch of dialogue:

> "Look at that cloudless blue sky," Melvin said. "There doesn't seem to be any bottom to that blue. It's beautiful, isn't it?"
>
> "Yup," Hank muttered.
>
> "Remember yesterday?"
>
> "Yup."
>
> "I thought it would never stop raining."
>
> "Me too."

Once an exchange like that gets going, the author can dispense with the identifying tags, because each separate paragraph will mark the shift in speaker.

But except for the purposes of emphasis, transition, or dialogue, a one- or a two-sentence paragraph can rarely be justified. One sentence is hardly enough to qualify as both the topic sentence and the development of the idea posed by that topic. Many times even three- and four-sentence paragraphs are not adequately developed. You will frequently see one-, two-, and sometimes three-sentence paragraphs in a newspaper, but newspapers arbitrarily break up paragraphs into small units merely to facilitate reading. In the narrow columns of a newspaper, a five- or six-sentence paragraph would look forbiddingly dense. So the short paragraph is a convention used by all newspapers.

Judgment about whether a paragraph is adequately developed is, of course, a relative matter. Because some ideas need more development than others, no one can say how many sentences a paragraph needs to be adequately developed. Each paragraph must be judged on its own terms and in the context in which it appears. If a paragraph has a topic sentence, for instance, that sentence can dictate how long the paragraph needs to be. What was done in the previous paragraph and what will be done in the paragraph that follows may dictate how long the middle paragraph needs to be.

The sample paragraphs have all been taken out of context, but even so, we can sense the inadequate development of these skimpy paragraphs. Paragraph **1**, for instance, raises some expectations that are not satisfied. The first sentence mentions **many methods**, and we expect that the next sentence will go on to specify at least one of those many methods. Instead, the writer changes the subject: we are now told that these methods (unspecified) have proved ineffective. First of all, the writer has to decide whether he or she wants this paragraph to specify the many methods that the government has used to prevent tax frauds or whether it is preferable to show how or why the methods proved ineffective. Having settled on the topic of the paragraph, the writer can then make some decisions about how to develop the paragraph and how much to develop it.

Even if paragraph **2** were a summary paragraph that followed a paragraph (or several paragraphs) in which the writer had discussed the disadvantages of indulging in drugs, the reader could reasonably expect the writer to say something more about the notion presented in the second sentence. What kind of legal or moral responsibilities do addicts have to themselves? What kind of responsibilities do they have to their family and to society in general? Once addicts have been "hooked," can they still be held responsible for their actions? What are the consequences, for themselves and for society, of their refusing to be responsible for their actions? These questions suggest ways in which the writer might have expanded the thinly developed paragraph.

A reader may feel that paragraph **3** is developed as much as it needs to be. The writer has suggested the need for a definition of the term **illiteracy** and in the next sentence has provided a definition of the term. But even lacking the context of both the paragraph that went before and the paragraph that came after this one, we can judge this paragraph to be inadequately developed. The mere fact that the writer felt the need to seek a definition of a principal term before going on with the discussion indicates that the writer recognized the slipperiness of the term. The phrase that begins the second sentence, **For most people,** suggests that regardless of the common meaning of **illiteracy** (an inability to read and write), the term has other meanings for other people. What the reader expects to get in this paragraph and doesn't get is an exposition of the word's complex meanings. Refining the definition of the word **illiteracy** is one of the ways of expanding the paragraph.

The first step in developing a paragraph is to consider its central idea—whether that is expressed in a topic sentence or merely implied—and determine what that idea commits one to do. It sometimes helps to ask oneself questions like those that were asked above about the second sample paragraph. If such questioning establishes what one is committed to do in a para-

Paragraphing

graph, one can then make a choice of the appropriate means of developing the paragraph. Here is a list of the common ways in which writers develop their paragraphs:

(a)   **They present examples or illustrations of what they are discussing.**

(b)   **They cite data—facts, statistics, evidence, details, precedents—that corroborate or confirm what they are discussing.**

(c)   **They quote, paraphrase, or summarize the testimony of others about what they are discussing.**

(d)   **They relate an anecdote or event that has some bearing on what they are discussing.**

(e)   **They define terms connected with what they are discussing.**

(f)   **They compare or contrast what they are discussing with something else—usually something familiar to the readers—and point out similarities or differences.**

(g)   **They explore the causes or reasons for the phenomenon or situation they are discussing.**

(h)   **They point out the effects or consequences of the phenomenon or situation they are discussing.**

(i)   **They explain how something operates.**

(j)   **They describe the person, place, or thing they are discussing.**

Using one or other of these means of development, we could expand the inadequately developed sample paragraphs. Each of the following revisions constitutes one way in which the corresponding sample paragraph might have been expanded:

1   Most of the methods that the government has resorted to in order to prevent tax frauds have proved ineffective. For instance, the government tried the system of requiring restaurant owners to report

not only the salaries of waiters but also the amount of their daily tips. The waiters, of course, circumvented that system by never reporting the correct total of their tips. Cabdrivers, bellhops, doormen, and others whose chief source of income is tips are a problem too. The government tried setting a standard tip-per-transaction, but these employees rarely reported the correct number of customers they had served, and there was no way that the government could reliably check the figures that were reported. Those who are self-employed constitute the major problem for the Internal Revenue Service. All efforts to get the self-employed to keep and to report accurate or honest records of business transactions have proven futile. It seems that if you are determined enough and smart enough you can evade even the most ingenious efforts of the IRS to make you pay all the taxes that you should pay.

(*expanded by giving examples*)

2 Young people who develop an addiction to drugs should be made aware of their responsibilities for their actions. They must be taught that their insatiable appetite for drugs has consequences not only for themselves but also for family, friends, and society. Parents are the ones who are hurt the most by a son or daughter who gets hooked on drugs. They suffer deeply when they see someone they love become a slave to drugs; and they also feel ashamed and guilt-ridden for their child's addiction. Friends too suffer anguish and humiliation; but they suffer most from the loss of the companionship of a former friend. The effects on society are too numerous to specify completely, but they include the dangers from an addict's resort to violent crimes, the cost of maintaining special police forces, and the loss of a valuable contributing member to the community. Drug addicts don't just ruin themselves; they affect the lives of dozens of other people.

(*expanded by pointing out the effects or consequences of a situation*)

3 Before we seek answers to those questions, however, we should settle on a definition of the term *illiteracy*. For most people, *illiteracy* signifies a person's inability to read and write. But that general defi-

Paragraphing

nition does not reveal the wide range of disabilities covered by the term. There are those who cannot read or write anything in their native language. Others can read minimally, but they cannot write anything—not even their own name. A large number of people have minimal skills in reading and writing, but they cannot apply those skills to some of the ordinary tasks of day-to-day living—e.g. they cannot make sense of the written instructions on a can of weed-killer or fill out an application form. Such people are sometimes referred to as being "functionally illiterate." So whenever we discuss the problem of illiteracy with others, we should make sure what degree of disability people have in mind when they use the term *illiteracy*.

(expanded by defining or explaining a key term)

Punctuation

Graphic punctuation, which is the only kind dealt with in this section, is a feature of the written language exclusively. For the written language, it performs the kinds of functions that intonation (pitch, stress, pause, and juncture) performs for the spoken language. Punctuation and intonation can be considered as part of the grammar of a language because they join with other grammatical devices (word order, inflections, and function words) to help convey meaning. If writers would regard punctuation as an integral—and often indispensable—part of the expressive system of a language, they might cease to think of it as just another nuisance imposed on them by editors and English teachers.

In *Structural Essentials of English* (New York: Harcourt Brace Jovanovich, 1956), Harold Whitehall has neatly summarized the four main functions of graphic punctuation:

☐ **For LINKING parts of sentences and words.**
semicolon ;
colon :
dash ▬
hyphen (for words only) ▬

Punctuation

☐ For SEPARATING sentences and parts of sentences.

period **.**
question mark **?**
exclamation point **!**
comma **,**

☐ For ENCLOSING parts of sentences.

pair of commas **,** ... **,**

pair of dashes ▬ ... ▬

pair of parentheses **(** ... **)**

pair of brackets **[** ... **]**

pair of quotation marks **"** ... **"**

☐ For INDICATING omissions.

apostrophe (e.g. **don't, we'll, it's, we've**)
period (e.g. abbreviations, **Mrs., U.S.A. H. Robinson**)
dash (e.g. **John R—, D—n!**)
triple periods (**...** to indicate omitted words in a quotation)

Punctuation is strictly a convention. There is no reason in the nature of things why the mark **?** should be used in English to indicate a question. The Greek language, for instance, uses **;** (what we call a semicolon) to mark questions. Nor is there any reason in the nature of things why the single comma should be a separating device rather than a linking device. It is usage that has established the distinctive functions of the various marks of punctuation. And although styles of punctuation have changed somewhat from century to century and even from country to country, the conventions of punctuation set forth in the following section are the prevailing conventions in the United States in the last quarter of the twentieth century. Although publishers of newspapers, magazines, and books often have style manuals that prescribe, for their own editors and writers, a style of punctuation that may differ in some particulars from the prevailing conventions, writers who observe the conventions of punctuation set forth in this section can rest assured that they are following the predominant system in the United States.

60

Put a comma in front of the coordinating conjunction that joins the independent clauses of a compound sentence.

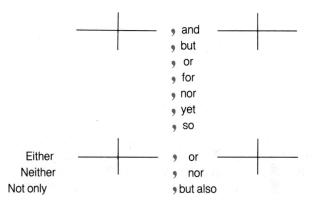

Examples of compound sentences that need a comma:

1 He disliked this kind of cruel humor yet he continued to tease her unmercifully.

Punctuation

2 Alice's embarrassment amused Julian so he deliberately pursued the conversation with the Dirty Old Man across the aisle.

3 He returned the book for his mother refused to pay any more fines.

4 The decision about whether to attend college should be left entirely to the children and their parents should make every effort to reconcile themselves to the decision.

5 It was snowing outside and in the building Kazuko felt safe.

6 Either the senators will reject the proposal or they will modify it in such a way as to make it innocuous.

This convention of the comma comes into play only in compound sentences (sentences composed of two or more independent clauses) or in compound-complex sentences (sentences composed of two or more independent clauses and at least one dependent clause). According to **62**, pairs of words, phrases, or clauses (except independent clauses) joined by one of the coordinating conjunctions should *not* be separated with a comma.

This practice of using a comma probably developed because in many compounded sentences, the absence of the comma could lead to an initial misreading of the sentence. In sentence **1**, for instance, it would be quite natural for us to read **for** as a preposition and consequently to read the sentence this way: **He returned the book for his mother**. . . . But when we came to the verb **refused**, we would realize that we had misread the syntax of the sentence, and we would have to back up and reread the sentence. Likewise, in sentence **4**, we tend to read the sentence in this way: . . . **should be left entirely to the children and their parents**. . . . But when we read on, we realize that the absence of a comma before the conjunction **and** has trapped us into a misreading of the syntax of the sentence. A comma placed before the coordinating conjunction that joins the independent clauses of a compound sentence will prevent such misreadings.

Some handbooks authorize you to omit this separating comma under certain conditions. However, if you *invariably* insert a comma before the coordinating conjunction that joins the independent clauses, you never have to pause to consider whether those conditions are present, and you can be confident that your sentence will always be read correctly the first time. So the safest practice is *always* to insert the comma before the coordinating conjunction or before the second of the correlative conjunctions (**either . . . or; neither . . . nor; not only . . . but also**) that join the main clauses of a compound or compound-complex sentence.

Here are the sample sentences with the comma inserted in the proper place:

1 He disliked this kind of cruel humor, yet he continued to tease her unmercifully.

2 Alice's embarrassment amused Julian, so he deliberately pursued the conversation with the Dirty Old Man across the aisle.

3 He returned the book, for his mother refused to pay any more fines.

4 The decision about whether to attend college should be left entirely to the children, and their parents should make every effort to reconcile themselves to the decision.

5 It was snowing outside, and in the building Kazuko felt safe.

6 Either the senators will reject the proposal, or they will modify it in such a way as to make it innocuous.

61

Introductory words, phrases, or clauses should be separated from the main (independent) clause by a comma.

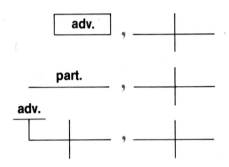

Examples of introductory words, phrases, and clauses that need a comma:

Underneath the papers were scorched.
(*introductory word*)

I tiptoed into the house. Inside the front room looked as though it had been recently painted by a group of three-year-olds.
(*introductory word*)

In addition to the logical errors Doris had made several miscalculations in addition and subtraction.
(*introductory prepositional phrase*)

As we went by the church revealed all of its redbrick Georgian elegance.
(*introductory adverbial clause*)

After hurriedly gathering the crowd decided to rush the gates.
(*introductory verbal phrase*)

6 Although she vehemently protested the violence was not as destructive as he predicted it would be.
  (*introductory adverbial clause*)

The reason this convention developed is that the comma facilitates the reading of the sentence and often prevents an initial misreading. Without the "protective" comma, the syntax of the six sample sentences above would probably be misread on the first reading. The likelihood is that you read the sample sentences this way the first time:

1 **Underneath the papers . . .**

2 **Inside the front room . . .**

3 **In addition to the logical errors [that] Doris had made . . .**

4 **As we went by the church . . .**

5 **After hurriedly gathering the crowd . . .**

6 **Although she vehemently protested the violence . . .**

The insertion of a comma after each of these introductory elements would have prevented that kind of misreading.

Even in those instances, however, where there is little or no chance of an initial misreading, the insertion of a comma after the introductory word, phrase, or clause will facilitate the reading of the sentence. If you read the following sentences twice, the first time without the comma, the second time with the comma after the introductory word, phrase, or clause, you will discover that it is easier to read and understand the sentences that have a comma after the introductory element:

Besides the crowd wasn't impressed by his flaming oratory.

Having failed to impress the crowd with his flaming oratory he tried another tactic.

After he saw that his flaming oratory had not impressed the crowd he tried another tactic.

Punctuation

Here now are the sample sentences with a comma inserted after the introductory word, phrase, or clause:

1 Underneath , the papers were scorched.
2 I tiptoed into the house. Inside , the front room looked as though it had been recently painted by a group of three-year-olds.
3 In addition to the logical errors , Doris had made several miscalculations in addition and substraction.
4 As we went by , the church revealed all of its redbrick Georgian elegance.
5 After hurriedly gathering , the crowd decided to rush the gates.
6 Although she vehemently protested , the violence was not as destructive as he predicted it would be.

If writers *always* insert a comma after an introductory word, phrase, or clause, they will not have to consider each time whether it would be safe to omit the comma, and they can be confident that their sentence will not be misread.

62

Pairs of words, phrases, or dependent clauses joined by one of the coordinating conjunctions should not be separated with a comma.

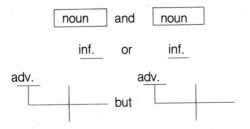

Examples of pairs incorrectly separated by a comma;

1 The mother **,** and the father appeared in court **,** and testified about their son's activities.

2 There was nothing they could do to prevent the gas attack **,** or to protect themselves against the gas once it had been released.

3 The men who are able to work **,** but who are not willing to work will not be eligible to receive monthly welfare checks.

4 Marian was happiest when she was free of her parents' scrutiny **,** or while she was working in her garden.

The principle behind this convention is that what has been joined by one means (the coordinating conjunction) should not then be separated by another means (the comma, a separating device). The function of the coordinating conjunction is to join units of equal rank (e.g. nouns with nouns, verbs with verbs, prepositional phrases with prepositional phrases, adjective clauses with adjective clauses). Once pairs of coordinate units have been joined by the conjunction, it makes no sense to separate them with a comma—as has been done in all the sample sentences above.

A pair of *independent* clauses is not covered by this rule. According to **60**, a comma should be inserted before the coordinating conjunction, because in this structure the omission of the comma could lead—and often does lead—to an initial misreading of the sentence. But there are almost no instances where the use of a comma would prevent the misreading of pairs of words, phrases, or dependent clauses joined by a coordinating conjunction. As a matter of fact, sentence 1 is harder to read because of the comma that separates the two nouns of the subject (**mother** and **father**) and the two verbs of the predicate (**appeared** and **testified**). The commas used in that sentence only confuse the reader.

Punctuation

An exception to this convention occurs in the case of suspended structures, as in the following sentence:

> This account of an author's struggles with ❟ and her anxieties about ❟ her writing fascinated me.

The phrases **struggles with** and **anxieties about** are called *suspended structures* because they are left "hanging" until the noun phrase **her writing**, which completes them grammatically, occurs. If this sentence could have been written

> This account of an author's struggles and anxieties about her writing fascinated me.

there would not be, according to **62**, a comma in front of the **and** that joins the pair of nouns **struggles** and **anxieties**. Here the preposition **about** fits idiomatically with **anxieties** but does not fit idiomatically with **struggles**. In such cases, writers are faced with a choice. Either they can complete both structures and write

> This account of an author's struggles with her writing and her anxieties about her writing fascinated me.

Or, if they prefer to avoid the repetition of **her writing**, they can choose to use suspended structures, and they can alert the reader to the structures by putting a comma after **with** and after **about**:

> This account of an author's struggles with, and anxieties about, her writing fascinated me.

In this case, inserting a comma before the conjunction **and**, which joins the two phrases, makes it easier for us to read the sentence.

With this exception, the joining device (the conjunction) and the separating device (the comma) should not work against one another.

Here are the sample sentences with the superfluous commas deleted:

1 The **mother** and the **father appeared** in court and **testified** about their son's activities.
   (*two nouns and two verbs joined by **and***)

2 There was nothing they could do **to prevent the gas attack** or **to protect themselves** against the gas once it had been released.
   (*two infinitive phrases joined by **or***)

3 The men **who are able to work** but **who are not willing to work** will not be eligible to receive monthly welfare checks.
   (*two adjective clauses joined by **but***)

4 Marian was happiest **when she was free of her parents' scrutiny** or **while she was working in her garden**.
   (*two adverb clauses joined by **or***)

63

Use a comma to separate a series of coordinate words, phrases, or clauses.

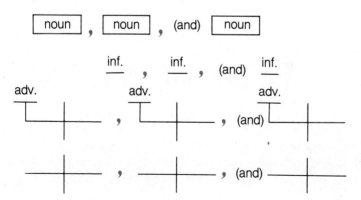

Punctuation

*(The parentheses around **and** in the diagrams above indicate that the coordinating conjunction between the last two members of a series may sometimes be dispensed with. For instance, the phrasing **The tall, robust, gray-haired soldier rose to speak** is stylistically preferable to **The tall, robust, and gray-haired soldier rose to speak**.)*

Examples of series lacking one or more commas:

1 Could he cope with the challenges posed by war, poverty, pollution and crime?
   (*a series of nouns*)

2 He would have to terminate the war, alleviate the plight of the poor, arrest the contamination of the environment and hobble the criminal.
   (*series of infinitive phrases, with **to** understood in the last three members of the series*)

3 If she is willing to work if she is resourceful enough to formulate sensible policies if she subordinates her own interests to the interests of the community, she can rescue the nation from the despair that now prevails.
   (*series of adverb clauses*)

4 She wanted to save the nation, she knew she could save it and eventually she did save it.
   (*series of independent clauses*)

Whereas the convention stated in **62** says that *pairs* of coordinate words, phrases, or clauses should not be separated with a comma, the convention governing a *series* of coordinate words, phrases, and clauses says that these units should be separated with commas. (*A series is to be understood as a sequence of three or more coordinate units.*) Built on the principle of parallelism (see **27**), the series always involves words, phrases, or clauses of a similar kind. So a series should never couple nouns with adjectives, prepositional phrases with infinitive phrases, adjective clauses with adverb clauses, etc.

The convention that will be recommended here follows this formula:

a, b, and c.

Another acceptable formula for the series is

a, b and c

where no comma is used between the last two members of the series when they are joined by a coordinating conjunction. The formula **a, b, and c** is adopted here because the alternative formula (**a, b and c**) sometimes leads to ambiguity. Consider the following example, which uses the **a, b and c** formula:

> Please send me a gross each of the red, green, blue, orange and black ties.

The shipping clerk who received that order might wonder whether five gross of ties (**red, green, blue, orange, black**) were being ordered or only four gross (**red, green, blue, orange-and-black**). If five gross were being ordered, a comma after **orange** would specify the order unambiguously; if four gross were being ordered, hyphens should have been used to signify the combination of colors.

A more common instance of the ambiguity that is sometimes created by the use of the **a, b and c** formula is the following:

> He appealed to the administrators, the deans and the chairpersons.

In this sentence, it is not clear whether he appealed to three different groups (**administrators, deans, chairpersons**)—a meaning that would have been clearly indicated by the **a, b, and c** formula—or to only one group, **administrators,** who are then specified in the two appositives **deans** and **chairpersons**.

Punctuation

Since there is never any chance of ambiguity if you use the **a, b, and c** formula, you would be well advised to adopt this option for punctuating a series.

Here are the sample sentences revised to make them conform to the **a, b, and c** formula:

1 Could he cope with the challenges posed by war, poverty, pollution, and crime?

2 He would have to terminate the war, alleviate the plight of the poor, arrest the contamination of the environment, and hobble the criminal.

3 If she is willing to work, if she is resourceful enough to formulate sensible policies, if she subordinates her own interests to the interests of the community, she can rescue the nation from the despair that now prevails.

4 She wanted to save the nation, she knew she could save it, and eventually she did save it.

64

Nonrestrictive adjective clauses should be enclosed with a pair of commas.

Examples of nonrestrictive adjective clauses that should be enclosed with commas:

1 My oldest brother **who is a chemist** was hurt in an accident last week.

2 The shopkeeper caters only to American tourists **who usually have enough money to buy what they want** and to aristocratic families.

3 Norman Mailer's book **which most reviewers considered juvenile in its pronouncements** was severely panned by feminist-movement groups.

4 The townspeople threaten the strangers **who are looking at the young girl**

A nonrestrictive adjective clause is one that supplies information about the noun that it modifies but information that is not needed to identify or specify the particular person, place, or thing that is being talked about. (The four **that** clauses in this last sentence, for instance, are *restrictive* adjective clauses— clauses that supply *necessary* identifying or specifying information about the nouns that they modify.)

In sentence 1, the adjective clause **who is a chemist** supplies additional information about **my oldest brother**, but this information is not needed to identify which of the brothers was hurt in the accident, because the adjective **oldest** sufficiently identifies the brother being talked about.

One test to determine whether an adjective clause is nonrestrictive is to read the sentence without it, and if the particular person, place, or thing being talked about is sufficiently identified by what is left, the adjective clause can be considered nonrestrictive—and, according to the convention, should be marked off with enclosing commas. If, for instance, you were to drop the adjective clause from sentence 1 and say **My oldest brother was hurt in an accident last week**, your readers would not have to ask, "Which one of your brothers was hurt?" The brother that was hurt is specified by the adjective **oldest**, since there can be only one oldest brother. The clause **who is a chemist** merely supplies some additional but nonessential information about the oldest brother.

Punctuation

Another test to determine whether an adjective clause is nonrestrictive is the *intonation* test. Read these two written versions of sentence **2** aloud:

He caters to American tourists, who have enough money to buy what they want, and to aristocratic families.

He caters to American tourists who have enough money to buy what they want and to aristocratic families.

In reading the first sentence aloud, native speakers of the language would pause briefly after the words **tourists** and **want** (that is, in the places where the commas are) and would lower the pitch of their voices slightly in enunciating the clause **who have enough money to buy what they want**. In reading the second sentence aloud, native speakers would read right through without a pause and would not lower the pitch of their voices in reading the adjective clause.

In writing, it makes a *significant* difference whether the adjective clause in a sentence is marked off with commas or not. *With* the enclosing commas, sentence **2**, for instance, means this: He caters to American tourists (who, incidentally, usually have enough money to buy what they want) and to aristocratic families. *Without* the enclosing commas, the sentence means this: He caters only to those American tourists who have enough money to buy what they want (he doesn't cater to any American tourists who don't have enough money to buy) and to aristocratic families. Those two meanings are quite different from one another, and for that reason, it is extremely important, in a written text, whether or not the adjective clause is marked off with commas.

Likewise, it is important whether or not the adjective clause in sentence **4** is marked off with commas. Without the comma before the **who** clause, the sentence means that the townspeople threaten only those strangers who are looking at the young girl (with the implication that some are not looking at her). But it was clear from the context in which that sentence occurred that the writer meant to say that the townspeople threatened *all* the strangers—all of whom were looking lasciviously at the young girl. The way the writer should have signaled this latter meaning was to put a comma before the **who** clause, thus indicating that this adjective clause was to be read as a nonrestrictive clause.

There are some instances in which the adjective clause is almost invariably nonrestrictive:

(a) Where the antecedent is a **proper noun,** the adjective clause is usually nonrestrictive:

Martin Chuzzlewit, who is a character in Dicken's novel, . . .

New York City, which has the largest urban population in the United States, . . .

The College of William and Mary, which was founded in 1693, . . .

(b) Where, in the nature of things, there could be **only one such** person, place, or thing, the adjective clause is usually nonrestrictive:

My mother, who is now forty-six years old, . . .

Their birthplace, which is Jamestown, . . .

His fingerprints, which are on file in Washington, . . .

(c) Where the identity of the antecedent has been clearly established by the **previous context,** the adjective clause is usually nonrestrictive:

My brother, who has hazel eyes, . . . (where it is clear from the context that you have only one brother)

The book, which never made the bestseller list, . . . (where the previous sentence has identified the particular book being talked about)

Such revolutions, which never enlist the sympathies of the majority of the people, . . . (where the kinds of revolutions being talked about have been specified in the previous sentences or paragraphs)

Punctuation

Which is the usual relative pronoun that introduces nonrestrictive adjective clauses. **That** is the more common relative pronoun used in restrictive adjective clauses. **Who** (or its inflected forms **whose** and **whom**) is the usual relative pronoun when the antecedent is a person; **that,** however, may also be used when the antecedent is a person and the clause is restrictive: either "the men whom I admire" or "the men that I admire."

Here are revisions of the sample sentences with the nonrestrictive adjective clauses properly marked off with enclosing commas. (Incidentally, sentence **4** does not have the second of the pair of enclosing commas because the adjective clause occurs at the end of the sentence rather than, as the others do, somewhere in the middle of the sentence.)

1 My oldest brother **,** who is a chemist **,** was hurt in an accident last week.

2 The shopkeeper caters only to American tourists **,** who usually have enough money to buy what they want **,** and to aristocratic families.

3 Norman Mailer's book **,** which most reviewers considered juvenile in its pronouncements **,** was severely panned by feminist-movement groups.

4 The townspeople threaten the strangers **,** who are looking at the young girl.

65

Restrictive adjective clauses should not be marked off with a pair of commas.

adj.

(no comma)   (no comma)

Examples of adjective clauses that should not be marked off with a pair of commas:

1 Middle-aged people **,** who have slow reflexes **,** should be denied a driver's license.

2 The poem is about a girl **,** who has been in Vietnam and has rejoined her family.

3 All streets, alleys, and thoroughfares **,** that are in the public domain **,** should be maintained by the city.

A restrictive adjective clause is one that identifies or specifies the particular person, place, or thing being talked about. It "restricts" the noun that it modifies; it "defines"—that is, "draws boundaries around"—the noun being talked about. Nonrestrictive clauses, as we saw in **64**, give *additional* information about the nouns that they modify, but they do not serve to *identify* or *specify* the noun that they modify.

In sentence **1**, the adjective clause **who have slow reflexes** is restrictive because it identifies, defines, designates, specifies *which* middle-aged people should be denied a driver's license. The writer of that sentence did not intend to say that *all* middle-aged people should be denied a driver's license, but with the commas enclosing the adjective clause, the sentence does suggest that all of them should not be allowed to drive. The

Punctuation

writer meant to say that only those middle-aged people who have slow reflexes should be denied a driver's license. Leaving out the enclosing commas will make the sentence say what the writer intended to say.

The commas in sentences **2** and **3** should also be omitted. The **who** clause in sentence **2** "restricts" the kind of girl that the poem is about. If the commas enclosing the **that** clause in sentence **3** are omitted, the sentence will say what the writer obviously intended to say: that the city is responsible for maintaining only those streets, alleys, and thoroughfares that are in the public domain.

If you were speaking those three sentences, your voice would do what the presence or the absence of the commas does. If the commas are left out—as they should be—your voice would join the adjective clause to the noun or nouns that it modifies by running on without a pause after the nouns. With the commas, your voice would pause momentarily at those junctures, and a different meaning would be conveyed.

According to the convention, restrictive adjective clauses modifying nonhuman nouns should be introduced with the relative pronoun **that** rather than with **which**:

Governments, which are instituted to protect the rights of men, should be responsive to the will of the people.
(*nonrestrictive*)

Governments that want to remain in favor with their constituents must be responsive to the will of the people.
(*restrictive*)

Here is another distinctive fact about the phrasing of restrictive and nonrestrictive clauses: the relative pronoun may sometimes be omitted in restrictive clauses, but it may never be omitted in nonrestrictive clauses. Note that it is impossible in English to drop the relative pronouns **who** and **whom** from the following nonrestrictive clauses:

John, who is my dearest friend, won't drink with me.

John, whom I love dearly, hardly notices me.

(In the first sentence, however, the clause **who is my dearest friend** could be reduced to an appositive phrase: **John,** *my dearest friend***, won't drink with me**.)

In restrictive adjective clauses, we sometimes have the option of using or not using the relative pronoun:

The one whom I love dearly hardly notices me.
(*with the relative pronoun*)

The one that I love dearly hardly notices me.
(*with the relative pronoun*)

The one I love dearly hardly notices me.
(*without the relative pronoun*)

In restrictive adjective clauses like these, where the relative pronoun serves as the object of the verb of the adjective clause, the relative pronoun may be omitted. The relative pronoun in restrictive clauses may also be omitted if it serves as the object of a preposition in the adjective clause: "The man I gave the wallet to disappeared" (here the understood *whom* or *that* serves as the object of the preposition **to**). However, the relative pronoun may *not* be omitted when it serves as the subject of the restrictive adjective clause:

He who exalts himself shall be humbled.
(***who*** *cannot be omitted*)

The money that was set aside for scholarships was squandered on roads.
(***that*** *cannot be omitted*)

Here are the sample sentences with the separating commas deleted:

1 Middle-aged people who have slow reflexes should be denied a driver's license.

2 The poem is about a girl who has been in Vietnam and has rejoined her family.

3 All streets, alleys, and thoroughfares that are in the public domain should be maintained by the city.

66

If the independent clauses of a compound sentence are not joined by one of the coordinating conjunctions, they should be joined by a semicolon.

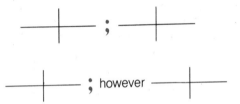

Examples of compound sentences that should be joined by a semicolon:

1 This refutation is based on an appeal to reason however, one must remember that an emotional appeal can also move people to reject an argument.

2 All the students spontaneously supported the team, they wanted to show their loyalty, even though they were disappointed with the outcome of the game.

3 She loved her father, in fact, she practically worshiped him.

The coordinating conjunctions are **and, but, or, nor, for, yet, so.** In the absence of one of those words, the independent clauses of a compound sentence should be spliced together with a punctuation device: the semicolon.

66 Semicolon, Compound Sentence

Words and phrases like **however, therefore, then, indeed, nevertheless, consequently, thus, moreover, furthermore, in fact, on the other hand, on the contrary** are not coordinating conjunctions; they are called *conjunctive adverbs*. Conjunctive adverbs provide logical links between sentences and between parts of sentences, but they do not function as grammatical splicers. Unlike coordinating conjunctions, which must always be placed *between* the two elements they join, conjunctive adverbs enjoy some freedom of movement in the sentence.

In sentence 1, the word **however** is placed between the two independent clauses, but evidence that this conjunctive adverb is not serving as the grammatical splicer of the two clauses is provided by the fact that **however** can be shifted to another position in the sentence: **This refutation is based on an appeal to reason; one must remember, however, that an emotional appeal can also move people to reject an argument.** The coordinating conjunction **but**, on the other hand, which is equivalent in meaning to **however**, could occupy no other position in the sentence than *between* the end of the first clause (after the word **reason**) and the beginning of the next clause (before the word **one**).

Nor can the independent clauses of a compound sentence be joined by a comma, because the comma is a separating device, not a joining device. Compound sentences so punctuated—like sentence 2—are called **comma splices** (see 30). As indicated in 60, if a compound sentence is joined by one of the coordinating conjunctions, a comma should be put in front of the conjunction to mark off the end of one independent clause and the beginning of the next independent clause. But whenever a coordinating conjunction is not present to join the independent clauses, a semicolon must be used to join them. The semicolon serves both to mark the division between the two clauses and to join them.

Punctuation

Sometimes it is advisable to use both a semicolon and a co-ordinating conjunction to join the independent clauses of a compound sentence. When the clauses are unusually long and have commas within them, a semicolon placed before the co-ordinating conjunction helps to demarcate the end of one clause and the beginning of the next one, as in this example:

> Struggling to salvage what was left of the semester, he pleaded with his English teacher, who was notoriously softhearted, to grant him an extension of time on his written assignments, quizzes, and class reports **; but** he forgot that, even with the best of intentions, he had only so many hours every day when he could study and only a limited reserve of energy.

The coordinating conjunction **but** serves to join the two main clauses of the compound sentence, but the use of the semi-colon in addition to the conjunction makes it easier to read the sentence.

Here are the sample sentences with the splicing semicolon inserted in the proper place:

1 This refutation is based on an appeal to reason; however, one must remember that an emotional appeal can also move people to reject an argument.

2 All the students spontaneously supported the team; they wanted to show their loyalty, even though they were disappointed with the out-come of the game.

3 She loved her father; in fact, she practically worshiped him.

67

Whenever you use a semicolon, be sure that you have an independent clause on both sides of the semicolon.

Examples of failure to observe this convention:

1 She played the guitar expertly; although she couldn't read a note of music.

2 Americans spend far too many hours as spectators of sports instead of as participants in them; watching meaningless drivel on television instead of spending that time reading a book.

3 The two series of poems also differ in style; the *Songs of Experience* being more vague and complex than the *Songs of Innocence.*

4 An industry like this benefits everyone, from the poor, for whom it creates employment; to the rich, who are made richer by it.

This convention is the corollary of **66**. It cautions against using the semicolon to join elements of unequal rank. Accordingly, if there is an independent clause on one side of the semicolon, there must be a balancing independent clause on the other side.

In all of the examples above, a semicolon has been used to join units of *unequal* rank. In all four sentences, there is an independent clause on the *left-hand* side of the semicolon; however, there is no independent clause on the *right-hand* side of the semicolon in any of those sentences. What is on the right-hand side of the semicolon could be called a sentence fragment (see **29**).

Punctuation

In sentence **1**, there is the independent clause **she played the guitar expertly** on the left-hand side of the semicolon, but on the right-hand side of the semicolon, there is only the adverb clause **although she couldn't read a note of music**. That adverb clause belongs with, depends on, the first clause. Since it is an integral part of the first clause, it should be *joined* with that clause. The effect of the semicolon is to make the adverb clause part of *another* clause that begins after the semicolon. But on the right-hand side of the semicolon, there is no independent clause that the subordinate, dependent adverb clause can be a part of. One way to correct the sentence is to supply an independent clause, on the right-hand side of the semicolon, that the adverb clause can adhere to—e.g. **She played the guitar expertly; although she couldn't read a note of music, she simply had a knack for playing stringed instruments**. The other way to correct the sentence is to substitute a comma for the semicolon.

Sentences **2, 3,** and **4** could also be corrected by substituting a comma for the semicolon. But in **2**, it would probably be better to supply an independent clause on the right-hand side of the semicolon. So revised, the sentence would have an independent clause on *both* sides of the semicolon.

Here are the sample sentences revised:

1 She played the guitar expertly, although she couldn't read a note of music.

2 Americans spend far too many hours as spectators of sports instead of as participants in them; they spend far too many hours watching meaningless drivel on television instead of spending that time reading a book.

3 The two series of poems also differ in style, the *Songs of Experience* being more vague and complex than the *Songs of Innocence*.

4 An industry like this benefits everyone, from the poor, for whom it creates employment, to the rich, who are made richer by it.

68

Use a colon after a grammatically complete lead-in sentence that formally announces a subsequent enumeration, explanation, illustration, or extended quotation.

The following sentences either need a colon or use a colon improperly:

1 The courses I am taking this quarter are: English, sociology, economics, political science, and psychology.

2 His approach works like this ——after displaying his product and extolling its virtues, he asks the homemaker if she has a small rug that she would like to have cleaned.

3 Examples of the diction used to evoke the horror of the scene include vivid images like: "coughing like hags," "thick green light," "guttering," "white eyes writhing in his face," "gargling from froth-corrupted lungs."

4 The reaction of the crowd signified only one thing, apathy.

A colon signals that what *follows* it is a specification of what was formally announced in the clause on the left-hand side of the colon. What distinguishes the colon from the dash as a symbolic device is that the colon throws the reader's attention *forward*, whereas the dash as a linking device throws the reader's attention *backward* (see 69). Although a word, a phrase, or a clause or a series of words, phrases, or clauses can follow the colon, there must be an independent clause (a grammatically complete sentence) on the left-hand side of the colon.

Punctuation

In accord with this principle, sentence **1** should not have been punctuated the way it was; that punctuation makes no more sense than punctuating a sentence in this way:

My name is: John Adams.

In both cases, the words following the colon are needed to complete the sentence grammatically. So either the colon must be dropped altogether, or enough words must be added to make the clause on the left-hand side of the colon a grammatically complete sentence—in sentence **1**, *are these* or *are as follows*.

In sentence **3**, the quoted phrases following the colon are needed to complete the prepositional phrase that begins with **like**. Therefore, either drop the colon or add a completing word like **these** before the colon. Since the lead-in clause in sentence **2** throws the reader's attention forward, the dash after **this** should be replaced by a colon. Likewise, the comma in the fourth sentence should be replaced by a colon.

A colon is conventionally used after the lead-in sentence that introduces an extended quotation in a research paper. Here is an example of that use:

Toward the end of the preface, Dr. Johnson confessed that he abandoned his earlier expectation that his dictionary would be able to "fix the language":

Those who have been persuaded to think well of my design will require that it should fix our language and put a stop to those alterations which time and chance have hitherto been suffered to make in it without opposition. With this consequence I will confess that I flattered myself for a while, but now begin to fear that I have indulged expectation which neither reason nor experience can justify.

Here are the sample sentences properly punctuated with a colon:

1 The courses I am taking this quarter are as follows: English, sociology, economics, political science, and psychology.

2 His approach works like this: after displaying his product and extolling its virtues, he asks the homemaker if she has a small rug that she would like to have cleaned.

3 Examples of the diction used to evoke the horror of the scene include vivid images like these: "coughing like hags," "thick green light," "guttering," "white eyes writhing in his face," "gargling from froth-corrupted lungs."

4 The reaction of the crowd signified only one thing: apathy.

69

Use a dash when the word or word-group that follows it constitutes a summation, an amplification, or a reversal of what went before it.

Examples of sentences that need to be punctuated with a dash:

1 English, psychology, history, and philosophy, these were the courses I took last quarter.

2 If he was pressured, he would become sullen and tight-lipped, a reaction that did not endear him to the president or the Senate.

3 Time and time again, she would admit that her critics were right, that she should have realized her mistakes, that she should have read the danger signs more accurately and then gone ahead with her original plans.

Unlike the colon (see **68**), which directs the reader's attention forward, the dash usually directs the reader's attention back-

Punctuation

ward. What follows the dash, when it is used as a linking device, looks back to what preceded it for the particulars or details that spell out the meaning or invest the meaning with pungency or irony.

The colon and the dash are usually not interchangeable marks of punctuation. They signal a different relationship between the word-groups that precede them and those that follow them. After much practice in writing, one develops a sense for the subtle distinction in relationships that is signaled by the punctuation in the following two sentences:

The reaction of the crowd signified only one thing: apathy.

The people clearly indicated their indifference to the provocative speech—an apathy that later came back to haunt them.

In the first sentence, the lead-in clause before the colon clearly alerts the reader to expect a specification of what is hinted at in that clause. In the second sentence, there is no such alerting of the reader in the lead-in clause; but following the dash, there is an unexpected commentary on what was said in the lead-in clause, a summary commentary that forces the reader to look backward and that receives a special emphasis by being set off with a dash. The colon and the single dash are both linking devices, but they signal different kinds of thought relationships between parts of the sentence.

Writers should also be cautioned to avoid using the dash as a catchall mark of punctuation, one that is indiscriminately substituted for periods, commas, semicolons, etc.

Here now are the sample sentences with a dash inserted in the proper place:

1 English, psychology, history, and philosophy —these were the courses I took last quarter.

2 If he was pressured, he would become sullen and tight-lipped —a reaction that did not endear him to the president or the Senate.

3 Time and time again, she would admit that her critics were right, that she should have realized her mistakes, that she should have read the danger signs more accurately—and then gone ahead with her original plans.

70

Use a pair of dashes to enclose abrupt parenthetical elements that occur within a sentence.

—— ——

Examples of parenthetical elements that should be enclosed with a pair of dashes:

1 In some instances, although no one will admit it, the police over-reacted to the provocation.

2 What surprised everyone when the measure came to a vote was the chairperson's reluctance, indeed, downright refusal, to allow any riders to be attached to the bill.

3 One of them (let me call him Jim Prude) is clean-shaven and dresses like an Ivy Leaguer of the early 1950s.

4 Their unhappiness is due to the ease with which envy is aroused and to the difficulty, or should I say impossibility, of fighting against it.

5 Yet despite the similarities in their travelogues (for indeed the same trip inspired both works), the two reports differ in some key aspects.

The three devices used to set off parenthetical elements in written prose are commas, parentheses, and dashes. The kind of parenthetical element that should be enclosed with a pair of dashes is the kind that interrupts the normal syntactical flow of the sentence. What characterizes all of the parenthetical elements in the examples above is that they abruptly arrest the

Punctuation

normal flow of the sentence to add some qualifying or rectifying comment. The rhetorical effect of the enclosing dashes is to alert the reader to the interruption and thereby to help the reader read the sentence.

A pair of parentheses is another typographical device used to mark off parenthetical elements in a sentence. Enclosure within parentheses is used mainly for those elements that merely add information or identification, as in sentences like these:

> All the companies that used the service were charged a small fee (usually $500) and were required to sign a contract (an "exclusive-use" agreement).

> The manager of each franchise is expected to report monthly to NARM (National Association of Retail Merchants) and to "rotate" (take turns doing various jobs) every two weeks.

The typographical device used to set off the mildest kind of interrupting element is a pair of commas. Whether to enclose a parenthetical element with commas or with parentheses or with dashes is often more a matter of stylistic choice than a matter of grammatical necessity. There are degrees of interruption and emphasis, and with practice, a writer develops an instinct for knowing when to mark off parenthetical elements with commas (lowest degree of interruption and emphasis), when to mark them off with parentheses (middle degree), and when to mark them off with dashes (highest degree). Consider the degrees of interruption and emphasis in the following sentences:

> That agency, as we have since learned, reported the incident directly to the Department of Justice.

> During the postwar years (at least from 1946 to 1952), no one in the agency dared challenge a directive from higher up.

> When the order was challenged, the attorney general—some claim it was his wife—put a call through to the president.

Here are the revisions of the sample sentences with the parenthetical elements enclosed with dashes:

1 In some instances—although no one will admit it—the police overreacted to the provocation.

2 What surprised everyone when the measure came to a vote was the chairperson's reluctance—indeed, downright refusal—to allow any riders to be attached to the bill.

3 One of them—let me call him Jim Prude—is clean-shaven and dresses like an Ivy Leaguer of the early 1950s.

4 Their unhappiness is due to the ease with which envy is aroused and to the difficulty—or should I say impossibility—of fighting against it.

5 Yet despite the similarities in their travelogues—for indeed the same trip inspired both works—the two reports differ in some key aspects.

71

A dash is made on the typewriter with two unspaced hyphens and with no space before the dash or after the dash. (In handwriting, the dash should be made slightly longer than a hyphen.)

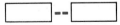

Examples of incorrect ways of forming the dash on a typewriter:

```
She forgot-if she ever knew-the functions of
the various marks of punctuation.
```

Punctuation

```
She forgot - if she ever knew - the functions of
the various marks of punctuation.

She forgot -- if she ever knew -- the functions
of the various marks of punctuation.

She forgot - - if she ever knew - - the func-
tions of the various marks of punctuation.
```

Because a typewriter does not have a separate key for a dash, you have to make a dash with two hyphens. Do not hit the spacebar on the typewriter before the first hyphen, *between* the first and second hyphen, or *after* the second hyphen. In short, do not hit the spacebar at all in forming the dash on the typewriter. When you are handwriting a text, you have to distinguish a dash from a hyphen by making the dash slightly longer than the hyphen.

Here is an illustration of the proper way to form the dash on the typewriter:

```
She forgot--if she ever knew--the functions of
the various marks of punctuation.
```

Mechanics

The graphic devices dealt with in this section might be, and often are, classified as punctuation. But because such graphic devices as italics, capitalization, and numbers are not correlated—as punctuation marks are—with the intonational patterns of the spoken language, these devices are grouped in a separate section under the heading Mechanics. In the spoken language, a word printed with an initial capital letter is pronounced no differently from the same word printed with an initial lower-case letter. Nor is the italicized title of a book pronounced any differently from that same title printed without italics. (Italics used for emphasizing a word or phrase, however, do correspond to stress in the spoken language.) Even quotation marks, which one might regard as correlated with the spoken language, do not correspond to anything the voice does when it quotes direct speech.

But whether one classifies these graphic devices as punctuation or as mechanics is immaterial. What is important to remember is that these devices are part of the written language exclusively and that they facilitate the reading of that language.

Mechanics

Most readers would have at least momentary difficulty making sense of the following string of words:

> Jill cried buckets as many as you can fetch Jack thought I don't have to please you over there she continued nuts pails they're called yelled Jack

If the proper punctuation and mechanics were used with that string of words, readers would be spared the momentary difficulty:

> Jill cried, ''Buckets! As many as you can fetch!'' Jack thought, ''I don't have to!'' ''Please, you over there!'' she continued. ''Nuts! *pails* they're called!'' yelled Jack.

Deprived of the resources that the human voice possesses to clarify the meaning of words as spoken, writers should be eager to use all those typographical devices that make it easier for readers to grasp what the writers are trying to convey.

80

The period or the comma always goes inside the closing quotation mark.

Examples of sentences with misplaced quotation marks:

1 The author announces at the beginning of her article that she is going to cite only ''facts''.

2 ''I know'', she said, ''that you are telling me a barefaced lie''.

3 Mrs. Robinson's ''bearded, sandaled, unwashed hippies'', many of whom had traveled over a thousand miles to the festival, represented an aggregation of straight-*A* students.

80 Closing Quotation Mark, with Period and Comma

This is a clear case where usage, rather than logic, has established the prevailing convention. Many reputable British editors and publishers put the period or comma *outside* the closing quotation mark, especially when the quotation marks enclose something less than a complete sentence—e.g. a word or a phrase, such as in sentences **1** and **3** above. But the American convention is almost universally to put the period or comma *inside* the closing quotation mark.

The advantage of such consistency is that you never have to pause and ask yourself, "Is this a case where the period goes inside or outside the quotation mark?" Whether it is a single word or a phrase or a dependent clause or an independent clause, the period or comma always goes *inside* the closing quotation mark.

In handwriting or in typewriting, take care to put the period or comma *clearly* inside the quotation mark, not *under* it, as in sentence **2**. In the case of a quotation within a quotation, both the single-stroke quotation mark and the double-stroke quotation mark go *outside* the period or the commas, as in this example:

> "I read recently," he said, "that Patrick Henry never said, 'Give me liberty or give me death.' "

Here are the revisions of the sample sentences with the proper placement of the closing quotation mark in relation to the period or the comma:

1 The author announces at the beginning of her article that she is going to cite only "facts."

2 "I know," he said, "that you are telling me a barefaced lie."

3 Mrs. Robinson's "bearded, sandaled, unwashed hippies," many of whom had traveled over a thousand miles to the festival, represented an aggregation of straight-*A* students.

81

The colon or semicolon always goes outside the closing quotation mark.

'';'' ''';

Examples of a misplaced colon or semicolon in relation to the closing quotation mark:

1 She called this schedule of activities her "load:" work, study, exercise, recreation, and sleep.

2 He told his taunters, "I refuse to budge;" his knees, however, were shaking even as he said those words.

Whereas the period or the comma always goes *inside* the closing quotation mark, the colon or the semicolon always goes outside it. Whenever writers have occasion to use quotation marks with a colon or a semicolon, they have only to recall that the convention governing the relationship of the colon or the semicolon to the closing quotation mark is just the opposite of the convention for the period and the comma.

Here are the revisions of the sample sentences with the colon and the semicolon placed in the right position in relation to the closing quotation mark:

1 She called this schedule of activities her "load": work, study, exercise, recreation, and sleep.

2 He told his taunters, "I refuse to budge"; his knees, however, were shaking even as he said those words.

82

The question mark sometimes goes inside, sometimes outside, the closing quotation mark.

?"   "?

Examples of the question mark placed wrongly in relation to the closing quotation mark:

1 Who was it that said, "I regret that I have but one life to lose for my country?"

2 He asked her bluntly, "Will you marry me"?

3 When will they stop asking, "Who then is responsible for the war"?

Although a period or a comma always goes inside the closing quotation mark and a colon or a semicolon always goes outside it, you have to consider each case individually before deciding whether to put the question mark inside or outside the closing quotation mark. Fortunately, the criteria for determining whether it goes inside or outside the quotation mark are fairly simple to apply:

(a)   When the whole sentence, but not the unit enclosed in quotation marks, is a question, the question mark goes *outside* the closing quotation mark. (See sentence 1.)

(b)   When only the unit enclosed in quotation marks is a question, the question mark goes *inside* the closing quotation mark. (See sentence 2.)

(c)   When the whole sentence and the unit enclosed in quotation marks are both questions, the question mark goes *inside* the closing quotation mark. (See sentence 3.)

Whenever the question mark occurs at the end of a sentence, it serves as the terminal punctuation for the entire sentence. In **(b)**, you do not add a period outside the closing quotation mark, and in **(c)**, you do not add another question mark outside the closing quotation mark.

Here are the sample sentences corrected in accord with the criteria set forth in **(a)**, **(b)**, and **(c)**:

1 Who was it that said, "I regret that I have but one life to lose for my country **''?**

2 He asked her bluntly, "Will you marry me **?''**

3 When will they stop asking, "Who then is responsible for the war **?''**

83

The titles of books, newspapers, magazines, professional journals, plays, long poems, movies, radio programs, television programs, long musical compositions, works of art, and the names of ships and airplanes should be *underlined*.

Examples of titles that should be underlined:

1 The critics have always rated Hemingway's "A Farewell to Arms" above his "For Whom the Bell Tolls."

2 To support her contention, she quoted a passage from an anonymous article in Newsweek.

3 My parents insisted on watching "All in the Family."

4 Charles Darwin took a historic trip on the Beagle.

Printers use *italics*—a special typeface that slants slightly to the right—to set off certain words in a sentence (or certain sentences in a paragraph) from the body of words or sentences, which are printed in roman type (upright letters). The word *italics* in this and the previous sentence is printed in italics. In handwriting or typewriting, one italicizes words by underlining them.

One of the uses of italic type is to set off the words that appear in certain kinds of names and titles. Most often, writers have occasion to use italics for the titles of book- or pamphlet-length published materials. Besides being a convention, the use of italics for titles can also protect meaning in some instances. If someone wrote "I don't really like Huckleberry Finn," a reader might be uncertain (unless the context gave a clue) whether the writer was revealing a dislike for Mark Twain's novel or for the character of that name in the novel. Simply by underlining (italicizing) the proper name, the writer could indicate unambiguously that she or he disliked the novel, not the character.

How does one decide whether a poem is long enough to have its title underlined? As with most relative matters, the extreme cases are easily determinable. Obviously, a sonnet would not qualify as a long poem, but Milton's *Paradise Lost* would. It is the middle-length poem that causes indecision. A reliable rule of thumb is this: if the poem was ever published as a separate book or if it could conceivably be published as a separate book, it can be considered long enough to have its title underlined. According to that guideline, T. S. Eliot's *The Wasteland* would be considered a long poem, but his "The Love Song of J. Alfred Prufrock" would be considered a short poem and therefore should be enclosed in quotation marks (see **84**). But if you cannot decide whether a poem is "long" or "short," either underline the title or enclose it in quotation marks and use that system consistently throughout the paper.

Here are the sample sentences, with the titles underlined (italicized):

Mechanics

1 The critics have always rated Hemingway's <u>A Farewell to Arms</u> above his <u>For Whom the Bell Tolls</u>.

   (titles of novels)

2 To support her contention, she quoted a passage from an anonymous article in <u>Newsweek</u>.

   (title of a magazine)

3 My parents insisted on watching <u>All in the Family</u>.

   (title of a television show)

4 Charles Darwin took a historic trip on the <u>Beagle</u>.

   (name of a ship)

84

The titles of articles, essays, short poems, songs, and chapters of books should be enclosed in quotation marks.

Examples of titles that need to be enclosed with quotation marks:

1 Thomas Gray's Elegy Written in a Country Churchyard is reputed to be the most anthologized poem in the English language.

2 Hollis Alpert's <u>Movies Are Better Than the Stage</u> first appeared in the <u>Saturday Review of Literature</u>.

3 'Raindrops Keep Falling on My Head' set exactly the right mood for the bicycle caper in <u>Butch Cassidy and the Sundance Kid</u>.

The general rule here is that the titles of published material that is *part* of a book or a periodical should be enclosed in quotation marks.

The title of a paper that you write should not be enclosed in quotation marks, nor should it be underlined. If your title contains elements that are normally underlined or enclosed in quotation marks, those elements, of course, should be underlined or enclosed in quotation marks.

The right and the wrong formats of a title for a paper submitted as a class assignment or for publication are illustrated here in typescript:

WRONG: "The Evolution of Courtly Love
              in Medieval Literature"

              The Evolution of Courtly Love
              in Medieval Literature

RIGHT: The Evolution of Courtly Love
              in Medieval Literature

              The Evolution of Courtly Love
              in Chaucer's Troilus and Criseyde

              Courtly Love in Herrick's "Corinna's Going
              a-Maying" and Marvell's "To His Coy Mistress"

              The Shift in Meaning of the Word Love
              in Renaissance Lyrics

              "One Giant Step for Mankind"--Historic Words
              for a Historic Occasion

Here are the revised sentences with the titles enclosed in quotation marks:

1 Thomas Gray's " Elegy Written in a Country Churchyard " is reputed to be the most anthologized poem in the English language.
   (*title of a short poem*)

2 Hollis Alpert's " Movies Are Better Than the Stage " first appeared in the Saturday Review of Literature.
   (*title of an article in a periodical*)

Mechanics

3   "Raindrops Keep Falling on My Head" set exactly the right mood for the bicycle caper in <u>Butch Cassidy and the Sundance Kid</u>.
(*title of a song*)

85

Underline (italicize) words referred to as words.

Examples of words that should be underlined (italicized).

1   She questioned the appropriateness of **honesty** in this context.
2   <u>The American Heritage Dictionary</u> defines **dudgeon** as "a sullen, angry, or indignant humor."
3   Unquestionably, **trudged** is a more specific verb than **walked**
4   Look, for example, at his use of purely subjective words like **marvelous, exquisite**, and **wondrous**

One of the uses of the graphic device of underlining (italics) is to distinguish a word being used *as a word* from that same word used as a symbol for a thing or an idea. Looking at two similar sentences can help us to see what difference in meaning is created by underlining or not underlining some word in the sentences:

> She questioned the appropriateness of honesty in this context.
>
> She questioned the appropriateness of <u>honesty</u> in this context.

Both of these sentences have the same words in the same order. The only difference between them is that in the second sentence, one of the words is underlined (italicized). That underlining of the word **honesty** makes for a difference in the meaning of the two sentences. The first sentence signifies that what is being challenged is the appropriateness of the thing (the abstract quality) designated by the word **honesty**; the second

85 Underlining, for Words as Words

sentence signifies that what is being questioned is the appropriateness of the word only. Underlining (italicizing) the word **honesty** helps the reader to read the sentence as the writer intended it to be read—namely, that it was the word, not the virtue, that was being questioned.

An alternative but less common device for marking words used as words is to enclose the words in quotation marks, as in this example:

> The heavy use of such sensory diction as ''juicy,'' ''empurpled,'' ''smooth,'' ''creaked,'' ''murmuring'' helps to evoke the scene and make it palpable to the reader.

Since both devices are authorized by convention, the writer should adopt one system and use it consistently. The use of italics is probably the safer of the two systems, however, because quotation marks are also used to enclose quoted words and phrases, as in the sentence

> We heard her say ''yes.''

(Here **yes** is not being referred to as a word but is a quotation of what she said.)

Here are the sample sentences revised to include the underlining (italicizing) of words being referred to as words:

1 She questioned the appropriateness of honesty in this context.

2 The American Heritage Dictionary defines dudgeon as ''a sullen, angry, or indignant humor.''

3 Unquestionably, trudged is a more specific verb than walked.

4 Look, for example, at his use of purely subjective words like marvelous, exquisite, and wondrous.

Mechanics

86

Underline (italicize) foreign words and phrases, unless they have become naturalized or Anglicized.

Examples of foreign words and phrases that should be underlined (italicized):

1 Why does the advertiser, whose mouthpiece is the copywriter, allow himself to be presented before the public as a poet **malgré lui**?

2 The advice to begin a short story as close to the climax as possible is a heritage of Horace's advice to begin a narrative **in medias res** rather than **ab ovo**

3 There had been a remarkable revival in the late 1960s of the **Weltschmerz** that characterized the poetry of the Romantics.

So that the reader will not be even momentarily mystified by the sudden intrusion of strange-looking words into a stream of English words, printers use italics to underscore foreign words and phrases. The graphic device of italics does not ensure, of course, that the reader will be able to translate the foreign expression, but it does prevent confusion by alerting the reader to the presence of non-English words.

Some foreign words and phrases, like habeas corpus, divorcee, mania, siesta, subpoena, have been used so often in an English context that they have been accepted into the vocabulary as "naturalized" English words and therefore as not needing to be underlined (italicized). Dictionaries have a system for indicating which foreign words and phrases have become naturalized and which have *not* become naturalized. Since dictionaries sometimes differ in their judgments about the naturalized status of certain foreign expressions, the writer in such doubtful cases may put the foreign word or phrase in ordinary (roman) type—that is, without underlining or italicizing.

An exception to the rule is that proper nouns designating foreign persons, places, and institutions, even when they retain their native spelling and pronunciation, are *always* set forth without underlining (italics).

Here are the sample sentences with their foreign words and phrases properly underlined:

1 Why does the advertiser, whose mouthpiece is the copywriter, allow himself to be presented before the public as a poet malgré lui?

2 The advice to begin a short story as close to the climax as possible is a heritage of Horace's advice to begin a narrative in medias res rather than ab ovo.

3 There had been a remarkable revival in the late 1960s of the Weltschmerz that characterized the poetry of the Romantics.

87

Compound words should be hyphenated.

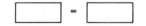

Examples of compound words that need to be hyphenated:

1 Because I had the normal **six year old's** "sweet tooth," I was irresistibly lured by the candy store.

2 She was attracted to **antiEstablishment** movements because they lacked **policy making** administrators.

3 They scheduled the examinations in three **quarter hour** segments.

4 She preferred **eighteenth century** literature because of its urbanity.

5 A **five** or **six story** building should be all you need for that kind of plant operation.

6 Jim Paisley was the only **new car** dealer in town.

Mechanics

English reveals its Germanic origins in its tendency to form compounds—that is, to take two or more words and join them to create a single unit that designates a thing or a concept quite different from what the individual words designate. A familiar example is the word basketball. When the two distinct words *basket* and *ball* were first joined to designate an athletic game or the kind of ball used in that game, the words were linked by a hyphen: *basket-ball*. When repeated use had made this new compound familiar to readers, the hyphen was dropped, and the two words were printed as a single word, with no break between the two constituent parts.

Dozens of words in English have made this transition from a hyphenated compound to a single amalgamated word (e.g. *postoffice, skyscraper, briefcase, airport*). But hundreds of compounds are still printed with a hyphen, either because they have not been used enough to achieve status as unmarked hybrids or because the absence of a hyphen would lead to ambiguity. A reliable dictionary will indicate which compounds have made the passage and which have not.

With the exception of those words that have become recognized amalgams, a hyphen should be used to link

(a) two or more words functioning as a single grammatical unit.

his **never-say-die** attitude (adjective)

the junkyard had a huge **car-crusher** (noun)

the hoodlums **pistol-whipped** him (verb)

he conceded the point **willy-nilly** (adverb)

(b) two-word numbers (from 21 to 99) when they are written out.

twenty-one, thirty-six, forty-eight, ninety-nine

(c) combinations with prefixes **ex-** and **self-.**

ex-president, ex-wife, self-denial, self-contradictory

(d)   combinations with prefixes like **anti-, pro-, pre-, post-,** when the second element in the combinations begins with a capital letter or a number.

anti-Establishment, pro-American, pre-1929, post-1945

(e)   combinations with prefixes like **anti-, pro-, pre-, re-, semi-, sub-, over-,** when the second element begins with the letter that occurs at the end of the prefix.

anti-intellectual, pro-oxidant, pre-election, re-entry, semi-independent, sub-basement, over-refined

(f)   combinations where the unhyphenated compound might be mistaken for another word.

re-cover (the chair)

recover (the lost wallet)

re-sign (the contract)

resign (the office)

co-op

coop

With the exceptions noted in **(d)** and **(e)**, compounds formed with prefixes now tend to be written as a single word (for example, *antiknock*, *preconscious*, *subdivision*, *postgraduate*). From extensive reading, one develops a sense for those compounds that have been used often enough to become a single word in English.

Frequently in writing, only a hyphen will clarify ambiguous syntax. In sentence **3**, for instance, a reader would have difficulty determining whether the examination was divided into three segments of fifteen minutes each (a meaning that would be clearly signaled by this placement of the hyphen: **three quarter-hour segments**) or whether it was divided into segments of forty-five minutes duration (a meaning that is clearly

Mechanics

signaled by this placement of hyphens: **three-quarter-hour segments**). There is a similar ambiguity in sentence **6**, **Jim Paisley was the only new car dealer in town.** A speaker would be able to clarify the ambiguous syntax of that sentence by the appropriate intonation of the voice. But in writing, only a hyphen will make clear whether the writer meant to say that Jim Paisley was the only new **car-dealer** in town or that he was the only **new-car** dealer in town.

Sentence **5** shows how to hyphenate when there is more than one term on the left side of the hyphenation (**five-, six-**). In this way, **story** need not be repeated (as in **A five-story or six-story building. . .**). In typing, one inserts a space after the hyphen if the hyphen is not immediately followed by the word it is meant to join (**five- or;** NOT: **five-or**).

Here are the revisions of the sample sentences with the hyphens inserted in all the compound words:

1 Because I had the normal six⁻year⁻old's "sweet tooth," I was irresistibly lured by the candy store.

2 She was attracted to anti⁻Establishment movements because they lacked policy⁻making administrators.

3 They scheduled the examinations in three quarter⁻hour segments.

4 She preferred eighteenth⁻century literature because of its urbanity.

5 A five⁻ or six⁻story building should be all you will need for that kind of plant operation.

6 Jim Paisley was the only new⁻car dealer in town.

88

A word can be broken and hyphenated at the end of a line only at a syllable-break; a one-syllable word can never be broken and hyphenated.

Examples of words improperly syllabified:

1 bell-igerent
2 stopp-ing
3 rigo-rous
4 a-bout
5 comm-unity
6 wrench-ed

For the writer, two valuable bits of information are supplied by the initial entry of every word in the dictionary: (1) the spelling of the word, (2) the syllabification of the word. The word **belliger-ent**, for instance, is entered this way in the dictionary: **bel·lig·er·ent**. If that word occurred at the end of a line and you saw that you could not get the whole word in the remaining space, you could break the word and hyphenate it at any of the syllables marked with a raised period. But you could not break the word in any of the following places: **bell·igerent, belli·gerent, bellige·rent**.

Since the syllabification of English words is often unpredictable, it is safest to consult a dictionary when you are in doubt about where syllable-breaks occur. But after a while, you learn certain "tricks" about syllabification that save you a trip to the dictionary. A word can usually be broken

(a)   after a prefix (**con-, ad-, un-, im-**).
(b)   before a suffix (**-tion, -ment, -less, -ous, -ing**).

Mechanics

(c) between double consonants (**oc-cur-rence, cop-per, stop-ping, prig-gish**).

One-syllable words, however, can never be divided and hyphenated, no matter how long they are. So if you come to the end of a line and find that you do not have enough space to squeeze in single-syllable words like **horde, grieve, stopped, quaint, strength, wrenched,** leave the space blank and write the whole word on the next line. You have no choice.

Even in the interest of preserving a right-hand margin, you should not divide a word so that only one or two letters of it stand at the end of the line or at the beginning of the next line. Faced with divisions like **a-bout, o-cean, un-healthy, grass-y, dioram-a, flor-id, smok-er, live-ly,** you should put the whole word on that line or on the next line. Remember that the hyphen itself takes up one space.

Here are the sample words hyphenated in the right place or not syllabified at all:

1 bel-lig-er-ent
2 stop-ping
3 rigor-ous
4 about
5 com-mu-nity
6 wrenched

89

Observe the conventions governing the use of numbers in written copy.

Examples of violations of the conventions:

1 **522** men reported to the recruiting center.

2 During the first half of the **20th** century, **28** 4-year colleges and **14** **2**-year colleges adopted collective-bargaining agencies.

3 The cocktail party started at **four** P.M. **in the afternoon.**

4 An account of the Wall Street crash of October **twenty-ninth, nineteen hundred and twenty-nine** begins on page **fifty-five**

5 About **six and a half** % of the stores were selling a gross of **three-by-five** index cards for more than **thirty-six dollars and thirty-eight cents**

The most common conventions governing the use of numbers in written copy are as follows:

(a) Do not begin a sentence with an arabic numeral; spell out the number or recast the sentence:

Five hundred twenty-two men reported to the recruiting center.

OR: A total of **522** men reported to the recruiting center.

(b) Spell out any number of less than three digits (or any number under 101) when the number is used as an adjective modifying a noun:

During the first half of the **twentieth** century, **twenty-eight four**-year colleges and **fourteen two**-year colleges adopted collective-bargaining agencies.

(c) Always use arabic numerals with A.M. and P.M. and do not add the redundant **o'clock** and **morning** or **afternoon**:

The cocktail party started at **4:00** P.M.

OR: The cocktail party started at **four o'clock in the afternoon.**

(d) Use arabic numerals for dates and page numbers:

An account of the Wall Street crash of October **29, 1919** begins on page **55.**

(e) Use arabic numerals for addresses (618 N. 29th St.), dollars and cents ($4.68, $0.15 or 15 cents), decimals (3.14,

Mechanics

0.475), degrees (52°F.), measurements (especially when abbreviations are used: 3″ × 5″, 3.75 mi., 2 ft. 9 in., 6′2″ tall, but *six feet tall*), percentages (6% or 6 percent, but always use **percent** with fractional percentages—6½ percent or 6.5 percent):

> About **6½ percent** of the stores were selling a gross of **3** ″ × **5** ″ index cards for more than **$36.38.**

90

Observe the conventions governing the capitalization of certain words.

Examples of words that need to be capitalized:

1 president Gerald R. Ford informed the members of congress that he was appointing ms. Shirley Temple Black as the united states ambassador to ghana.

2 The title of the article in the *New Yorker* was "The time of illusion."

3 Dr. Thomas J. Cade, a professor in the division of biological sciences at Cornell university, has been supervising the breeding of peregrines captured in the arctic, the west, and the pacific northwest.

4 The prime vacation time for most Americans is the period between the fourth of July and labor day.

5 The korean troops resisted the incursion of the communist forces.

In general, the convention governing capitalization is that the first letter of the proper name (that is, the particular or exclusive name) of persons, places, things, institutions, agencies, etc. should be capitalized. While the tendency today is to use lowercase letters for many words that formerly were written or printed with capital letters (for instance, *biblical reference* in-

stead of *Biblical reference*), the use of capital letters still prevails in the following cases:

(a) The first letter of the first word of a sentence.

They were uncertain about which words should be capitalized.

(b) The first letter of the first word of every line of English
verse.

Little fly,
Thy summer's play
My thoughtless hand
Has brushed away.

(c) All nouns, pronouns, verbs, adjectives, adverbs, and
first and last words of titles of publications and other artistic
works.

Remembrance of Things Past (see **83**)
"**T**he **P**lace of the **E**nthymeme in **R**hetorical **T**heory" (see **84**)
"**A T**ent **T**hat **F**amilies **C**an **L**ive **I**n"
The Return of the Pink Panther

(d) The first name, middle name or initial, and last name of
a person, real or fictional.

T. S. Eliot   **S**ylvia **M**arie **M**ikkelsen
David **C**opperfield   **A**chilles

(e) The names and abbreviations of villages, towns, cities,
counties, states, nations, and regions.

Chillicothe, **O**hio   **F**ranklin **C**ounty
U.S.A.   **S**oviet **U**nion
Indo-**C**hina   **A**rctic **C**ircle

Mechanics

the **W**estern **W**orld   **S**outh **A**merica
the **M**idwestern states the **S**outh (but: we drove
          south)

(f) The names of rivers, lakes, falls, oceans, mountains, deserts, parks.

the **M**ississippi **R**iver **A**tlantic
the **G**rand **T**etons   **Y**ellowstone **N**ational **P**ark
Lake **E**rie   **V**ictoria **F**alls

(g) The names and abbreviations of businesses, industries, institutions, agencies, schools, political parties, religious denominations, and philosophical, literary, and artistic movements.

University of **N**ebraska **D**emocrats
the **R**epublican convention **C.I.A.**
Dow **C**hemical **C**orporation **J**ohn **W**iley & **S**ons, **P**ublishers
Communist(s) (but: a com- **S**mithsonian **I**nstitution
munist ideology)   **J**apan **A**ir **L**ines
Victorian literature   the **P**entagon
Thomistic philosophy   **P**ure **L**and **B**uddhism

(h) The titles of historical events, epochs, and periods.

Renaissance   **T**hirty **Y**ears' **W**ar
World **W**ar II   **I**ce **A**ge
the **M**iddle **A**ges   the **B**attle of **G**ettysburg
Reformation   the **D**epression

(i) Honorary and official titles when they precede the name of the person.

Rabbi **B**alfour **B**rickner **B**ishop **T**suji
the **D**uke of **C**ornwall **G**eneral **P**atton

90 Capitalization, of Certain Words

Pope John Paul II   the Chief Justice
His (Her) Excellency   Queen Elizabeth

(j) The names of weekdays, months, holidays, holy days,
and other special days or periods.

Christmas Eve   Memorial Day
Passover   the Fourth of July
Lent   National Book Week
Mardi Gras   the first Sunday in June

(k) The names and abbreviations of the books and divisions of the Bible and other sacred books (no italics for these
titles).

Genesis   Pentateuch
Matt. (Gospel of Matthew)   Acts of the Apostles
Epistle to the Romans   Koran
King James Version   Scriptures
Talmud   Bhagavad Gita
Book of Job   Lotus Sutra
Pss. (Psalms)   Science and Health

Exceptions: Do not capitalize words like the underlined in the
following examples:

the African coast (but: the   the river Elbe (but: the Elbe
West Coast)   River)
northern Wisconsin   the federal government
the senator from Wyoming   the presidential itinerary
the municipal library   the county courthouse

Here are the revisions of the sample sentences, with all the
proper names capitalized:

1 President Gerald R. Ford informed the members of Congress that

Never-Say Neverisms

he was appointing Ms. Shirley Temple Black as the United States ambassador to Ghana.

2 The title of the article in the *New Yorker* was "The Time of Illusion."

3 Dr. Thomas J. Cade, a professor in the Division of Biological Sciences at Cornell University, has been supervising the breeding of peregrines captured in the Arctic, the West, and the Pacific Northwest.

4 The prime vacation time for most Americans is the period between the Fourth of July and Labor Day.

5 The Korean troops resisted the incursion of the Communist forces.

Never-Say Neverisms

William Safire

(If you have absorbed the lessons of this handbook, you will be able to detect what is wrong in each of the following proscriptions, which William Safire calls "never-say neverisms."*)

1. Remember to never split an infinitive.

2. The passive voice should never be used.

3. Avoid run-on sentences they are hard to read.

4. Don't use no double negatives.

5. Use the semicolon properly, always use it where it is appropriate; and never where it isn't.

6. Reserve the apostrophe for it's proper use and omit it when its not needed.

7. Do not put statements in the negative form.

8. Verbs has to agree with their subjects.

9. No sentence fragments.

*From William Safire, "The Fumblerules of Grammar," *The New York Times Magazine*, November 4, 1979, p.16, and "Fumblerule Follow-Up," November 25, 1979, p. 14. © 1979 by The New York Times Company. Reprinted by permission.

10. Proofread carefully to see if you any words out.

11. Avoid commas, that are not necessary.

12. If you reread your work, you will find on rereading that a great deal of repetition can be avoided by rereading and editing.

13. A writer must not shift your point of view.

14. Eschew dialect, irregardless.

15. And don't start a sentence with a conjunction.

16. Don't overuse exclamation marks!!!

17. Place pronouns as close as possible, especially in long sentences, as of ten or more words, to their antecedents.

18. Hyphenate between syllables and avoid un-necessary hyphens.

19. Write all adverbial forms correct.

20. Don't use contractions in formal writing.

21. Writing carefully, dangling participles must be avoided.

22. It is incumbent on us to avoid archaisms.

23. If any word is improper at the end of a sentence, a linking verb is.

24. Steer clear of incorrect forms of verbs that have snuck in the language.

25. Take the bull by the hand and avoid mixed metaphors.

26. Avoid trendy locutions that sound flaky.

27. Never, ever use repetitive redundancies.

28. Everyone should be careful to use a singular pronoun with singular nouns in their writing.

29. If I've told you once, I've told you a thousand times, resist hyperbole.

30. Also, avoid awkward or affected alliteration.

31. Don't string too many prepositional phrases together unless you are walking through the valley of the shadow of death.

32. Never use a long word when a diminutive one will do.

Never-Say Neverisms

33. If a dependent clause precedes an independent clause put a comma after the dependent clause.

34. One will not have needed the future perfect in one's entire life.

35. Unqualified superlatives are the worst of all.

36. If this were subjunctive, I'm in the wrong mood.

37. Always pick on the correct idiom.

38. "Avoid overuse of 'quotation "marks." ' "

39. The adverb always follows the verb.

40. Last but not least, avoid clichés like the plague; seek viable alternatives.

41. Surly grammarians insist that all words ending in "ly" are adverbs.

42. De-accession euphemisms.

43. In statements involving two word phrases, make an all out effort to use hyphens.

44. It is not resultful to transform one part of speech into another by prefixing, suffixing, or other alterings.

45. Avoid colloquial stuff.

Glossary of Usage

Many of the entries here deal with pairs of words that writers often confuse because the words look alike or sound alike. Ascertain the distinctions between these confusing pairs and then invent your own memorizing devices to help you make the right choice in a particular case. In all cases of disputed usage, the most conservative position on that usage is presented so that you can decide whether you can afford to run the risk of alienating that segment of your readers who subscribe to the conservative position.

affect, effect. The noun form is almost always **effect** (*The effect of that usage was to alienate the purists*). The wrong choices are usually made when writers use the verb. The verb **effect** means "to bring about," "to accomplish" (*The prisoner effected his escape by picking a lock*). The verb **affect** means "to influence" (*The weather affected her moods*).

allusion, illusion. Think of **allusion** as meaning "indirect reference" (*He made an allusion to her parents*). Think of **illusion** as meaning "a deceptive impression" (*He continued to entertain this illusion about her ancestry*).

Glossary of Usage

alot, a lot. This locution should always be written as two words (*A lot of the natives lost faith in the government*).

alright, allright, all right. **All right** is the only correct way to write this expression (*He told his mother that he was all right*).

altogether, all together. **Altogether** is the adverb form in the sense of "completely" (*She was not altogether happy with the present*). **All together** is the adjective form in the sense of "collectively" (*The students were all together in their loyalty to the team*).

among. See **between**.

amount of, number of. When you are speaking of masses or bulks, use **amount of** (*They bought a large amount of sugar*). When you are speaking of persons or things that can be counted one by one, use **number of** (*They bought a large number of cookies*). See **fewer, less**.

as, like. See **like**.

because of. See **due to**.

beside, besides. Both of these words are used as prepositions, but **beside** means "at the side of" (*They built a cabin beside a lake*), and **besides** means "in addition to" (*They bought a jacket besides a pair of boots*).

between. The conservative position is that between should be used only when two persons or things are involved (*They made a choice between the Democrat and the Republican*).

can't help but. Conservatives regard this expression as an instance of a double negative (**can't** and **but**). They would rewrite the sentence *She can't help but love him* as *She can't help loving him*.

center around. One frequently sees and hears this expression (e.g. *His interest centered around his work*). The expression seems to violate the basic metaphor from which it derives. How can something center **around** something else? Say instead *"His interest centered on his work"* or *"His interest centered upon his work."*

continual, continuous. There is a real distinction between these two adjectives. Think of **continual** as referring to something that occurs repeatedly (i.e. with interruptions). For instance, a noise that occurred every three or four minutes would be a "continual noise"; a noise that persisted without interruption for an hour would be a "continuous noise." **Continual** is stop-and-go; **continuous** is an uninterrupted flow.

could of, should of, would of. In the spoken language, these forms sound very much like the correct written forms. In writing, use the correct forms **could have, should have, would have** or, in informal contexts, the contractions **could've, should've, would've**.

data. The word **data**, like the words **criteria** and **phenomena**, is a plural noun and therefore demands the plural form of the demonstrative adjective (*these data, those data*) and the plural form of the verb (*These data present convincing evidence of his guilt. The data were submitted by the committee*).

different from, different than. In British usage, **different than** is more likely to be used than **different from** when a clause follows the expression (e.g. *This treatment is different than we expected*). In conservative American usage, **different from** is preferred to **different than**, whether the expression is followed with a noun phrase (*The British usage is different from the American usage*) or with a noun clause (*This treatment is different from what we expected*).

disinterested, uninterested. Careful writers still make a distinction between these two words. For them, **disinterested**

means "unbiased," "impartial," "objective" (*The mother could not make a disinterested judgment about her son*). **Uninterested**, for them, means "bored," "indifferent to" (*The students were obviously uninterested in the lecture*).

due to, because of.   Many writers use **due to** and **because of** interchangeably. Some writers, however, observe the conservative distinction between these two expressions: **due to** is an adjectival construction, and **because of** is an adverbial construction. Accordingly, they would always follow any form of the verb **to be** (**is, were, has been,** etc.) with **due to** (*His absence last week was due to illness*), they would always follow transitive and intransitive verbs with the adverbial construction **because of** (*She missed the party because of illness. He failed because of illness*). Sometimes, they substitute **owing to** or **on account of** for **because of**.

effect.   See **affect**.

fewer, less.   Use **fewer** with countable items (*Louise has fewer hats than Emily does*). Use **less** when speaking of mass or bulk (*Elmer has less sand in his garden than Andrew does*). See **amount of, number of**.

human, humans.   Those who take a conservative view of language have not yet accepted **human** or **humans** as a noun. They would rewrite "The natives made no distinction between animals and humans" as "The natives made no distinction between animals and human beings." In their view, **human** should be used only as an adjective.

imply, infer.   There is a definite difference in meaning between these two verbs. **Imply** means "to hint at," "to suggest" (*She implied that she wouldn't come to his party*). **Infer** means "to deduce," "to draw a conclusion from" (*He inferred from the look on her face that she wouldn't come to his party*).

kind of, sort of. Do not use the article **a** or **an** with either of these phrases (*He suffered some kind of a heart attack. She got the sort of an ovation she deserved*). **Kind of** and **sort of** in the sense of "rather" or "somewhat" (*He was kind of annoyed with his teacher*) should be reserved for an informal or a colloquial context.

lend, loan. The conservative position is that **loan** should be used exclusively as a noun (*He took out a loan from the bank*) and that **lend** should be used exclusively as a verb (*The bank lends him the downpayment*).

less. See **fewer**.

lie, lay. **Lie** (past tense **lay**, past participle **lain**) is an intransitive verb meaning "to rest," "to recline" (*The book lies on the table. It has lain there for three days*). **Lay** (past tense **laid**, past participle **laid**) is a transitive verb (i.e. must be followed by an object) meaning "to put down" (*She lays the book on the table. Yesterday she laid the book on the mantelpiece*).

like, as. Avoid the use of **like** as a subordinating conjunction (*At a party, he behaves like he does in church*). Use **like** exclusively as a preposition (*At a party, he behaves like a prude*). **As** is the appropriate subordinating conjunction with clauses (*At a party, he behaves as he does in church*).

literally. Originally, **literally** was used as an adverb meaning the opposite of **figuratively**. In recent years, some people have been using the word as an intensifier (*She literally blew her top*). Careful writers still use the word in its original sense of "actually" (*The mother literally washed out her son's mouth with soap*).

loose, lose. These words look alike but do not sound alike. Here is a device to help you remember the difference in meaning. The two *o*'s in **loose** are like two marbles dumped out of a can (*The dog broke its leash and ran loose in the backyard*). The word **lose** has lost one of its *o*'s (*I always lose my wallet when I go to a carnival*). If these memorizing devices do not help you keep the two words straight, invent your own device.

past, passed. These words are more sound-alikes than look-alikes. The word with the *-ed* is the only one that can be used as a verb (*His car passed mine on the freeway*). The word **past** is versatile: it can be used as a noun (*I recalled my sordid past*), as an adjective (*I recalled the past events*), and as a preposition (*His car sped past mine like a bullet*), but it is never used as a verb.

principal, principle. These words sound alike, but they are spelled differently, and they have different meanings. Whether used as a noun or as an adjective, **principal** carries the meaning of "chief." The chief of a high school is the **principal**. The adjective that means "chief" is always *principal* (*The principal is the principal administrative officer of a high school*). The word **principle** is used only as a noun and means "rule," "law" (*A manufacturer shouldn't ignore the basic principles of physics*).

quote(s). In formal contexts, use **quotation(s)** instead of the colloquial contraction **quote(s)**.

reason is because. This phrasing constitutes an example of faulty predication (see section **40**). Write "the reason is that . . ."

reason why. This phrasing is redundant. Instead of writing "The reason why I am unhappy is that I lost my wallet," drop the redundant **why** and write "The reason I am unhappy is that I lost my wallet."

respectfully, respectively. Choose the correct adverb for what you want to say. **Respectfully** means "with respect"

(*She answered her mother respectfully*). **Respectively** means "the previously mentioned items in the order in which they are listed" (*Mary Sarton, Emily Doan, and Sarah Fowler were the first, second, and third presidents of the Guild, respectively*).

should of. See **could of**.

so, such. Avoid the use of **so** or **such** as an unqualified intensifier, as in sentences like "She was so happy," "It was such a cold day." If you must use an intensifier, use such adverbs as **very, exceedingly, unusually** (*She was very happy. It was an unusually cold day*). If you use **so** or **such** to modify an adjective, your readers have a right to expect you to complete the structure with a *that*-clause of result (*She was so happy that she clapped her hands for joy. It was so cold that we clapped our hands to keep warm*).

sort of. See **kind of**.

supposed to, used to. Because it is difficult to hear the *-d* when these phrases are spoken, writers sometimes write "He was suppose to come yesterday. He use to come at noon." Always add the *-d* to these words.

their, there, they're. All three words are pronounced alike. The wrong one is chosen in a particular instance, not because the writer does not know better but because the writer has been careless or inattentive. There [their? they're?] is no need to review the different meanings of these very common words.

try and. In the spoken medium, one frequently hears utterances like "Try and stay within the white lines if you can." Purists still insist that we write "Try to stay within the white lines if you can." So if we want to be "proper," we should always write **try to** instead of **try and**.

used to. See **supposed to**.

Glossary of Usage

whose, who's.   Since the two words are pronounced alike, it is understandable that writers sometimes make the wrong choice. The word spelled with the apostrophe is the contraction of "who is" (*Who's the principal actor? Who's playing the lead role?*) **Whose** is (1) the interrogative pronoun (*Whose hat is this?*), (2) the possessive case of the relative pronoun **who** (*John is the man whose son died last week*), (3) an acceptable possessive form of the relative pronoun **which** (*Our flag, whose broad stripes and bright stars we watched through the perilous fight, was gallantly streaming over the ramparts*).

would of.   See **could of**.

Index

Index

Index

Index

Index

Index

Index

Index

PROOFREADERS' MARKS

⌒	close up space
ℐ	delete
⌒ℐ	delete and close up space
#	separate with a space
∧	insert here what is indicated in the margin
¶	start new paragraph
no ¶	no paragraph; run in with previous paragraph
⊙/	insert period
⋀/	insert comma
;/	insert semicolon
:/	insert colon
$\frac{1}{M}$/	insert em dash
$\frac{1}{M}$/$\frac{1}{M}$	insert pair of em dashes
=/	insert hyphen
⌄/	insert apostrophe
cap	use capital letter here
lc	use lowercase letter here
ital	set in italic type
rom	set in roman type
sc	set in small capitals
bf	set in boldface type
tr	transpose letters or words

Reference Chart, continued